DATE			

The Art of Digital Audio

John Watkinson

Focal Press

London & Boston

For Anne

Focal Press
is an imprint of the Butterworth Group
which has principal offices in
London, Boston, Singapore, Sydney, Toronto, Wellington

First published 1988

British Library Cataloguing in Publication Data

Watkinson, John
   The art of digitial audio.
   1. Sound—Recording and reproducing—Digital techniques
   I. Title
   621.389'3   TK881.4

   ISBN 0–240–51270–7

Library of Congress Cataloging in Publication Data

Watkinson, John.
   The art of digital audio.

   Bibliography: p.
   Includes index.
   1. Sound—Recording and reproducing—
Digital techniques.   I. Title.
TK7881.4.W38 1988   621.389'3   87-32771
ISBN 0-240-51270-7

Photoset by August Filmsetting, Haydock, St Helens
Printed and bound in Great Britain by Butler and Tanner, Frome, Somerset

Preface

History abounds with stories of men and women who had dreams of how things should be done for the better. Not all such dreams came to fruition; the cold light of economic reality, difficulty of implementation and conservatism will sort the weak from the tenacious.

There were those who dreamed that sound could be conveyed in a better way than permitted by the existing analog technology: not by some gradual perfecting of an existing mechanism, but by a totally different approach which would wipe away existing problems at a stroke. It would require many and diverse skills from fields which had not previously had any relevance to audio: computation, laser optics, mass storage, communications theory and error correction.

The people who successfully realised these dreams mastered all these disciplines, and overcame the obstacles to information flow imposed by jargon and idiomatic use of words. In doing so they elevated themselves from engineers to artists, and have thus inspired the title of this book. There can be few people in the developed world who have not been touched by their art, either directly by the Compact Disc, or indirectly by listening to material which has been digitally recorded.

Digital audio is still developing, but it has reached a point where there is something solid to discuss. There are products in the marketplace which are dependable workhorses rather than laboratory curiosities. People use them to make a living, recording music with breathtaking clarity. Standards have been agreed for many common areas, and controversy over basic theory has largely ceased.

This book describes all of the essential theory of digital audio, and a good deal of practice, but it is not a history book. Nor is it, I suppose, a conventional textbook, largely because I have had so much difficulty with conventional books. I am told that a conventional book has to choose its target audience and stick to that academic level. The need for understanding in digital audio is too wide and the subject is too interdisciplinary for that.

How could I neglect the needs of those who are new to the subject by assuming existing knowledge? How could I make it comprehensible only to those who choose to express things mathematically? The answer in both cases is that I could not, and so every concept begins with the basic mechanism involved, and defines its terminology. If I thus risk being accused of condescension, so be it, for those who understand where previously they did not will defend me.

Readers who are mathematically inclined will soon be able to convert my words to equations: so much easier than going the other way.

There are few stated facts here, since facts are easily forgotten. Instead, there are reasons, arguments and mechanisms from which facts can be deduced. The deduction of facts from concepts is a powerful approach which can be used all the way from basics to advanced techniques, so there is also plenty in this book for the expert. The level at which treatment of a subject is left should be sufficient to make the many quoted references a logical next step for those interested in deep study.

In the interests of clarity, the words used here have been carefully chosen, so they will not necessarily be the ones used in casual parlance. The inevitable misnomers will be identified instead of continuing their misleading lives. The language is a touch transatlantic, in that I prefer analog and program to the more ornate English spellings, but I still cannot accept that colour can be spelled without the 'u'. Perhaps I can make amends by using the word disk everywhere it is not Compact?

Acknowledgements

I must first thank Denis Mee and Eric Daniel, for it was their invitation to supply a small chapter on digital audio for their definitive work on magnetic recording[1] which spurred me on to do a self-contained work.

The role of the Audio Engineering Society in providing a forum for discussion of digital audio through conventions and publications is deeply appreciated.

I am eternally grateful to the many people who have suggested and supplied reference material, and have found time to discuss difficult subjects as well as giving encouragements. In particular I should like to thank Toshi Doi and John Ajimine of Sony Corporation, Roger Lagadec, now also with Sony, Kees Schouhamer-Immink of NV Philips, Roger Wood of IBM, John Mallinson of CMRR San Diego, Tony Griffiths of Decca, Guy McNally of Digital Audio Research Ltd. and Tim Shelton of the BBC.

Francis Rumsey of the University of Surrey kindly suggested the title.

John Watkinson
Burghfield Common, England, January 1988

---

[1] Mee, C.D. and Daniel, E.D., *Magnetic Recording – Vol. II*. New York: McGraw-Hill (1987)

Contents

Chapter 1

Why digital?

1.1 The advantages of digital audio

Understandably, the first techniques to be used for sound processing and recording were analog: initially mechanical cylinders and disks, which had no signal processing at all, and later magnetic wire, tape and optical film soundtracks which depended on gain and equalization stages provided by vacuum-tube amplifiers. In those days it was not necessary to specify that such equipment was analog as there was no different equipment with which it might be confused. Magnetic analog recording as it is known today was essentially hammered out in the heat and pressure of the Second World War along with the turbojet engine, radar and the atomic bomb. Since then analog sound processing and recording has undergone a process of gradual refinement. The multi-track recorder and its complementary mixing console became standard for the recording of certain types of music and modern systems are capable of an extremely high standard of reproduction. This has been achieved by the study of every shortcoming in the analog recording process and the introduction of some measure to reduce it, and it is not necessary in this book merely to repeat such excellent work. The important point to appreciate is that analog signal processing and recording is now a mature technology, and the state-of-the-art curve has become asymptotic to the limits determined by the physics of the process. The law of diminishing returns applies in such cases.

As there is now another audio technology, which has come to be known as digital, the previous technology has to be referred to as analog. It is convenient to attempt here some kind of definition of the fundamental differences between these two technologies.

In an analog system, information is conveyed by the infinite variation of some continuous parameter, such as the voltage on a wire or the strength of flux. When it comes to recording, distance along the medium is a further analog of time. However much the signal is magnified, more and more detail will be revealed until a point is reached where the actual value is uncertain because of noise. A parameter can only be a true analog of the original if the conversion process is linear, otherwise harmonic distortion is introduced. If the speed of the medium is not constant there will not be a true analog of time.

It is a characteristic of an analog system that the degradations at the output are the sum of all the degradations introduced in each stage through which the signal has passed. This sets a limit to the number of stages a signal can pass

1

through before it becomes too impaired to be worth listening to. Down at signal level, all impairments can be reduced to the addition of some unwanted signal such as noise or distortion, and timing instability such as group-delay effects and jitter. In an analog system, such effects can never be separated from the original signal; in the digital domain they can be eliminated.

In a digital audio system, the information is in binary form. The signals sent have only two states, and change at predetermined times according to a stable clock. If the binary signal is degraded by noise, this will be rejected at the receiver, as the signal is judged solely on whether it is above or below some threshold. However, the signal will be conveyed with finite bandwidth, and this will restrict the rate at which the voltage changes. Superimposed noise can move the point at which the receiver judges that there has been a change of state. Time instability has this effect too. This instability is also rejected because, on receipt, the signal is reclocked by the stable clock, and all changes in the system will take place at the edges of that clock. Fig.1.1 shows that however many stages a

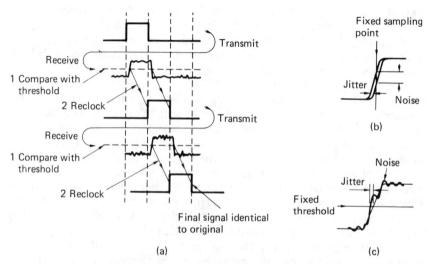

(a)

(b)

(c)

Figure 1.1 (a) A binary signal is compared with a threshold and reclocked on receipt, thus the meaning will be unchanged.
(b) Jitter on a signal can appear as noise with respect to fixed timing.
(c) Noise on a signal can appear as jitter when compared with a fixed threshold.

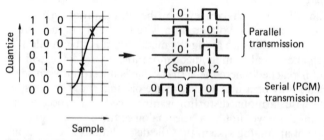

Figure 1.2 When a signal is carried in numerical form, either parallel or serial, the mechanisms of Figure 1.1 ensure that the only degradation is in the conversion processes.

binary signal passes through, it still comes out the same, only later. It is possible to convey an analog waveform down such a signal path. That analog waveform has to be broken into evenly spaced time elements (a process known as sampling) and then each sample is expressed as a whole number, or integer, which can be carried by binary digits (bits for short). Fig.1.2 shows that the signal path may either convey sample values in parallel on several wires, where each wire carries a binary signal representing a different power of two, or serially in one channel, at higher speed, a process called pulse code modulation (PCM). The only drawback of this scheme is that a single high-quality audio channel requires about one million bits per second. Digital audio only became viable when advances in high-density recording made such a data rate available at reasonable cost.

In simple terms, the signal waveform is conveyed in a digital recorder as if someone had measured the voltage at regular intervals with a digital voltmeter and written the readings in binary on a roll of paper. The rate at which these measurements are made and the accuracy of the meter now wholly determine the quality of the system, because once a parameter is expressed as discrete numbers, those numbers can be conveyed unchanged through a recording process. This dependence on the quality of conversion is the price paid to make quality independent of the signal path. As it is so critical to sound quality, a whole chapter of this book is dedicated to sampling and conversion.

A magnetic head cannot know the meaning of signals which are passed through it, so there is no distinction at the head/medium interface between analog and digital recording. Thus a digital signal will suffer all the degradations that beset an analog signal: particulate noise, distortion, dropout, modulation noise, print-through, crosstalk and so on. However, there is a difference in the effect of these degradations on the meaning of the signals. As stated, digital recording uses a binary code, and the presence or absence of a flux change is the only item of interest. Provided that flux change can generate a playback pulse which is sensibly bigger than the noise, the numerical meaning will be unchanged by reasonable distortions of the waveform. In other words, a bit is still a bit, whatever its shape. This implies that the bits on the medium can be very small indeed, and can be packed very close together; hence the required data rate of a million bits per second is achievable. If the trivial example of the paper tape recording is pursued further, suppose that the tape upon which the voltages were written became crumpled up. If it were smoothed out, the numbers would still be legible, and could be copied without error to a new piece of paper. By comparison, if a photograph is crumpled up, it will look like a crumpled-up photograph for evermore.

Large disturbances of the recording, such as dropout or severe interference, may cause flux changes to be missed, or simulate ones which did not exist. The result is that some of the numbers recorded will be incorrect. In numerical systems, provision of an error-correction system is feasible; in analog systems it is not. The human ear is highly sensitive to the kind of noise caused by bit errors, and a properly engineered error-correction system is absolutely essential to return the corrupted numbers to their original value. It is probably true to say that, without error-correction systems, digital audio would not be technically feasible.

In the digital domain, signals can be easily conveyed and stored in circuitry. Speed variations in recorders cause the numbers to appear at a fluctuating rate.

The use of a temporary store allows those numbers to be read out at constant rate, a process known as timebase correction. In this way wow, flutter and phase errors between tracks, caused by tape weave and azimuth error, can be eliminated.

The ease with which pure delay can be achieved in the digital domain led to one of the first applications of digital audio. This was the vinyl-disk-cutter delay, which allowed a disk cutter to look ahead and coarsen its groove pitch in advance of a loud passage of music. Previously a special tape deck with an advanced head had been necessary. Pure delay also allowed the realization of the digital reverberator—another one of the first digital products. The ease with which delay is provided also allows linear phase filters to be created very simply, because the group delay problems of analog filters cannot occur. Filters can be constructed which work with mathematical precision and freedom from component drift and with a response that can be easily changed.

The main advantages of digital audio recording can be summarized as follows (they are not in order of importance because this will change with the application):

* The quality of a digital audio recording is independent of the head and medium in a properly engineered system. Audio frequency response, linearity and noise are determined only by the quality of the conversion processes. Exceptional dynamic range and linearity are readily achieved, combined with freedom from modulation noise, print-through and crosstalk. The independence of the quality from the medium also means that a recorder will not sound different if different brands of tape are used, provided that they all have acceptable error rates.

* A digital recording is no more than a series of numbers, and hence can be copied through an indefinite number of generations without degradation. This implies that the life of a recording can be truly indefinite, because even if the medium begins to decay physically, the sample values can be copied to a new medium with no loss of information.

* The use of error-correction techniques eliminates the effects of dropout. In consumer products, error correction can be used to advantage to ease the handling requirements.

* The use of timebase correction on replay eliminates wow and flutter, and can be further used to synchronize more than one machine to sample accuracy.

* The use of digital recording and error correction allows the signal- to-noise ratio of the recorded tracks to be relatively poor. The tracks can be narrow and hence achieve a saving in tape consumption despite the greater bandwidth.

* It is possible to construct extremely precise and stable filters and equalizers with inherent phase linearity.

1.2 The opportunities

Digital audio does far more than merely compare favourably with analog. Its most exciting aspects are the tremendous possibilities which are denied to analog technology. Once in the digital domain, the original sound is just a series of numbers, and these can be stored, conveyed and processed in many and varied ways. The computer industry has spent decades perfecting machines to store, convey and process streams of numbers at high speed and at a cost which continues to fall. Digital audio can take full advantage of such techniques. Recordings can be stored on computer disk drives, magnetic or optical, whose radially moving heads allow rapid random access to the information. For rapid editing of audio, this is far superior to waiting for tape recorders to wind and rewind. An edit can be effected by reading samples from two sources and fading between them in digital circuitry. The edit can be simulated, so that the outcome can be heard, and the edit point can be moved around at will until the result is satisfactory. The final edited version can be recorded on a different medium if necessary, leaving the source material intact.

Using computer technology to construct a mixing console releases the full potential of software control. The configuration of an analog desk is fixed by its construction; a digital desk can be configured as the operator pleases, simply by choosing the order of the routines which process the samples.

The cable and satellite communications networks around the world are increasingly being used for digital transmission, and a packet of digital audio information can pass through as easily as a Telex message or a bank transaction. Provided the original numbers are fed in the correct order at the correct rate to the final destination, for conversion to sound, it does not matter how they have been conveyed. Let us take an extreme example. A stereo recording could be made digitally, the left-channel samples recorded on a computer laser disk sent to the airport, and the right-channel samples recorded on a computer Winchester disk. While the left channel is flying the Atlantic, the right channel is transmitted over a cheap low-speed modem link to a receiving computer at the other side of the world. When the laser disk arrives from the airport, it will be possible to listen to a perfect stereo reproduction of the original recording, because in the digital domain it is easy to reassemble sample streams and correctly phase channels irrespective of how they have been conveyed. In reality no-one would employ such a topsy-turvy route, except perhaps to prove a point. But the worlds of digital audio, digital video, communication and computation are closely related, and that is where the real potential lies. People who expect to use digital machines just as they would analog machines are going to be very surprised if they fail to realize these facts.

1.3 Some typical machines outlined

Some outlines of typical digital audio machines follow to illustrate what is possible, and to put the major chapters of this book into perspective.

Fig.1.3 shows some of the ways in which a digital recording can be made, starting with the sampling and quantizing processes explained in Chapter 2. Once in digital form, the data are formed into blocks, and the encoding section of the error-correction system supplies additional bits designed to protect the data against errors. These blocks are then converted into some form of channel code which combines the data with clock information so that it is possible to identify how many bits were recorded even if several adjacent bits are identical. Chapter 6 deals with the extensive subject of channel coding.

The coded data are recorded on some medium, which can be optical or magnetic, disk or tape, rotary head, moving head or stationary head. Some media are erasable; some can only be recorded once. Chapter 8 is concerned with rotary-head recorders; Chapter 9 treats stationary-head recorders. Magnetic-disk drives are detailed in Chapter 12, along with the allied subjects of

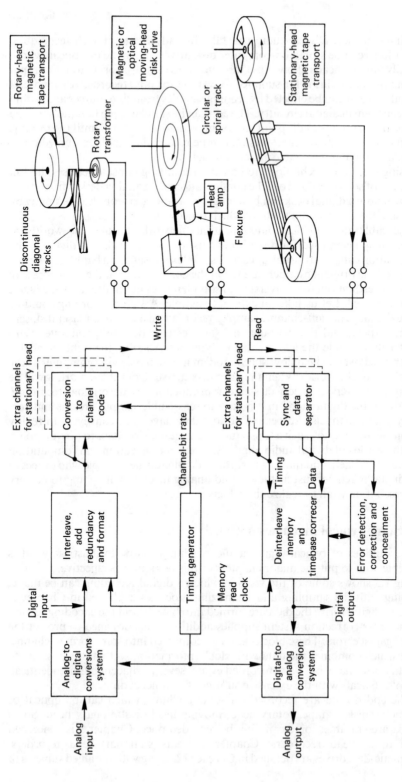

Figure 1.3 Basic digital audio recording. The essential processes in digital recording are largely independent of the kind of medium used. As shown here, audio can be recorded with stationary or rotary heads, and on disk or tape. Stationary-head recorders often distribute the data from one audio channel over several tracks to reduce tape speed. The actual medium used will determine the nature of the channel-code and error-correction strategy.

recordable and erasable optical media. The important subject of Compact Disc is explained in detail in Chapter 13.

Upon replaying the recording of the hypothetical machine of Fig.1.3, the errors caused by various mechanisms will be detected, corrected or concealed using the extra bits appended during the encoding process. Chapter 7 treats the subject of error correction as comprehensively as possible without becoming lost in the mathematics.

The replayed digital recording may be processed before being heard again or re-recorded. Simple manipulations of digital audio, such as gain control and mixing, are covered in Chapter 3; more advanced processes, such as digital filtering and sampling-rate conversion, occupy Chapter 4.

The digital recorder and the digital mixer may well be two different units of different manufacture, and it is necessary to provide some standard interconnection between them in the digital domain. Chapter 5 details digital communications between equipment.

1.4 Disadvantages

In this comparison of digital and analog technologies, the emphasis so far has been on the advantages of digital audio. In the interests of fairness and truth we must also look at some of the problems of digital audio.

(1) Many stationary-head digital audio recorders support tape-cut editing, but, for reasons which will be made clear in Chapter 7, digital recorders will never be as amenable to splicing as analog recorders.

(2) Digital recorders must use thin tape with a fine surface finish to allow the very short wavelength recordings needed. The backcoat must be reasonably smooth to avoid damaging the recorded layer when tape is wound on the reel. This conflicts with the need for a rough backcoat to allow neat spooling at high speed. Digital stationary-head recorders will probably never be able to spool as fast as their analog brothers.

(3) Digital channel codes are designed to restrict the range of frequencies recorded on the medium, and the playback circuits are equalized to accept these frequencies. It causes great difficulty if a digital recording has to be played at a speed which differs from normal by more than about 10–15%. Analog recorders are clearly superior in this respect.

(4) In general, digital audio recorders will not play backwards, although a computerized editor could be programmed to reverse the order of samples in a recording held in memory.

(5) Since standard sampling rates are needed for interchange of digital recordings, there is a conflict with the requirement to synchronize to video signals, since these have different frequencies in different standards.

(6) Inevitably, digital recorders are more complex than analog recorders, and this has implications for maintenance and repair.

Further reading

For an excellent introduction to digital audio, with an exhaustive list of references, the reader is recommended to:

BLOOM, P.J., High-quality digital audio in the entertainment industry: an overview of achievements and challenges. *IEEE Acoust. Speech Signal Process Magazine,* **2**, 2–25 (1985)

Chapter 2

Conversion

It was shown in Chapter 1 that the essence of digital audio is that the quality is independent of the storage or transmission medium, and is determined instead by the accuracy of conversion between the analog and digital domains. This chapter will examine in detail the theory and practice of this critical aspect of digital audio.

The acuity of the human ear is astonishing. It can detect tiny amounts of distortion, and will accept an enormous dynamic range. The only criterion for quality that we have is that if the ear cannot detect impairments, we must say that the reproduced sound is perfect. Usually, people's ears are at their most sensitive between about 2 kHz and 5 kHz, and although some people can detect 20 kHz at high level, there is much evidence to suggest that most listeners cannot tell if the upper frequency limit of sound is 20 kHz or 16 kHz.[1,2] For a long time it was thought that frequencies below about 40 Hz were unimportant, but it is becoming clear that reproduction of frequencies down to 20 Hz improves reality and ambience.[3] A digital system can deliver a response down to DC if necessary. The dynamic range of the ear is obtained by a logarithmic response, and certainly exceeds 100 dB. At the extremes of this range, the ear is either straining to hear or is suffering pain, neither of which can be described as pleasurable or entertaining, and it is hardly necessary to produce recordings of this dynamic range for the consumer since, among other things, he is unlikely to have anywhere to listen to them.

Probably more important than dynamic range is the sensitivity of the ear to distortion. The ear behaves as a kind of spectrum analyser, with frequency bands about 100 Hz wide below 500 Hz and from one sixth to one third of an octave wide, proportional to frequency, above this. In the presence of a complex spectrum, it appears to protect itself from information overload by failing to register energy in some bands when there is more energy in a nearby band. This is the phenomenon of auditory masking, defined as the decreased audibility of one sound in the presence of another. The information reduction achieved is considerable; masking can take place even when the masking tone ceases before the masked sound appears. Another example of the slowness of the ear is the Haas effect, in which the source of a sound is attributed to the first arriving wavefront even though a later echo is much louder. Since distortion results in energy moving from one frequency band to another, a knowledge of masking is essential to estimate how audible the effect of distortion will be. Before digital techniques were used for high-quality audio, it was thought that the principles of digitizing were adequately understood, but the disappointing results of some early digital audio machines showed that this was not so. The ear could detect the minute imperfections of filters and converters, which could be neglected in, for example, instrumentation applications. A more rigorous study of digitization was soon applied, and the essentials of it can be found here. The important topic of oversampling is also shown here to be soundly based on information theory, and its significant inherent advantages for audio are discussed.

2.1 Types of digitization

An analog signal is continuous in time, and infinitely variable in voltage, whereas a digital signal is time-discrete, and its voltage changes in steps. These two dimensions, time and voltage, are quite distinct, and can be treated separately.

There are several methods of converting an analog waveform to a bit stream, and it is more useful to compare them than to contrast them because they are related; in advanced conversion systems it is possible to move from one system to another to combine the advantages of both. Fig.2.1 and Fig.2.2 introduce the

Analog to PCM digital conversion

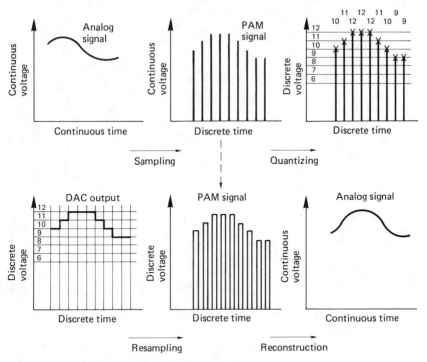

PCM digital to analog conversion

Figure 2.1 The major processes in PCM conversion. Note that the quantizing step can be omitted to examine sampling and reconstruction independently of quantizing (dotted arrow).

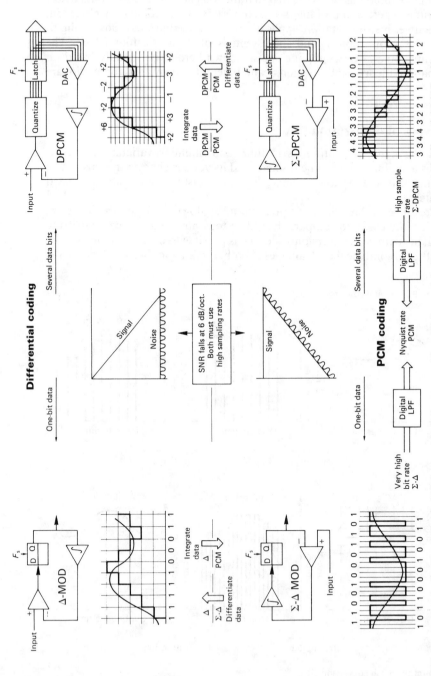

Figure 2.2 The four main alternatives to simple PCM conversion are compared here. Delta modulation is a one-bit case of differential PCM, and conveys the slope of the signal. The digital output of both can be integrated to give PCM. Σ–Δ (sigma-delta) is a one-bit case of Σ-DPCM. The application of integrator before differentiator makes the output true PCM, but tilts the noise floor; hence these can be referred to as 'noise-shaping' converters.

major processes involved in conversion in both directions. Conversion from continuous to discrete time is known as sampling; the reverse process is known as reconstruction. The expression of an analog sample value as a number is called quantizing, but there is no term for the opposite process. The sampling process produces pulses whose amplitude is an analog quantity. It is as if a stream of constant-height pulses had been amplitude-modulated by the input signal; hence the term pulse amplitude modulation, universally abbreviated to PAM. When the height of these pulses is quantized and expressed as a number code, the result is known as pulse code modulation, again better known by the abbreviation PCM. In principle this is exactly the same as logging the variations in a slowly changing voltage by recording the readings of a digital voltmeter every few seconds, only the speed is increased for audio. Fig.2.1 also shows that it is possible to go straight back to the analog domain from a PAM signal, bypassing the quantizing stage altogether and supporting the intention here to treat the time and voltage dimensions separately.

The amplitude of the signal which can be conveyed in this way only depends on the number range of the quantizer, and is independent of the frequency of the input. Similarly, the amplitude of the unwanted signals introduced by the quantizing process is also largely independent of input frequency.

In differential pulse code modulation (DPCM), the parameter which is quantized is the difference between the previous absolute sample value and the current one. This process limits the maximum rate at which the input signal voltage can change, and thus the permissible signal amplitude falls at 6 dB per octave. The unwanted signal amplitude is constant again, so as input frequency rises, ultimately the signal level available will fall down to it.

It is possible to produce a DPCM signal from a PCM signal by simply subtracting successive samples; this is digital differentiation. Similarly the reverse process is possible by using an accumulator to compute sample values from the differences received. The problem with this approach is that it is very easy to lose the baseline of the signal if it commences at some arbitrary time, and a digital high-pass filter is necessary to prevent unwanted offsets.

If DPCM is taken to the extreme case where only a binary output signal is available then the process is described as delta modulation. The meaning of the binary signal is that the analog input is above or below the accumulation of previous bits. The characteristics of the system show the same trends as DPCM, except that there is severe limiting of the rate of change of the input signal. Since the decoder must also accumulate all the difference bits to provide an analog output, this function can be performed by an integrator.

If an integrator is placed in the input to a delta modulator, the integrator's response loss of 6 dB per octave parallels the amplitude limit of 6 dB per octave, thus the system amplitude limit becomes independent of frequency. This integration is responsible for the term delta sigma modulation, since in mathematics sigma is used to denote summation. The transmitted signal is now the amplitude of the input, not the slope; thus the receiving integrator can be dispensed with, and all that is necessary is an LPF to smooth the bits. Unfortunately the removal of the integration stage now means that the unwanted signal amplitude rises at 6 dB per octave, ultimately meeting the level of the wanted signal.

This principle of using an input integrator can also be applied to a true DPCM system and the result should perhaps be called sigma DPCM. The dynamic range improvement over delta sigma modulation is 6 dB for every extra bit in the code. Because the level of the unwanted signal rises at 6 dB per octave, just as in delta sigma modulation, the system is sometimes referred to as a 'noise-shaping' converter, although it will be seen later in this chapter that the use of the word 'noise' is not wholly appropriate. The output of a sigma DPCM system is again the absolute signal amplitude, and a DAC will be needed to receive it, because it is a binary code.

As the differential group of systems suffer from a wanted signal that converges with the unwanted signal as frequency rises, they all must use high sampling rates.[4] It is possible to convert from sigma DPCM to conventional PCM by reducing the sampling rate digitally. This has some advantages which will become evident when oversampling is discussed (section 2.10).

2.2 Information content of audio

The sound conveyed through a digital system travels as a stream of bits. Because the bits are discrete, it is easy to quantify the flow, just by counting the number per second. It is much harder to quantify the amount of information in an analog signal (from a microphone, for example) but if this were done using the same units, it would be possible to decide just what bit rate was necessary to convey that signal without loss of information. If a signal can be conveyed without loss of information, and without picking up any unwanted signals on the way, it will have been transmitted perfectly.

The connection between analog signals and information capacity was made by Shannon, in one of the most significant papers in the history of this technology,[5] and those parts which are important for this subject are repeated here. The principles are straightforward, and offer an immediate insight into the

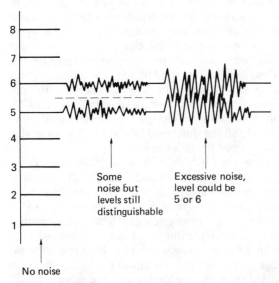

Figure 2.3 To receive eight different levels in a signal unambiguously, the pk–pk noise must be less than the difference in level. Signal-to-noise ratio must be at least 8:1 or 18 dB to convey eight levels. This can also be conveyed by three bits ($2^3 = 8$). For sixteen levels, SNR would have to be 24 dB, which would be conveyed by four bits.

relative performances and potentials of different modulation methods, including digitizing.

Fig.2.3 shows an analog signal with a certain amount of superimposed noise, as is the case for all real audio signals. Noise is defined as a random superimposed signal which is not correlated with the wanted signal. To avoid pitfalls in digital audio, this definition must be adhered to with what initially seems like pedantry. The noise is random, and so the actual voltage of the wanted signal is uncertain; it could be anywhere in the range of the noise amplitude. If the signal amplitude is, for the sake of argument, sixteen times the noise amplitude, it would only be possible to convey sixteen different signal levels unambiguously, because the levels have to be sufficiently different that noise will not make one look like another. It is possible to convey sixteen different levels in all combinations of four data bits, and so the connection between the analog and quantized domains is established.

The choice of sampling rate (the rate at which the signal voltage must be examined to convey the information in a changing signal) is important in any system; if it is too low, the signal will be degraded, and if it is too high, the number of samples to be recorded will rise unnecessarily, as will the cost of the system. Here it will be established just what sampling rate is necessary in a given situation, initially in theory, then taking into account practical restrictions. By multiplying the number of bits needed to express the signal voltage by the rate at which the process must be updated, the bit rate of the digital data stream resulting from a particular analog signal can be determined.

2.3 Sampling and aliasing

In Fig.2.4(a) a high sampling rate is intuitively adequate to convey the waveform, whereas in (b) there is clearly a problem. The output waveform is now at a new frequency. To explain this phenomenon we need to study the spectrum of a sampled signal. Fig.2.5(a) shows the spectrum of the unmodulated sampling pulses. The first entry in the spectrum is the sampling rate, but since the sample is vanishingly short in duration, the spectrum is infinite, and consists of harmonics of the sampling rate. As stated, the input signal amplitude modulates the sampling impulses. As might be expected, this produces sidebands, upper and lower, but these appear about all of the harmonics to give the spectrum of Fig.2.5(b). Also shown is the necessary response of the reconstruction filter which must reject the sidebands and pass only the baseband signal.

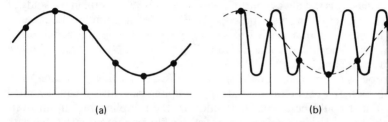

(a)   (b)

Figure 2.4 At (a), the sampling is adequate to reconstruct the original signal. At (b) the sampling rate is inadequate, and reconstruction produces the wrong waveform (dotted). Aliasing has taken place.

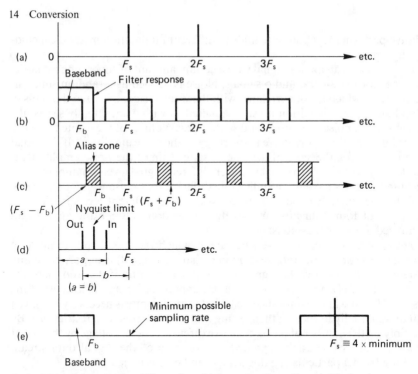

Figure 2.5 (a) Spectrum of sampling pulses. (b) Spectrum of samples. (c) Aliasing due to sideband overlap. (d) Beat-frequency production. (e) 4 × oversampling.

In Fig.2.5(c) the sampling rate has been reduced too far, and there is a region of overlap (shaded) between the baseband and the sidebands. The reconstruction filter can no longer separate them, and the result is aliasing. Fig.2.5(d) shows that if an excessive frequency is put into a sampling system, the output will be a beat (difference) frequency between input and sampling rate. If a perfect filter is available, then the sampling rate must only exceed twice the basebandwidth and no aliasing will occur. Although this was described by Shannon it is almost always referred to as the Nyquist Theory in digital audio documentation. In the Soviet Union, the theory is attributed to Kotelnikov, whose work was almost simultaneous to that of Shannon. A striking example of aliasing is the tendency of spoked wheels to appear to be turning at the wrong speed when seen on film or TV. The movie camera is a sampling system, and the spoke frequency of a rapidly turning wheel may be beyond the Nyquist frequency. Aliasing is not always harmful, however; it is very useful in the study of rotating machinery using a stroboscope. In Fig.2.5(e) the sampling rate used is greatly in excess of that needed to satisfy Nyquist. This is the definition of oversampling. The ratio of the actual sampling rate to the Nyquist rate is known as the oversampling factor.

The process of reconstruction is shown in Fig.2.6. The low-pass filter must have a cut-off frequency of one-half the sampling rate in a Nyquist-limited system, but it could be a smaller fraction of the sampling rate in an over-sampling system. The impulse response of such a filter is a $\sin x/x$ curve, but with the interesting property that the voltage of the impulse is zero at the position of all other samples. Clearly there is no interference between samples at the sample

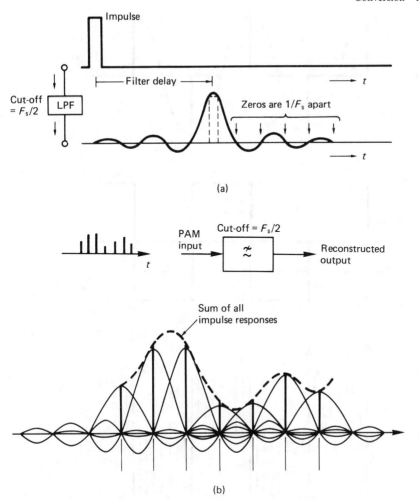

Figure 2.6 The impulse response of a low-pass filter which cuts off at $F_s/2$ has zeros at $1/F_s$ spacing which correspond to the position of adjacent samples, as shown in (b). The output will be a signal which has the value of each sample at the sample instant, but with smooth transitions from sample to sample.

instants; thus the output waveform of the filter will join up the peaks of all the impulses. The figure shows how the various impulses add in the filter to produce all intermediate voltages between samples.[6]

This reconstruction process only takes place as described if the input to the filter is a series of impulses of negligible duration. In practice this is never achieved. Fig.2.7 and Fig.2.8 show that an impulse of finite width can be thought of as a large number of infinitely small impulses, side by side. The $\sin x/x$ curves due to these impulses now interfere with adjacent sample impulses. The result is a roll-off of high frequencies. This phenomenon is known as the aperture effect; it has exactly the same result as the loss due to finite head-gap in magnetic recording, and the same equations apply. If the impulses

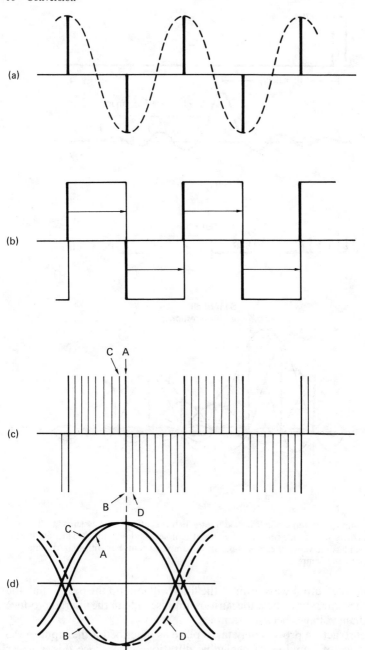

Figure 2.7 The mechanism of aperture effect which causes high-frequency losses when impulse has finite period. (a) Maximum-frequency sine wave in samples of zero duration. (b) Zero-order hold version of above (100% aperture). (c) Consider rectangular pulse as infinite number of delta functions. (d) Result of low-pass filtering some of above impulses. A cancels B completely. C cancels D partially.

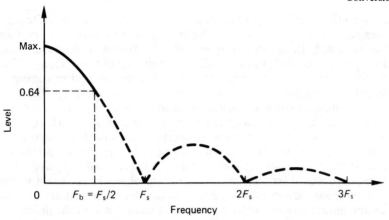

Figure 2.8 Frequency response with 100 % aperture nulls at multiples of sampling rate. Area of interest is up to half sampling rate.

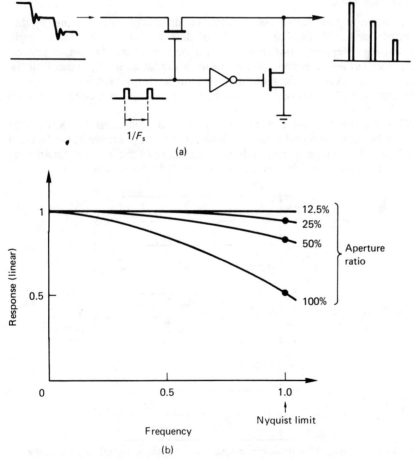

Figure 2.9 (a) Resampling circuit eliminates transients and reduces aperture ratio.
(b) Response of various aperture ratios.

are the same width as the sample period, the frequency response rolls off to zero at the sampling rate as a sin x/x curve. The filter, however, will only respond up to half the sampling rate, where the output will be 0.64 of the maximum or some 4 dB down. Many DACs produce such a zero-order hold waveform which appears like a staircase. The process of resampling can be used to convert a zero-order hold signal into one with narrower impulses, as in Fig.2.9. The duty cycle of the switch is known as the aperture ratio. Fig.2.7 also shows the frequency responses due to various aperture ratios. In digital audio, where linearity of frequency response is important, an aperture ratio of as little as $\frac{1}{8}$ may be used, which minimizes the amount of equalization necessary. It is important not to take resampling too far, since with impulses of negligible duration, the frequency response would be very linear, but the signal would be buried in the noise of the reconstruction filter. The term resampling is sometimes used to mean sampling-rate conversion, but the context usually makes the difference clear.

2.4 Quantizing

Fig.2.10 shows that the process of quantizing divides the voltage range up into quantizing intervals Q. These may be of differing size for particular applications, e.g. telephony, but in this case it becomes very difficult to process sample values arithmetically. Hence in most digital audio equipment all the quantizing intervals are the same, and the term 'uniform quantising' is applied. The term 'linear quantising' will also be found, but this is a contradiction in terms.

Whatever the exact voltage of the input signal, the quantizer will express it as the number of the interval it falls in. When that number arrives at the DAC, it will create the voltage corresponding to the centre of the interval. Quantizing thus makes errors, which cannot exceed $\pm\frac{1}{2}Q$. If the output of the DAC is

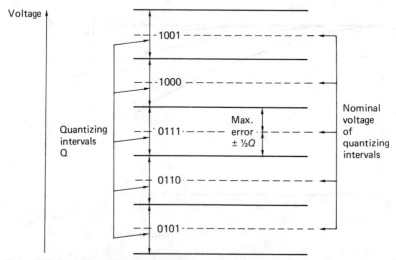

Figure 2.10 Quantizing. All voltages within a particular quantizing interval are assigned the same number, which corresponds to the voltage of the centre of the interval. The maximum quantizing error cannot exceed $\pm\frac{1}{2}Q$.

resampled to avoid aperture effect, the impulses from the DAC can be compared with the impulses at the input sampling stage. The difference between the two will be an impulse train (Fig.2.11) which can be thought of as an unwanted signal added by the quantizing process to a perfect signal. This is the quantizing error signal; it warrants considerable study since it has some unexpected characteristics.

Where the input signal exercises the range of the quantizer, and has a complex waveform (such as that produced by the sound of an orchestra, for example) the size of the quantizing error will be anywhere between $-\frac{1}{2}Q$ and $+\frac{1}{2}Q$ with uniform probability, as in Fig.2.11(c). This probability density function should be contrasted with that of thermal noise in electronic components, which has a Gaussian shape. Since in this case the unwanted signal is uncorrelated with the information, it is appropriate to call it noise. However, the large signal case is the one where noise is of the least interest, since the presence of the signal masks noise. Nevertheless many treatments of quantizing proceed to make the simple connection between the number of bits in the word, n, and the signal-to-noise ratio, namely $6.02n + 1.76$ dB. There are two shortcomings to this simplistic approach. First, the noise power calculated has an infinite spectrum, and no account is taken of the effect of the reconstruction filter on this spectrum.

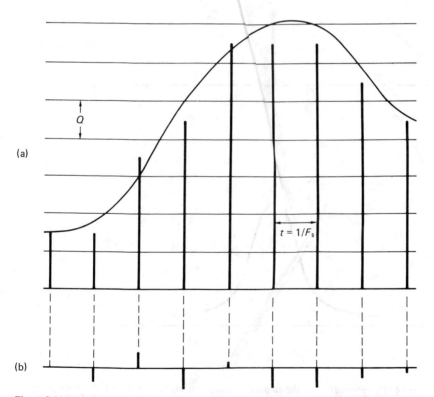

Figure 2.11 At (a) an arbitrary signal is represented to finite accuracy by PAM needles whose peaks are at the centre of the quantizing intervals. The errors caused can be thought of as an unwanted signal (b) added to the original.

Secondly, and much more importantly, the mathematics only holds if the probability density function of the quantizing error is uniform. At low levels, and particularly with pure or simple signals, the quantizing error ceases to be random, and becomes a function of the input signal. Once an unwanted signal

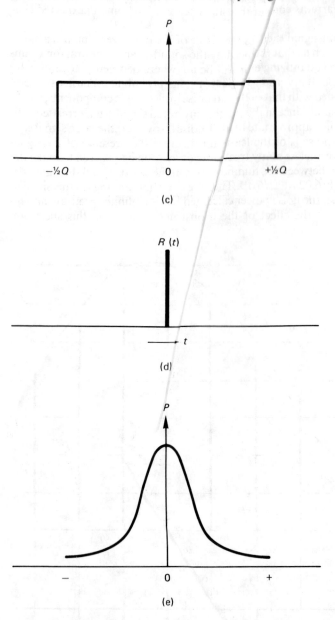

(c)

(d)

(e)

Figure 2.11 (*continued*) At (c) the amplitude of a quantizing error needle will be from $-\frac{1}{2}Q$ to $+\frac{1}{2}Q$ with equal probability. For large complex signals the autocorrelation function $R(t)$ has one spike as at (d), giving a uniform spectrum. Note, however, that white noise in analog circuits generally has Gaussian amplitude distribution, shown at (e).

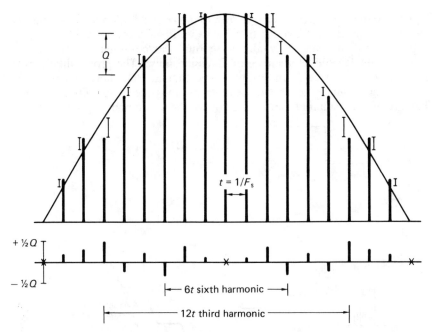

Figure 2.12 Mathematically derived quantizing error waveform for sine wave sampled at a multiple of itself. The numerous autocorrelations between quantizing errors show that there are harmonics of the signal in the error, and that the error is not random, but deterministic.

becomes a deterministic function of the wanted signal, it has to be referred to as distortion rather than noise. As the level of the analog input is reduced, the quantizing error becomes less random, and noise modulation occurs. Where more than one frequency is present in the input there will be intermodulation products. The distinctive gravelly effect that results has come to be known as granulation.

The harmonics caused by these non-linear processes can alias with the sampling rate to produce anharmonic frequencies in the audible spectrum which are often called birdsinging. Where the sampling rate is a multiple of the signal frequency, the effect is harmonic distortion. It is easy to demonstrate this phenomenon graphically (Fig.2.12). The quantizing error has been determined from the signal. Strong correlations between quantizing errors can be seen and the resultant harmonics of the signal are visible. This result is true for a perfect quantizer, and the effect can be demonstrated easily by temporarily disabling some of the low-order bits in a system. In practice, it is difficult to obtain a perfectly deterministic quantizing error because of noise in the input signal. This has a randomizing effect on the quantizing error, and reduces the distortion accordingly. Fig.2.13 shows that the effect of dither is to smear the transfer function of the quantizer horizontally. Where the RMS noise voltage is one-third of a quantizing interval,[7] the quantizing error will be as random as the noise, and the quantizing process becomes perfectly linear. Another way of describing the effect is to say that the voltage of the input between quantizing intervals is conveyed in the duty cycle of the binary switching.

This randomizing technique is known as *dither*; in addition to linearizing the system it also defines the signal-to-noise ratio. If sufficient noise is not already superimposed on the input signal, a noise source can be built into the converter. A diode can be used as a source of Gaussian noise. The probability density function of the dither is important. If rectangular PDF noise is created by connecting a digitally generated pseudo-random sequence to a DAC, the probability of the resultant quantizing error will be the combined probabilities of

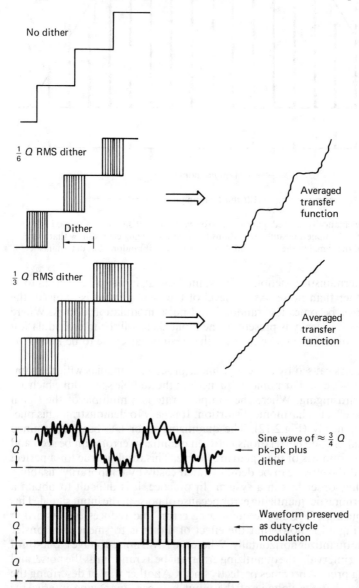

Figure 2.13 The use of wideband dither of $\frac{1}{3}Q$ RMS linearizes the transfer function and produces noise instead of distortion. This can be proved by time-averaging. Noise reduces with averaging; distortion would not.

the dither and the undithered quantizing error. Since the pseudo-random generator output cannot be correlated with the undithered quantizing error, the combination of the two results in a triangular probability density function. The result will be slight noise modulation: the amplitude of the noise changes with signal amplitude, although the linearizing effect is unimpaired. If sufficient Gaussian dither is used to produce a linear system, namely $\frac{1}{3}Q$ RMS, the signal-to-noise ratio can easily be shown to be $6.02n$ dB. For most practical purposes, 6 dB per bit is an adequate assessment of signal to noise, but only if suitable dither is employed.

In an extension of the application of dither, Blesser[8] has suggested digitally generated dither which is converted to the analog domain and added to the input signal prior to quantizing. That same digital dither is then subtracted from the digital quantizer output. The effect is that the transfer function of the quantizer is smeared diagonally (Fig.2.14). The significance of this diagonal smearing

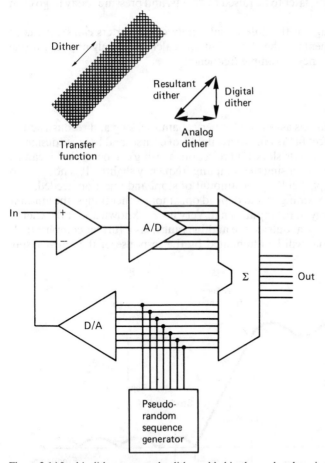

Figure 2.14 In this dither system, the dither added in the analog domain shifts the transfer function horizontally, but the same dither is subtracted in the digital domain, which shifts the transfer function vertically. The result is that the quantizer staircase is smeared diagonally as shown top left. There is thus no limit to dither amplitude, and excess dither can be used to improve differential linearity of the converter.

is that the amplitude of the dither is not critical. However much dither is employed, the noise amplitude will remain the same. If dither of several quantizing intervals is used, it has the effect of making all the quantizing intervals in an imperfect converter appear to have the same size. The importance of correctly dithering a quantizer cannot be emphasized enough, since failure to dither irrevocably distorts the converted signal: there can be no process which will subsequently remove that distortion.

In principle a sample can be quantized into any number range desired, but it is convenient to use binary circuitry to handle and store the numbers, and accordingly quantizing ranges will always be some power of two. The appropriate range is hard to define since, as with any signal which will be assessed by a human being, results are subjective. It is tempting to take the signal-to-noise ratio of an equivalent analog system and divide by six to obtain the number of bits. This approach was not found to be successful for audio: hence the initial machines with 14 bits, later to be raised to 16 bits, and pressure today to go even further.

The dynamic range of the differential family of converters can be deduced using similar arguments to the above, but any calculation only applies for one ratio of signal frequency to sample frequency.

2.5 Filter design

The discussion so far has assumed that perfect anti-aliasing and reconstruction filters are used. Perfect filters are not available, of course, and because designers must use devices with finite slope and rejection, aliasing can occur, but it can be made less significant by raising the sampling frequency slightly. It is not easy to specify such filters, particularly the amount of stopband rejection needed. The amount of aliasing resulting would depend on, among other things, the amount of out-of-band energy in the input signal. Very little is known about the energy in typical source material outside the audible range. As a further complication, an out-of-band signal will be attenuated by the response of the anti-aliasing

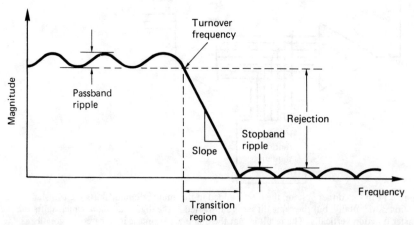

Figure 2.15 The important features and terminology of low-pass filters used for anti-aliasing and reconstruction.

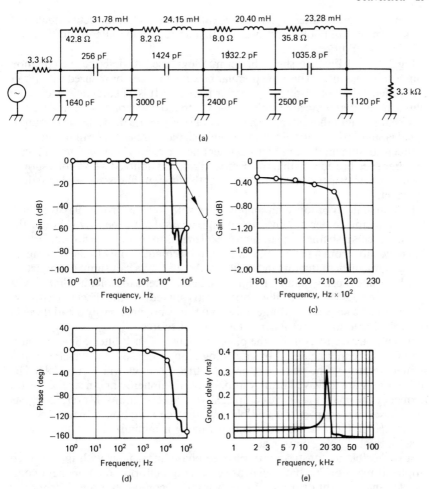

Figure 2.16 (a) Circuit of typical nine-pole elliptic passive filter with frequency response at (b) shown magnified in the region of cutoff at (c). Note phase response at (d) beginning to change at only 1 kHz, and group delay at (e), which require compensation for quality applications. Note that in the presence of out-of-band signals, aliasing might only be 60 dB down. A thirteen-pole filter manages in excess of 80 dB, but phase response is worse.

filter to that frequency, but the residual signal will then alias, and the reconstruction filter will reject it according to its attenuation at the new frequency to which it has aliased. To take the opposite extreme, if a microphone were used which had no response at all above the audio band, no anti-aliasing filter would be needed.

It could be argued that the reconstruction filter is unnecessary, since all the images are outside the range of human hearing, but the slightest nonlinearity in subsequent stages would result in gross intermodulation distortion. The possibility of damage to tweeters and beating with the bias systems of analog tape recorders must also be considered. It would, however, be acceptable to bypass one of the filters involved in a copy from one digital machine to another via the analog domain, although a digital transfer is of course to be preferred.

The nature of the filters used has a great bearing on the subjective quality of the system. Entire books have been written about analog filters, and they will only be treated briefly here.

Fig.2.15 and Fig.2.16 show the terminology used to describe the common elliptic low pass filter. These are popular because they can be realized with fewer components than other filters of similar response. It is a characteristic of these elliptic filters that there are ripples in the passband and stopband. Lagadec and Stockham[9] found that filters with passband ripple cause dispersion: the output signal is smeared in time and, on toneburst signals, pre-echoes can be detected. In much equipment the anti-aliasing filter and the reconstruction filter will have the same specification, so that the passband ripple is doubled with a corresponding increase in dispersion. Sometimes slightly different filters are used to reduce the effect.

It is difficult to produce an analog filter with low distortion. Passive filters using inductors suffer nonlinearity at high levels due to the B/H curve of the cores. It seems a shame to go to such great lengths to remove the nonlinearity of magnetic tape from a recording using digital techniques only to pass the signal through magnetic inductors in the filters. Active filters can simulate inductors which are linear using op-amp techniques, but they tend to suffer nonlinearity at high frequencies where the falling open-loop gain reduces the effect of feedback. Active filters also can contribute noise, but this is not necessarily a bad thing in controlled amounts, since it can act as a dither source.

It is instructive to examine the phase response of such filters. Since a sharp cut-off is generally achieved by cascading many filter sections which cut at a similar frequency, the phase responses of these sections will accumulate. The phase may start to leave linearity at only a few kilohertz, and near the cut-off frequency the phase may have completed several revolutions. Meyer[10] suggests that these phase errors are audible and that equalization is necessary. An advantage of linear phase filters is that ringing is minimized, and there is less possibility of clipping on transients.

It is possible to construct a ripple-free phase-linear filter with the required stopband rejection,[8,11] but is expensive of design effort and component complexity, and it might drift out of specification as components age. The money may be better spent in avoiding the need for such a filter. Much effort can be saved in analog filter design by using oversampling. As shown in Fig.2.17 a high sampling rate produces a large spectral gap between the baseband and the first lower sideband. The anti-aliasing and reconstruction filters need only have a gentle roll-off, causing minimum disturbance to phase linearity in the baseband,

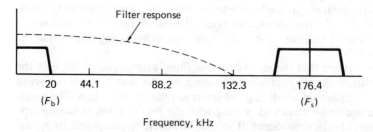

Figure 2.17 In this 4× oversampling system, the large separation between baseband and sidebands allows a gentle roll-off reconstruction filter to be used.

and the Butterworth configuration, which does not have ripple or dispersion, can be used. The penalty of oversampling is that an excessive data rate results. It is necessary to reduce the rate using a digital LPF. Reference to Chapter 4 will show that certain digital filters are inherently phase-linear and, using LSIs, can be inexpensive to construct. The audible superiority of oversampling converters means that they will be increasingly used in the future, which is why the subject is more prominent here than the treatment of filter design.

2.6 Choice of sampling rate

The Nyquist criterion is only the beginning of the process which must be followed to arrive at a suitable sampling rate. The slope of available filters will compel designers to raise the sampling rate above the theoretical Nyquist rate. For consumer products, the lower the sampling rate the better, since the cost of the medium is directly proportional to the sampling rate: thus sampling rates near to twice 20 kHz are to be expected. For professional products, there is a need to operate at variable speed for pitch correction. When the speed of a digital recorder is reduced, the offtape sampling rate falls, and Fig.2.18 shows that with a minimal sampling rate the first image frequency can become low enough to pass the reconstruction filter. If the sampling frequency is raised without changing the response of the filters, the speed can be reduced without this problem. It follows that variable-speed recorders, generally those with stationary heads, must use a higher sampling rate.

In the early days of digital audio research, the necessary bandwidth of about one megabit per second per audio channel was difficult to store. Disk drives had the bandwidth, but not the capacity for long recording time, attention therefore turned to the video recorder. In Chapter 8 it will be seen that these were adapted to store audio samples by creating a pseudo-video waveform which could convey binary as black and white. The sampling rate of such a system is constrained to relate simply to the field rate and field structure of the television standard used, so that an integer number of samples can be stored on each usable TV line in the field. Unfortunately there are two standards, 525 lines at 59.94 Hz and 625 lines at 50 Hz, and it is not possible to find a frequency which is a common multiple of the two and is low enough to use as a sampling rate.

The allowable sampling rates in a pseudo-video system can be deduced by multiplying the field rate by the number of active lines in a field (blanked lines cannot be used) and again by the number of samples in a line. By careful choice of parameters it is possible to use 525/59.94 or 625/50 video with only a slight difference in sampling rate.

In 59.94 Hz video, there are 35 blanked lines, leaving 490 lines per frame, or 245 lines per field for samples. If three samples are stored per line, the sampling rate becomes:
$$59.94 \times 245 \times 3 = 44.0559 \text{ kHz}$$
In 50 Hz video, there are 37 lines of blanking, leaving 588 active lines per frame, or 294 per field, so the sampling rate becomes:
$$50.00 \times 294 \times 3 = 44.1 \text{ kHz}$$
There is a 0.1 % difference between these two rates, which means that for some purposes a recording made at one rate can be played at the other.

These two rates are used by consumer PCM adaptors corresponding to the EIAJ format, which record six samples per line to allow stereo operation, and

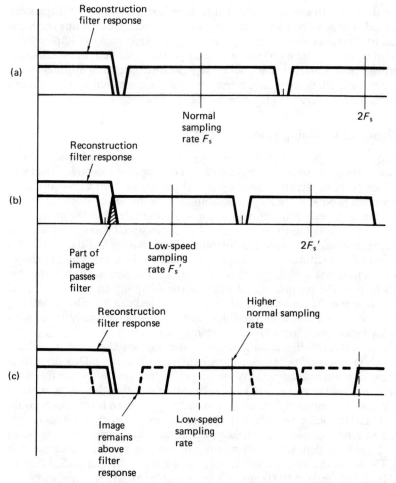

Figure 2.18 At normal speed, the reconstruction filter correctly prevents images entering the baseband, as at (a). When speed is reduced, the sampling rate falls, and a fixed filter will allow part of the lower sideband of the sampling frequency to pass. If the sampling rate of the machine is raised, but the filter characteristic remains the same, the problem can be avoided, as at (c).

allow the use of a VCR of the video format of the country of sale, since it was expected that the consumer would require to use the same VCR either for regular video recording or for PCM audio.

44.1 kHz came to be the sampling rate of the Compact Disc. Even though CD has no video circuitry, the equipment used to make CD masters is video-based, and determines the sampling rate. Oddly enough, the VCRs used for CD production run at 525/60.00 *not* 59.94 Hz, so the sampling rate is given by:

$$60 \times 245 \times 3 = 44.1 \, \text{kHz}$$

The strange situation arises that it is possible to lock a 60 Hz-based VCR for CD mastering to the PAL or SECAM video system at 50 Hz via the sampling rate, but it is not possible to lock to 59.94 Hz NTSC.

With these sampling rates having been established so early, it was natural to suggest higher rates for professional use which had a simple relationship to them. The argument was that digital sampling-rate conversion is eased if the rates are related. The professional frequencies of 50.34965...kHz and 50.4 kHz are obtained by multiplying the pseudo-video frequencies derived earlier by $\frac{8}{7}$.

For landlines to FM stereo broadcast transmitters having a 15 kHz audio bandwidth, the sampling rate of 32 kHz is more than adequate, and has been in use for some time in the United Kingdom and Japan. The professional sampling rate of 48 kHz was proposed as having a simple relationship to 32 kHz, being far enough above 40 kHz for variable-speed operation, and having a simple relationship with PAL video timing which would allow digital video recorders to store the convenient number of 960 audio samples per video field. The important work done on variable sampling-rate converters (see Chapter 4) demonstrated that there was no longer a need to have simple relations between sampling rates, and so 48 kHz came to be the accepted sampling rate for professional audio.

The absence of degradation when copying means that pirated digital audio recordings are difficult to tell from the original. There has accordingly been a great deal of pressure from music publishers to make consumer digital recorders have a sampling rate different from Compact Disc. The RDAT format in its consumer version will only record at 48 kHz, but it can play only at 44.1 kHz, so that software for Compact Disc can be published on prerecorded RDAT tapes. The digital sampling-rate converter will remain a relatively expensive item, but even if a pirate organization obtained one, prerecorded RDAT tapes at 48 kHz would arouse suspicion.

Although in a perfect world the adoption of a single sampling rate might have had virtues, for practical and economic reasons digital audio now has essentially three rates to support: 32 kHz for broadcast, 44.1 kHz for CD/EIAJ/RDAT replay only, and 48 kHz for professional/digital VTR/RDAT record/play.[12]

2.7 Basic digital-to-analog conversion

The reverse of the quantizing process will be discussed first, since ADCs often use DACs in feedback loops.

There are two main ways of obtaining an analog signal from PCM data. One is to control binary-weighted currents and sum them; the other is to control the length of time a fixed current flows into an integrator. The two methods are contrasted in Fig.2.19. They look simple, but are of no use for audio in these forms because of practical limitations. In Fig.2.19(c), the binary code is about to have a major overflow, and all the low-order currents are flowing. In Fig. 2.19(d), the binary input has increased by one, and only the most significant current flows. This current must equal the sum of all the others plus one least-significant current to an accuracy of rather better than one least-significant current. In this simple four-bit example, the necessary accuracy is only one part in sixteen, but for a sixteen bit system it would become one part in 65 536, or about 0.0015 %. This degree of accuracy is almost impossible to achieve, let alone maintain in the presence of ageing and temperature change.

The integrator-type converter in this four-bit example is shown in Fig.2.19(e); it requires a clock for the counter which allows it to count up to the maximum in less than one sample period. This will be more than sixteen times the sampling

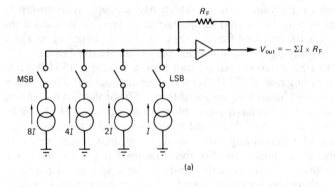

(a)

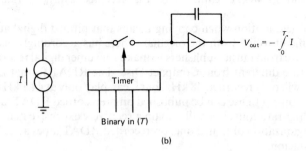

(b)

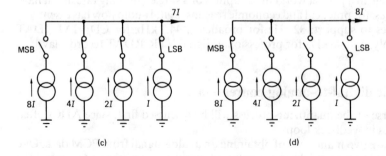

(c)

(d)

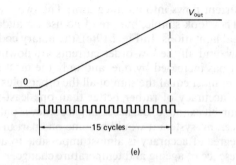

(e)

Figure 2.19 Elementary conversion: (a) weighted current DAC; (b) timed integrator DAC; (c) current flow with 0111 input; (d) current flow with 1000 input; (e) integrator ramps up for fifteen cycles of clock for input 1111.

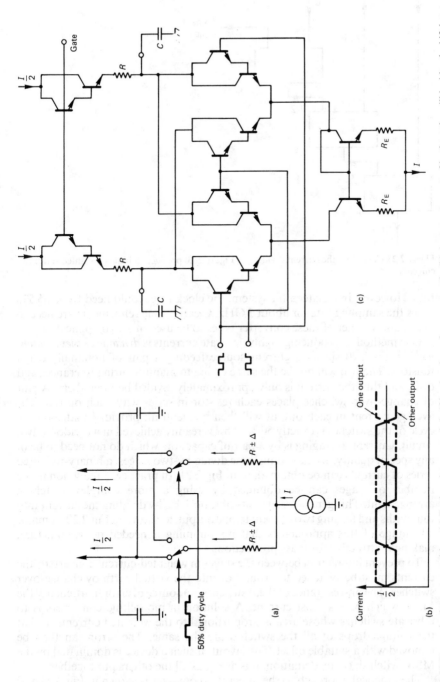

Figure 2.20 Dynamic element matching. (a) Each resistor spends half its time in each current path. (b) Average current of both paths will be identical if duty cycle is accurately 50%. (c) Typical monolithic implementation. Note clock frequency is arbitrary.

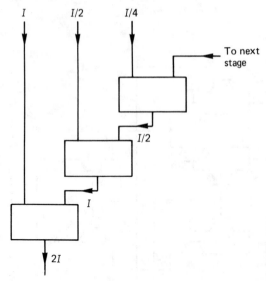

Figure 2.21 Cascading the current dividers of Figure 2.20 produces a binary weighted series of currents.

rate. However, in a sixteen bit system, the clock rate would need to be 65 536 times the sampling rate, or about 3 GHz. Clearly some refinements are necessary to allow either of these converter types to be used in audio applications.

One method of producing highly accurate currents is *dynamic element matching*[13,14]. Fig.2.20 shows a current source feeding a pair of nominally equal resistors. The two will not be the same owing to manufacturing tolerances and drift, and thus the current is only approximately divided between them. A pair of change-over switches places each resistor in series with each output. The average current in each output will then be identical, provided that the duty cycle of the switches is exactly 50 %. This is readily achieved in a divide-by-two circuit. Current-averaging is by a pair of capacitors which do not need to be of any special quality. By cascading these divide-by-two stages, a binary-weighted series of currents can be obtained, as in Fig.2.21. In practice, a reduction in the number of stages can be obtained by using a more complex switching arrangement. This generates currents of ratio 1:1:2 by dividing the current into four paths and feeding two of them to one output, as shown in Fig.2.22. A major advantage of this approach is that no trimming is needed in manufacture, making it attractive for mass production.

To prevent interaction between the stages in weighted-current converters, the currents must be switched to ground or into the virtual earth by change-over switches. The on-resistance of these switches is a source of error, particularly the MSB, which passes most current. A solution in monolithic converters is to fabricate switches whose area is proportional to the weighted current, so that the voltage-drops of all the switches are the same. The error can then be removed with a suitable offset. The layout of such a device is dominated by the MSB switch since, by definition, it is as big as all the others put together.

The practical approach to the integrator converter is shown in Fig.2.23 and Fig.2.24 where two current sources whose ratio is 256 to 1 are used; the larger is timed by the high byte of the sample and the smaller is timed by the low byte.

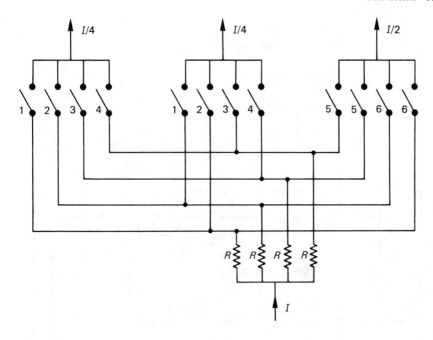

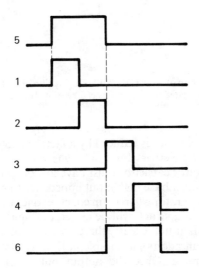

Figure 2.22 More complex dynamic element matching system. Four drive signals (1, 2, 3, 4) of 25% duty cycle close switches of corresponding number. Two signals (5, 6) have 50% duty cycle, resulting in two current shares going to right-hand output. Division is thus into 1:1:2.

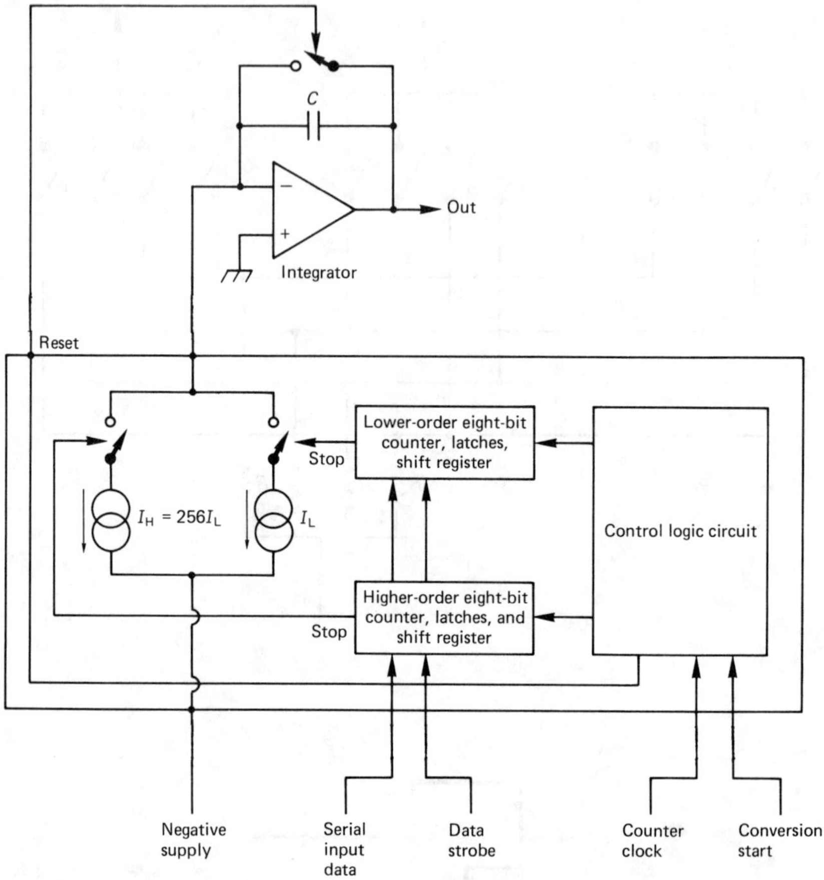

Figure 2.23 Simplified diagram of Sony CX-20017. The high-order and low-order current sources (I_H and I_L) and associated timing circuits can be seen. The necessary integrator is external.

The necessary clock frequency is reduced by a factor of 256. Any inaccuracy in the current ratio will cause errors, but tracking is easier to achieve in a monolithic device. The integrator capacitor must have low dielectric leakage, and the operational amplifier must have high input impedance to prevent nonlinearity.

The output of the integrator will remain constant once the current sources are turned off, and an analog switch will be closed during the voltage plateau to produce the resampled output. Clearly this device cannot produce a zero-order hold output without an additional sample-hold stage, so it is naturally complemented by resampling. Once the output pulse has been gated to the reconstruction filter, the capacitor is discharged with a further switch in preparation for the next conversion. The conversion count must take place in rather less than one sample period to permit the resampling and discharge phases. A clock frequency of about 20 MHz is adequate for a sixteen bit 48 kHz unit, which permits the ramp to complete in 12.8 μs, leaving 8 μs for resampling and reset.

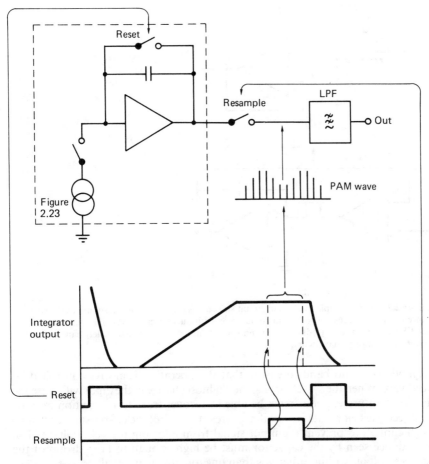

Figure 2.24 In an integrator converter, the output level is only stable when the ramp finishes. An analog switch is necessary to isolate the ramp from subsequent circuits. The switch can also be used to produce a PAM (pulse amplitude modulated) signal which has a flatter frequency response than a zero-order hold (staircase) signal.

2.8 Basic analog-to-digital conversion

Many of the ADCs described here will need a finite time to operate, whereas an instantaneous sample must be taken from the input. The solution is to use a track/hold circuit, which is shown in simple form in Fig.2.25. When the switch is closed, the output will follow the input, and when the switch opens the capacitor holds the voltage of the signal at that instant. In practice, the shortcomings of this simple arrangement are too great for audio use. In particular, the time constant of the capacitor with the on-resistance of the switch results in long settling time. The effect can be minimized by putting the switch inside a feed-back loop as shown in Fig.2.25(b), since the series resistance of the switch will then be divided by the open-loop gain of the buffer. The specification of the buffer amplifier is stringent, since it requires adequate open-loop gain well

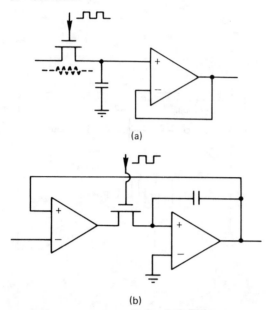

(a)

(b)

Figure 2.25 (a) The simple track-hold circuit shown has poor frequency response as the resistance of the FET causes a roll-off in conjunction with the capacitor. At (b) the resistance of the FET is now inside a feedback loop and will be eliminated, provided the left-hand op-amp never runs out of gain or swing.

beyond the audio band to ensure that the operation is always controlled by feedback. When the switch opens, the slightest change in the input will cause the buffer to saturate, and it must be able to recover from this condition rapidly. The feedback eliminates the switch on-resistance, but the off-resistance must be high enough to prevent the input signal from affecting the held voltage. The impedance seen by the capacitor must be high enough to keep droop of the sample voltage within rather less than one quantizing interval.

The clock which drives the switch must have very low jitter, or noise may be superimposed on the sample values. The mechanism is illustrated in Fig.2.26, where a changing signal is being sampled. The mistiming due to clock jitter causes the wrong voltage to be sampled. The effect clearly rises with the rate of change of input voltage; therefore the amount of noise caused will depend on the spectrum of the input, making it a form of modulation noise. It is difficult to specify the clock jitter tolerance, since the worst-case assumptions demand an accuracy within about 100 ps!

Fig.2.27 shows the various events during a track/hold sequence, and catalogues the various sources of inaccuracy. The track/hold stage is extremely difficult to design because of the accuracy required in audio applications. In particular it is difficult to meet the droop specification for a system of more than sixteen bits accuracy. Whenever such performance bottlenecks are found, it is tempting to look for an alternative method which avoids the problems. This alternative will be found in oversampling.

The general principle of a quantizer is that different quantized voltages are compared with the unknown analog input until the closest quantized voltage is found. The code corresponding to this becomes the output.

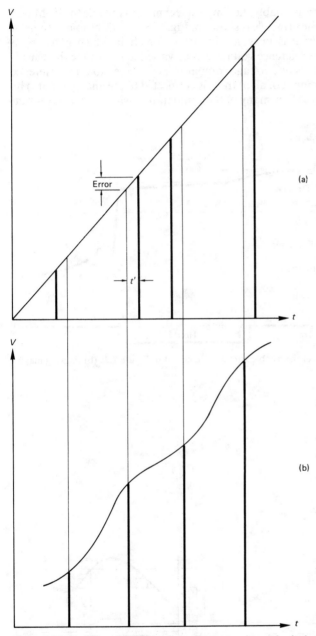

Figure 2.26 The effect of sampling timing jitter on noise, and calculation of the required accuracy for a sixteen-bit system. (a) Ramp sampled with jitter has error proportional to slope. (b) When jitter is removed by later circuits, error appears as noise added to samples. For a sixteen-bit system there are $2^{16}Q$, and the maximum slope at 20 kHz will be $20\,000\pi \times 2^{16}Q$/sec. If jitter is to be neglected, the noise must be less than $\frac{1}{2}Q$, thus timing accuracy t' multiplied by maximum slope $= \frac{1}{2}Q$ or $20\,000\pi \times 2^{16}Qt' = \frac{1}{2}Q$

$$\therefore t' = \frac{1}{2 \times 20\,000 \times \pi \times 2^{16}} = 121 \text{ ps.}$$

The flash converter is probably the simplest technique available for PCM and DPCM conversion. The principle is shown in Fig.2.28. The threshold voltage of every quantizing interval is provided by a resistor chain which is fed by a reference voltage. This reference voltage can be varied to determine the sensitivity of the input. There is one voltage comparator connected to every reference voltage, and the other input of all of these is connected to the analog input. The input voltage determines how many of the comparators will have a true output.

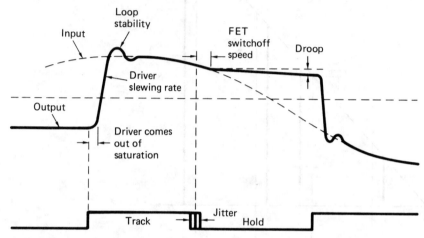

Figure 2.27 Characteristics of the feedback track/hold circuit of Figure 2.25 (b) showing major sources of error.

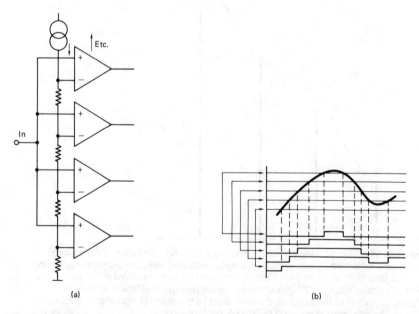

Figure 2.28 The flash converter. At (a) each quantizing interval has its own comparator, resulting in waveforms of (b). A priority encoder is necessary to convert the comparator outputs to a binary code.

As one comparator is necessary for each quantizing interval, then, for example, in an eight bit system there will be 255 binary comparator outputs, and it is necessary to use a priority encoder to convert these to a binary code. Although the device is simple in principle, it contains a lot of circuitry, and can only be practicably implemented on a chip. A sixteen bit device would need a ridiculous 65 535 comparators, and thus these converters are not practicable for direct audio conversion, although they will be used in DPCM and in oversampling

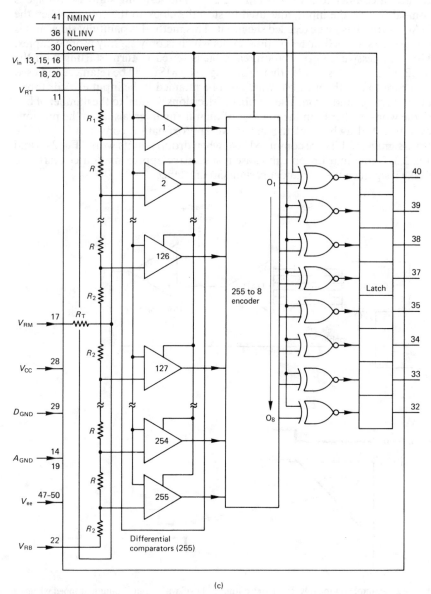

(c)

Figure 2.28 (*continued*) Shown at (c) is a typical eight-bit flash converter primarily intended for video applications (Courtesy TRW).

converters. The analog signal has to drive a lot of inputs, and a low-impedance driver is essential to avoid restricting the slewing rate of the input. The extreme speed of a flash converter is a distinct advantage in oversampling. Because computation of all bits is performed simultaneously, no track/hold circuit is required, and droop is eliminated.

Reduction in component complexity can be achieved by quantizing serially. The most primitive method of generating different quantized voltages is to connect a counter to a DAC as in Fig.2.29. The resulting staircase voltage is compared with the input, and used to stop the clock to the counter when the DAC output has just exceeded the input. This method is painfully slow, and is not used, as a much faster method exists which is only slightly more complex. Using successive approximation, each bit is tested in turn, starting with the MSB. If the input is greater than half range, the MSB will be retained, and used as a base to test the next bit, which will be retained if the input exceeds three-quarters range and so on. The number of decisions is equal to the number of bits in the word, rather than the number of quantizing intervals, as in the previous example. A drawback of the successive approximation converter is that the least-significant bits are computed last, when droop is at its worst. Fig.2.30 and Fig.2.31 show that droop can cause a successive approximation converter to make a significant error under certain circumstances.

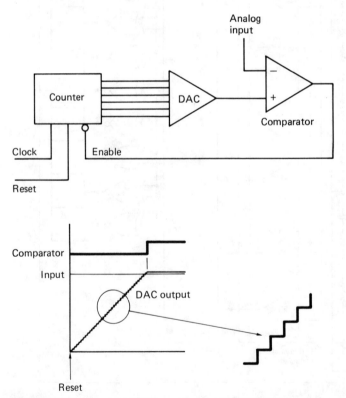

Figure 2.29 Simple ramp ADC compares output of DAC with input. Count is stopped when DAC output just exceeds input. This method, although potentially accurate, is much too slow for digital audio.

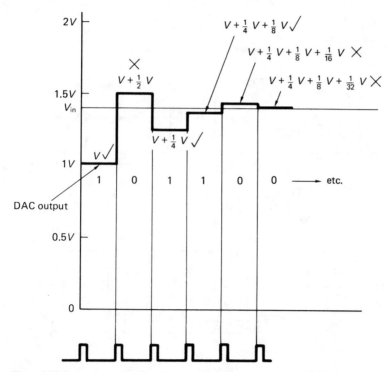

Figure 2.30 Successive approximation tests each bit in turn, starting with the most significant. The DAC output is compared with the input. If the DAC output is below the input ($\checkmark$) the bit is made 1; if the DAC output is above the input ($\times$) the bit is made zero.

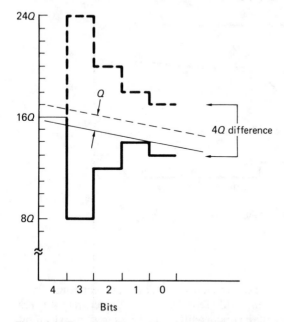

Figure 2.31 Two drooping track/hold signals (solid and dotted lines) which differ by one quantizing interval Q are shown here to result in conversions which are $4Q$ apart. Thus droop can destroy the monotonicity of a converter. Low-level signals (near the midrange of the number system) are especially vulnerable.

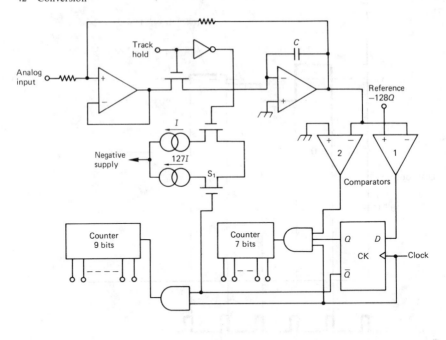

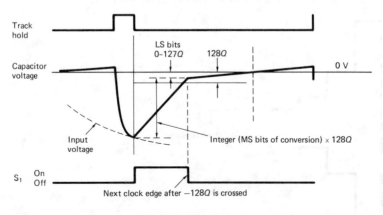

Figure 2.32 Dual-ramp ADC using track/hold capacitor as integrator.

A-to-D conversion can also be performed using the dual-current-source type DAC in a feedback system; the major difference is that the two current sources must work sequentially rather than concurrently. Fig.2.32 shows a sixteen bit application in which the capacitor of the track/hold circuit is also used as the ramp integrator. The system operates as follows. When the track/hold FET switches off, the capacitor C will be holding the sample voltage. Two currents of ratio 128:1 are capable of discharging the capacitor. Due to this ratio, the smaller current will be used to determine the least significant seven bits, and the larger current will determine the nine most significant bits. The currents are provided by current sources of ratio 127:1. When both run together, the current produced is 128 times that from the smaller source alone. This approach means that the current can be changed simply by turning off the larger source, rather than by attempting a changeover.

With both current sources enabled, the high-order counter counts up until the capacitor voltage has fallen below the reference of $-128\,Q$ supplied to comparator 1. At the next clock edge, the larger current source is turned off. Waiting for the next clock edge is important, because it ensures that the larger source can only run for entire clock periods, which will discharge the integrator by integer multiples of $128\,Q$. The integrator voltage will overshoot the $128\,Q$ reference, and the remaining voltage on the integrator will be less than $128\,Q$ and will be measured by counting the number of clocks for which the smaller current source runs before the integrator voltage reaches zero. This process is termed residual expansion. The break in the slope of the integrator voltage gives rise to the alternative title of gear-change converter. Following ramping to ground in the conversion process, the track/hold circuit must settle in time for the next conversion. In this sixteen bit example, the high-order conversion needs a maximum count of 512, and the low order needs 128: a total of 640. Allowing 25 % of the sample period for the track/hold circuit to operate, a 48 kHz converter would need to be clocked at some 40 MHz. This is rather faster than the clock needed for the DAC using the same technology.

2.9 Imperfections of converters

An ADC cannot be more accurate than the DAC it contains, and because of the higher operating speed, and the imperfections of the track/hold process, ADCs are generally responsible for more signal degradation than DACs. The two devices have the same transfer function, since they are only distinguished by the direction of operation, and therefore the same terminology can be used to classify the shortcomings of both.

Fig.2.33 shows the transfer functions resulting from the main types of converter error:

(a) *Offset error*. A constant appears to have been added to the digital signal. This has no effect on sound quality, unless the offset is gross, when the symptom would be premature clipping. DAC offset is of little consequence, but ADC offset is undesirable since it can cause an audible thump if an edit is made between two signals having different offsets. Offset error is sometimes cancelled by digitally averaging the converter output and feeding it back to the analog input as a small control voltage. Alternatively, a digital high-pass filter can be used.

(b) *Gain error*. The slope of the transfer function is incorrect. Since converters are referred to one end of the range, gain error causes an offset error. The gain stability is probably the least important factor in a digital audio converter, since ears, meters and gain controls are logarithmic.

(c) *Linearity* (also known as *integral linearity*). The deviation of the transfer function from a straight line (ignoring the quantizing steps). It has exactly the

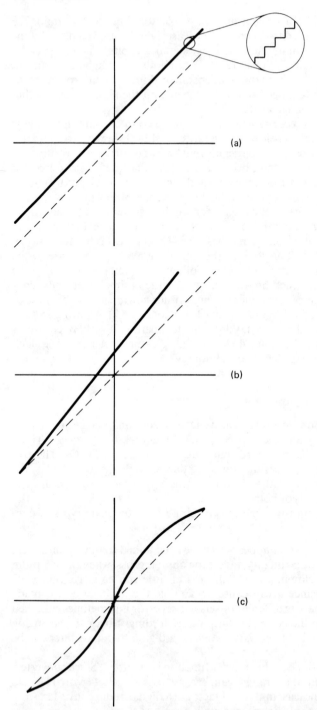

Figure 2.33 Main converter errors (solid line) compared with perfect transfer function (dotted line). These graphs hold for ADCs and DACs, and the axes are interchangeable; if one is chosen to be analog, the other will be digital.

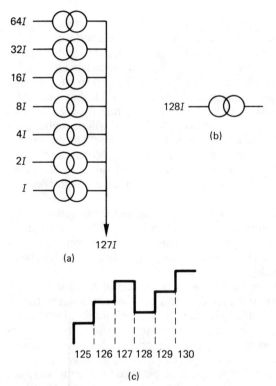

Figure 2.34 (a) Equivalent circuit of DAC with 127^{10} input. (b) DAC with 128^{10} input. On a major overflow, here from 127^{10} to 128^{10}, one current source ($128I$) must be precisely I greater than the sum of all the lower-order sources. If $128I$ is too small, the result shown at (c) will occur. This is non-monotonicity.

same significance as linearity in analog circuits, since if it is inadequate, harmonic distortion will be caused. Subclassifications of linearity which are used are *differential nonlinearity*, which is the amount by which adjacent quantizing intervals differ in size, and *monotonicity*, which is a special case of differential nonlinearity. Non-monotonicity means that the output does not increase for an increase in input. Fig.2.34 shows how this can happen. With a converter input code of 01111111 (127 decimal), the seven low-order current sources of the converter will be on. The next code is 10000000 (128 decimal), where only the eighth current source is operating. If the current it supplies is in error on the low side, the analog output for 128 may be less than that for 127. If a device has better than $\frac{1}{2}Q$ linearity it must be monotonic.

(d) *Absolute accuracy*. The difference between actual and ideal output for a given input. For audio this is rather less important than linearity. For example, if all the current sources in a converter have good thermal tracking, linearity will be maintained, even though the absolute accuracy drifts.

2.10 Oversampling theory

The information in an analog signal is two-dimensional; it was shown earlier that the number of levels which can be resolved unambiguously represents one dimension, and the bandwidth represents the other dimension. Fig.2.35 shows that it is an area which is the product of bandwidth and signal-to-noise ratio expressed linearly. The figure also shows that the same amount of information can be conveyed down a channel with 6 dB less SNR if the bandwidth used is doubled, with 12 dB less SNR if bandwidth is quadrupled, and so on, provided that the modulation scheme used is perfect. This theory predicts that if an audio signal is spread over a much wider bandwidth by, for example, the use of an FM broadcast transmitter, the SNR of the demodulated signal will be higher than that of the channel it passes through, and this is clearly the case. The theory also predicts that stereo FM will have more hiss; since two channels of audio are now using the same transmitter bandwidth, each one can have only half the information capacity, so it will lose 6 dB of SNR. In practice things are slightly worse, because the process is not perfect.

The information in an analog signal can be conveyed using some analog modulation scheme in any combination of bandwidth and SNR which yields the appropriate channel capacity. In digital audio, a signal having only two states, known as a binary channel, will be used, needing only a poor SNR, but a correspondingly high bandwidth.

It is useful to examine information capacity in the digital domain. Fig.2.36 shows several examples. A single binary digit can only have two states; thus it can only convey two pieces of information, perhaps 'yes' or 'no'. Two binary digits together can have four states, and can thus convey four pieces of information, perhaps 'spring summer autumn or winter', which is two pieces of information per bit. Three binary digits grouped together can have eight combinations, and convey eight pieces of information, perhaps 'doh re mi fah so lah te or doh', which is nearly three pieces of information per digit. Clearly the further this principle is taken, the greater the benefit. In a sixteen bit system, each bit is worth 4K pieces of information. It is always more efficient, in

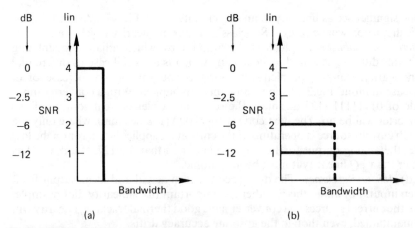

(a)   (b)

Figure 2.35 The number of levels which can be resolved in a voltage signal determines the amount of information at any instant. The bandwidth determines the rate at which that information can be conveyed; hence the overall information capacity is the product of linear SNR and bandwidth. If a given input signal at (a) is modulated in some perfect way, it may be conveyed down a channel with one-half the signal-to-noise ratio (− 6 dB) if the bandwidth is doubled, or with one-quarter the signal-to-noise ratio (− 12 dB) if the bandwidth is quadrupled.

0 = No 1 = Yes	00 = Spring 01 = Summer 10 = Autumn 11 = Winter	000 do 001 re 010 mi 011 fa 100 so 101 la 110 te 111 do	0000 0 0001 1 0010 2 0011 3 0100 4 0101 5 0110 6 0111 7 1000 8 1001 9 1010 A 1011 B 1100 C 1101 D 1110 E 1111 F	0000 ⋮ FFFF Digital audio sample values
No of bits 1	2	3	4	16
Information per word 2	4	8	16	65536
Information per bit 2	2	≈3	4	4096

Figure 2.36 The amount of information per bit increases disproportionately as wordlength increases. It is always more efficient to use the longest words possible at the lowest word rate. It will be evident that sixteen-bit PCM is 2048 times as efficient as delta modulation. Over-sampled data is also inefficient for storage.

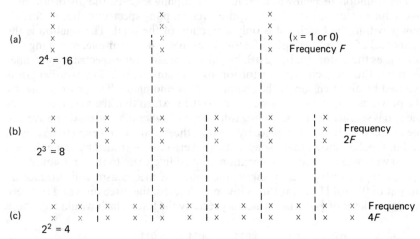

Figure 2.37 Information rate can be held constant when frequency doubles by removing one bit from each word. In all cases here it is $16F$. Note bit rate of (c) is double that of (a). Data storage in oversampled form is inefficient.

information-capacity terms, to use the combinations of long binary words than to send single bits for every piece of information. This is one reason why PCM is more popular than delta modulation, despite the simplicity of implementation of the latter. PCM simply makes more efficient use of the capacity of the binary channel.

Information theory is necessary to understand oversampling. The storage or transmission system is usually going to be PCM, where the sampling rate is a little more than twice the audio bandwidth. In the converters, the sampling rate will be higher, because of the advantages stated earlier in the construction of the analog filters. There are other advantages because, when the sampling rate is raised, information theory suggests that the wordlength of the samples can be reduced. Fig.2.37 shows the reverse case of Fig.2.36. The information rate is held constant, and as the sampling rate doubles, one bit can be removed from the wordlength. Thus by using oversampling, not only can the problems of analog filters be overcome, but also the wordlength of the converters is reduced, making them easier to construct. Note that the theory only predicts what is possible; it is not a guarantee of success. Oversampling simply means raising the sampling rate. Further mechanisms are needed to take advantage of the wordlength reduction.

2.11 An oversampling DAC

Consider a system which oversamples by a factor of four. Starting with sixteen-bit PCM, the 4 × oversampling will permit the use of a fourteen-bit converter, but only if the wordlength is reduced optimally. Simple truncation of wordlength gives the same result as if the original audio had been quantized into fewer levels in the first place. For every bit lost, the same amount of distortion will be obtained with a level 6.02 dB higher. Simple truncation, then, does not allow the results predicted by information theory.

The roundoff mechanism used in oversampling spreads the distortion products due to truncation over the entire oversampling spectrum; thus distortion power within the baseband is only a fraction of the total. The fraction is the reciprocal of the oversampling factor. Thus in our 4 × example, removing two bits raises the distortion by 12 dB, but this is spread over a spectrum four times as great, thus reducing the distortion by the same 12 dB. The wordlength is reduced by an extension of the technique of rounding up. The error caused by the previous truncation is carried over to the next, so that the average error of the two is smaller. As the sampling rate is much higher than normal, the averaging process will have taken place by the time the signal has returned to baseband audio. Fig.2.38 shows that the accumulated error is controlled by using the bits which were neglected in the truncation, and adding them to the next sample. In this example, with a steady input, the roundoff mechanism will produce an output of 01110111 . . . . If this is low-pass filtered, the three ones and one zero result in a level of $\frac{3}{4}$ of a bit, which is precisely the level which would have been

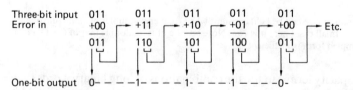

Figure 2.38 By adding the error caused by truncation to the next value, the resolution of the lost bits is maintained in the duty cycle of the output. Here, truncation of 011 by two bits would give continuous zeros, but the system repeats 0111, 0111, which, after filtering, will produce a level of three quarters of a bit.

obtained by direct conversion of the full digital input. Thus the information capacity is maintained even though two bits have been removed. This process is often referred to as noise shaping, but this is a misnomer, as failure to perform these steps results in harmonic distortion. The term time averaging is also used to describe this kind of resolution extension.

In the oversampling system used in Philips Compact Disc players[15] the aperture effect in the DAC is used as part of the reconstruction filter response, in conjunction with a third-order Bessel filter. Equalization of the frequency response is by the digital filter which produces the oversampled data. The operation of digital filters is described in Chapter 4, where it will be seen that their frequency response is proportional to the sampling rate. If a digital recorder is played at a reduced speed, the response of the digital filter will reduce automatically, and prevent images passing the reconstruction process. If oversampling were to become universal, there would then be no need for the 48 kHz sampling rate.

2.12 Oversampling ADCs

The use of oversampling to extend the resolution of ADCs is subject to the same limits set by information theory, but it is harder to approach the limit in ADCs than in DACs.

If a perfect quantizer is used, no amount of oversampling will increase the resolution of the system, since a perfect quantizer is blind to all changes of input within one quantizing interval, and looking more often is of no help. It was shown earlier that the use of dither would linearize a quantizer, so that input changes much smaller than the quantizing interval would be reflected in the output. Dither must be employed to minimize distortion in conventional quantizers. Resolution cannot be extended in ADCs unless some signal is added to the analog input.

Fig.2.39 shows the example of a white-noise-dithered quantizer, oversampled by a factor of four. Since dither is correctly employed, it is valid to speak of the unwanted signal as noise. The noise power extends over the whole baseband up to the Nyquist limit. If the basebandwidth is reduced by the oversampling factor of four back to the bandwidth of the original analog input, the noise bandwidth will also be reduced by a factor of four, and the noise power will be one quarter of that produced at the quantizer. One-quarter noise power implies one half the noise voltage, so the SNR of this example has been increased by 6 dB, the equivalent of one extra bit in the quantizer. Information theory predicts that an oversampling factor of four would allow an extension by two bits, so it can be concluded that this method is sub-optimal.

The division of the noise by a larger factor is the only route left open, since all the other parameters are fixed by the signal bandwidth required. The reduction of noise power resulting from a reduction in bandwidth is only proportional if the noise is white, i.e. it has uniform power spectral density (PSD). If the noise from the quantizer is made spectrally non-uniform, the oversampling factor will no longer be the factor by which the noise power is reduced. The goal is to concentrate noise power at high frequencies, so that after low-pass filtering in the digital domain to the audio input bandwidth, the noise power will be reduced by more than the oversampling factor. The sigma DPCM converter has

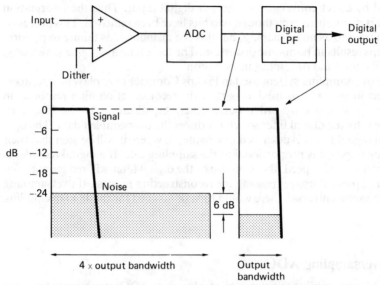

Figure 2.39 In this simple oversampled converter, 4× oversampling is used. When the converter output is low-pass filtered, the noise power is reduced to one quarter, which in voltage terms is 6 dB. This is a sub-optimal method and is not used.

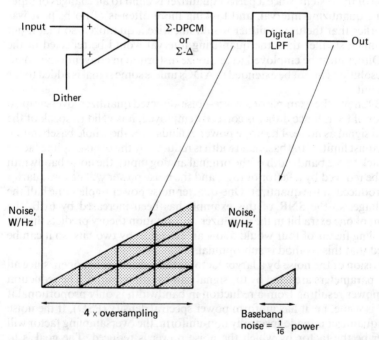

Figure 2.40 In a Σ–DPCM or Σ–Δ converter, noise amplitude increases by 6 dB/octave, noise power by 12 dB/octave. In this 4× oversampling converter, the digital filter reduces bandwidth by four, but noise power is reduced by a factor of sixteen. Noise voltage falls by a factor of 4 or 12 dB.

a natural application here; as seen earlier its noise spectrum rises at 6 dB per octave. Fig.2.40 shows an oversampling system using a sigma DPCM converter and an oversampling factor of four. The sampling spectrum shows that the noise is concentrated at frequencies outside the audio part of the oversampling baseband. Since the scale used here means that noise power is represented by the area under the graph, the area left under the graph after the filter shows the noise-power reduction. Using the relative areas of similar triangles shows that the reduction has been by a factor of sixteen. The corresponding noise-voltage reduction would be a factor of four, or 12 dB, in a white-noise system, being exactly that permitted by four times oversampling, but because of the rise of 6 dB per octave in the PSD of the noise, the SNR will be 3 dB worse at the edge of the audio band. This 3 dB loss remains the same whatever the oversampling factor; therefore the greater the oversampling factor, the less significant the loss. The noise injected by the vital dither process will be of the same order anyway, and the digital low-pass filter will introduce some noise, so that the slope of 6 dB per octave will not continue back to the origin; it will level out. The performance of such a system is thus not far short of the information-theory limit for a dithered converter. A sixteen-times oversampling system using this technique allows a resolution extension of 21 dB. The number of bits needed to express this greater resolution will be four; thus the effective quantizing intervals of the system have been made one-sixteenth the size of the quantizer steps. The amount of white-noise dither on the analog input must be reduced accordingly. Adams[16] has described a system based on these principles using an oversampling factor of 128 to achieve a true eighteen-bit accurate conversion with exceptional phase linearity. At the time of writing this probably represents the state of the art in audio converters.

2.13 Spectral coding

There have been studies and proposals made on the subject of spectral recording, but it can be said to be in its infancy at the moment. The basic principle of spectral recording is that instead of trying to record the pressure waveform, which changes at frequencies up to 20 kHz, the sound spectrum is recorded because it changes much less frequently.[17] The coding process consists of periodically calculating the spectrum or Fourier transform of the input, and storing it digitally as a series of centre frequencies and levels. On replay the spectral information is used to control frequency synthesizers which reproduce the sound pressure waveform. In practice the masking characteristics of the ear are exploited so that low-level spectral entries which are present in the waveform but which could not be perceived by the ear are omitted from the recording; the storage requirement is thus greatly reduced compared with that of conventional digital audio recording. The data reduction offered is most promising, as it is several orders of magnitude, but the current problem to be overcome is the sheer amount of computation required in a traditional digital computer to derive the Fourier transform.[18] Spectral recording cannot currently be done in real time, since several hours of CPU time are required for a few minutes of sound waveform. If new methods of calculating transforms, perhaps using optical techniques, become available, then spectral recording will become more significant.

References

1. MURAOKA, T., IWAHARA, M. and YAMADA, Y., Examination of audio bandwidth requirements for optimum sound signal transmission. *J. Audio Eng. Soc.*, **29**, 2–9 (1982)
2. MURAOKA, T., YAMADA, Y. and YAMAZAKI, M., Sampling frequency considerations in digital audio. *J. Audio Eng. Soc.*, **26**, 252–256, (1978)
3. FINCHAM, L.R., The subjective importance of uniform group delay at low frequencies. Presented at the 74th Audio Engineering Society Convention. (New York, 1983), preprint 2056(H-1)
4. ADAMS, R.W., Companded predictive delta modulation: a low-cost technique for digital recording. *J.Audio Eng. Soc.*, **32** 659–672 (1984)
5. SHANNON, C.E., A mathematical theory of communication. *Bell System Tech. J.*, **27** 379 (1948)
6. BETTS, J.A., *Signal Processing Modulation and Noise.* Sevenoaks: Hodder and Stoughton (1970), Ch.6
7. VANDERKOOY, J. and LIPSHITZ, S.P., Resolution below the least significant bit in digital systems with dither. *J. Audio Eng. Soc.*, **32**, 106–113 (1984)
8. BLESSER, B., Advanced A-D conversion and filtering: data conversion. In *Digital Audio*, edited by B.A. Blesser, B. Locanthi and T.G. Stockham Jr, 37–53. New York: Audio Engineering Society (1983)
9. LAGADEC, R. and STOCKHAM, T.G.,Jr, Dispersive models for A-to-D and D-to-A conversion systems. Presented at the 75th Audio Engineering Society Convention (Paris, 1984), preprint 2097(H-8)
10. MEYER, J., Time correction of anti-aliasing filters used in digital audio systems. *J. Audio Eng. Soc.*, **32**, 132–137 (1984)
11. LAGADEC, R., WEISS, D. and GREUTMANN, R., High-quality analog filters for digital audio. Presented at the 67th Audio Engineering Society Convention (New York, 1980), preprint 1707(B-4)
12. ANON., AES recommended practice for professional digital audio applications employing pulse code modulation: preferred sampling frequencies. AES5-1984 (ANSI S4.28-1984), *J. Audio Eng. Soc.*, **32**, 781–785, (1984)
13. v.d. PLASSCHE, R.J., Dynamic element matching puts trimless convertors on chip. *Electronics* (16 Jun 1983)
14. v.d. PLASSCHE, R.J. and GOEDHART, D., A monolithic 14 bit D-A convertor. *IEEE J. Solid-State Circuits*, **SC-14**, 552–556 (1979)
15. v.d. PLASSCHE, R.J. and DIJKMANS, E.C., A monolithic 16 bit D-A conversion system for digital audio. In *Digital Audio*, op. cit., 54–60 (see ref. 8)
16. ADAMS, R.W., Design and implementation of an audio 18-bit A-D convertor using over-sampling techniques. Presented at the 77th Audio Engineering Society Convention (Hamburg, 1985), preprint 2182
17. RANADA, D., New hi-fi horizons. *Stereo Review* 68–70 and 117 (Dec. 1984)
18. SCHROEDER, E.F. and VOESSING, W., High-quality digital audio encoding with 3 bits/sample using adaptive transform coding. Presented at the 80th Audio Engineering Society Convention (Montreux, 1986), preprint 2321

Chapter 3

Digital audio coding and processing

The conversion process expresses the analog input as a binary code. In this chapter the choice of code is shown to be governed by the requirements of digital signal processing, which is applied to the sample stream from a converter to perform the functions of level meters, attenuators and operational amplifiers.

The subject of timebase correction is uncommon in analog audio, but is fundamental to digital recording, and is treated in some depth here. A brief introduction to binary arithmetic and logic is included, for those who are approaching the subject for the first time.

3.1 Introduction to logic

The strength of binary logic is that the signal has only two states, and considerable noise and distortion can be tolerated before the state becomes uncertain. At every logical element, the signal is compared with a threshold, and thus can pass through any number of stages without being degraded. The two states of the signal when measured with an oscilloscope are simply two voltages, usually referred to as high and low. The actual voltage levels will depend on the type of logic chips in use, and on the supply voltage used. Within logic, these levels are not of much consequence, and it is only necessary to know them when interfacing between different logic families or when driving external devices. The pure logic designer is not interested at all in these voltages, only in their meaning. Just as the electrical waveform from a microphone represents sound pressure, so the waveform in a logic circuit represents the truth of some statement. As there are only two states, there can only be *true* or *false* meanings. The true state of the signal can be assigned by the designer to either voltage state. When a high voltage represents a true logic condition and a low voltage represents a false condition, the system is known as *positive logic*, or *high true logic*. This is the usual system, but sometimes the low voltage represents the true condition and the high voltage represents the false condition. This is known as *negative logic* or *low true logic*. Provided that everyone is aware of the logic convention in use, both work equally well.

Negative logic is often found in the TTL logic family, because in this technology it is easier to sink current to ground than to source it from the power supply. Fig.3.1 shows that if it is necessary to connect several logic elements to a

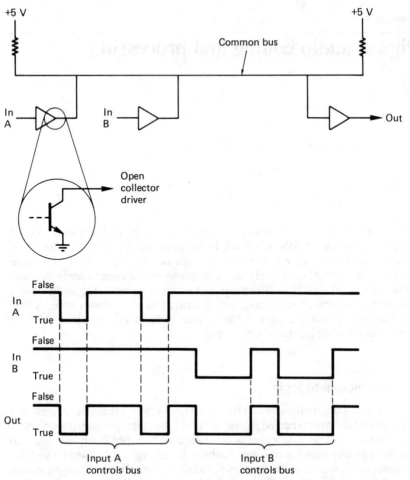

Figure 3.1 Using open-collector drive, several signal sources can share one common bus. If negative logic is used, the bus drivers turn off their output transistors with a false input, allowing another driver to control the bus. This will not happen with positive logic.

common bus so that any one can communicate with any other, an open collector system is used, where high levels are provided by pull-up resistors and the logic elements only pull the common line down. If positive logic were used, when no device was operating the pull-up resistors would cause the common line to take on an absurd true state; whereas if negative logic is used, the common line pulls up to a sensible false condition when there is no device using the bus.

In logic systems, all complex devices can be configured from combinations of a few fundamental gates. It is not profitable to spend too much time arguing which are the really fundamental ones, since most can be made from combinations of others. Table 3.1 shows the important simple gates and their derivatives, and introduces the logical expressions to describe them, which can be compared with the truth-table notation. The figure also shows the important fact that when negative logic is used, the OR gate function interchanges with that of the AND gate. Sometimes schematics are drawn to reflect which voltage state represents the true condition. In the so-called intentional logic scheme, a negative logic signal always starts and ends at an inverting 'bubble'. If an AND function is required between two negative logic signals, it will be drawn as an AND symbol with bubbles on all the terminals, even though the component used will be a positive logic OR gate. Opinions vary on the merits of intentional logic.

If numerical quantities need to be conveyed down the two-state signal paths described here, then the only appropriate numbering system is binary, which has only two symbols, 0 and 1. Just as positive or negative logic could be used for the truth of a logical binary signal, it can also be used for a numerical binary signal. Normally, a high voltage level will represent a binary 1 and a low voltage will represent a binary 0, described as a 'high for a one' system. Clearly a 'low for

Table 3.1 The basic logic gates compared.

Positive logic name	Boolean expression	Positive logic symbol	Positive logic truth table			Plain English
Inverter or NOT gate	$Q = \bar{A}$		A	Q		Output is opposite of input
			0	1		
			1	0		
AND gate	$Q = A \cdot B$		A	B	Q	Output true when both inputs are true only
			0	0	0	
			0	1	0	
			1	0	0	
			1	1	1	
NAND (Not AND) gate	$Q = \overline{A \cdot B}$ $= \bar{A} + \bar{B}$		A	B	Q	Output false when both inputs are true only
			0	0	1	
			0	1	1	
			1	0	1	
			1	1	0	
OR gate	$Q = A + B$		A	B	Q	Output true if either or both inputs true
			0	0	0	
			0	1	1	
			1	0	1	
			1	1	1	
NOR (Not OR) gate	$Q = \overline{A + B}$ $= \bar{A} \cdot \bar{B}$		A	B	Q	Output false if either or both inputs true
			0	0	1	
			0	1	0	
			1	0	0	
			1	1	0	
Exclusive OR (XOR) gate	$Q = A \oplus B$		A	B	Q	Output true if inputs are different
			0	0	0	
			0	1	1	
			1	0	1	
			1	1	0	

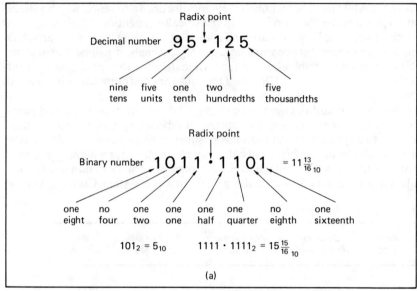

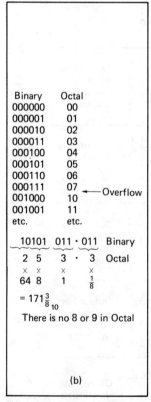

Binary	Octal
000000	00
000001	01
000010	02
000011	03
000100	04
000101	05
000110	06
000111	07 ◄── Overflow
001000	10
001001	11
etc.	etc.

10101 011 · 011   Binary

 2 5 3 · 3   Octal

64 8 1 $\frac{1}{8}$

$= 171\frac{3}{8}_{10}$

There is no 8 or 9 in Octal

(b)

Binary	Hex	Decimal
0000	0	0
0001	1	1
0010	2	2
0011	3	3
0100	4	4
0101	5	5
0110	6	6
0111	7	7
1000	8	8
1001	9	9
1010	A	10
1011	B	11
1100	C	12
1101	D	13
1110	E	14
1111	F	15

1100 0000 1111 1111 1110 1110   Binary

 C 0 F F E E   Hex

 0 15 15 14 14

65 536 4096 256 16

12

1048576   = 12 648 430₁₀

(c)

Figure 3.2 (a) Binary and decimal. (b) In octal, groups of three bits make one symbol 0–7. (c) In hex, groups of four bits make one symbol 0–F. Note how much shorter the number is in hex.

a one' system is just as feasible. Decimal numbers have several columns, each of which represents a different power of ten; in binary the column position specifies the power of two. Fig.3.2 shows some binary numbers and their equivalent in decimal. The radix point has the same significance in binary: symbols to the right of it represent one half, one quarter and so on. Binary is convenient for electronic circuits, which do not get tired, but numbers expressed in binary become very long, and writing them is tedious and error-prone. The octal and hexadecimal notations are both used for writing binary since conversion is so simple. A binary number is split into groups of three or four digits starting at the least significant end, and the groups are individually converted to octal or hexadecimal digits. Since sixteen different symbols are required in hex, the letters A-F are used for the numbers above nine.

A number of binary digits or bits are needed to express a binary number. These bits can be conveyed at the same time by several signals to form a parallel system, which is most convenient inside equipment because it is fast, or one at a time down a single signal path, which is slower, but convenient for cables between pieces of equipment because the connectors require fewer pins. When a binary system is used to convey numbers in this way, it can be called a digital system.

3.2 Binary codes

For audio use, the prime purpose of binary numbers is to express the values of the samples which represent the original analog sound-pressure waveform. There will be a fixed number of bits in the sample, which determines the number range. For example, in a sixteen-bit system, there are 65 536 different numbers. Each number represents a different analog signal voltage, and care must be

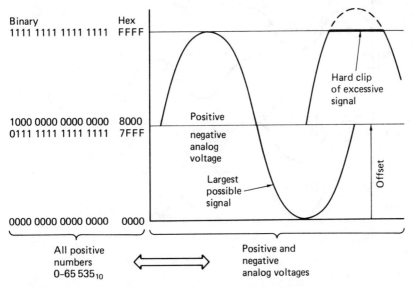

Figure 3.3 Offset-binary coding is simple but causes problems in digital audio processing. It is seldom used.

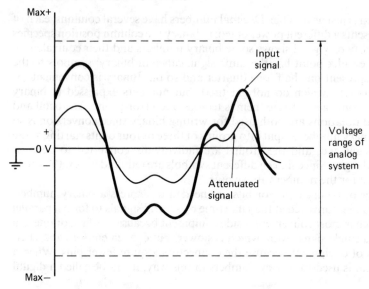

Figure 3.4 Attenuation of an audio signal takes place with respect to midrange.

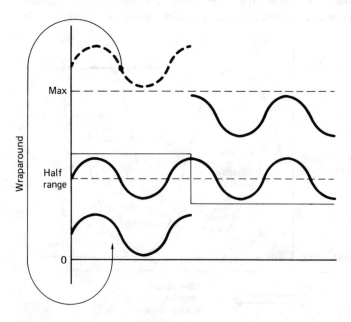

Figure 3.5 If two pure binary data streams are added to simulate mixing, offset or overflow will result.

taken during conversion to ensure that the signal does not go outside the converter range, or it will be clipped. In Fig.3.3, it will be seen that in a simple system, the number range goes from 0000 hex, which represents the largest negative voltage, through 7FFF hex, which represents the smallest negative voltage, through 8000 hex, which represents the smallest positive voltage, to FFFF hex, which represents the largest positive voltage. Effectively, the number range of the converter has been shifted so that positive and negative voltages in a real audio signal can be expressed by binary numbers which are only positive. This approach is called offset binary, and is perfectly acceptable where the signal has been digitized only for recording or transmission from one place to another, after which it will be converted back to analog. Under these conditions it is not necessary for the quantizing steps to be uniform, provided both ADC and DAC are constructed to the same standard. In practice, it is the requirements of signal processing in the digital domain which make both non-uniform quantizing and offset binary unsuitable.

Fig.3.4 shows that an audio signal voltage is referred to midrange. The level of the signal is measured by how far the waveform deviates from midrange, and attenuation, gain and mixing all take place around midrange. It is necessary to add sample values from two or more different sources to perform the mixing function, and adding circuits assume that all bits represent the same quantizing interval so that the sum of two sample values will represent the sum of the two original analog voltages. In non-uniform quantizing this is not the case, and such signals cannot readily be processed. Fig.3.5 shows that, if two offset binary sample streams are added together in an attempt to perform digital mixing, the result will be an offset which may lead to an overflow. Similarly, if an attempt is made to attenuate by, say, 6 dB by dividing all of the sample values by two, Fig.3.6 shows that a further offset results. The problem is that offset binary is referred to one end of the range. What is needed is a numbering system which operates symmetrically about the centre of the range.

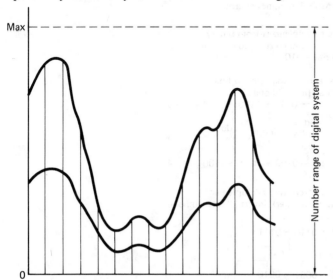

Figure 3.6 The result of an attempted attenuation in pure binary code is an offset. Pure binary cannot be used for digital audio processing.

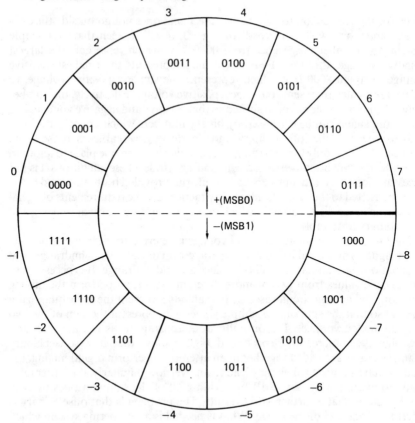

Figure 3.7 In this example of a four-bit two's complement code, the number range is from −8 to +7. Note that the MSB determines polarity.

(a) **Conversion to two's complement from binary**
Positive numbers: add leading zeros to determine sign bit.
Example: $101_2 = 5_{10} = 0101_{2C}$

Negative numbers: add leading zeros to final
wordlength; invert all bits; add one.
Example 1: $11_2 = 3_{10} \rightarrow 0011 \rightarrow 1100 \rightarrow 1101_{2C} = -3$

add
leading   invert   add
zeros   1

Example 2: $100_2 = 4_{10} \rightarrow 0100 \rightarrow 1011 \rightarrow 1100_{2C} = -4$

(b) **Conversion to binary from two's complement**
If MSB = 1 (Negative Number), invert all bits; add one.

Example 1: $1001 \rightarrow 0110 \rightarrow 0111 = -7_{10}$

invert   add
1

Example 2: $1110 \rightarrow 0001 \rightarrow 0010 = -2_{10}$

Figure 3.8 (a) Binary to two's complement conversion. (b) Two's complement to binary.

(c)   4   4   0100
$$\frac{-6}{-2} \equiv \frac{+(-6)}{-2} \equiv \frac{+\ 1010}{1110}$$

$$\frac{-8}{-5} \quad \frac{1000}{1011}$$
$$+3 \equiv 0011$$

$$\frac{-3}{3} \quad \frac{1101}{0011}$$
$$+6 \equiv 0110$$

C C

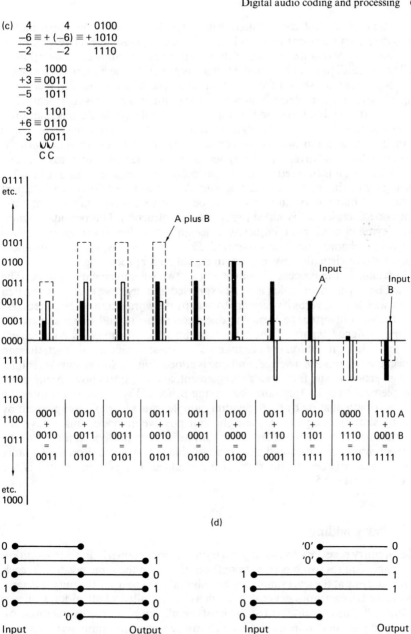

(d)

0001   0010   0010   0011   0011   0100   0011   0010   0000   1110 A
 +   +   +   +   +   +   +   +   +   +
0010   0011   0011   0010   0001   0000   1110   1101   1110   0001 B
 =   =   =   =   =   =   =   =   =   =
0011   0101   0101   0101   0100   0100   0001   1111   1110   1111

Input 20₁₀   Output 40₁₀

$20_{10} \times 2 = 40_{10}$

(e)

Input 12₁₀   Output 3₁₀

$12_{10} \div 4 = 3_{10}$

(f)

Figure 3.8 (*continued*) (c) Some examples. (d) Using two's complement arithmetic, single values from two waveforms are added together with respect to midrange to give a correct mixing function. (e) Multiplication or (f) division by two by bit-shifting compounds to 6 dB gain change.

In the two's complement system, which has this property, the upper half of the pure binary number range has been defined to represent negative quantities. If a pure binary counter is constantly incremented and allowed to overflow, it will produce all the numbers in the range permitted by the number of available bits, and these are shown for a four-bit example drawn around the circle in Fig.3.7. In two's complement, however, the number range this represents does not start at zero, but starts on the opposite side of the circle. Zero is midrange, and all numbers with the most significant bit set are considered negative. Two's complement notation can also be considered as an offset binary code with the most significant bit inverted. This system allows two sample values to be added, where the result is referred to the system midrange; this is analogous to adding analog signals in an operational amplifier. A further asset of two's complement notation is that binary subtraction can be performed using only adding logic. The two's complement is added to perform a subtraction. This permits a significant saving in hardware complexity, since only carry logic is necessary and no borrow mechanism need be supported. For these reasons, two's complement notation is in virtually universal use in digital audio processing.

Fortunately the process of conversion to two's complement is simple. The signed binary number which is to be expressed as a negative number is written down with leading zeros if necessary to occupy the wordlength of the system. All bits are then inverted, to form the one's complement, and one is added. To return to signed binary, if the most significant bit of the two's complement number is false, no action need be taken. If the most significant bit is set, the sign is negative, all bits are inverted, and one is added. Fig.3.8 shows some examples of conversion to and from two's complement, and illustrates how adding two's complement samples simulates the mixing process. Fig.3.8 also illustrates the process of attenuating by 6 dB, dividing sample values in two's complement by two by shifting one place to the right. For positive numbers, this is easy; for negative numbers, the necessary right shift must carry in a one at the left of the number, not a zero. It should also be noted that in two's complement, if a radix point exists, numbers to the right of it are added. For example 1100.1 is not -4.5, it is $-4 + 0.5 = -3.5$.

3.3 Binary adding

The circuitry necessary for adding binary numbers is shown in Fig.3.9. Addition in binary requires two bits to be taken at a time from the same position in each word, starting at the least significant bit. Should both be ones, the output is zero, and there is a carry-out generated. Such a circuit, called a half adder, is shown in Fig.3.9(a) and is suitable for the least-significant bit of the calculation. All higher stages will require a circuit which can accept a carry input as well as two data inputs. This is known as a full adder (Fig.3.9(b)). Multibit full adders are available in chip form, and have carry-in and carry-out terminals to allow them to be connected in parallel to operate on long wordlengths. Such a device is also convenient for producing the two's complement of a signed binary number, in conjunction with a set of inverters. The adder chip has one set of inputs grounded, and the carry-in permanently held true, such that it adds one to the one's complement number from the inverter.

When mixing by adding sample values, care has to be taken to ensure that if

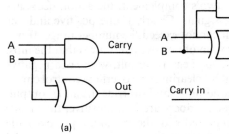 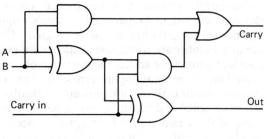

(a)

Data A	Bits B	Carry in	Out	Carry out
0	0	0	0	0
0	0	1	1	0
0	1	0	1	0
0	1	1	0	1
1	0	0	1	0
1	0	1	0	1
1	1	0	0	1
1	1	1	1	1

(b)

A MSB

B MSB

High when
A and B negative
but adder output
positive

High when
A and B positive
but adder output
negative

Adder
MSB

Input A

Two's
complement

Σ

Out

Input B

Maximum
positive
value

Maximum
negative
value

(c)

Figure 3.9 (a) Half adder; (b) full-adder circuit and truth table; (c) comparison of sign bits prevents wraparound on adder overflow by substituting clipping level.

the sum of the two sample values exceeds the number range the result will be clipping rather than wraparound. In two's complement, the action necessary depends on the polarities of the two signals. Clearly if one positive and one negative number are added, the result cannot exceed the number range. If two positive numbers are added, the symptom of positive overflow is that the most significant bit sets, causing an erroneous negative result, whereas a negative overflow results in the most significant bit clearing. The overflow control circuit will be designed to detect these two conditions, and override the adder output. If the MSB of both inputs is zero, the numbers are both positive, thus if the sum has the MSB set, the output is replaced with the maximum positive code (0111 . . .). If the MSB of both inputs is set, the numbers are both negative, and if the sum has no MSB set, the output is replaced with the maximum negative code (1000 . . .). These conditions can also be connected to warning indicators. Fig.3.9(c) shows this system in hardware. The resultant clipping on overload is sudden, and sometimes a PROM is included which translates values around and beyond maximum to soft-clipped values below or equal to maximum.

3.4 Level metering

In the digital domain it will be necessary to display the level of a signal for the same reasons that analog equipment has level meters. In the analog domain, the two main methods are the *volume unit* (VU) meter and the *peak program meter* (PPM) which differ primarily in the decay time of the reading due to a peak. In order to give a true representation of the level of an audio signal, full-wave rectification must be used to catch positive and negative peaks, before any

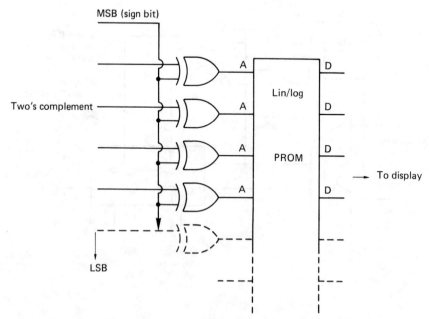

Figure 3.10 Rectification of a two's complement sample stream by examining the sign bit, and selectively inverting the remaining bits.

attack and decay circuits. It is possible to full-wave rectify a two's complement sample stream. This is shown in Fig.3.10 where the most significant bit of the sample is examined, since it is the sign bit. If the sign bit is false, the remaining bits of the sample pass unchanged, but if it is set, the number is negative, and all the other bits will be inverted by the exclusive OR gates, to return to signed binary. Strictly speaking, one should be added to the result, but the error caused by not doing so is so minute that it is usually neglected. The full-wave-rectified sample stream produced is a series of numbers which specify how far the signal voltage is from zero. For audio applications, a logarithmic relationship between level and display is required so that the meter can be calibrated in dB relative to some standard level. In analog meters, the logarithmic current/voltage relationship of a diode is sometimes used, or the scale markings can be made nonlinear. Happily this is unnecessary with a digital rectified sample stream. In binary, if a number is doubled, exactly one more bit is necessary to convey it. Since a gain increase of 6 dB (or to be pedantic 6.02 dB) doubles the sample values, it will bring into use an extra bit in the word. All that is necessary is to determine the position of the most significant one in the rectified word, and a digital logarithmic level in 6 dB steps is obtained directly.

The level thus obtained will generally be displayed on an optoelectronic device such as a bar LED or a fluorescent indicator. There are fifteen bits in the rectified word from a sixteen-bit system, and so a fifteen-segment indicator is adequate to display level. However, it is common to decode rectified values which are very close to the digital ceiling of all ones to illuminate a sixteenth indicator, usually red, which warns that the signal is about to, or has, hit the stops and may be clipping. The attack time of an analog meter is a compromise between a desirable value of zero, and the practicable rate at which a mechanical moving coil meter can be accelerated. Optoelectronic displays have no such inertia; thus the attack time can be made to be the minimum possible, which is one sample period. It is normal to interconnect the individual LEDs in the bar display such that the most significant LED causes all those below it to illuminate also. This results in a bar of light whose length varies with level. Having no inertia, such a simple system has a decay time of one sample too, and decay has to be simulated electronically. Fig.3.11 shows how this can be done. A shift register is loaded with the most significant one in the rectified word, and slowly shifted down, so that the display decays one 6 dB step per shift following a single peak sample. The state of the display is compared at each new sample with the most significant one from that sample. If the new sample is lower in level than the decaying level from the previous peak, no action is taken. If the new sample is higher in level, it is latched into the shift register. The clock rate of the shift register determines the decay time constant. If long, the PPM action can be simulated; if shorter, the VU action can be simulated. In practice it is possible to have the best of both worlds. In a combined VU/PPM digital level meter, the PPM readout is a single illuminated segment which slowly shifts down with the long PPM time constant. On the same display, the VU level is displayed as a bar of segments illuminated from the bottom upwards. On tones and steady material, the display appears as an ordinary bar LED, but following a brief transient, the length of the bar will contract rapidly, leaving the single segment further up the scale, holding the peak. The action is particularly noticeable if pre-emphasis is in use in the analog domain prior to sampling, since this will make the samples appear more peaky to a digital meter, and it is important that

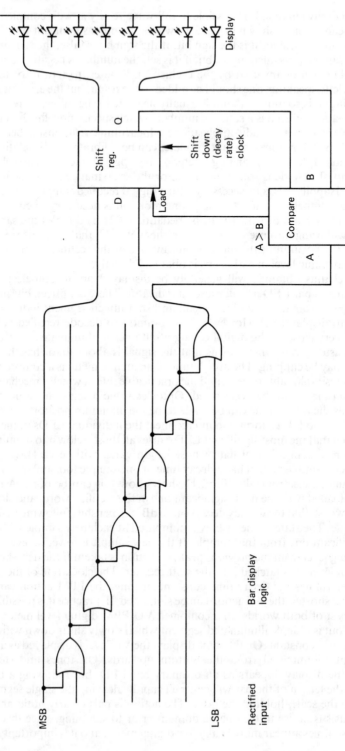

Figure 3.11 The rectified sample values drive a series of OR gates such that the input creates a bar of illuminated segments. If a higher value occurs, the comparator will cause the shift register to load, giving fast attack. In the absence of input the register shifts down to give decay.

the fact is noticed if clipping is to be avoided. Meters of this kind are not restricted to digital signals alone, since it is possible to use them on analog signals by employing suitable A to D converters. As the samples are needed only to drive the meter, the musicality of the converter is of little consequence, and an instrumentation type will suffice.[1]

There has been some controversy over the labelling of digital level meters, but once the characteristics of digital systems are appreciated, the best choice becomes reasonably obvious. The dynamic range of a digitally conveyed sound cannot exceed the upper limit set by the largest digital code the system offers, beyond which it will clip, and the lower limit where the signal will be lost in the dither noise of the converter. A sixteen-segment LED indicator, as described, embraces that range in 6 dB steps, and it can be argued that no labelling is necessary whatsoever because the lights speak for themselves. The best signal-to-noise ratio will be obtained when as many segments as possible are on except the top one. On the equipment built at Decca Records and used for classical record and Compact Disc production, the level meters have no markings whatsoever.

If markings are needed on a digital level meter, the best scheme is to have 0 dB at the top, so that all levels are below it. This is the approach used for the digital meters on Studer and JVC recorders. The reasoning is as follows. An analog tape recorder has a noise floor just like a dithered digital system, but at the top levels the signal becomes progressively more distorted as saturation of the tape is approached. The level meters of an analog recorder often show 0 dB at the level just below the onset of this distortion, and the range of levels between this and saturation is called headroom. A digital system does not need any headroom, because it remains perfectly linear until the onset of clipping. The best recording will, in theory, be made when the largest sample just reaches the end of the quantizing range, although in practice the occasional clipped peak is inaudible. If no headroom is needed, then 0 dB might just as well be at the top of the scale. This argument is equally valid for the broadcast environment, where the level of signals fed to transmitters has to be controlled to prevent clipping in AM and overdeviation in FM, both of which increase the channel bandwidth beyond permitted limits. Since the output level of a digital system cannot exceed the limits set by the largest sample value allowed by the wordlength, it is a simple matter to arrange the sensitivity of the transmitter input to reach full drive on such a signal, and overdriving cannot occur. No headroom is necessary, and again there is no reason why the maximum level should not be labelled 0 dB.

3.5 Gain control

Using a digital level meter, the gain of an analog input can be adjusted to make a recording of maximum signal-to-noise ratio. At some later time, the recording may be played back and mixed with other recordings, and the desired effect can only be achieved if the gain of each recording can be set independently. Gain is controlled in the digital domain by multiplying each sample value by some fixed coefficient. If that coefficient is less than one, attenuation will result; if it is greater than one, amplification can be obtained.

Multiplication in binary circuits is difficult. It can be performed by repeated adding, but this is too slow to be of any use. In fast multiplication, one of the

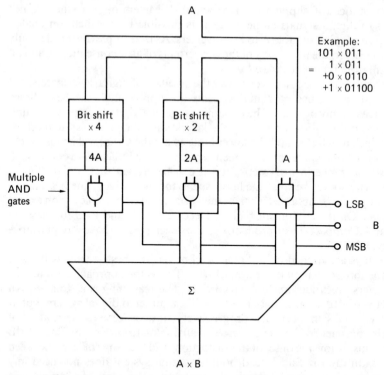

Figure 3.12 Structure of fast multiplier: The input A is multiplied by 1, 2, 4, 8 etc by the bit-shifting technique of Figure 3.8 (e). The digits of the B input then determine which multiples of A should be added together by enabling AND gates between the shifters and the adder. For long wordlengths, the number of gates required becomes enormous, and the device is best implemented in a chip.

inputs will be simultaneously multiplied by one, two, four etc., by hard-wired bit shifting. Fig.3.12 shows that the other input bits will determine which of these powers will be added to produce the final sum, and which will be neglected. If multiplying by five, the process is the same as multiplying by four, multiplying by one, and adding the two products. This is achieved by adding the input to itself shifted two places. As the wordlength of such a device increases, the complexity increases exponentially, so this is a natural application for an integrated circuit. It is probably true that digital audio would not have been viable without such chips.

In a digital mixer, the gain coefficients will originate in the hand-operated faders, but may not travel directly, as in an automated desk the coefficients may be stored on a floppy disk, or on one track of a multitrack recorder. It is possible to obtain coefficients from an analog fader by feeding the end of the track with a stable DC voltage and digitizing the voltage on the wiper, but direct digital faders are also available. In these devices, a grating is moved with respect to several light beams, one for each bit of the coefficient. The interruption of the beams by the grating is monitored by photocells. It is not possible to encode such a grating in pure binary, as Fig.3.13(a) shows that this generates transient false codes due to mechanical tolerances. The solution is to use a non sequential binary code, where only one bit changes at a time between adjacent states. This approach avoids transients. One such code is the Gray code, shown in Fig.3.13(b), which is used extensively in shaft encoders for machine control. The Gray code can be converted back to binary in a suitable PROM, available as a standard chip. For audio use, a logarithmic characteristic is required on faders, and this can be achieved in two ways: the PROM can be programmed to convert directly from Gray code to logarithmic binary, or the grating on the fader can be made nonlinear.

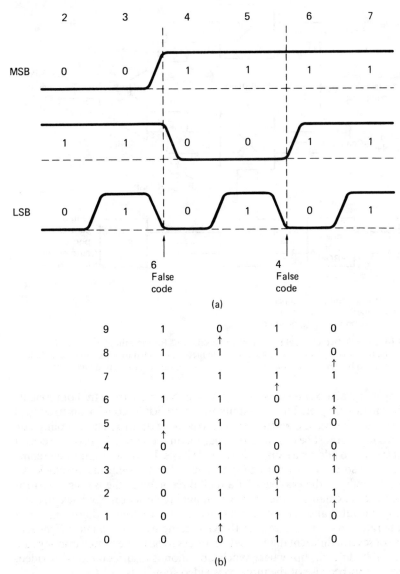

(a)

9	1	0	1	0
8	1	1	1	0
7	1	1	1	1
6	1	1	0	1
5	1	1	0	0
4	0	1	0	0
3	0	1	0	1
2	0	1	1	1
1	0	1	1	0
0	0	0	0	0

(b)

Figure 3.13 (a) Binary cannot be used for position encoders because mechanical tolerances cause false codes to be produced. (b) In Gray code, only one bit (arrowed) changes in between positions, so no false codes can be generated.

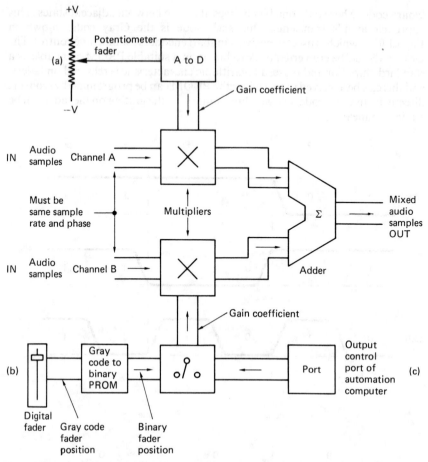

Figure 3.14 A simple two-channel mixer requires coefficients for the gain of each channel. These can be provided by: (a) conventional potentiometer connected to ADC; (b) digital fader and Gray code to binary conversion; (c) gain settings stored in an automated mix system.

A simple digital mixer is shown in Fig.3.14, constructed from the components described in this chapter. The two inputs are multiplied by coefficients to control their respective levels, and added together to achieve the mix. The sampling rate of the two inputs must be exactly the same, and in the same phase, or the circuit will not be able to add on a sample-by-sample basis. If the two inputs have come from different sources, they must be synchronized by the same master clock. An obvious difficulty is the playback of a digital recorder at the wrong speed for pitch correction. Changing the speed of a digital recorder on playback changes the sampling rate, and to obtain a standard rate to feed a digital mixer, a sampling rate converter is necessary to avoid going back into analog. Synchronization of several different digital audio sources to have the same sampling rate is not terribly difficult, but where synchronization is also required with video, problems occur because of the numerous video standards.

Some thought must be given to the wordlength of the system. If a sample is attenuated, it will develop bits which are below the radix point. For example, if a sixteen-bit sample is attenuated by 24 dB, the sample value will be shifted four places down. Extra bits must be available within the mixer to accommodate this shift. Generally, mixers work with an internal wordlength of about 24 bits. When several attenuated sources are added together to produce the final mix, the result will be a 24-bit sample stream. As the output will generally need to be of the same format as the input, the wordlength must be shortened. This must be done very carefully.

3.6 Digital dither

When a sample value is attenuated, the extra low-order bits made available preserve the resolution of the signal and the dither in the least significant bit which linearizes the system. If several such sample streams are added together, the random element in the low-order bits may now be some way below the least significant bit in the shortened word. If the word is simply truncated by ignoring the low-order bits below the desired wordlength, the result will be quantizing distortion, because the dither component has been removed. The wordlength of samples must be shortened so as to replace the lost dither, a process called digital dithering. A pseudo-random sequence generator is necessary, which is compared with the last bit to be retained and those below it. The comparison, as shown in Fig.3.15, rounds up or down to yield the least significant bit of the shortened word, which has a linearizing random component. The probability density of the pseudo-random sequence is important. Vanderkooy and Lipshitz[2] found that uniform probability density produced noise modulation, in

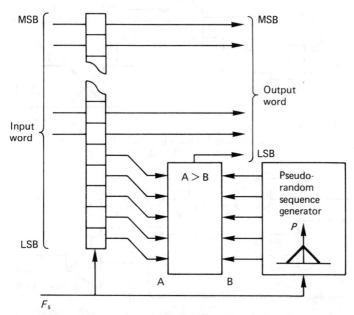

Figure 3.15 In order to shorten the wordlength of a sample correctly, the least significant bit must contain a random element to prevent quantizing distortion. By comparing the triangular probability pseudo-random sequence with the low-order bits, the resulting LSB contains information from those bits in the form of duty cycle modulation.

which the amplitude of the random component varies as a function of the amplitude of the samples. A triangular probability-density function obtained by adding together two pseudo-random sequences eliminated the noise modulation to yield a signal-independent white-noise component in the least significant bit. It is vital that such steps are taken when sample wordlength is to be reduced.

3.7 Mixing and crossfading

In some applications, such as splice-handling by stationary-head recorders, a crossfade in the digital domain is necessary. Fig.3.16(a) shows that this could be performed with two multipliers, one fed with a descending set of coefficients and one fed with an ascending set. In practice this would be wasteful, because a simple rearrangement of the expression for the crossfade produces a new equation which has only one product. This rearranged expression can be implemented with only one multiplier as in Fig.3.16(b).

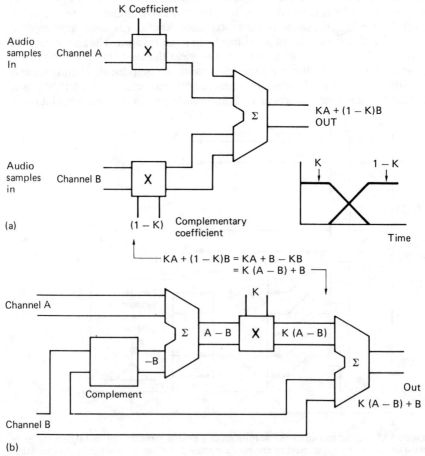

Figure 3.16 Crossfade at (a) requires two multipliers. Reconfiguration at (b) requires only one multiplier.

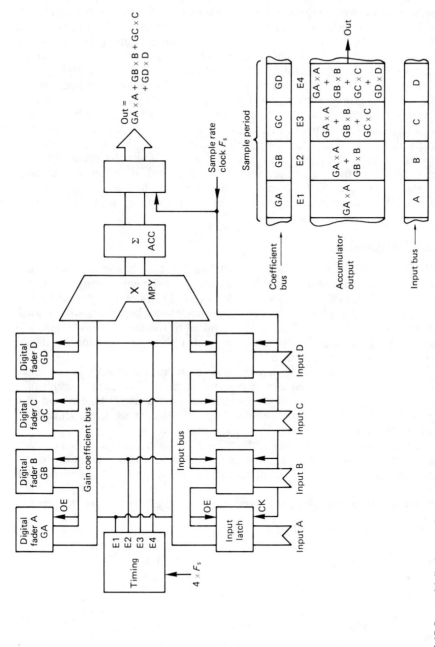

Figure 3.17 One multiplier/accumulator can be time-shared between several signals by operating at a multiple of sampling rate. In this example, four multiplications are performed during one sample period.

In practice a digital mixer would not have one multiplier for every input. Multiplier chips are expensive, but can work much faster than the relatively low frequencies used in audio sampling. Fig.3.17 shows that a more economical system results when a time-shared bus system is used with only one multiplier followed by an accumulator. In one sample period, each of the input samples is fed in turn to the lower input of the multiplier, at the same time as the correspon- ding coefficient is fed to the upper input. The products from the multiplier are accumulated during the sample period, so that at the end of the sample period, the accumulator holds the sum of all the products, which is the digitally mixed sample. The process then repeats for the next sample period. To facilitate the sharing of common circuits by many signals, the so-called tri-state logic devices can be used. These devices, in addition to having low- and high-output drive capability, can also adopt a high-impedance state on their output terminals under the control of an external signal. The outputs of such devices can be wired in parallel, and the state of the parallel connection will be the state of the device whose output is enabled. Clearly only one output can be enabled at a time, and this will be ensured by a sequencer circuit connected to all the device enables.

3.8 Companding

One of the fundamental concepts of digital audio is that the signal-to-noise ratio of the channel can be determined by selecting a suitable wordlength. For this reason professional digital recorders do not need to employ companding, and any debate about subjective effects such as noise modulation is neatly avoided. However, the bit rate is directly proportional to the sample wordlength, and where there is a restriction on channel bandwidth or storage capacity, digital companding may have to be used.

In editors for rotary-head digital audio recorders based on VCRs, the exact edit point has to be located using a memory, because VCRs cannot readily play at variable speed or backwards. In order to store a useful time period in a memory of reasonable cost, companding will often be used, particularly on earlier machines when memory was more expensive.

In the Video 8 system, the PCM audio has to share the tape with an analog video signal, and since it is a consumer product, tape consumption is at a premium. Companding is used in this system, and is explained in more detail in Chapter 10.

Broadcasters wishing to communicate over long distances are restricted to

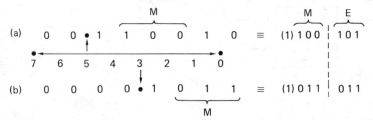

Figure 3.18 In this example of floating-point notation, the radix point can have eight positions determined by the exponent E. The point is placed to the left of the first '1', and the next four bits to the right form the mantissa M. As the MSB of the mantissa is always 1, it need not always be stored.

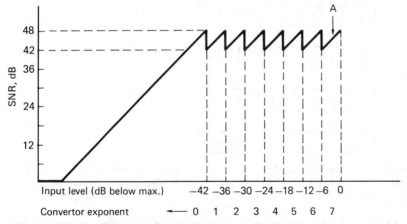

Figure 3.19 In this example of an eight-bit mantissa, three-bit exponent system, the maximum SNR is 6 dB × 8 = 48 dB with maximum input of 0 dB. As input level falls by 6 dB, the converter noise remains the same, so SNR falls to 42 dB. Further reduction in signal level causes the converter to shift range (point A in the diagram) by increasing the input analog gain by 6 dB. The SNR is restored, and the exponent changes from 7 to 6 in order to cause the same gain change at the receiver. The noise modulation would be audible in this simple system. A longer mantissa word is needed in practice.

the data rate conveniently available in the digital telephone network. Using companding, the BBC is able to pass six high-quality audio channels down the available telephone channels of 2048 kbits/s.[3] Companded samples are also used to distribute the sound accompanying television broadcasts by putting two PCM samples inside the line-synchronizing pulses, thus obtaining a sampling rate of twice the TV line rate.[4]

Just as sampling and quantizing are orthogonal processes, there are companding processes in both time and voltage. Samples may be compressed individually, or adjacent samples may be grouped together and compressed as a block. The compression of a sample can be done in two related ways.

In conversion-table companding, the range of values in which an input sample finds itself determines the factor by which it will be multiplied. For example, a sample value with the most significant bit reset could be multiplied by two to shift the bits up one place. If the two most significant bits are reset, the value could be multiplied by four and so on. Constants are then added to allow the range of the compressed sample value to determine the expansion necessary.

In floating point notation (Fig.3.18), a binary number is represented as a mantissa, which is always a binary fraction with one just to the right of the radix point, and an exponent, which is the power of two the mantissa has to be multiplied by to obtain the fixed-point number. Clearly the signal-to-noise ratio is now defined by the number of bits in the mantissa, and as shown in Fig.3.19, this will vary as a sawtooth function of signal level, as the best value, obtained when the mantissa is near overflow, is replaced by the worst value when the mantissa overflows and the exponent is incremented. Floating-point notation is at its most useful when several adjacent samples are assembled into a block so that the largest sample value determines a common exponent for the whole block. This technique is known as floating-point block coding (Fig.3.20). A relative of this process is the near instantaneous companding of the BBC

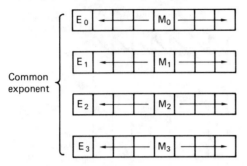

Figure 3.20 Floating-point block coding. A common exponent of four bits $E_0 - E_3$ is stored in four bytes leaving space for 4×7 bit mantissae. All four will be multiplied by the same exponent to return to fixed point.

NICAM system, where the magnitude of the largest sample in a one-millisecond block is used to determine the degree of compression.[5]

Such techniques cause an increase in program-modulated noise, but with care this can be inaudible due to masking. As its name suggests, an edit-point location memory serves only to help choose the time at which the edit is to be made and the edited sound does not need to pass through it. There is less necessity for high quality, and a higher degree of compression can be used. Chapter 8 gives an example of this approach.

3.9 Timebase correction

In Chapter 1 it was stated that a strength of digital technology is the ease with which delay can be provided. Accurate control of delay is the essence of timebase correction, necessary whenever the instantaneous time of arrival or rate from a data source does not match the destination. In magnetic tape recording, the destination will almost always have perfectly regular timing, namely the replay sampling rate generator, and timebase correction consists of aligning jittery offtape signals with the stable reference. In the Compact Disc, spindle runout causes variations in the data rate from the pickup. Rotary-head recorders suffer from impulsive jitter due to the heads striking the tape. All digital audio recorders, including disk drives, assemble data into blocks to facilitate editing and error correction as well as to permit head switching between blocks in rotary-head machines. Owing to the spaces between blocks, data arrive in bursts on replay, but must be fed to the output converters in an unbroken stream at the sampling rate. In this way, wow and flutter are rendered unmeasureable.

In computer hard-disk drives, which are used in digital audio editing systems, the data from the disk blocks arrive at a reasonably constant rate, but cannot necessarily be accepted at a steady rate by the logic because of contention for the use of buses and memory by the different parts of the system. In this case a further timebase corrector, usually referred to as a silo, is necessary.

Although delay is easily implemented, it is not possible to advance a data stream. Most real machines cause instabilities balanced about the correct timing: the output jitters between too early and too late. Since the information cannot be advanced in the corrector, only delayed, the solution is to run the machine in advance of real time. In this case, correctly timed output signals will need a nominal delay to align them with reference timing. Early output signals will receive more delay, and late output signals will receive less delay.

3.10 RAM timebase correction

There are three basic ways of obtaining delay in the digital domain: shift registers, memories and first-in-first-out devices (FIFOs).

The basic memory element in logic circuits is the latch, which is constructed from two gates, and can be set or reset. A more useful variant is the D-type latch which remembers the state of the input at the time a separate clock either changes state for an edge-triggered device, or after it goes false for a level-triggered device. D-type latches are commonly available with four or eight latches to the chip. A shift register can be made by connecting them one after the other, so that data are delayed by the number of stages in the register.

Where large numbers of bits are to be stored, cross-coupled latches are less suitable because they are more complicated to fabricate inside integrated circuits than dynamic memory.

In large random access memories (RAMs), the data bits are stored as the presence or absence of charge in a tiny capacitor. The charge will suffer leakage, and the value would become indeterminate after a few milliseconds. Where the delay needed is less than this, decay is of no consequence, as data will be read out before they have had a chance to decay. Where longer delays are necessary, such memories must be refreshed periodically by reading the bit value and writing it back to the same place. Most modern RAM chips have suitable circuitry built in. Large RAMs store thousands of bits, and it is clearly impractical to have a connection to each one. Instead, the desired bit has to be addressed before it can be read or written. The size of the chip package restricts the number of pins available, so that large memories use the same address pins more than once. The bits are arranged internally as rows and columns, and the row address and the column address are specified sequentially on the same pins. Fig.3.21 shows some examples of different memory devices.

The shift-register approach and the memory approach to delay are very similar, as a shift register can be thought of as a memory whose address increases automatically when clocked. The data rate and the maximum delay determine the capacity of the memory required. Fig.3.22 shows that the addressing of the memory is by a counter that overflows endlessly from the end of the memory back to the beginning, giving the memory a ring-like structure. The write address is determined by the incoming data, and the read address is determined by the outgoing data. This means that the memory has to be able to read and write at the same time. The switching between read and write involves not only a data multiplexer but also an address multiplexer. In general (Fig.3.23) the arbitration between read and write will be done by signals from the stable side of the TBC, which in the case of digital-recorder replay will be the read side. The stable side of the memory will read a sample when it demands, and the writing will be locked out for that period. The input data cannot be interrupted in many applications, however, so a small buffer silo is installed before the memory, which fills up as the writing is locked out, and empties again as writing is permitted. Alternatively, the memory will be split into blocks, such

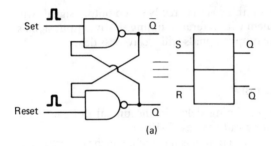

(a)

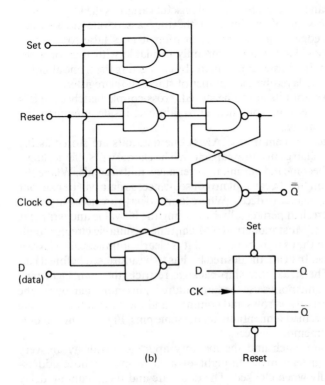

(b)

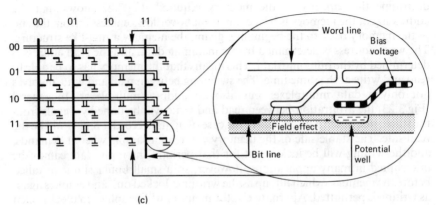

(c)

Figure 3.21 (*facing page*) Digital semiconductor memory types. At (a), one data bit can be stored in a simple set–reset latch, which has little application because the D-type latch at (b) can store the state of the single data input when the clock occurs. These devices can be implemented with bipolar transistors of FETs, and are called static memories because they can store indefinitely. They consume a lot of power.

At (c), a bit is stored as the charge in a potential well in the substrate of a chip. It is accessed by connecting the bit line with the field effect from the word line. The single well where the two lines cross can then be written or read. These devices are called dynamic RAMs because the charge decays, and they must be read and rewritten (refreshed) periodically.

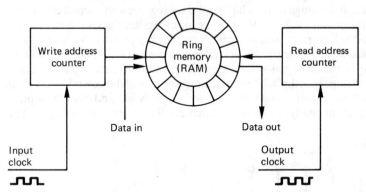

Figure 3.22 TBC memory is addressed by a counter which periodically overflows to give a ring structure. Memory allows read side to be non-synchronous with write side.

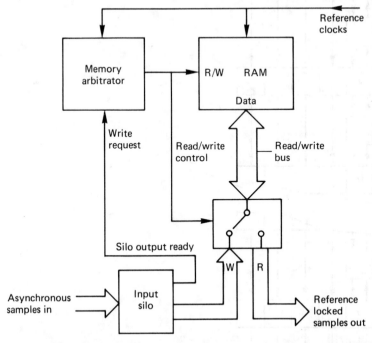

Figure 3.23 In a RAM-based TBC, the RAM is reference-synchronous, and an arbitrator decides when it will read and when it will write. During reading, asynchronous input data backs up in the input silo, asserting a write request to the arbitrator. Arbitrator will then cause a write cycle between read cycles.

that when one block is reading a different block will be writing and the problem does not arise.

3.11 FIFO timebase correction

Fig.3.24 shows the operation of a FIFO chip, colloquially known as a silo because the data are tipped in at the top on delivery and drawn off at the bottom when needed. Each stage of the chip has a data register and a small amount of logic, including a data-valid or V bit. If the input register does not contain data, the first V bit will be reset, and this will cause the chip to assert 'input ready'. If data are presented at the input, and clocked into the first stage, the V bit will set, and the 'input ready' signal will become false. However, the logic associated with the next stage sees the V bit set in the top stage, and if its own V bit is clear, it will clock the data into its own register, set its own V bit, and clear the input V bit, causing 'input ready' to reassert, when another word can be fed in. This

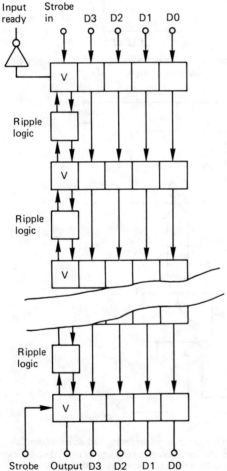

Figure 3.24 Structure of FIFO or silo chip. Ripple logic controls propagation of data down silo.

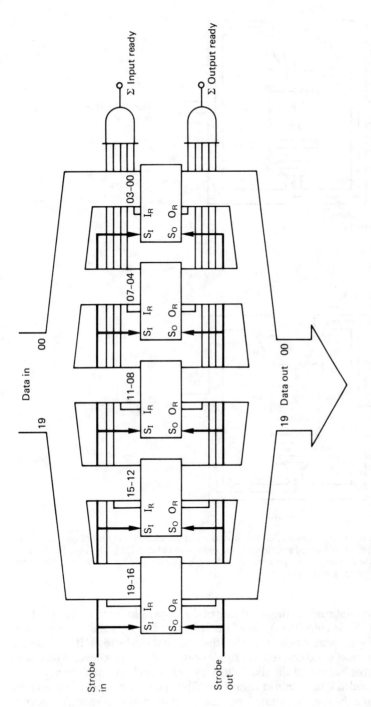

Figure 3.25 In this example, a twenty-bit wordlength silo is made from five parallel FIFO chips. The asynchronous ripple action of FIFOs means that it is necessary to 'and' together the ready signals.

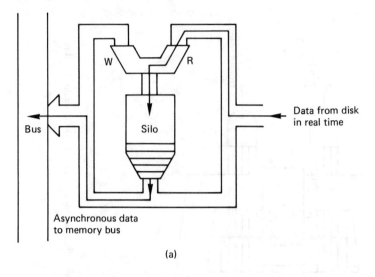

(a)

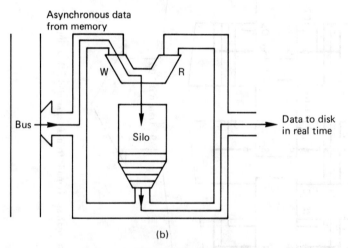

(b)

Figure 3.26 In order to guarantee that the drive can transfer data in real time at regular intervals (determined by disk speed and density) the silo provides buffering to the asynchronous operation of the memory access process. At (a) the silo is configured for a disk read. The same silo is used at (b) for a disk write.

process then continues as the word moves down the silo, until it arrives at the last register in the chip. The V bit of the last stage becomes the 'output ready' signal, telling subsequent circuitry that there are data to be read. If this word is not read, the next word entered will ripple down to the stage above. Words thus stack up at the bottom of the silo. When a word is read out, an external signal must be provided which resets the bottom V bit. The 'output ready' signal now goes false, and the logic associated with the last stage now sees valid data above, and loads down the word when it will become ready again. The last register but one will now have no V bit set, and will see data above itself and bring that

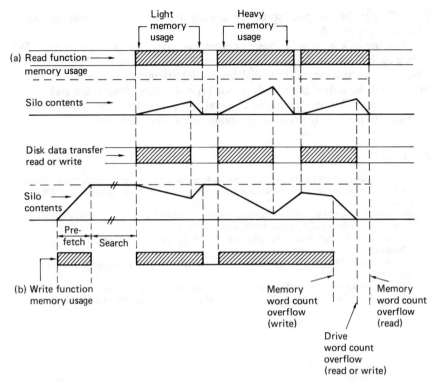

Figure 3.27 The silo contents during read functions (a) appear different from those during write functions (b). In (a), the control logic attempts to keep the silo as empty as possible; in (b) the logic prefills the silo and attempts to keep it full until the memory word count overflows.

down. In this way a reset V bit propagates up the chip while the data ripple down, rather like a hole in a semiconductor going the opposite way to the electrons. Silo chips are usually available in four-bit wordlengths, but can easily be connected in parallel to form longer words. Silo chips are asynchronous, and paralleled chips will not necessarily all work at the same speed. This problem is easily overcome by 'anding' together all of the input-ready and output-ready signals and parallel-connecting the strobes. Fig.3.25 shows this mode of operation.

When used in a hard-disk system, a silo will allow data to and from the disk, which is turning at constant speed (Fig.3.26). When reading the disk, the silo starts empty, and if there is bus contention, the silo will start to fill. Where the bus is free, the disk controller will attempt to empty the silo into the memory. The system can take advantage of the interblock gaps on the disk, containing headers, preambles and redundancy, for in these areas there are no data to transfer, and there is some breathing space to empty the silo before the next block. In practice the silo need not be empty at the start of every block, provided it never becomes full before the end of the transfer. If this happens some data are lost and the function must be aborted. The block containing the silo overflow will generally be re-read on the next revolution. In sophisticated systems, the silo has a kind of dipstick, and can interrupt the CPU if the data get too deep.

The CPU can then suspend some bus activity to allow the disk controller more time to empty the silo.

When the disk is to be written, a continuous data stream must be provided during each block, as the disk cannot stop. The silo will be prefilled before the disk attempts to write, and the disk controller attempts to keep it full. In this case all will be well if the silo does not become empty before the end of the transfer. Fig.3.27 shows the silo of a typical disk controller with the multiplexers necessary to put it in the read data stream or the write data stream.

References

1. KOVINIC, M. and VASILJEVIC, D., A novel approach to the digital solution of the peak program meter. Presented at the 77th Audio Engineering Society Convention (Hamburg, 1985), pre-print 2210(G-5)
2. VANDERKOOY, J. and LIPSHITZ, S.P., Digital dither. Presented at the 81st Audio Engineering Society Convention (Los Angeles, 1986), preprint 2412(C-8)
3. MCNALLY, G.W., Digital audio in broadcasting. *IEEE Acoust. Speech Signal Process Magazine*, **2**, 26–44 (1985)
4. JONES, A.H., A PCM sound-in-syncs distribution system. General description. *BBC Res. Dept Rept*, 1969/35
5. CAINE, C.R., ENGLISH, A.R. and O'CLAREY, J.W.H. NICAM-3: near-instantaneous companded digital transmission for high-quality sound programmes. *J. IERE*, **50**, 519–530 (1980)

Chapter 4

Advanced digital audio processing

Chapter 3 dealt with the important basics of multiplication, addition and delay for these are the foundation of all digital filtering. In this chapter, the use of digital filters for oversampling, sampling-rate conversion and equalization will be explained, followed by a look at some ways in which digital mixing consoles and special effects can be implemented.

4.1 Phase linearity

One of the strengths of digital signal processing is that filtering can be performed with stable binary logic instead of the inductors and capacitors needed for analog filters. In analog filtering, the frequency response is usually the most quoted parameter, followed by the phase response and the impulse response. These last two are the most difficult to get right in an analog filter.

Fig.4.1 shows that impulse response testing tells a great deal about a filter. In a perfect filter, all frequencies should experience the same time delay; this is the group delay. If not, there is a group-delay error. As an impulse contains an infinite spectrum, a filter fed with an impulse will separate the different frequencies in time if it suffers from group-delay error.

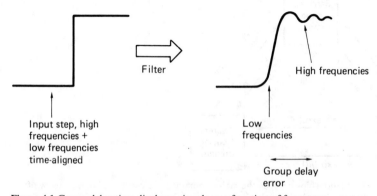

Figure 4.1 Group delay time displaces signals as a function of frequency.

A pure delay will cause a phase shift proportional to frequency, and a filter with this characteristic is said to be phase-linear. The impulse response of a phase-linear filter is symmetrical. If a filter suffers from group-delay error it cannot be phase-linear. It is almost impossible to make a phase-linear analog filter, and many filters have a group-delay equalization stage following them which is often as complex as the filter itself. In the digital domain it is reasonably straightforward to make a phase-linear filter, and phase equalization becomes unnecessary. Because of the sampled nature of the signal, whatever the response at low frequencies may be, all digital channels act as low-pass filters cutting off at the Nyquist limit, or half the sampling frequency.

4.2 Transforms and convolution

It is necessary to understand the principles of filter operation so that the performance of proposed designs can be evaluated without having to build hardware for test. Just as techniques exist for designing analog filters, there are comparable techniques for designing digital filters. The use of mathematics is

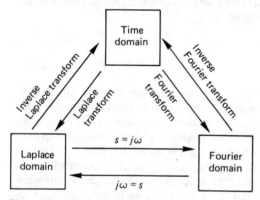

Figure 4.2 (a) The major domains for consideration of a time-continuous signal in analog filter design.

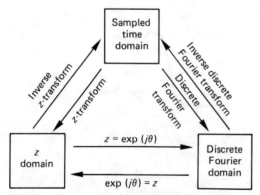

Figure 4.2 (b) The relationships between the major domains to be considered in the theory of filters for time-discrete (sampled) signals.

inescapable, but it has been kept to a minimum here. The principles involved can be understood by referring only to the graphic examples in this chapter.

A digital audio signal contains sampled or discrete-time domain information; the audio engineer is often more concerned with the frequency response of filters, and the designer is concerned with how a certain response will be achieved. All three can be satisfied by different aspects of a unified filter theory which allows filter operation to be computed in any of three different domains. Fig.4.2 shows the relationships of the time, frequency (Fourier transform) and s-plane (Laplace transform) domains in an analog filter, and the corresponding relationships of discrete time, discrete frequency (DFT) and z-plane domains in sampled systems.

The time domain will be treated first, by comparison with analog circuitry. Fig.4.3 shows a simple RC network and its corresponding impulse response. If an infinitely short pulse is supplied to the input, the capacitor will store the energy of the pulse, which leaks away through the resistor to give the familiar exponential decay curve. The figure also shows what happens when a square wave is used as an input. The resultant waveform can be calculated because the input signal and the impulse response are equally simple.

When the input signal and the impulse response are both complicated functions of time, this approach becomes almost impossible. In the time domain, the output waveform represents the convolution of the input waveform and the impulse response. Convolution can be understood by a graphic example shown in Fig.4.4. The most important step in performing a graphical convolution is to reverse the impulse response in time so that it is a mirrored version of itself. The impulse response is then slid through the input pulse. The output voltage, as the impulse slides through, is given by the shaded area where the two pulses overlap.

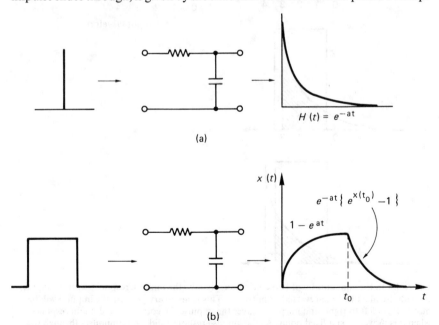

$$H(t) = e^{-at}$$

(a)

$$x(t)$$

$$e^{-at}\{ e^{x(t_0)} - 1 \}$$

$$1 - e^{at}$$

$$t_0$$

(b)

Figure 4.3 (a) The impulse response of a simple RC network is an exponential decay. This can be used to calculate the response to a square wave, as in (b).

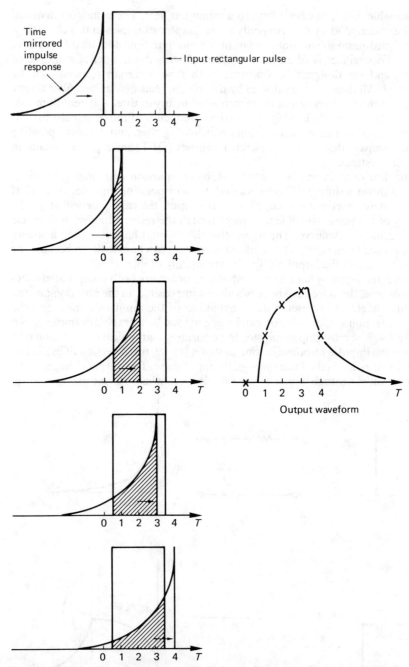

Figure 4.4 In the convolution of two continuous signals (the impulse response with the input), the impulse must be time-reversed or mirrored. This is necessary because the impulse will be moved from left to right, and mirroring gives the impulse the correct time-domain response when it is moved past a fixed point. As the impulse response slides continuously through the input waveform, the area where the two overlap determines the instantaneous output amplitude. This is shown for five different times by the crosses on the output waveform.

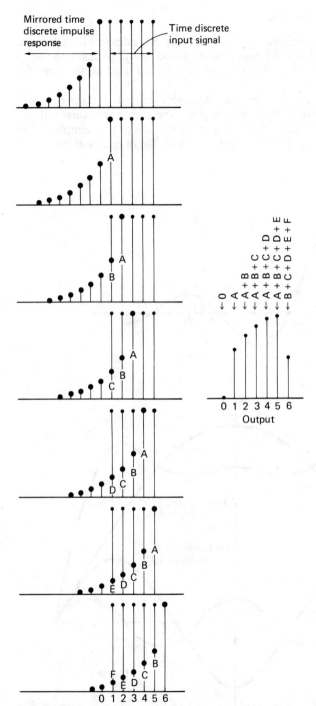

Figure 4.5 In time-discrete convolution, the mirrored impulse response is stepped through the input one sample period at a time. At each step, the sum of the cross products is used to form an output value. As the input in this example is a constant-height pulse, the output is simply proportional to the sum of the coincident impulse response samples. This figure should be compared with Figure 4.4.

The same process can be undertaken in the sampled or discrete time domain. The impulse response (Fig.4.5) is now a series of discrete samples, as is the input signal. The only constraint is that the sampling period must be the same for both.

The impulse response no longer slides through the input, because positions where samples do not coincide are meaningless. The impulse response is therefore moved through the input signal in a series of steps of one sample period each. At each step, the area of the graph still yields the output, but the area is

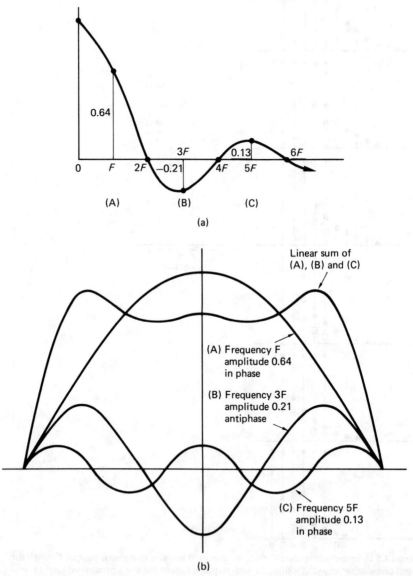

Figure 4.6 At (a) the spectrum of a squarewave is a sin x/x shape, showing that there are no even harmonics. At (b) the first three components are shown separately, then added to form a ringing squarewave.

evaluated more easily. Since the sample periods are identical, the output sample is given by adding up the lengths of all of the relevant impulse samples. If the input signal were more complicated, such that successive samples were different, it would be necessary to multiply the lengths of superimposed input and impulse samples together before adding them up. In mathematical terms, the output sample values represent the convolution of the input and impulse response by summing the coincident cross-products.

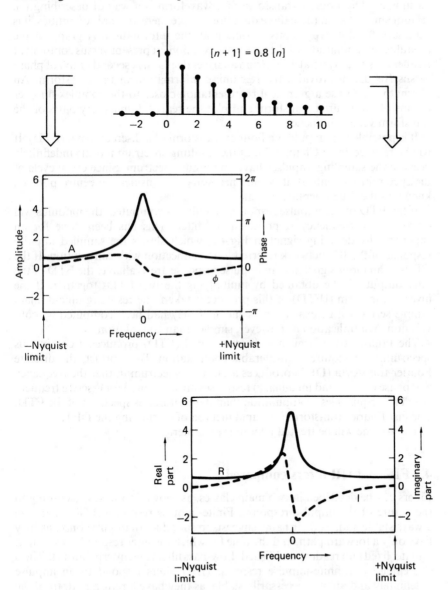

Figure 4.7 When a Fourier analysis is made of the time-discrete input shown, the spectrum is complex, and can be drawn either as an amplitude and phase response (left) or as a real and imaginary response (right). (Courtesy *Philips Technical Review*)

In the time domain the response of a filter is predicted by convolution. As the digital filter works in exactly this way, it might be better to say that time-domain calculations are no more than a simulation of the operation of the filter.

The frequency domain will now be related to the time domain. Fourier analysis holds that all waveforms can be represented by the sum of a number of sinusoidal signals of different amplitudes, phases and frequencies. Fig.4.6 shows the example of building up a square wave from component frequencies or harmonics. The Fourier transform of a waveform is a way of describing the relationship between these three quantities. Since there are three quantities, it is necessary to plot two graphs to obtain all the information. A graph of the modulus (or magnitude) of the sine-wave component present versus component frequency is exactly what a spectrum analyser displays. A second graph of phase versus frequency provides the remaining information in the transform. An alternative is to use a graphical representation closer to the complex-number origins of the Fourier transform and plot the real and imaginary parts of the transform versus frequency.

It is possible to compute the Fourier transform of a discrete signal (FTD). It will be recalled from Chapter 2 that the resulting spectrum repeats indefinitely because the sampling impulses have an infinite spectrum. Since every cycle of the spectrum is identical, it is only necessary to consider the centre portion, known as the fundamental interval.

If the FTD of the impulse response of a filter is computed, the modulus will represent the frequency response of the filter. This has been done for an exponentially decaying signal in Fig.4.7, which shows the sampled impulse response of the RC network referred to in connection with convolution. If the FTDs of an input signal and an impulse response are available, the FTD of the filter output will be obtained by multiplying the two FTDs together. If the inverse transform (IFTD) of this product is taken, the resulting time-domain sample series will be exactly the same as if they had been computed by convolution. Multiplication is, however, simpler than convolution.

The Fourier transform of a discrete signal (FTD) produces a continuous spectrum, and requires considerable computation. By contrast, the discrete Fourier transform (DFT) produces a sampled spectrum in that the frequency and phase (or real and imaginary) responses are computed for discrete frequencies. This requires less computation than the continuous spectrum of the FTD. The fast Fourier transform is a rapid method of calculating the DFT.

The z-plane will be treated later in the chapter.

4.3 FIR and IIR filters compared

Filters can be described in two main classes, as shown in Fig.4.8, according to the nature of the impulse response. Finite-impulse response (FIR) filters are always stable and, as their name suggests, respond to an impulse once, as they have only a forward path, and the time for which the filter responds to an input is finite, fixed and readily established. Low-pass filters and interpolators fall into this category. Infinite-impulse response (IIR) filters respond to an impulse indefinitely and are not necessarily stable, as they have a return path from the output to the input. For this reason they are also called recursive filters. Digital reverberators and equalizers employ recursive filters.

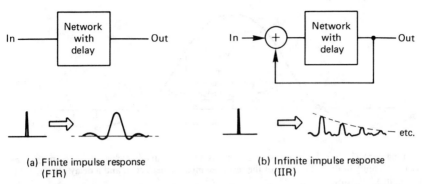

(a) Finite impulse response
(FIR)

(b) Infinite impulse response
(IIR)

Figure 4.8 A FIR filter (a) responds only only to an input, whereas the output of an IIR filter (b) continues indefinitely rather like a decaying echo.

4.4 FIR filters

A FIR filter works by graphically constructing the impulse response for every input sample. It is first necessary to establish the correct impulse response. Fig.4.9(a) shows an example of a low-pass filter which cuts off at $\frac{1}{4}$ of the sampling rate. The impulse response of a perfect low-pass filter is a $\sin x/x$ curve, where the time between the two central zero crossings is the reciprocal of the cut-off frequency. According to the mathematics, the waveform has always existed, and carries on for ever. The peak value of the output coincides with the input impulse. This means that the filter is not causal, because the output has changed before the input is known. Thus in all practical applications it is necessary to truncate the extreme ends of the impulse response, which causes an aperture effect, and to introduce a time delay in the filter equal to half the duration of the truncated impulse in order to make the filter causal. As an input impulse is shifted through the series of registers in Fig.4.9(b), the impulse response is created, because at each point it is multiplied by a coefficient as in Fig.4.9(c). These coefficients are simply the result of sampling and quantizing the desired impulse response. Clearly the sampling rate used to sample the impulse must be the same as the sampling rate for which the filter is being designed. In practice the coefficients are calculated, rather than attempting to sample an actual impulse response, although this would be possible if a particular analog filter had to be duplicated in the digital domain. The coefficient wordlength will be a compromise between cost and performance. Because the input sample shifts across the system to create the shape of the impulse response, the configuration is also known as a transversal filter. In operation with real sample streams, there will be several consecutive sample values in the filter registers at any time in order to convolve the input with the impulse response, and this should be compared with the convolution shown in Fig.4.5.

Simply truncating the impulse response causes an abrupt transition from input samples which matter and those which do not. This aperture effect results in a tendency for the response to peak just before the cut-off frequency. This peak is known as Gibb's phenomenon; it causes ripples in both passband and stopband.[1,2] As a result, the length of the impulse which must be considered will depend not only on the frequency response, but also on the amount of ripple

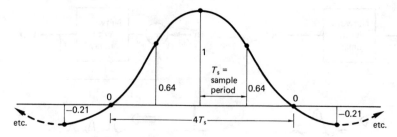

Figure 4.9 (a) The impulse response of an LPF is a sin x/x curve which stretches from − infinity to + infinity in time. The ends of the response must be neglected, and a delay introduced to make the filter causal.

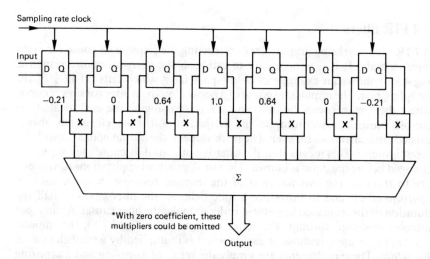

Figure 4.9 (b) The structure of an FIR LPF. Input samples shift across the register, and at each point are multiplied by different coefficients.

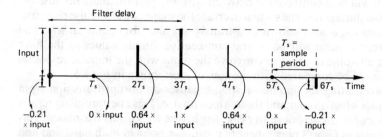

Figure 4.9 (c) When a single unit sample shifts across the circuit of Figure 4.9 (b), the impulse response is created at the output as the impulse is multiplied by each coefficient in turn.

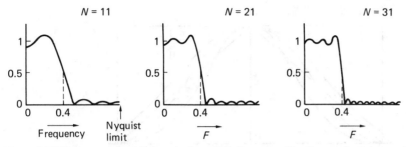

Figure 4.10 The truncation of the impulse in an FIR filter caused by the use of a finite number of points (*N*) results in ripple in the response. Shown here are three different numbers of points for the same impulse response. The filter is an LPF which rolls off at 0.4 of the fundamental interval. (Courtesy *Philips Technical Review*)

which can be tolerated. If the relevant period of the impulse is measured in sample periods, the result will be the number of points needed in the filter.

Fig.4.10 compares the performance of filters with different numbers of points. A typical digital audio FIR filter may have as many as 96 points.

Rather than simply truncate the impulse response in time, it is better to make a smooth transition from samples which do not count to those that do. This can be done by multiplying the coefficients in the filter by a window function which peaks in the centre of the impulse. Fig.4.11 shows some different window functions and their responses. Clearly the rectangular window is the same as truncation, and the response is shown at I. A linear reduction in weight from the centre of the window to the edges characterizes the Bartlett window II, which trades ripple for an increase in transition-region width. At III is shown the Hanning window, which is essentially a raised cosine shape. Not shown is the similar Hamming window, which offers a slightly different trade-off between ripple and the width of the main lobe. The Blackman window introduces an extra cosine term into the Hamming window at half the period of the main cosine period, reducing Gibb's phenomenon and ripple level, but increasing the width of the transition region. The Kaiser window is a family of windows based on the Bessel function, allowing various trade-offs between ripple ratio and main lobe width. Two of these are shown in IV and V. The drawback of the Kaiser windows is that they are complex to implement.

For audio applications, the equiripple filter is the preferred characteristic, and the coefficients can be optimized by computer simulation. One of the best-known techniques used is the Remez exchange algorithm, which converges on the optimum coefficients after a number of iterations.

In the example of Fig.4.12, the low-pass filter of Fig.4.9 is shown with a Bartlett window. Acceptable ripple determines the number of significant sample periods embraced by the impulse. This determines in turn both the number of points in the filter, and the filter delay. For the purposes of illustration, the number of points is much smaller than would normally be needed in an audio application. As the impulse is symmetrical, the delay will be half the impulse period. The impulse response is a $\sin x/x$ function, and this has been calculated in the figure. The $\sin x/x$ response is next multiplied by the window function to give the windowed impulse response. If the coefficients are not quantized finely enough, it will be as if they had been calculated inaccurately, and the performance of the filter will be less than expected. Fig.4.13 shows an example of

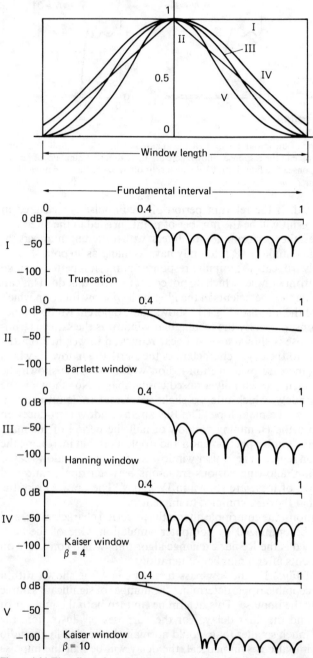

Figure 4.11 The effect of window functions. At top, various window functions are shown in continuous form. Once the number of samples in the window is established, the continuous functions shown here are sampled at the appropriate spacing to obtain window coefficients. These are multiplied by the truncated impulse response coefficients to obtain the actual coefficients used by the filter. The amplitude responses I–V correspond to the window functions illustrated. (Responses courtesy *Philips Technical Review*)

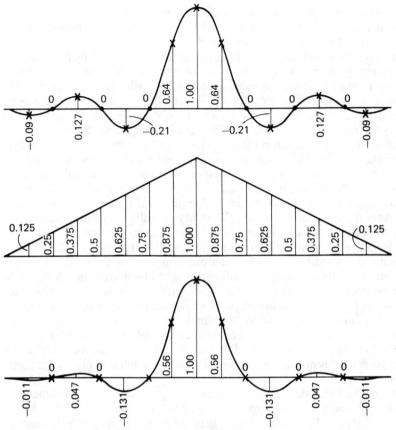

Figure 4.12 A truncated sin x/x impulse (top) is multiplied by a Bartlett window function (centre) to produce the actual coefficients used (bottom).

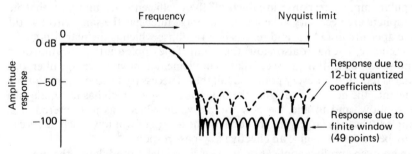

Figure 4.13 Frequency response of a 49-point transversal filter with infinite precision (solid line) shows ripple due to finite window size. Quantizing coefficients to 12 bits reduces attenuation in the stopband. (Responses courtesy *Philips Technical Review*)

quantizing coefficients. Conversely, raising the wordlength of the coefficients increases cost.

The FIR structure is inherently phase linear because there is rigid time control due to the way samples are shifted through the filter. The individual samples in a digital system do not know in isolation what frequency they represent, and they can only pass through the filter at a rate determined by the clock. Because of this inherent phase-linearity, a FIR filter can be designed for a specific impulse response, and the frequency response will follow.

The frequency response of the filter can be changed at will by changing the coefficients. A programmable filter only requires a series of PROMs to supply the coefficients; the address supplied to the PROMs will select the response. The frequency response of a digital filter will also change if the clock rate is changed, so it is often less ambiguous to specify a frequency of interest in a digital filter in terms of a fraction of the fundamental interval rather than in absolute terms.

The configuration shown in Fig.4.9(c) serves to illustrate the principle. Where the number of points in the filter is large, as in digital audio, the number and cost of multipliers needed for a configuration of this kind would be prohibitive, and a more cost-effective solution is to use one multiplier and multiplex the samples and coefficients in time so that the multiplier runs much faster than the sampling rate. As computer processors have the ability to multiply and accumulate, and delay can be achieved by leaving data in registers or memory, it is also possible to write software which will make a computer act as a digital filter. A new computation is required for every output sample, and to provide synchronization in real-time systems, the software will be in a subroutine which will be called by interrupts at the sample rate. The computer must be able to execute the subroutine before the next interrupt. Where the impulse response is symmetrical, it is often possible to reduce the number of multiplications, because the same product can be used twice, at equal distances before and after the centre of the window. This is known as folding the filter. The implementation of a programmable filter is now only a matter of selecting a different file for the coefficients.

The cost of FIR filters using complicated impulse shapes is sometimes prohibitive, especially if a prototype is required before LSIs are available. In this case it is still possible to take advantage of the phase linearity of FIR filters by restricting the available responses to those which require little hardware.[3] One such device is the so-called moving-average filter (Fig.4.14), which has a rectangular impulse response in which all the coefficients are unity, so that no multipliers are necessary. The moving-average filter has the same effect as the finite aperture in DACs, and results in a response which is the magnitude of a $\sin x / x$ curve. The figure also shows the origin of the ripple due to truncation of an impulse response. It might seem that to implement a moving average filter, one adder is required for every point, but all that is necessary to convert one output value into the next is to subtract the old input sample which has just gone past the window, and to add the new sample value which has just entered. The complexity is then largely independent of the length of window. Such filters can easily be cascaded to give an effective low-pass response.[4]

In an oversampling application using a sigma delta modulator, the input to the filter may be one-bit samples at a very high rate. These samples will need to be low-pass filtered as part of the sampling-rate reduction. In the special case of one-bit samples, a series of samples can form the address of a ROM which is programmed at that location with the weighted sum of the address bits. This makes implementation much simpler. Such filters are invariably linear -phase with symmetrical impulse responses, and lend themselves to folding.[5] In hardware, folding requires reversing the sequence of samples after the centre of the window, and a last-in-first-out (LIFO) register is placed at the fold.

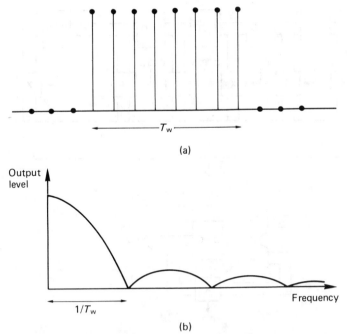

(a)

(b)

Figure 4.14 At (a) the impulse response of moving average filter has all coefficients equal to one, so no multipliers are necessary. (b) The frequency response of a moving average filter is the familiar sin x/x curve of an aperture function.

4.5 IIR filters

The next example is an FIR filter which simulates an RC network. Because an RC network is causal, i.e. the output cannot appear before the input, the impulse response is asymmetrical, and represents an exponential decay, as shown in Fig.4.15(a). The asymmetry of the impulse response confirms the expected result that this filter will not be phase-linear. The implementation of the filter is exactly the same as the example of Fig.4.12; only the coefficients have been changed. The simulation of RC networks is common in digital audio for the purposes of equalization or provision of tone controls. A large number of points are required in an FIR filter to create the long exponential decays necessary, and the FIR filter is at a disadvantage here because an exponential decay can be computed as every output sample is a fixed proportion of the previous one. Fig.4.15(b) shows a much simpler hardware configuration, where the output is returned in attenuated form to the input. The response of this circuit to a single sample is a decaying series of samples, in which the rate of decay is controlled by the gain of the multiplier. If the gain is one, the output can carry on indefinitely. For this reason, the configuration is known as an infinite impulse response (IIR) filter. If the gain of the multiplier is slightly more than one, the output will increase exponentially after a single non-zero input until the end of the number range is reached. Unlike FIR filters, IIR filters are not necessarily stable. FIR filters are easy to understand, but difficult to make in audio applications; IIR filters are easier to make, because less hardware is needed, but they are harder to understand.

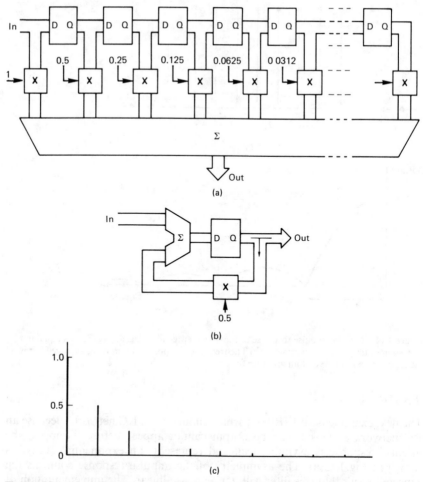

Figure 4.15 At (a) an FIR filter is supplied with exponentially decaying coefficient to simulate an RC response. At (b) the configuration of an IIR or recursive filter uses much less hardware (or computation) to give the same response, shown in (c).

One major consideration when recursive techniques are to be used is that the accuracy of the coefficients must be much higher. This is because an impulse response is created by making each output some fraction of the previous one, and a small error in the coefficient becomes a large error after several recursions. This error between what is wanted and what results from using truncated coefficients can often be enough to make the actual filter unstable whereas the theoretical model is not.

By way of introduction to this class of filters, the characteristics of some useful configurations will be discussed. It will be seen that parallels can be drawn with some classical analog circuits.

The terms phase lag and phase lead are used to describe analog circuit characteristics, and they are also applicable to digital circuits. Fig.4.16(a) shows a first-order lag network containing two multipliers, a register to provide one sample period of delay, and an adder. As might be expected, the characteristics

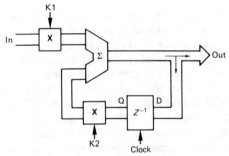

Figure 4.16 (a) First-order lag network IIR filter. Note recursive path through single sample delay latch.

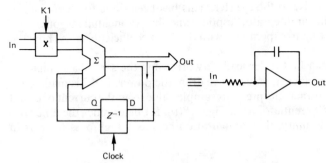

Figure 4.16 (b) The arrangement of (a) becomes an integrator if K2 = 1, since the output is always added to the next sample.

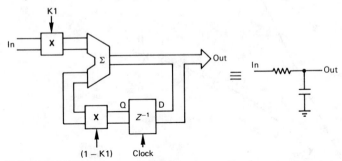

Figure 4.16 (c) When the two coefficients sum to unity, the system behaves as an RC lag network.

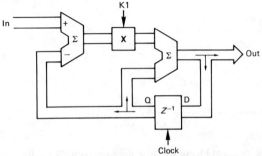

Figure 4.16 (d) The same performance as in (c) can be realized with only one multiplier by reconfiguring as shown here.

of the circuit can be transformed by changing the coefficients. If K2 is greater than unity, the circuit is unstable, as any non-zero input causes the output to increase exponentially. Making K2 equal to unity (Fig.4.16(b)) produces a digital integrator, because the current value in the latch is added to the input to form the next value in the latch. The coefficient K1 determines the time constant in the same way that the RC network does for the analog circuit. Fig.4.16(c) shows the case where K1 + K2 = 1; the response will be the same as an RC lag network. In this case it will be more economical to construct a different configuration shown in Fig.4.16(d) having the same characteristics but eliminating one stage of multiplication. The operation of these configurations can be verified by computing their responses to an input step. This is simply done by applying some constant input value, and deducing how the output changes for each applied clock pulse to the register. This has been done for two cases in Fig.4.17 where the linear integrator response and the exponential responses can be seen. It is interesting to experiment with different coefficients to see how the results change.

Fig.4.18(a) shows a first-order lead network using the same basic building blocks. Again, the coefficient values have dramatic power. If K2 is made zero, the circuit simply subtracts the previous sample value from the current one, and so becomes a true differentiator as in Fig.4.18(b). K1 determines the time constant. If K2 is made unity, the configuration acts as a high-pass filter as in Fig.4.18(c).

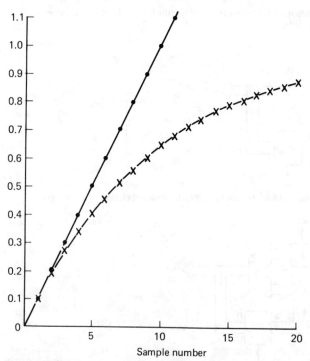

Figure 4.17 The response of the configuration of Figure 4.16 to a unit step. With K2 = 1, the system is an integrator, and the straight line shows the output with K1 = 0.1. With K1 = 0.1 and K2 = 0.9, K1 + K2 = 1 and the exponential response of an RC network is simulated.

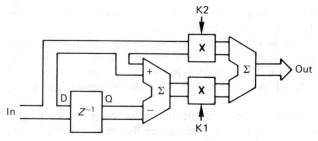

Figure 4.18 (a) First-order lead configuration. Unlike the lag filter this arrangement is always stable, but as before the effect of changing the coefficients is dramatic.

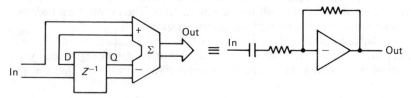

Figure 4.18 (b) When K2 of (a) is made zero, the configuration subtracts successive samples, and thus acts as a differentiator.

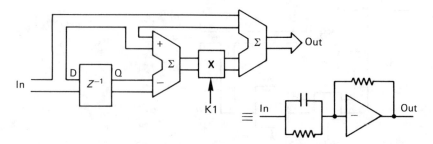

Figure 4.18 (c) Setting K2 of (a) to unity gives the high-pass filter response shown here.

4.6 The z-transform

Whereas it was possible to design effective FIR filters with relatively simple theory, the IIR filter family are too complicated for that. The z-transform is particularly appropriate for IIR digital filter design because it permits a rapid graphic assessment of the characteristics of a proposed filter. This graphic nature of the z-plane also lends itself to explanation so that an understanding of filter concepts can be obtained without their becoming obscured by mathematics.

Digital filters rely heavily on delaying sample values by one or more sample periods. One tremendous advantage of the z-transform is that a delay which is difficult to handle in the time domain corresponds to a multiplication in the z-domain. This means that the transfer function of a circuit in the z-domain can often be written down by referring to the block diagram, which is why a register causing a sample delay is usually described by z^{-1}.

The circuit configuration of Fig.4.16(c) is repeated in Fig.4.19(a). For simplicity in calculation, the two coefficients have been set to 0.5. The impulse response of this circuit will be found first, followed by the characteristics of the circuit in the z-plane which will immediately give the frequency and phase response.

The impulse response can be found graphically by supplying a series of samples as input which are all zero except for one which has unity value. This has been done in the figure, where it will be seen that once the unity sample has entered, the output y will always be one half the previous output, resulting in an exponential decay.

Where there is a continuous input to the circuit, the output will be one half the previous output y plus one half the current input x. The output then becomes the convolution of the input and the impulse response.

It is possible to express the operation of the circuit mathematically. Time is discrete, and is measured in sample periods, so the time can be expressed by the number of the sample n. Accordingly the input at time n will be called $x[n]$ and

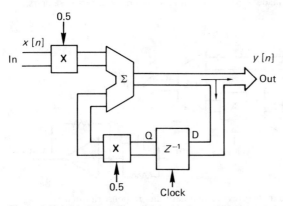

Figure 4.19 (a) A digital filter which simulates an RC network. In this example the coefficients are both 0.5.

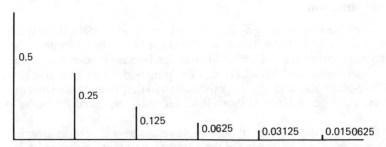

Figure 4.19 (b) The response of (a) to a single unity-value sample. The initial output of 0.5 is due to the input coefficient. Subsequent outputs are always 0.5 of the previous sample, owing to the recursive path through the latch.

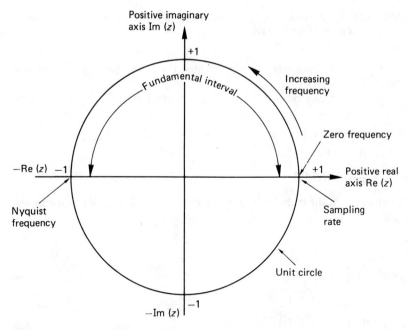

Figure 4.19 (c) The z-plane showing real and imaginary axes. Frequency increases anti-clockwise from $\mathrm{Re}(z) = +1$ to the Nyquist limit at $\mathrm{Re}(z) = -1$, returning to $\mathrm{Re}(z) = +1$ at the sampling rate. The origin of aliasing is clear.

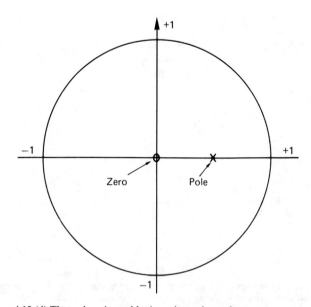

Figure 4.19 (d) The z-plane is used by inserting poles and zeros.

the corresponding output will be called $y[n]$. The previous output is called $y[n-1]$. It is then possible to write:

$$y[n] = 0.5\,x[n] + 0.5\,y[n-1]$$

This is called a recurrence relationship, because if it is repeated for all values of n, a convolution results.

The relationship can be transformed into an expression in z, referring to Fig.4.19(b).

$$y[n] = y[z],\ x[n] = x[z]$$

and $y[n-1] = z^{-1}y[z]$

so that $y[z] = 0.5x[z] + 0.5z^{-1}y[z]$ \hfill (4.1)

As with any system the transfer function is the ratio of the output to the input. Thus:

$$H[z] = \frac{y[z]}{x[z]}$$

Rearranging Eqn.4.1 gives:

$$y[z] - 0.5z^{-1}y[z] = 0.5x[z]$$

$$y[z]\,(1 - 0.5z^{-1}) = 0.5x[z]$$

$$\frac{y[z]}{x[z]} = \frac{0.5}{1 - 0.5z^{-1}} = \frac{1}{2 - z^{-1}} = \frac{z}{2z - 1}$$

Thus:

$$H[z] = \frac{z}{2z - 1}$$ \hfill (4.2)

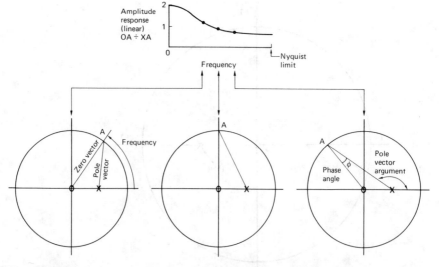

Figure 4.19 (e) Some examples of response of the circuit of (a) using the z plane. The zero vector is divided by the pole vector to obtain the amplitude response, and the phase response is the difference between the arguments of the two vectors.

The term in the numerator would make the transfer function zero when it became zero, whereas the terms in the denominator would make the transfer function infinite if they were to become zero. These result in poles.

Poles and zeros are plotted on a z-plane diagram. The basics of the z-plane are shown in Fig.4.19(c). There are two axes at right angles, the real axis $Re(z)$ and the imaginary axis $Im(z)$. Upon this plane is drawn a circle of unit radius whose centre is at the intersection of the axes. Frequency increases anticlockwise around this circle from 0 Hz at $Re(z) = +1$ to the Nyquist limit frequency at $Re(z) = -1$. Negative frequency increases clockwise around the circle reaching the negative Nyquist limit at $Re(z) = -1$. Essentially the circle on the z-plane is produced by taking the graph of a Fourier spectrum and wrapping it round a cylinder. The repeated spectral components at multiples of the sampling frequency in the Fourier domain simply overlap the fundamental interval when rolled up in this way, and so it is an ideal method for displaying the response of a sampled system, since only the response in the fundamental interval is of interest. Fig.4.19(d) shows that the z-plane diagram is used by inserting poles (X) and zeros (0).

In Eqn 4.2, $H[z]$ can be made zero only if z is zero; therefore a zero is placed on the diagram at $z = 0$. $H[z]$ becomes infinite if z is 0.5, because the denominator becomes zero. A pole (X) is placed on the diagram at $Re(z) = 0.5$. It will be recalled that 0.5 was the value of the coefficient used in the filter circuit being analysed. The performance of the system can be analysed for any frequency by drawing two vectors. The frequency in question is a fraction of the sampling rate and is expressed as an angle which is the same fraction of 360 degrees. A mark is made on the unit circle at that angle; a pole vector is drawn from the pole to the mark, and the zero vector is drawn from the zero to the mark. The amplitude response at the chosen frequency is found by dividing the magnitude of the zero vector by the magnitude of the pole vector. A working approximation can be made by taking distances from the diagram with a ruler. The phase response at that frequency can be found by subtracting the argument of the pole vector from the argument of the zero vector, where the argument is the angle between the vector and the positive real z axis. The phase response is clearly also the angle between the vectors. In Fig.4.19(e) the resulting diagram has been shown for several frequencies, and this has been used to plot the frequency and phase response of the system. This is confirmation of the power of the z-transform, because it has given the results of a Fourier analysis directly from the block diagram of the filter with trivial calculation. There cannot be more zeros than poles in any realizable system, and the poles must remain within the unit circle or instability results.

Fig.4.20(a) shows a slightly different configuration which will be used to support the example of a high-pass filter. High-pass filters with a low cut-off frequency are used extensively in digital audio to remove DC components in sample streams which have arisen due to convertor drift.

Using the same terminology as the previous example:

$$u[n] = x[n] + Ku[n-1]$$

so that in the z-domain:

$$u[z] = x[z] + Kz^{-1}u[z] \tag{4.3}$$

Also: $y[n] = u[n] - u[n-1]$

So that in the z-domain:

$$y[z] = u[z] - z^{-1}u[z] = u[z]\,(1 - z^{-1})$$

Therefore:

$$\frac{y[z]}{u[z]} = 1 - z^{-1} \qquad\qquad (4.4)$$

From Eqn. 4.3: $u[z] - Kz^{-1}u[z] = x[z]$

Therefore:

$$u[z]\,(1 - Kz^{-1}) = x[z]$$

and $\dfrac{u[z]}{x[z]} = \dfrac{1}{1 - Kz^{-1}} \qquad\qquad (4.5)$

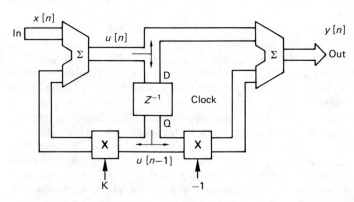

Figure 4.20 (a) Configuration used as a high-pass filter to remove DC offsets in audio samples.

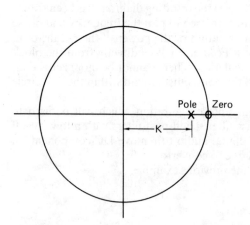

Figure 4.20 (b) The coefficient K determines the position of the pole on the real axis. It would normally be very close to the zero.

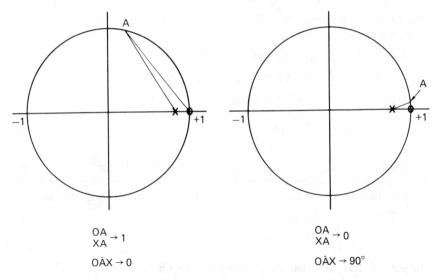

$$\frac{OA}{XA} \to 1$$

$$O\hat{A}X \to 0$$

$$\frac{OA}{XA} \to 0$$

$$O\hat{A}X \to 90°$$

Figure 4.20 (c) In the passband, the closeness of the pole and zero means the vectors are almost the same length, so the gain tends to unity and the phase shift is small (left). In the stop band, the gain falls and the phase angle tends to 90°.

From Eqns. 4.4 and 4.5:

$$\frac{y[z]}{x[z]} = \frac{y[z]}{u[z]} \times \frac{u[z]}{x[z]} = \frac{1 - z^{-1}}{1 - Kz^{-1}}$$

Since the numerator determines the position of the pole, this will be at $z = 1$, and the zero will be at $z = K$ because this makes the denominator go to zero. Fig.4.20(b) shows that if the pole is put close to the zero by making K almost unity, the filter will only attenuate very low frequencies. At high frequencies, the ratio of the length of the pole vector to the zero vector will be almost unity, whereas at very low frequencies the ratio falls steeply becoming zero at DC. The phase characteristics can also be established. At high frequencies the pole and zero vectors will be almost parallel, so phase shift will be minimal. It is only in the area of the zero that the phase will change.

4.7 Bandpass filters

The low- and high-pass cases have been examined, and it has been seen that they can be realised with simple first-order filters. Bandpass circuits will now be discussed; these will generally involve higher-order configurations. Bandpass filters are used extensively for presence filters and their more complex relative the graphic equalizer, and are essentially filters which are tuned to respond to a certain band of frequencies more than others.

Fig.4.21(a) shows a bandpass filter, which is essentially a lead filter and a lag filter combined. The coefficients have been made simple for clarity; in fact two of them are set to zero. The adder now sums three terms, so the recurrence relationship is given by:

$$y[n] = x[n] - x[n-2] - 0.25y[n-2]$$

Since in the z transform $x[n-1] = z^{-1}x[n]$,

$$y[z] = x[z] - z^{-2}x[z] - 0.25z^{-2}y[z]$$

$$H[z] = \frac{y[z]}{x[z]} = \frac{1 - z^{-2}}{1 + 0.25z^{-2}} = \frac{z^2 - 1}{z^2 + 0.25}$$

As before, the position of poles and zeros is determined by finding what values of z will cause the denominator or the numerator to become zero. This can be done by factorizing the terms. In the denominator the roots will be complex:

$$\frac{z^2 - 1}{z^2 + 0.25} = \frac{(z+1)(z-1)}{(z+j0.5)(z-j0.5)}$$

Fig.4.21(b) illustrates that the poles have come off the real axis of the z-plane, and then appear as a complex conjugate pair, so that the diagram is essentially symmetrical about the real axis. There are also two zeros, at RE + 1 and Re − 1.

With more poles and zeros, the graphical method of determining the frequency response becomes more complicated. The procedure is to multiply together the lengths of all the zero vectors, and divide by the product of the lengths of all the pole vectors. The process is shown in Fig.4.21(c). The frequency response shows an indistinct peak at half the Nyquist frequency. This is because the poles are some distance from the unit radius.

A more pronounced peak can be obtained by placing the poles closer to unit radius. In contrast to the previous examples, which have accepted a particular configuration and predicted what it will do, this example will decide what response is to be obtained and then compute the coefficients needed. Fig.4.22(a) shows the z-plane diagram. The resonant frequency is one third of the Nyquist limit, or 60 degrees around the circle, and the poles have been placed at a radius of 0.9 to give a peakier response.

It is possible to write down the transfer function directly from the position of the poles and zeros:

$$H[z] = \frac{(z+1)(z-1)}{(z - r\,e^{j\omega T})(z - r\,e^{-j\omega T})}$$

$$= \frac{z^2 - 1}{z^2 - rz\cos\omega T + r^2} = \frac{y[z]}{x[z]}$$

$$y[z](z^2 - 2rz\cos\omega T + r^2) = x[z](z^2 - 1)$$

$$y[z]z^2 = x[z]z^2 - x[z] + y[z]2rz\cos\omega T - y[z]r^2$$

$$y[z] = x[z] - x[z]z^{-2} + y[z]2rz^{-1}\cos\omega T - y[z]r^2z^{-2}$$

As $\cos 60 = 0.5$, the recurrence relationship can be written:

$$y[n] = x[n] - x[n-2] + 0.9y[n-1] - 0.81y[n-2]$$

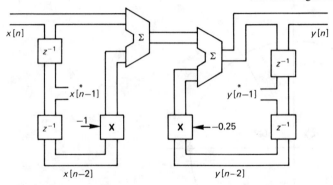

Figure 4.21 (a) Simple bandpass filter combining lead and lag stages. Note that two terms marked * have zero coefficients, reducing the complexity of implementation.

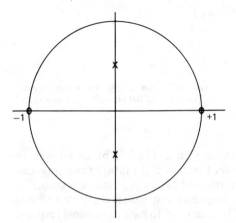

Figure 4.21 (b) Bandpass filters are characterised by poles which are away from the real axis.

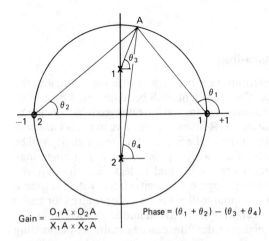

$$\text{Gain} = \frac{O_1 A \times O_2 A}{X_1 A \times X_2 A} \qquad \text{Phase} = (\theta_1 + \theta_2) - (\theta_3 + \theta_4)$$

Figure 4.21 (c) With multiple poles and zeros, the computation of gain and phase is a little more complicated.

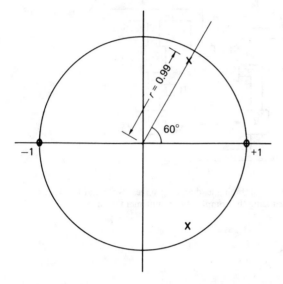

Figure 4.22 (a) The peak frequency chosen here is one-sixth of the sample rate, which requires the poles to be on radii at ±60° from the real axis. The radius of 0.9 places the poles close to the unit cycle, resulting in a pronounced peak.

The configuration necessary can now be seen in Fig.4.22(b), along with the necessary coefficients. Since the transfer function is the ratio of two quadratic expressions, this arrangement is often referred to as a biquadratic section.

As with the previous example, the frequency response is computed by multiplying the vector lengths, and it will be seen in (c) to have the desired response. The impulse response has been computed for a single non-zero input sample in Fig.4.22(d), and this will be seen to ring with a period of six samples as expected.

4.8 Higher-order filters: cascading

In the example above, the calculations were performed with precision, and the result was as desired. In practice, the coefficients will be represented by a finite wordlength, which means that some inaccuracy will be unavoidable. Owing to the recursion of previous calculations, IIR filters are sensitive to the accuracy of the coefficients, and the higher the order of the filter, the more sensitivity will be shown. In the worst case, a stable filter with a pole near the unit circle may become unstable if the coefficients are represented to less than the required accuracy. Whilst it is possible to design high-order digital filters with a response fixed for a given application, programmable filters of the type required for audio are seldom attempted above the second order to avoid undue coefficient sensitivity. The same response as for a higher-order filter can be obtained by cascading second-order filter sections. For certain applications, such as graphic equalizers, filter sections might be used in parallel.

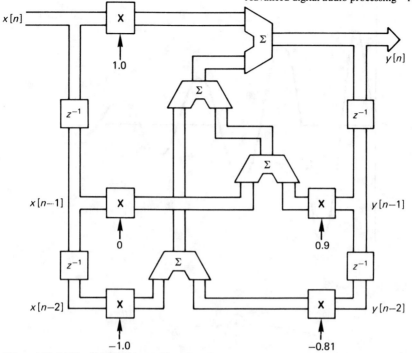

Figure 4.22 (b) The biquadratic configuration shown here implements the recurrence relationship derived in the text: $y[n] = x[n] - x[n-2] + 0.9y[n-1] - 0.81y[n-2]$

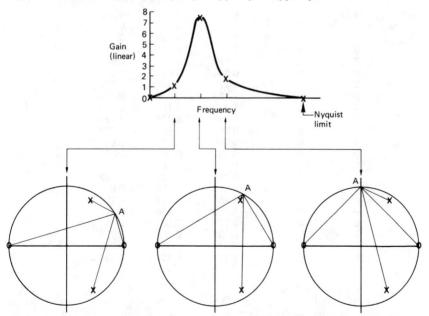

Figure 4.22 (c) Calculating the frequency response of the filter of (b). The method of Figure 4.21 (c) is used. Note how the pole vector becomes very short as the resonance is reached. As this is in the denominator, the response is large. The instability resulting from a pole on or outside the unit circle is thus clearly demonstrated.

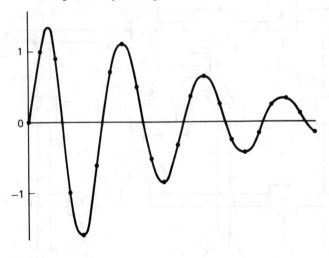

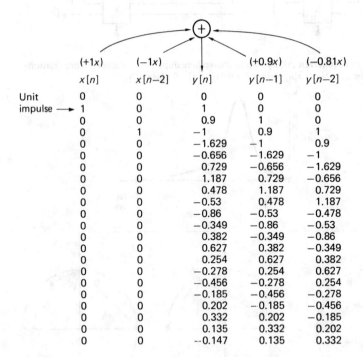

	(+1x)	(−1x)		(+0.9x)	(−0.81x)
	x[n]	x[n−2]	y[n]	y[n−1]	y[n−2]
Unit	0	0	0	0	0
impulse →	1	0	1	0	0
	0	0	0.9	1	0
	0	1	−1	0.9	1
	0	0	−1.629	−1	0.9
	0	0	−0.656	−1.629	−1
	0	0	0.729	−0.656	−1.629
	0	0	1.187	0.729	−0.656
	0	0	0.478	1.187	0.729
	0	0	−0.53	0.478	1.187
	0	0	−0.86	−0.53	−0.478
	0	0	−0.349	−0.86	−0.53
	0	0	0.382	−0.349	−0.86
	0	0	0.627	0.382	−0.349
	0	0	0.254	0.627	0.382
	0	0	−0.278	0.254	0.627
	0	0	−0.456	−0.278	0.254
	0	0	−0.185	−0.456	−0.278
	0	0	0.202	−0.185	−0.456
	0	0	0.332	0.202	−0.185
	0	0	0.135	0.332	0.202
	0	0	−0.147	0.135	0.332

Figure 4.22 (d) The response of the filter of (b) to a unit impulse has been tabulated by using the recurrence relation. The filter rings with a period of six samples, as expected.

A further issue which demands attention is the effect of truncation of the wordlength within the data path of the filter. Truncation of coefficients causes only a fixed change in the filter performance which can be calculated. The same cannot be said for data-path truncation. When a sample is multiplied by a coefficient, the necessary wordlength increases dramatically. In a recursive filter the output of one multiplication becomes the input to the next, and so on, making the theoretical wordlength required infinite. By definition, the required wordlength is not available within a realizable filter. Some low-order bits of the product will be lost, which causes noise or distortion depending on the input signal. A series cascade will produce more noise of this kind than a parallel implementation.[6]

In some cases, truncation can cause oscillation. Consider a recursive decay following a large input impulse. Successive output samples become smaller and smaller, but if truncation takes place, the sample may be coarsely quantized as it becomes small, and at some point will not be the correct proportion of the previous sample. In an extreme case, the decay may reverse, and the output samples will grow in magnitude until they are great enough to be represented accurately in the truncation, when they will again decay. The filter is then locked in an endless loop known as a limit cycle.[7] It is a form of instability which cannot exist on large signals because the larger a signal becomes, the smaller the effect of a given truncation. It can be prevented by the injection of digital dither at an appropriate point in the data path. The randomizing effect of the dither destroys the deterministic effect of truncation and prevents the occurrence of the limit cycle.

In the opposite case from truncation due to losing low-order sample bits, products are also subject to overflow if sufficient high-order bits are not available after a multiplication.[8] A simple overflow results in a wraparound of the sample value, and is most disturbing as well as being a possible source of large-amplitude limit cycles. The saturating adders described in Chapter 3 find an application in digital filters, since the output clips or limits instead of wrapping, and limit cycles are prevented. In order to balance the requirements of truncation and saturation, the output of one stage may be shifted one or more binary places before entering the next stage. This process is known as scaling, since shifting down in binary divides by powers of two; it can be used to prevent overflow. Conversely if the coefficients in use dictate that the high-order bits of a given multiplier output will never be exercised, a shift up may be used to reduce the effects of truncation.

The configuration shown in Fig.4.22 is not the only way of implementing a two-pole two-zero filter. Fig.4.23 shows some alternatives. In the direct form 2 filter, the delays have exchanged places with the adders to give a structure which is sometimes referred to as the canonical form.

Filters can also be transposed to yield a different structure with the same transfer function. Transposing is done by reversing signal flow in all of the branches, the delays and the multipliers, and replacing nodes in the flow with adders and vice versa. Coefficients and delay lengths are unchanged. The transposed configurations are shown in Fig.4.22(c) and (d). The transposed direct form 2 filter has advantages for audio use,[9] since it has less tendency to problems with overflow, and can be made so that the dominant truncation takes place at one node, which eases the avoidance of limit cycles.

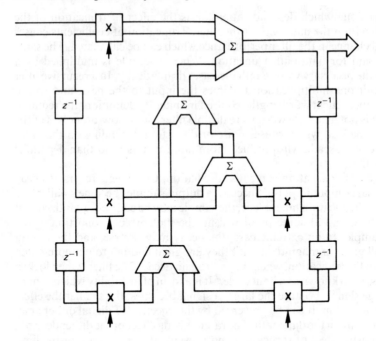

(a) Direct form

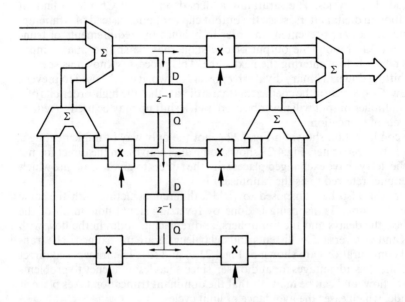

(b) Canonical form

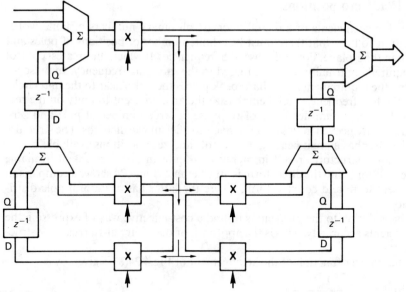

(c) Transposed direct form

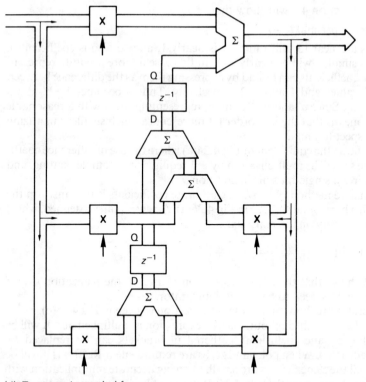

(d) Transposed canonical form

Figure 4.23 The same filter can be realized in the direct and canonical forms, (a) and (b), and each can be transposed, (c) and (d).

4.9 Pole/zero positions

Since the coefficients of a digital filter are all binary numbers of finite word-length, it follows that there must be a finite number of positions of poles and zeros in the z-plane. For audio use, the frequencies at which the greatest control is required are usually small compared to the sampling frequency. In presence filters, the requirement for a sharp peak places the poles near to the unit circle, and the low frequencies used emphasize the area adjacent to unity on the real axis. For maximum flexibility of response, a large number of pole and zero positions are needed in this area for given coefficient wordlengths. The structure of the filter has a great bearing on the pole and zero positions available.

Canonic structures result in highly non-uniform distributions of available pole positions, and the direct form is little better.[10] Fig.4.24 shows a comparison of direct form and coupled form, where the latter has a uniform pole distribution.

One solution to the problem is to find a cost-effective way of expressing the coefficients accurately. This is the approach of the Agarwal-Burrus filter structure.[11]

The transfer function of the arrangement of Fig.4.24(a) is given by:

$$H[z] = \frac{1}{1 + az^{-1} + bz^{-2}}$$

Reference to section 4.7 will show that

$$a = -2r \cos \omega T \text{ and } b = r^2$$

When poles are near to unit radius, r is nearly 1, and so also is coefficient b. When ωT is small, a will be nearly -2. In this case a more accurate representation of the coefficients can be had by expressing them as the difference between the wanted values and 1 and -2 respectively. Thus b becomes $1 - b'$ and a becomes $2 - a'$. Since a' and b' are small, representing them with a reasonable wordlength means that the low-order bit represents a much smaller quantizing step with respect to unity.

Fig.4.25 shows the equivalent of Fig.4.24(a) where the use of difference coefficients can be seen. The multiplication by -1 requires only complementing, and by -2 requires a single-bit shift in addition.

An alternative method of providing accurate coefficients is to transform the z-plane with a horizontal shift, as in Fig.4.26(a). A new z' plane is defined, where the origin is at unity on the real z-axis.

$$z' = z - 1 \text{ and } z'^{-1} = \frac{1}{z - 1} = \frac{z^{-1}}{1 - z^{-1}}$$

Fig.4.26(b) shows that the above expression is used in the realization of a z' stage, which will be seen to be a digital integrator.

The general expression for a biquadratic section is given in Fig.4.26(c). z^{-1} is replaced by $1/(z' + 1)$ throughout, and the expression is multiplied out. It will be seen that the z-plane coefficients gathered in brackets can be replaced by z'-plane coefficients. When poles and zeros are required near $\text{Re}[z] = 1$, it will be found that all the z' coefficients are small, allowing accurate multiplication with short-coefficient wordlengths. Fig.4.26(d) shows a filter constructed in this way. These configurations demonstrate their accuracy with minimal truncation noise and limit cycles.

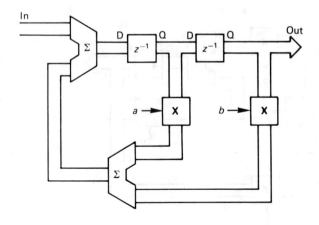

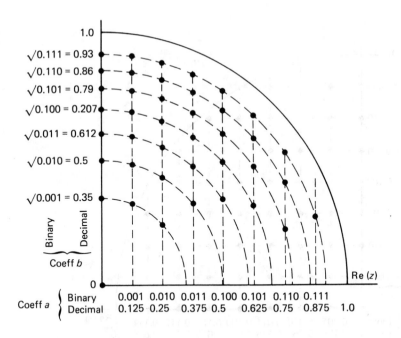

Figure 4.24 (a) A second-order, direct-form digital filter, with coefficients quantized to three bits (not including the sign bit). This means that each coefficient can have only eight values. As the pole radius is the square root of the coefficient b, the pole distribution is non-uniform, and poles are not available in the area near to $\text{Re}(z) = 1$ which is of interest in audio.

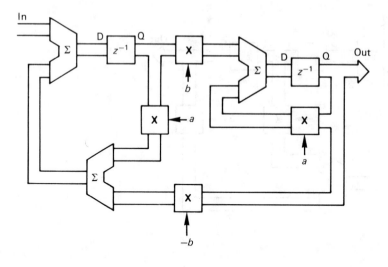

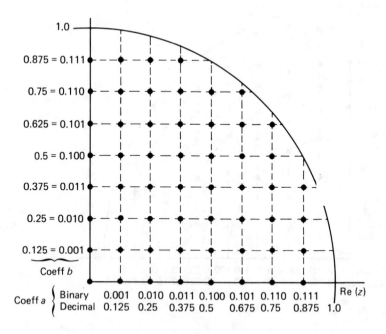

Figure 4.24 (b) In the coupled structure shown here, the realizable pole positions are now on a uniform grid, with the advantage of more pole positions near to $Re(z) = 1$, but the penalty that more processing is required.

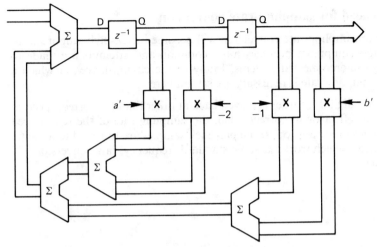

Figure 4.25 In the Agarwal–Burrus filter structure, advantage is taken of the fact that the coefficients are nearly 1 and 2 when the poles are close to unit radius. The coefficients actually used are the difference between these round numbers and the desired value. This configuration should be compared with that of Figure 4.24 (a).

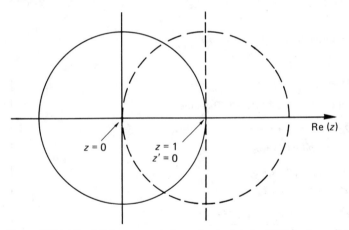

Figure 4.26 (a) By defining a new z' plane whose origin is at $\mathrm{Re}(z) = 1$, small coefficients in z' will correspond to poles near to $z = 1$.

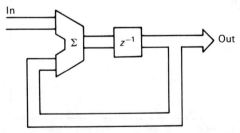

Figure 4.26 (b) The above configuration implements a z'^{-1} transfer function. It is in fact a digital integrator.

4.10 The need for sampling-rate conversion

The topic of sampling-rate conversion will become increasingly important as digital audio equipment becomes more common and attempts are made to create large interconnected systems. Many of the circumstances in which a change of sampling rate is necessary are set out here:

(1) When a digital recorder is played back at other than the correct speed to achieve some effect or to correct pitch, the sampling rate of the reproduced signal changes in proportion. If the playback samples are to be fed to a digital mixing console which works at some standard frequency, rate conversion will be necessary.

$$H[z] = \frac{a_0 + a_1 z^{-1} + a_2 z^{-2}}{1 + b_1 z^{-1} + b_2 z^{-2}}$$

Multiplying by z^2 throughout:

$$H[z] = \frac{a_0 z^2 + a_1 z + a_2}{z^2 + b_1 z + b_2}$$

Since $z = z' + 1$, then $z^2 = z'^2 = z'^2 + 2z' + 1$. Therefore:

$$H[z] = \frac{a_0(z'^2 + 2z' + 1) + a_1(z' + 1) + a_2}{z'^2 + 2z' + 1 + b_1(z' + 1) + b_2}$$

$$= \frac{a_0 z'^2 + 2a_0 z' + a_0 + a_1 z' + a_1 + a_2}{z'^2 + 2z' + 1 + b_1 z' + b_1 + b_2}$$

$$= \frac{a_0 + 2a_0 z'^{-1} + a_0 z'^{-2} + a_1 z'^{-1} + a_1 z'^{-2} + a_2 z'^{-2}}{1 + 2z'^{-1} + z'^{-2} + b_1 z'^{-1} + b_1 z'^{-2} + b_2 z'^{-2}}$$

$$= \frac{a_0 + (2a_0 + a_1)z'^{-1} + (a_0 + a_1 + a_2)z'^{-2}}{1 + (2 + b_1)z'^{-1} + (1 + b_1 + b_2)z'^{-2}}$$

$$= \frac{a'_0 + a'_1 z'^{-1} + a'_2 z'^{-2}}{1 + b'_1 z'^{-1} + b'_2 z'^{-2}}$$

where $a'_0 = a_0$ $\quad a'_1 = 2a_0 + a_1$ $\quad a'_2 = a_0 + a_1 + a_2$
$b'_1 = 2 + b_1$ $\quad b'_2 = 1 + b_1 + b_2$

Figure 4.26 (c) Conversion to the z' plane requires the coefficients in z to be combined as shown here.

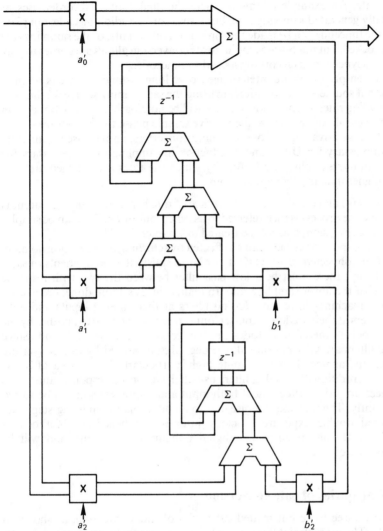

Figure 4.26 (d) Implementation of a z' plane filter. The z'^{-1} sections can be seen at centre. As the coefficients are all small, scaling (not shown) must be used.

(2) In the past, many different sampling rates were used on recorders which are now becoming obsolete. With sampling-rate conversion, recordings made on such machines can be played back and transferred to more modern formats at standard sampling rates.

(3) Different sampling rates exist today for different purposes. Rate conversion allows material to be exchanged freely between rates. For example, master tapes made at 48 kHz on multitrack recorders may be digitally mixed down to two tracks at that frequency, and then converted to 44.1 kHz for Compact Disc or RDAT mastering, or to 32 kHz for broadcast use.

(4) When digital audio is used in conjunction with film or video, difficulties arise because it is not always possible to synchronize the sampling rate with the

frame rate. An example of this is where the digital audio recorder uses its internally generated sampling rate, but also records studio timecode. On playback, the timecode can be made the same as on other units, or the sampling rate can be locked, but not both. Sampling-rate conversion allows a recorder to play back an asynchronous recording locked to timecode.

(5) When programs are interchanged over long distances, there is no guarantee that source and destination are using the same timing source. In this case the sampling rates at both ends of a link will be nominally identical, but drift in reference oscillators will cause the relative sample phase to be arbitrary.

(6) To take advantage of oversampling converters, an increase in sampling rate is necessary for DACs and a reduction in sampling rate is necessary for ADCs. In oversampling the factors by which the rates are changed are very much higher than in other applications.

In items (4) and (5) above, the difference of rate between input and output is small, and the process is then referred to as synchronization. This can be simpler than rate conversion, and will be treated in Chapter 5.

Sampling-rate conversion can be effected by returning to the analog domain. A DAC is connected to an ADC. In order to satisfy the requirements of sampling theory, there must be a low-pass filter between the two with response one-half of the lower sampling rate. In reality this is seldom done, because all practical machines have anti-aliasing filters at their analog inputs and anti-image filters at their analog outputs. Connecting one machine to another by the analog sockets therefore includes one unnecessary filter in the chain. Since analog filters are seldom optimal, the degradation caused by rate-converting through the analog domain is quite high, particularly in the area of phase response. Additionally, analog filters usually have a fixed response, and this is not necessarily the correct one if both input and output rates are to be varied significantly. The increase in noise due to an additional quantizing stage and additional double exposure to clock jitter is not beneficial. Methods of sampling-rate conversion in the digital domain are necessary and will be described here.

4.11 Categories of rate conversion

There are three basic but related categories of rate conversion, as shown in Fig.4.27. The most straightforward (a) changes the rate by an integer ratio, up or down. The timing of the system is thus simplified because all samples (input and output) are present on edges of the higher-rate sampling clock. Such a system is generally adopted for oversampling converters; the exact sampling rate immediately adjacent to the analog domain is not critical, and will be chosen to make the filters easier to implement.

Next in order of difficulty is the category shown at (b) where the rate is changed by the ratio of two small integers. Samples in the input periodically time-align with the output. Many of the early proposals for professional sampling rates were based on simple fractional relationships to 44.1 kHz such as $\frac{8}{7}$ so that this technique could be used. This technique is not suitable for variable-speed replay or for asynchronous operation.

The most complex rate-conversion category is where there is no simple relationship between input and output sampling rates, and indeed they are

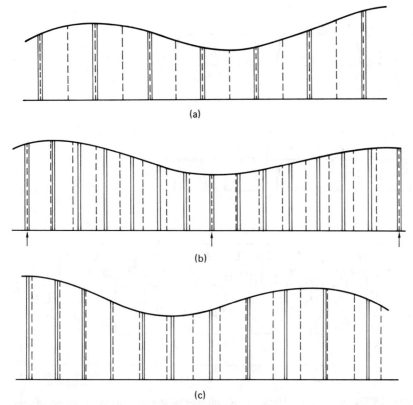

Figure 4.27 Categories of rate conversion. (a) Integer ratio conversion, where the lower-rate samples are always coincident with those of the higher rate. There are a small number of phases needed. (b) Fractional ratio conversion, where sample coincidence is periodic. A larger number of phases is required. Example here is conversion from 50.4 kHz to 44.1 kHz (8/7). (c) Variable ratio conversion, where there is no fixed relationship, and a large number of phases are required.

allowed to vary. This situation shown at (c), is known as variable-ratio conversion. The time relationship of input and output samples is arbitrary, and independent clocks are necessary. Once it was established that variable-ratio conversion was feasible, the choice of a professional sampling rate became very much easier, because the simple fractional relationships could be abandoned. The conversion fraction between 48 kHz and 44.1 kHz is 160:147 which is indeed not simple.

4.12 Integer ratio conversion

As the technique of integer-ratio conversion is used almost exclusively for oversampling in digital audio it will be discussed in that context. Sampling-rate reduction by an integer factor is dealt with first.

Fig.4.28(a) shows the spectrum of a typical sampled system where the sampling rate is a little more than twice the analog bandwidth. Attempts to reduce the sampling rate by simply omitting samples, a process known as decimation,

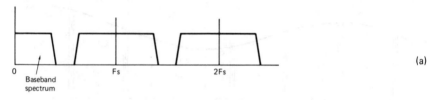

(a)

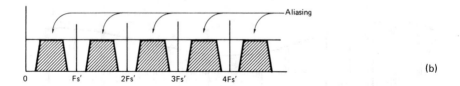

(b)

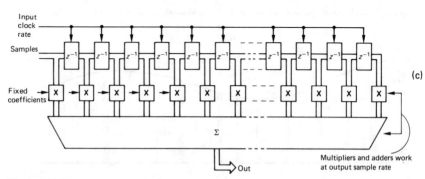

(c)

Figure 4.28 The spectrum of a typical digital audio sample stream at (a) will be subject to aliasing as in (b) if the baseband width is not reduced by an LPF. At (c) an FIR low-pass filter prevents aliasing. Samples are clocked transversely across the filter at the input rate, but the filter only computes at the output sample rate. Clearly this will only work if the two rates are related by an integer factor.

will result in aliasing, as shown in Fig.4.28(b). Intuitively it is obvious that omitting samples is the same as if the original sampling rate was lower. In order to prevent aliasing, it is necessary to incorporate low-pass filtering into the system where the cut-off frequency reflects the new, lower, sampling rate. An FIR type low-pass filter could be installed, as described earlier in this chapter, immediately prior to the stage where samples are omitted, but this would be wasteful, because for much of its time the FIR filter would be calculating sample values which are to be discarded. The more effective method is to combine the low-pass filter with the decimator so that the filter only calculates values to be retained in the output sample stream. Fig.4.28(c) shows how this is done. The filter makes one accumulation for every output sample, but that accumulation is the result of multiplying all relevant input samples in the filter window by an appropriate coefficient. The number of points in the filter is determined by the number of *input* samples in the period of the filter window, but the number of multiplications per second is obtained by multiplying that figure by the *output* rate. If the filter is not integrated with the decimator, the number of points has to be multiplied by the input rate. The larger the rate-reduction factor the more advantageous the decimating filter ought to be, but this is not quite the case, as the greater the reduction in rate, the longer the filter window will need to be to accommodate the broader impulse response.

When the sampling rate is to be increased by an integer factor, additional samples must be created at even spacing between the existing ones. There is no need for the bandwidth of the input samples to be reduced since, if the original sampling rate was adequate, a higher one must also be adequate.

Fig.4.29 shows that the process of sampling-rate increase can be thought of in two stages. First the correct rate is achieved by inserting samples of zero value at the correct instant, and then the additional samples are given meaningful values by passing the sample stream through a low-pass filter which cuts off at the Nyquist frequency of the original sampling rate. This filter is known as an interpolator, and one of its tasks is to prevent images of the lower input-sampling spectrum from appearing in the extended baseband of the higher-rate output spectrum.

How do interpolators work? Remember that, according to Nyquist, all sampled systems have finite bandwidth. An individual digital sample value is obtained by sampling the instantaneous voltage of the original analog waveform, and because it has zero duration, it must contain an infinite spectrum. However, such a sample can never be heard in that form because of the reconstruction process, which limits the spectrum of the impulse to the Nyquist limit. After reconstruction, one infinitely short digital sample actually represents a sin x/x pulse whose central peak width is determined by the response of the reconstruction filter, and whose amplitude is proportional to the sample value. This implies that, in reality, one sample value has meaning over a considerable timespan, rather than just at the sample instant. If this were not true, it would be impossible to build an interpolator.

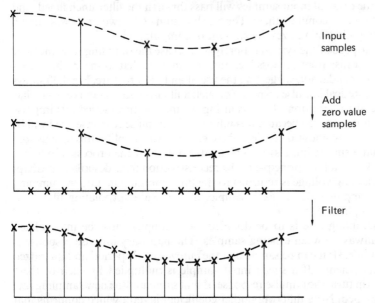

Figure 4.29 In integer ratio sampling, rate increase can be obtained in two stages. First zero value samples are inserted to increase the rate, and then filtering is used to give the extra samples real values. The filter necessary will be an LPF with a response which cuts off at the Nyquist frequency of the input samples.

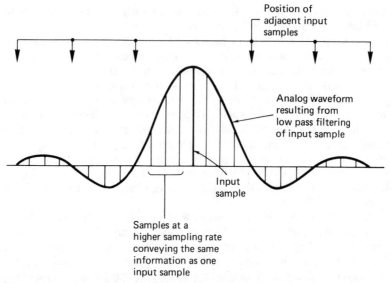

Figure 4.30 A single sample results in a sin x/x waveform after filtering in the analog domain. At a new, higher, sampling rate, the same waveform after filtering will be obtained if the numerous samples of differing size shown here are used. It follows that the values of these new samples can be calculated from the input samples in the digital domain in an FIR filter.

As in rate reduction, performing the steps separately is inefficient. The bandwidth of the information is unchanged when the sampling rate is increased; therefore the original input samples will pass through the filter unchanged, and it is superfluous to compute them. The combination of the two processes into an interpolating filter minimizes the amount of computation.

As the purpose of the system is purely to increase the sampling rate, the filter must be as transparent as possible, and this implies that a linear-phase configuration is mandatory, suggesting the use of an FIR structure. Fig.4.30 shows that the theoretical impulse response of such a filter is a sin x/x curve which has zero value at the position of adjacent input samples. In practice this impulse cannot be implemented because it is infinite. The impulse response used will be truncated and windowed as described earlier. To simplify this discussion, assume that a sin x/x impulse is to be used. To see how the process of interpolation works, recall the principle of the reconstruction filter described in Chapter 2. The analog voltage is returned to the time-continuous state by summing the analog impulses due to each sample. In a digital interpolating filter, this process is duplicated.[12]

If the sampling rate is to be doubled, new samples must be interpolated exactly halfway between existing samples. The necessary impulse response is shown in Fig.4.31; it can be sampled at the *output* sample period and quantized to form coefficients. If a single input sample is multiplied by each of these coefficients in turn, the impulse response of that sample at the new sampling rate will be obtained. Note that every other coefficient is zero, which confirms that no computation is necessary on the existing samples; they are just transferred to the output. The intermediate sample is computed by adding together the impulse responses of every input sample in the window. The figure shows how this mechanism operates. If the sampling rate is to be increased by a factor of

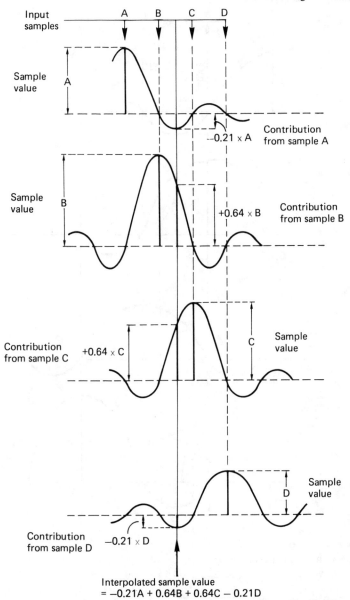

Input samples
A B C D

Sample value A

−0.21 × A

Contribution from sample A

Sample value B

+0.64 × B

Contribution from sample B

Contribution from sample C

+0.64 × C

C Sample value

Contribution from sample D

−0.21 × D

D Sample value

Interpolated sample value
= −0.21A + 0.64B + 0.64C − 0.21D

Figure 4.31 A two times oversampling interpolator. To compute an intermediate sample, the input samples are imagined to be sin x/x impulses, and the contributions from each at the point of interest can be calculated. In practice, rather more samples on either side need to be taken into account.

four, three sample values must be interpolated between existing input samples. Fig.4.32 shows that it is only necessary to sample the impulse response at one-quarter the period of input samples to obtain three sets of coefficients which will be used in turn. In hardware-implemented filters, the input sample which is passed straight to the output is transferred by using a fourth filter phase where all coefficients are zero except the central one which is unity.

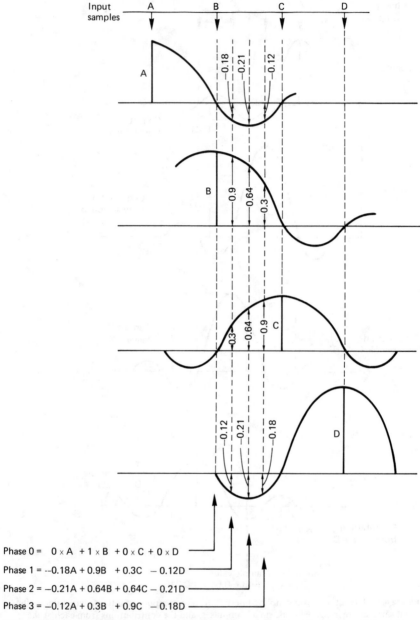

Phase 0 = $0 \times A$ $+ 1 \times B$ $+ 0 \times C$ $+ 0 \times D$

Phase 1 = $-0.18A + 0.9B$ $+ 0.3C$ $- 0.12D$

Phase 2 = $-0.21A + 0.64B + 0.64C - 0.21D$

Phase 3 = $-0.12A + 0.3B$ $+ 0.9C$ $- 0.18D$

Figure 4.32 In $4 \times$ oversampling, for each set of input samples, four phases of coefficients are necessary, each of which produces one of the oversampled values.

4.13 Fractional-ratio conversion

Fig. 4.27 showed that when the two sampling rates have a simple fractional relationship m/n, there is a periodicity in the relationship between samples in the two streams. It is possible to have a system clock running at the least-common multiple frequency which will divide by different integers to give each sampling rate.[13]

The existence of a common clock frequency means that a fractional-ratio converter could be made by arranging two integer-ratio converters in series. This configuration is shown in Fig.4.33(a). The input-sampling rate is multiplied by m in an interpolator, and the result is divided by n in a decimator. Although this system would work, it would be grossly inefficient, because only one in n of the interpolator's outputs would be used. A decimator followed by an interpolator would also offer the correct sampling rate at the output, but the intermediate sampling rate would be so low that the system bandwidth would be quite unacceptable.

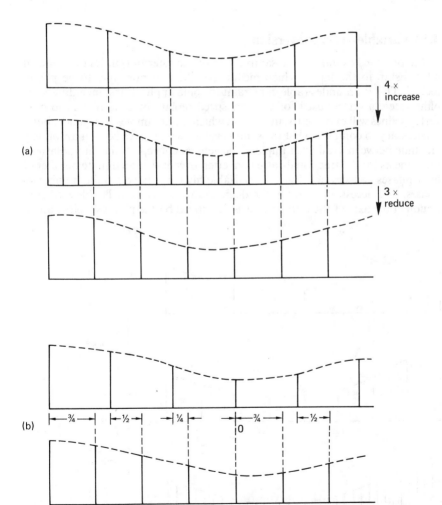

Figure 4.33 At (a), fractional ratio conversion of $\frac{3}{4}$ in this example is by increasing to 4 × input prior to reducing by 3 × . The inefficiency due to discarding previously computed values is clear. At (b), efficiency is raised since only needed values will be computed. Note how the interpolation phase changes for each output. Fixed coefficients can no longer be used.

As has been seen, a more efficient structure results from combining the processes. The result is exactly the same structure as an integer-ratio interpolator, and requires an FIR filter. The impulse response of the filter is determined by the lower of the two sampling rates, and as before it prevents aliasing when the rate is being reduced, and prevents images when the rate is being increased. The interpolator has sufficient coefficient phases to interpolate m output samples for every input sample, but not all of these values are computed; only interpolations which coincide with an output sample are performed. It will be seen in Fig.4.33(b) that input samples shift across the transversal filter at the input sampling rate, but interpolations are only performed at the output sample rate. This is possible because a different filter phase will be used at each interpolation.

4.14 Variable-ratio conversion

In the previous examples, the sample rate of the filter output had a constant relationship to the input, which meant that the two rates had to be phase-locked. This is an undesirable constraint in some applications, including sampling rate converters used for variable-speed replay. In a variable-ratio converter, values will exist for the instants at which input samples were made, but it is necessary to compute what the sample values would have been at absolutely any time between available samples. The general concept of the interpolator is the same as for the fractional-ratio converter, except that an infinite number of filter phases is necessary. Since a realizable filter will have a finite number of phases, it is necessary to study the degradation this causes. The desired continuous time axis of the interpolator is quantized by the phase spacing, and a

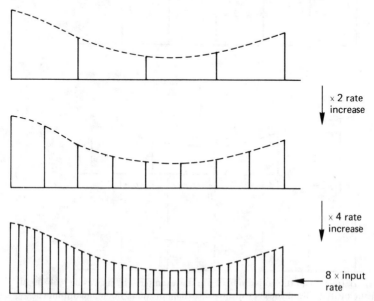

Figure 4.34 Cascading interpolators multiplies the factor of sampling rate increase of each stage.

sample value needed at a particular time will be replaced by a value for the nearest available filter phase. The number of phases in the filter therefore determines the time accuracy of the interpolation. The effects of calculating a value for the wrong time are identical to sampling with jitter, in that an error occurs proportional to the slope of the signal. The result is program-modulated noise. The higher the noise specification, the greater the desired time accuracy and the greater the number of phases required. The number of phases is equal to the number of sets of coefficients available, and should not be confused with the number of points in the filter, which is equal to the number of coefficients in a set (and the number of multiplications needed to calculate one output value).

In Chapter 2 the sampling jitter accuracy necessary for sixteen bit working was shown to be a few hundred picoseconds. This implies that something like 2^{15} filter phases will be required for adequate performance in a sixteen bit sampling-rate converter.[14] The direct provision of so many phases is difficult, since more than a million different coefficients must be stored; so alternative methods have been devised. When several interpolators are cascaded, the number of phases available is the product of the number of phases in each stage. For example, if a filter which could interpolate sample values halfway between existing samples were followed by a filter which could interpolate at one-quarter, one-half and three-quarters the input period, the overall number of phases available would be eight. This is illustrated in Fig.4.34. For a practical converter, four filters in series might be needed. To increase the sampling rate, the first two filters interpolate at fixed points between samples input to them, effectively multiplying the input sampling rate by some large factor as well as removing images from the spectrum; the second two work with variable coefficients, like the fractional-ratio converter described earlier, so that only samples coincident with the output clock are computed. To reduce the sampling rate, the positions of the two pairs of filters are reversed, so that the fixed-response filters

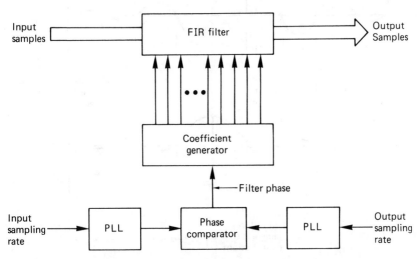

Figure 4.35 (a) In a variable-ratio converter, the phase relationship of input and output clock edges must be measured to determine the coefficients needed. Jitter on clocks prevents their direct use, and phase-locked loops must be used to average the jitter over many sample clocks.

perform the anti-aliasing function at the output sampling frequency. As mentioned earlier, the response of a digital filter is always proportional to the sampling rate.

When the sampling rate on input or output varies, the phase of the interpolators must change dynamically. The necessary phase must be selected to the stated accuracy, and this implies that the position of the relevant clock edge must be measured in time to the same accuracy. This is not possible because, in real systems, the presence of noise on binary signals of finite-rise time shifts the

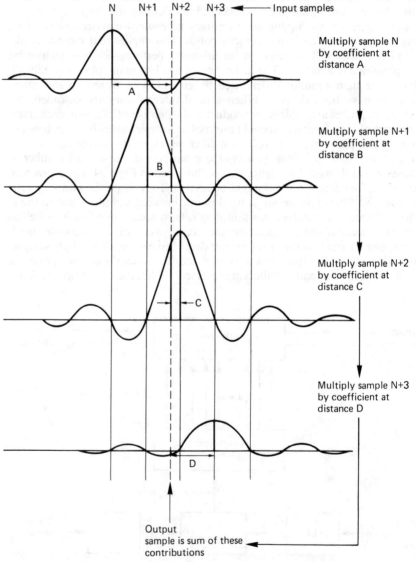

Figure 4.35 (b) The clock relationships in (a) determine the relative phases of output and input samples, which in conjunction with the filter impulse response determine the coefficients necessary.

time where the logical state is considered to have changed. The only way to measure the position of clocks in time without jitter is to filter the measurement digitally, and this can be done with a digital phase-locked loop. In a DPLL, some stable high-frequency clock is divided by a factor which depends on the phase error between the divider output and the sampling-clock input. After a settling period, the divider output will assume the same frequency as the sampling clock. If damping is provided by restricting the rate at which the division ratio can change in response to a phase error, the jitter on the sampling clock will be filtered out of the divider output, which can be used for measurement purposes. Two such DPLLs will be required, one for the input-sampling clock and one for the output. A jitter-free measurement can then be made of the phase of the output sample relative to the input samples. The penalty of using a damped phase-locked loop is that when either sampling rate changes, the loop will lag slightly behind the actual sampling clock. This implies that a phase error will occur, which will cause program-modulated noise. In practice the phase error changes so slowly that it cannot be classed as jitter; the resultant noise is subsonic, and less objectionable than the effects of sampling clock jitter. Fig.4.35 shows the essential stages of a variable- ratio converter of this kind.

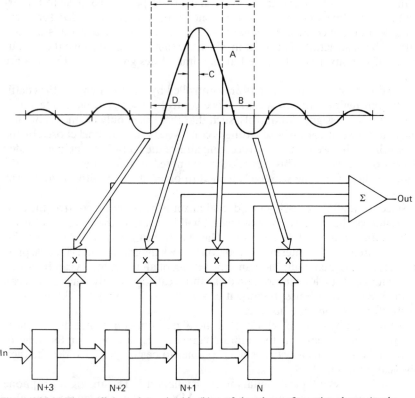

Figure 4.35 (c) The coefficients determined in (b) are fed to the configuration shown (or the equivalent implemented in software) to compute the output sample at the correct interpolated position. Note that actual filter will have many more points than this simple example shows.

When suitable processing speed is available, a digital computer can act as a filter, since each multiplication can be executed serially, and the results accumulated to produce an output sample. For simple filters, the coefficients would be stored in memory, but the number of coefficients needed for rate conversion precludes this. However, it is possible to compute what a set of coefficients should be algorithmically, and this approach permits single-stage conversion.

The two sampling clocks are compared as before, to produce an accurate relative-phase parameter. The lower sampling rate is measured to determine what the impulse response of the filter should be to prevent aliasing or images, and this is fed, along with the phase parameter, to a processor which computes a set of coefficients and multiplies them by a window function. These coefficients are then used by the single-filter stage to compute one output sample. The process then repeats for the next output sample.

4.15 Structure of digital mixing desks

Having dealt with a considerable amount of digital processing theory, it is appropriate to look now at the implementation of practical digital audio mixing desks.[15,16]

In analog audio mixers, the controls have to be positioned close to the circuitry for performance reasons; thus one control knob is needed for every variable, and the control panel is physically large. Remote control is difficult with such construction. The order in which the signal passes through the various stages of the mixer is determined at the time of design, and any changes are difficult.

In a digital mixer, all the filters are controlled by simply changing the coefficients, and remote control is easy. Since control is by digital parameters, it is possible to use assignable controls, such that there need only be one set of filter and equalizer controls, whose setting is conveyed to any channel chosen by the operator.[17] The use of digital processing allows the console to include a video display of the settings. This was seldom attempted in analog desks because the magnetic field from the scan coils tended to break through into the audio circuitry.

Since the audio processing in a digital mixer is by program control, the configuration of the desk can be changed at will by running the programs for the various functions in a different order. The operator can configure the desk to his own requirements by entering symbols on a block diagram on the video display, for example. The configuration and the setting of all the controls can be stored in memory or for a longer term, on disk, and recalled instantly. Such a desk can be in almost constant use, because it can be put back exactly to a known state easily after someone else has used it.

A further advantage of working in the digital domain is that delay can be controlled individually in the audio channels.[18] This allows for the time of arrival of wavefronts at various microphones to be compensated despite their physical position.

Fig.4.36 shows a typical digital mixer installation.[17] The analog microphone inputs are from remote units containing ADCs so that the length of analog cabling can be kept short. The input units communicate with the signal processor using digital fibre-optic links.

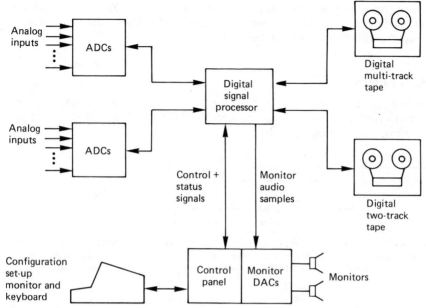

Figure 4.36 Digital mixer installation. The convenience of digital transmission without degradation allows the control panel to be physically remote from the processor.

The sampling rate of a typical digital audio signal is low compared to the speed at which typical logic gates can operate. It is sensible to minimize the quantity of hardware necessary by making each perform many functions in one sampling period. Although general-purpose computers can be programmed to process digital audio, they are not really suitable for the following reasons:

(1) The number of arithmetic operations in audio processing, particularly multiplications, is far higher than in data processing.

(2) Audio processing is done in real time; data processors do not generally work in real time.

(3) The program needed for an audio function generally remains constant for the duration of a session, or changes slowly, whereas a data processor rapidly jumps between many programs.

(4) Data processors can suspend a program on receipt of an interrupt; audio processors must work continuously for long periods.

(5) Data processors tend to be I/O limited, in that their operating speed is limited by the problems of moving large quantities of data and instructions into the CPU. Audio processors in contrast have a relatively small input and output rate, but compute intensively.

The above is a sufficient case for the development of specialized digital audio signal processors.[19,20] These units are implemented with more internal registers than data processors to facilitate multi-point filter algorithms. The arithmetic unit will be designed to offer high-speed multiply/accumulate using techniques such as pipelining, which allows operations to overlap.[21] The functions of the register set and the arithmetic unit are controlled by a microsequencer.

External control of a DSP will generally be by a smaller processor, often in the operator's console, which passes coefficients to the DSP as the operator moves the controls. In large systems, it is possible for several different consoles to control different sections of the DSP.[23]

4.16 Effects

In addition to equalization and mixing, modern audio production requires numerous effects, and these can be performed in the digital domain by simply mimicking the analog equivalent.

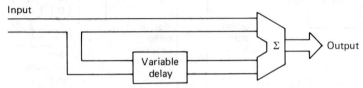

Figure 4.37 A simple configuration to obtain digital echo. The delay would normally be several tens of milliseconds. If the delay is made about 10 ms, the configuration acts as a comb filter, and if the delay is changed dynamically, a notch will sweep the audio spectrum resulting in flanging.

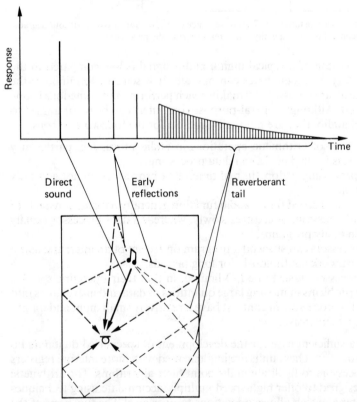

Figure 4.38 In a reverberant room, the signal picked up by a microphone is a mixture of direct sound, early reflections and a highly confused reverberant tail. A digital reverberator will simulate this with various combinations of recursive delay and attenuation.

One of the oldest effects is the use of a tape loop to produce an echo, and this can be implemented with memory or, for longer delays, with a disk drive (see Chapter 12). Fig.4.37 shows the basic configuration necessary for echo. If the delay period is dynamically changed from zero to about 10 ms, the result is flanging, where a notch sweeps through the audio spectrum. This was originally done by having two identical analog tapes running, and modifying the capstan speed with hand pressure! A relative of echo is reverberation, which is used to simulate ambience on an acoustically dry recording. Fig.4.38 shows that reverberation actually consists of a series of distinct early reflections, followed by the reverberation proper, which is due to multiple reflections. The early reflections are simply provided by short delays, but the reverberation is more difficult. A recursive structure is a natural choice for a decaying response, but simple recursion sounds artificial. The problem is that, in a real room, standing waves and interference effects cause large changes in the frequency response at each reflection. The effect can be simulated in a digital reverberator by adding various comb-filter sections which have the required effect on the response.

References

1. VAN DEN ENDEN, A.W.M. and VERHOECKX, N.A.M., Digital signal processing: theoretical background. *Philips Tech. Rev.*, **42**, 110–144, (1985)
2. MCCLELLAN, J.H., PARKS, T.W. and RABINER, L.R., A computer program for designing optimum FIR linear-phase digital filters. *IEEE Trans. Audio and Electroacoustics* **AU-21**, 506–526 (1973)
3. LIM, Y.C., Linear-phase digital audio tone control. *J. Audio Eng. Soc.*, **35**, 38–40 (1987)
4. ADAMS, R.W., Design and implementation of an 18 bit audio D/A convertor using oversampling techniques. Presented at the 77th Audio Engineering Society Convention (Hamburg, 1985), preprint 2182
5. VAN DER KAM, J.J., A digital decimating filter for analog to digital conversion of hi-fi audio signals. *Philips Tech. Rev.*, **42**, 230–238 (1986)
6. JACKSON, L.B., Roundoff noise analysis for fixed-point digital filters realized in cascade or parallel form. *IEEE Trans. Audio and Electroacoustics*, **AU-18**, 107–122 (1970)
7. PARKER, S.R., Limit cycles and correlated noise in digital filters. In *Digital Signal Processing*, Western Periodicals Co., 177–179 (1979)
8. CLAASEN, T.A.C.M., MECKLENBRAUKER, W.F.G. and PEEK, J.B.H., Effects of quantizing and overflow in recursive digital filters. *IEEE Trans. Acoust., Speech, Signal Process.*, **24**, 517–529 (1976)
9. MCNALLY, G.W., Digital audio: recursive digital filtering for high-quality audio signals. *BBC Res. Dept Report* RD 1981/10
10. RABINER, L.R. and GOLD, B., *Theory and Application of Digital Signal Processing*. New Jersey: Prentice-Hall (1975)
11. AGARWAL, R.C. and BURRUS, C.S., New recursive digital filter structures having very low sensitivity and roundoff noise. *IEEE Trans. Circuits. Syst.* **CAS-22**, 921–927 (1975)
12. CROCHIERE, R.E. and RABINER, L.R., Interpolation and decimation of digital signals — a tutorial review. *Proc. IEEE*, **69**, 300–331 (1981)
13. RABINER, L.R., Digital techniques for changing the sampling rate of a signal. In *Digital Audio*, edited by B. Blesser, B. Locanthi and T.G. Stockham Jr, pp.79–89, New York: Audio Engineering Society (1982)
14. LAGADEC, R., Digital sampling frequency conversion. In *Digital Audio*, edited by B. Blesser, B. Locanthi and T.G. Stockham Jr, pp.90–96, New York: Audio Engineering Society (1982)
15. RICHARDS, J.W., Digital audio mixing. *The Radio and Electron. Eng.*, **53**, 257–264 (1983)

16. RICHARDS, J.W. and CRAVEN, I., An experimental 'all digital' studio mixing desk. *J. Audio Eng. Soc.*, **30**, 117–126 (1982)

17. JONES, M.H., Processing systems for the digital audio studio. In *Digital Audio*, edited by B. Blesser, B. Locanthi and T.G. Stockham Jr, pp.221–225, New York: Audio Engineering Society (1982)

18. LIDBETTER, P.S., A digital delay processor and its applications. Presented at the 82nd Audio Engineering Society Convention (London, 1987), preprint 2474(K-4)

19. MCNALLY, G.W., COPAS – A high speed real time digital audio processor. *BBC Research Dept Report*, RD 1979/26

20. MCNALLY, G.W., Digital audio: COPAS-2, a modular digital audio signal processor for use in a mixing desk. *BBC Research Dept Report*, RD 1982/13

21. MOORER, J.A., The audio signal processor: the next step in digital audio. In *Digital Audio*, edited by B. Blesser, B. Locanthi and T.G. Stockham Jr, pp.205–215, New York: Audio Engineering Society (1982)

22. VANDENBULCKE, C. *et al.*, An integrated digital audio signal processor. Presented at the 77th Audio Engineering Society Convention (Hamburg, 1985), preprint 2181(B-7)

23. GOURLAOEN, R. and DELACROIX, P., The digital sound mixing desk: architecture and integration in the future all-digital studio. Presented at the 80th Audio Engineering Society Convention (Montreux, 1986), preprint 2327(D-1)

Chapter 5

Digital audio interconnects

Although digital recorders can be connected to an analog world by the use of converters, many of the advantages of the digital domain are lost if transfer of audio between digital machines has to be via analog signals. The importance of direct digital interconnection was realized early, and numerous incompatible methods were developed by various manufacturers until standardization was reached in the shape of the AES/EBU digital audio interface. This chapter is intended to assist in the process of connecting dissimilar digital machines, and so the details of common manufacturers' interconnects are given here in addition to a description of the AES/EBU standard. The chapter continues with an examination of methods for multitrack digital interconnects, and the problems of synchronization in large digital systems.

5.1 PCM-F1 Interconnect

Although intended as a high-end consumer product, the Sony PCM-F1 and its descendants were widely adopted by the audio industry, not least because of their low cost (see Chapter 8 for full description). Digital inputs and outputs were not provided as standard, but numerous companies have modified the equipment to give access to internal digital signals. The information given here is the interconnect standard used by Sony for digital signals into and out of converter chips. In the PCM-F1, which is a stereo machine, a single converter works at twice the sampling rate converting alternate channels. The signal structure reflects that philosophy. Fig.5.1 shows that there are three signals, one of which is a square-wave clock at the sampling rate. When the clock signal is high, the second signal conveys the left-channel sample, and when low, the right-channel sample. The data signal is simple bit-serial NRZ, with the most significant bit sent first. As two channels of sixteen bit samples must be conveyed, the bit rate is 32 times the word clock, and a signal at this frequency is also available. The figure shows the relationships between the signals. Bit clock falls at the centre of each bit cell, and would be used by receiving equipment to clock in the data bits. Word clock is used by the receiver to determine where sample boundaries are in the bit stream and to distinguish between left and right channels. The PCM-F1 can also work in fourteen bit mode, when it complies with the EIAJ format, and in this case, the two last bits in each sample will be zero. When

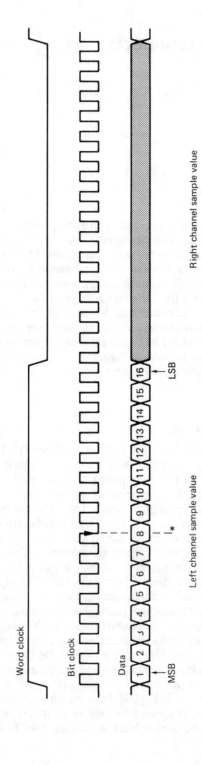

Figure 5.1 The digital signals available within the PCM-F1. Word clock determines the word boundaries, and separates left and right channels. Bit clock can be used to strobe in the NRZ data on a falling edge (shown *).

this is fed to a converter, the output level remains the same, but the resolution falls. The use of separate data and clock lines is perfectly in order within a piece of equipment as it was originally intended, but for interconnection purposes, it has little resistance to skew, and long cables are not advisable.

5.2 PCM-1610 interconnect

The PCM-1610 has been used extensively for Compact Disc mastering (see Chapter 8), and has a digital I/O format to allow interfacing to the CD cutter and to editors. Fig.5.2 shows that this format is more complex than that of the previous example. Each channel of the stereo signal is carried by a separate conductor with identical data structure. A square-wave word clock is provided at the sampling frequency, and one cycle of this describes the basic time slot used. The sampling rate is multiplied by 32 to obtain a bit-rate clock, but there are not 32 data bits in the time slot, because three bit cells are used by a synchro-nizing pattern. Accordingly 29 data bits can be conveyed in each time slot. The data bits are conveyed by serial NRZ, MSB first, and so the voltage on the line will only change at bit-cell boundaries. The synchronizing pattern is designed to have a central transition at the centre of a bit cell, and so it can be uniquely detected. The data signal is fed to a phase-locked loop, which updates its phase every time there is a transition between different data bits. When adjacent bits are identical, the loop flywheels in order to separate the bits. When the synchro-nizing pattern is fed in, the transition at the bit-cell centre causes a massive phase error in the loop which can be reliably detected to reset the bit counter which identifies the significance of the serial data bits. This is the correct way of receiv-ing the data. The use of word clock to clock-in data is not recommended as relative phase between word clock and the beginning of the time slot is not guaranteed.

The audio samples are placed in the first sixteen bits of the time slot, although the standard did cater for expansion to 20-bit samples. The remaining nine bits are available for control and user bits.

There is a block structure which repeats every 256 sample periods. At the beginning of every block, the 29th bit will be high to denote block sync. When this happens, the synchronizing pattern is inverted to guarantee a $1\frac{1}{2}$-bit run length. During the word containing the block flag, two data bits are implemen-ted, one for the emphasis flag, and one for the copy-prohibit flag, which is always zero in the PCM-1610.

When the block flag is low, the remaining eight bits in each word are available for user bits.

5.3 PCM-3324 interconnect

The PCM-3324 multitrack recorder used an identical signal structure, but a different electrical interface. This was a balanced line or differential signal. Interfacing with the PCM-1610 only requires the use of single-ended-to-differential driver chips, or vice versa. Since the PCM-1610 will only operate at 44.0559/44.1 kHz, clearly the 3324 will also have to operate at that rate.

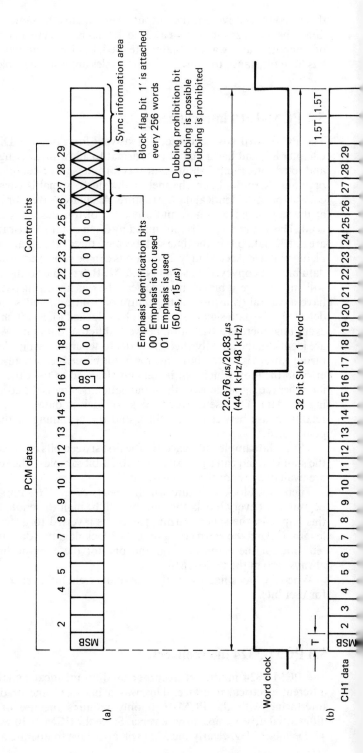

(a)

PCM data

Control bits

Sync information area

Block flag bit '1' is attached every 256 words

Dubbing prohibition bit
0 Dubbing is possible
1 Dubbing is prohibited

Emphasis identification bits
00 Emphasis is not used
01 Emphasis is used
(50 μs, 15 μs)

22.676 μs/20.83 μs
(44.1 kHz/48 kHz)

32 bit Slot = 1 Word

Word clock

(b)

CH1 data

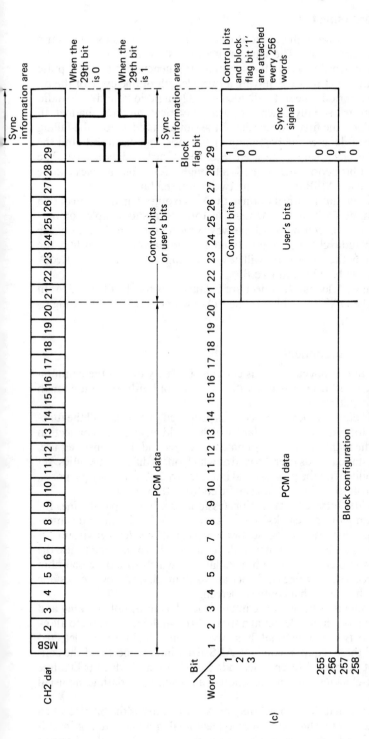

Figure 5.2 At (a) is the block content of the Sony 1610/3324 signal; (b) shows the synchronizing patterns used for data reception. At (c) user bits form a block which is synchronized every 256 sample periods. Note that PCM-1610 uses single-ended signal at 44.1 kHz only. PCM-3324 is differential signal and can also run at 48 kHz.

5.4 Melco interconnect

In the multitrack recorders adhering to ProDigi format, the Mitsubishi Electric Co. (Melco) interface is used. The signal structure is shown in Fig.5.3.

There is a single word clock at the sampling frequency, but this is a pulse signal rather than a square wave, having a pulse length of one cycle of the bit clock. The sample-period time slot is divided into 32-bit periods, and each audio channel is transmitted serially down a separate electrical interface channel. In sixteen-bit machines, the first sixteen bits of the slot are used, where the falling edge of word clock denotes the beginning of the most significant bit, and the falling edge of bit clock should be used to clock-in each individual bit. The remaining sixteen bit periods are unused, although twenty-bit samples can be accommodated, again MSB first, leaving twelve unused bits.

There is additional status information in the Melco output, in the form of two extra output channels which are identical in form to audio sample communication, but the two sixteen-bit words conveyed reflect the record status of the machine for each audio channel. If any channel of the machine is recording, the corresponding bit in the status word will be low. Channels 1–16 are in the Rec.A signal, and channels 17–32 are in Rec.B.

All signals in the Melco interconnect are balanced, as for the PCM-3324. In fact interfacing the DASH machine to the PD machine is reasonably straightforward.

5.5 AES/EBU interconnect

In all the above interconnects, there is enough similarity due to the common purpose to make interfacing possible with a little extra hardware, but enough difference to be irritating.

The AES/EBU digital audio interface[1] was proposed to embrace all the functions of existing formats in one standard which would ensure interconnection independent of the manufacture of equipment at either end. For consumer use, a corresponding standard has been arrived at which offers different facilities, yet retains compatibility with the professional interface so that, for many purposes, consumer and professional machines can be connected together.[2]

Many of the older interconnects for professional use have separate lines for bit clocks and sampling-rate clocks, which is acceptable for the short distances required for simple dubbing, but causes problems in the broadcast environment where long lines might be needed in a studio complex. It was desired to use the existing analog audio cabling in such installations, which would be 600 ohm balanced line screened, with one cable per audio channel, or in some cases one twisted pair per channel with a common screen.

If a single channel is to be used, the interconnect has to be self-clocking and self-synchronizing, i.e. the single signal must carry enough information to allow the boundaries between individual bits, words and blocks to be detected reliably. To fulfil these requirements, the AES/EBU interconnect and the consumer equivalent both use FM channel code (see Chapter 6) which is DC-free and strongly self-clocking. Synchronization is achieved by violating the usual encoding rules.

Using FM means that the channel frequency is the same as the bit rate when sending data ones. Tests showed that in typical analog audio-cabling installations, sufficient bandwidth was available to convey two digital audio channels

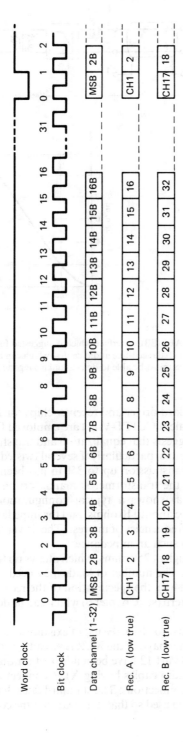

Figure 5.3 In the Mitsubishi format multitrack machines, the basic block has a frequency equal to the sampling rate, with a bit rate 32 times this. The first 16 or 20 bits of the block are used only. The falling edge of word clock denotes the beginning of a sample. Rec A and Rec B specify which channels of the machine are recording.

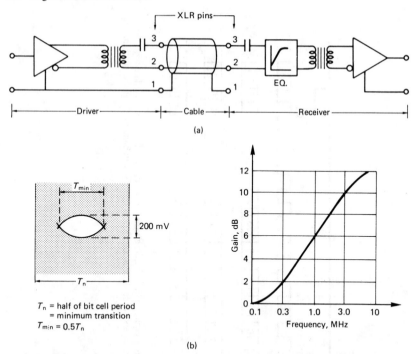

Figure 5.4 The configuration of the AES/EBU interface which is suggested for long cables. XLR pin connections are the same as balanced-line audio cables, which can be used. At (b) the minimum eye pattern which a receiver must be able to detect, and a suggested equalization response.

in one twisted pair. The standard driver and receiver chips for RS-422A[3] data communication (or the equivalent CCITT-V.11) are employed for professional use, but work by the BBC[4] suggests that equalization and transformer coupling are desirable for longer cable runs, particularly if several twisted pairs occupy a common shield. Successful transmission up to 350 m has been achieved with these techniques. The use of the transformer is mandatory in the equivalent EBU specification.[5] Fig.5.4(a) shows a typical configuration. The output impedance of the drivers will be about 110 ohms, and the impedance of the cable used should be similar at the frequencies of interest. The driver should produce between 3 and 10 V p − p into such an impedance.

The receiver impedance is high at 250 ohms, which allows up to four receivers to be driven from one source. The number of loads may need to be reduced if long cables are used. In Fig.5.4(b), the specification of the receiver is shown in terms of the minimum eye pattern (see Chapter 6) which can be detected without error.

The purpose of the standard is to allow the use of existing analog cabling, and as an adequate connector in the shape of the XLR is already in wide service, the recommendations of IEC 268 Part 12 have been adopted for digital audio use. Effectively, existing analog audio cables having XLR connectors can be used without alteration for digital connections. The standard does, however, require that suitable labelling should be used so that it is clear that the connections on a particular unit are digital.

The need to drive long cables does not generally arise in the domestic environment, and so a low-impedance balanced signal is not necessary. The electrical interface of the consumer format uses a 0.5 V peak single-ended signal, which can be conveyed down conventional audio-grade coaxial cable connected with phono plugs.

In Fig.5.5 the basic structure of the professional and consumer formats can be seen. One subframe consists of 32 bit-cells, of which four will be used by a synchronizing pattern. Up to 24-bit sample wordlength can be used, which should cater for all conceivable future developments, but normally 20-bit samples will be available with four auxiliary data bits, which might be used for a voice-grade channel in a professional application. In a consumer RDAT machine, subcode can be transmitted in bits 4–11, and the sixteen bit audio in bits 12–27.

In contrast with preceding formats, this format sends the least significant bit first. One advantage of this approach is that simple serial arithmetic is then possible on the samples because the carries produced by the operation on a given bit can be delayed by one bit period and then included in the operation on the next higher-order bit. There is additional complication, however, if it is proposed to build adaptors from one of the manufacturers' formats to the new format because of the word reversal. This problem is a temporary issue, as new machines are designed from the outset to have the standard connections.

Four status bits accompany each subframe. The validity flag will be reset if the associated sample is reliable. The parity bit produces even parity over the subframe, such that the total number of ones in the subframe is even. This allows for simple detection of an odd number of bits in error, and improves the probability of detection of sync. The user and channel-status bits are discussed later.

Two of the subframes described above make one frame, which repeats at the sampling rate in use. The first subframe will contain the sample from channel A, or from the left channel in stereo working. The second subframe will contain the sample from channel B, or the right channel. At 48 kHz, the bit rate will be 3.072 MHz.

In order to separate the audio channels on receipt the synchronizing patterns for the two subframes are different.

The channel status and user bits in each subframe form serial data streams with one bit of each per audio channel per frame. It is in the use of these bits that the differences between the professional and consumer interface standards are

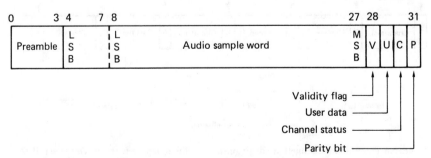

Figure 5.5 The basic subframe structure of the AES/EBU format. Sample can be twenty bits with four auxiliary bits, or 24 bits. LSB is transmitted first.

most pronounced. The channel status bits are given a block structure and synchronized every 192 frames, which at 48 kHz gives a block rate of 250 Hz, corresponding to a period of four milliseconds.

In professional applications, users are free to assign any desired format to the user bits, but it is recommended that the same block size is used, so that the user-block boundaries align with the channel-status block boundaries. This would minimize problems if the data structure was upset during synchronizing operations between systems with nonphased sampling clocks. It has been suggested that the user data is employed for labelling.[6] Labelling information is assembled into one or more 48-bit words which begin with a uniquely identifiable synchronizing pattern. Suggested uses of the labelling structure include:

Time and date of program origin
Program and identification number
Take number
Programme duration
Cue information
Act or scene number
Timecode-related information
Network information
Radio-data information
Generation number (for recording)
Copyright ownership code
Editing information
Signal source information (e.g. originating microphone)

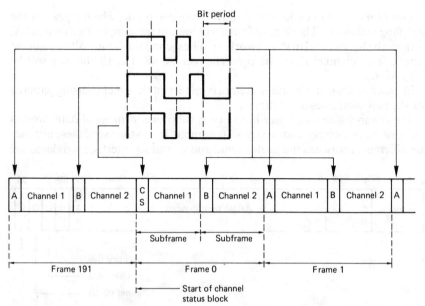

Figure 5.6 The A and B channels are distinguished by different sync patterns. Once every 192 blocks, the A sync is replaced by channel status block sync. Inverse of sync patterns is also valid; system is not polarity-conscious.

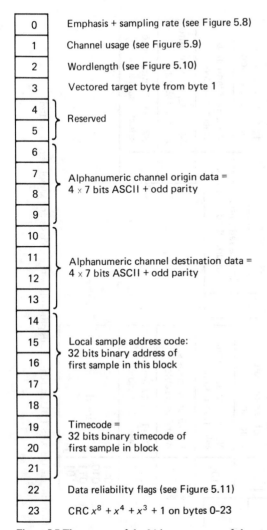

0	Emphasis + sampling rate (see Figure 5.8)
1	Channel usage (see Figure 5.9)
2	Wordlength (see Figure 5.10)
3	Vectored target byte from byte 1
4	Reserved
5	
6	
7	Alphanumeric channel origin data =
8	4 × 7 bits ASCII + odd parity
9	
10	
11	Alphanumeric channel destination data =
12	4 × 7 bits ASCII + odd parity
13	
14	
15	Local sample address code:
16	32 bits binary address of first sample in this block
17	
18	
19	Timecode =
20	32 bits binary timecode of first sample in block
21	
22	Data reliability flags (see Figure 5.11)
23	CRC $x^8 + x^4 + x^3 + 1$ on bytes 0–23

Figure 5.7 The content of the 24-byte sequence of channel-status data in the AES/EBU format.

In order to synchronize the channel-status blocks, the channel A sync pattern is replaced for one frame only by a third sync pattern. These three sync patterns are shown in Fig.5.6. As stated, there is a parity bit in each subframe, which means that the binary level at the end of a subframe will always be the same as at the beginning. Since the sync patterns have the same characteristic, the effect is that sync patterns always have the same polarity and the receiver can use that information to reject noise. The polarity of transmission is not specified, and indeed an accidental inversion in a twisted pair is of no consequence, since it is only the transition that is of importance, not the direction.

In the professional format, the sequence of channel-status bits over 192 sub-frames builds up a 24-byte channel-status block, shown in Fig.5.7. The first byte determines the use of emphasis and the sampling rate, with details in Fig.5.8. The second byte determines the channel usage, i.e. whether the data transmitted

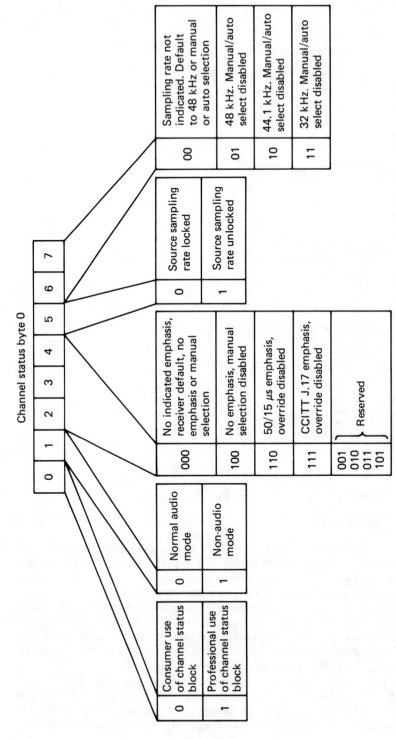

Figure 5.8 The first byte of the channel status information in the AES/EBU standard deals primarily with emphasis and sampling rate control.

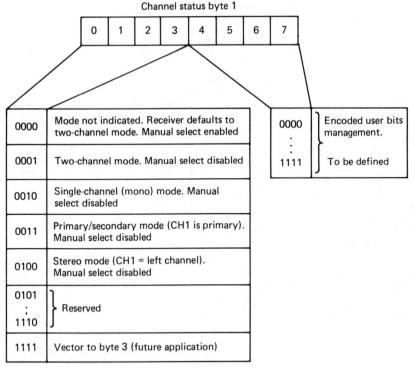

Figure 5.9 The secondary byte of the channel-status information currently deals with audio channel usage, but will be extended in the future to manage user bits.

are a stereo pair, two unrelated mono signals or a single mono signal. Fig.5.9 gives details. The third byte determines wordlength as in Fig.5.10.

There are two slots of four bytes each which are used for alphanumeric source and destination codes. These can be used for routing.

Bytes 14–17 convey a 32-bit sample address which increments every channel status frame. It effectively numbers the samples in a relative manner. Bytes 18–21 convey a similar number, but this is a time-of-day count, which starts from zero at midnight. With a sampling rate of 48 kHz, the binary count represents the number of four-millisecond intervals from midnight, and can easily be converted into, for example, EBU timecode by dividing by ten to obtain a count of 40 ms video frames. At other sampling frequencies, the division ratio would need to be modified appropriately.

The penultimate byte contains four flags which indicate that certain sections of the channel-status information are unreliable (see Fig.5.11). This allows the transmission of an incomplete channel-status block where the entire structure is not needed or where the information is not available. For example, setting bit 5 to a logical one would mean that no origin or destination data would be interpreted by the receiver, and so it need not be sent.

The final byte in the message is a CRCC which converts the entire channel-status block into a codeword (see Chapter 7).

For consumer use, a different version of the channel-status specification is used. Fig.5.12 shows that the serial data bits are assembled into twelve words of

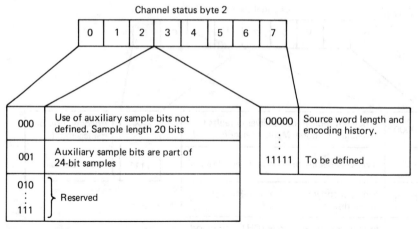

Figure 5.10 Byte 2 of channel status determines whether all 24 bits of the word slot are used for audio samples, or just 20 maximum.

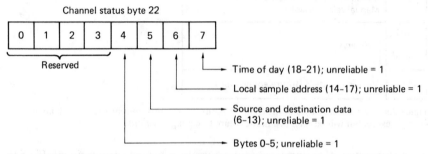

Figure 5.11 Byte 22 of channel status indicates if some of the information in the block is unreliable.

sixteen bits each. In the general format, the first six bits of the first word form a control code, and the next two bits permit a mode select for future expansion. At the moment only mode zero is standardized, and the three remaining codes are reserved.

Fig. 5.13 shows the bit allocations for mode zero. In addition to the control bits, there are a category code, a simplified version of the AES/EBU source field, a field which specifies the audio channel number for multichannel working, a sampling-rate field, and a sampling-rate tolerance field.

Originally the consumer format was incompatible with the professional format, since bit zero of channel status would be set to a one by a four-channel consumer machine, and this would confuse a professional receiver because bit zero specifies professional format. The EBU proposed to the IEC that the four-channel bit be moved to bit 5 of the consumer format, so that bit zero would always then be zero. This proposal is incorporated in the bit definitions of Fig. 5.12 and 5.13.

The category code specifies the type of equipment which is transmitting, and its characteristics. There are currently four categories; general purpose, two-channel CD player, two-channel PCM adaptor and two-channel digital tape recorder (RDAT or SDAT).

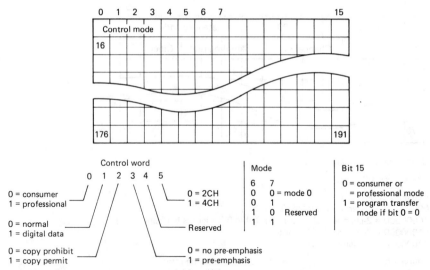

Figure 5.12 The general format of the consumer version of channel status. Bit 0 has the same meaning as in the professional format for compatibility. Bits 6–7 determine the consumer format mode, and presently only mode 0 is defined (see Figure 5.13).

Table 5.1 illustrates the format of the subframes in the general-purpose category.

When used with CD players, Table 5.2 applies. In this application, the extensive subcode data of a CD recording (see Chapter 13) can be conveyed down the interface. In every CD sync block, there are twelve audio samples, and eight bits of subcode, P–W. The P flag is not transmitted, since it is solely positioning information for the player; thus only Q–W are sent. Since the interface can carry one user bit for every sample, there is surplus capacity in the user-bit channel for subcode. A CD subcode block is built up over 98 sync blocks, and has a repetition rate of 75 Hz. The start of the subcode data in the user bit stream will be seen in Fig.5.14 to be denoted by a minimum of sixteen zeros, followed by a start bit which is always set to one. Immediately after the start bit, the receiver expects to see seven subcode bits, Q–W. Following these, another start bit and another seven bits may follow immediately, or a space of up to eight zeros may be left before the next start bit. This sequence repeats 98 times, when another sync pattern will be expected. The ability to leave zeros between the subcode symbols simplifies the handling of the disparity between user bit capacity and subcode bit rate. Fig.5.15 shows a representative example of a transmission from a CD player.

In a PCM adaptor, there is no subcode, and the only ancillary information available from the recording consists of copy-protect and emphasis bits. In other respects, the format is the same as the general-purpose format.

When an RDAT player is used with the interface, the user bits carry several items of information.[7] Once per drum revolution, the user bit in one subframe is raised when that subframe contains the first sample of the interleave block (see Chapter 8). This can be used to synchronize several RDAT machines together for editing purposes. Immediately following the sync bit, start ID will be transmitted when the player has found the code on the tape. This must be

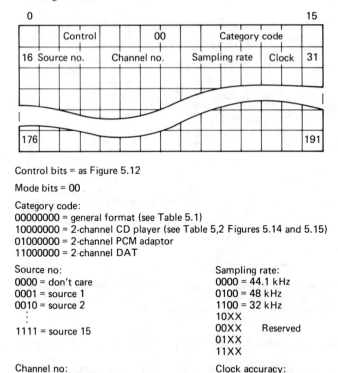

Control bits = as Figure 5.12

Mode bits = 00

Category code:
00000000 = general format (see Table 5.1)
10000000 = 2-channel CD player (see Table 5,2 Figures 5.14 and 5.15)
01000000 = 2-channel PCM adaptor
11000000 = 2-channel DAT

Source no:
0000 = don't care
0001 = source 1
0010 = source 2
⋮
1111 = source 15

Sampling rate:
0000 = 44.1 kHz
0100 = 48 kHz
1100 = 32 kHz
10XX
00XX   Reserved
01XX
11XX

Channel no:
0000 = don't care
1000 = A (left channel for stereo)
0100 = B (right channel for stereo)
1100 = C
⋮
1111 = 0

Clock accuracy:
00 = normal accuracy
10 = high accuracy
01 = variable speed

Figure 5.13 In Consumer mode 0, the significance of the first two sixteen-bit channel-status words is shown here. The category codes are expanded in Tables 5.1 and 5.2.

Table 5.1 The general category code causes the subframe structure of the transmission to be interpreted as below (see Figure 5.5) and the stated channel-status bits are valid.

Category code
00000000 = two-channel general format

Subframe structure

Two's complement, MSB in position 27, max 20 bits/sample
User bit channel = not used
V bit optional
Channel status left = Channel status right, unless channel number (Figure 5.13) is non-zero

Control bits in channel status
Emphasis = bit 3
Copy permit = bit 2

Sampling-rate bits in channel status
Bits 4–27 = according to rate in use

Clock-accuracy bits in channel status
Bits 28–29 = according to source accuracy

Table 5.2 In the CD category, the meaning below is placed on the transmission. The main difference from the general category is the use of user bits for subcode as specified in Figure 5.14.

Category code
10000000 = two-channel CD player

Subframe structure

Two's complement MSB in position 27, 16 bits/sample
User bit channel = CD subcode (see Figure 5.14)
V bit optional

Control bits in channel status
Derived from Q subcode control bits (see Chapter 13)

Sampling-rate bits in channel status
Bits 24–27 = 0000 = 44.1 kHz

Clock-accuracy bits in channel status
Bits 28–29 = according to source accuracy and use of variable speed

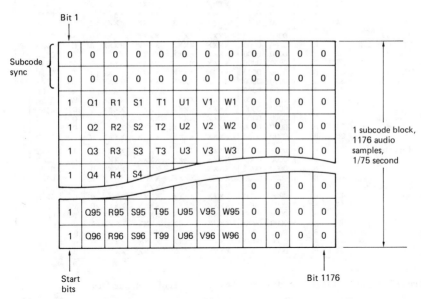

Figure 5.14 In CD, one subcode block is built up over 98 sync blocks. In this period there will be 1176 audio samples, and so there are 1176 user bits available to carry the subcode. There is insufficient subcode information to fill this capacity, and zero packing is used.

asserted for 300 ± 30 drum revolutions, or about ten seconds. In the third bit position the skip ID is transmitted when the player detects a skip command on the tape. This indicates that the player will go into fast forward until it detects the next start ID. The skip ID must be transmitted for 33 ± 3 drum rotations. Finally RDAT supports an end-of-skip command which terminates a skip when it is detected. This allows jump editing (see Chapter 9) to omit short sections of the recording.

RDAT can also transmit the track number (TNO) of the track being played down the user bit stream.

	Subframe no.	Pre-amble SYNC	Aux		LSB Audio samples MSB	V	U	C	P
Channel status →	1	CS	0000	0000	XXXX XXXX XXXX XXXX	0	0	C0L	P
block sync	2	B	0000	0000	XXXX XXXX XXXX XXXX	0	0	C0R	P
	3	A	0000	0000	XXXX XXXX XXXX XXXX	0	0	C1L	P
	4	B	0000	0000	XXXX XXXX XXXX XXXX	0	0	C1R	P
A = left →	5	A	0000	0000	XXXX XXXX XXXX XXXX	0	0	C2L	P
channel sample	6	B	0000	0000	XXXX XXXX XXXX XXXX	0	0	C2R	P
	7	A	0000	0000	XXXX XXXX XXXX XXXX	0	0	C3L	P
	8	B	0000	0000	XXXX XXXX XXXX XXXX	0	0	C3R	P
	9	A	0000	0000	XXXX XXXX XXXX XXXX	0	0	C4L	P
B = right →	10	B	0000	0000	XXXX XXXX XXXX XXXX	0	0	C4R	P
channel sample	11	A	0000	0000	XXXX XXXX XXXX XXXX	0	0	C5L	P
	12	B	0000	0000	XXXX XXXX XXXX XXXX	0	0	C5R	P
	13	A	0000	0000	XXXX XXXX XXXX XXXX	0	0	C6L	P
	14	B	0000	0000	XXXX XXXX XXXX XXXX	0	0	C6R	P
	15	A	0000	0000	XXXX XXXX XXXX XXXX	0	0	C7L	P
	16	B	0000	0000	XXXX XXXX XXXX XXXX	0	0	C7R	P
	17	A	0000	0000	XXXX XXXX XXXX XXXX	0	0	C8L	P
16 zeros	18	B	0000	0000	XXXX XXXX XXXX XXXX	0	0	C8R	P
in user bits	19	A	0000	0000	XXXX XXXX XXXX XXXX	0	0	C9L	P
= subcode	20	B	0000	0000	XXXX XXXX XXXX XXXX	0	0	C9R	P
sync word	21	A	0000	0000	XXXX XXXX XXXX XXXX	0	0	C10L	P
	22	B	0000	0000	XXXX XXXX XXXX XXXX	0	0	C10R	P
	23	A	0000	0000	XXXX XXXX XXXX XXXX	0	0	C11L	P
	24	B	0000	0000	XXXX XXXX XXXX XXXX	0	0	C11R	P
1 in user	25	A	0000	0000	XXXX XXXX XXXX XXXX	0	1	C12L	P
bits = subcode	26	B	0000	0000	XXXX XXXX XXXX XXXX	0	Q1	C12R	P
start bit	27	A	0000	0000	XXXX XXXX XXXX XXXX	0	R1	C13L	P
	28	B	0000	0000	XXXX XXXX XXXX XXXX	0	S1	C13R	P
U = Subcode	29	A	0000	0000	XXXX XXXX XXXX XXXX	0	T1	C14L	P
	30	B	0000	0000	XXXX XXXX XXXX XXXX	0	U1	C14R	P
	31	A	0000	0000	XXXX XXXX XXXX XXXX	0	V1	C15L	P
	32	B	0000	0000	XXXX XXXX XXXX XXXX	0	W1	C15R	P
	33	A	0000	0000	XXXX XXXX XXXX XXXX	0	0	C16L	P
Subcode	34	B	0000	0000	XXXX XXXX XXXX XXXX	0	0	C16R	P
space	35	A	0000	0000	XXXX XXXX XXXX XXXX	0	0	C17L	P
	36	B	0000	0000	XXXX XXXX XXXX XXXX	0	0	C17R	P
Start bit	37	A	0000	0000	XXXX XXXX XXXX XXXX	0	1	C18L	P
	38	B	0000	0000	XXXX XXXX XXXX XXXX	0	Q2	C18R	P
	39	A	0000	0000	XXXX XXXX XXXX XXXX	0	R2	C19L	P
	40	B	0000	0000	XXXX XXXX XXXX XXXX	0	S2	C19R	P
U = Subcode	41	A	0000	0000	XXXX XXXX XXXX XXXX	0	T2	C20L	P
	42	B	0000	0000	XXXX XXXX XXXX XXXX	0	U2	C20R	P
	43	A	0000	0000	XXXX XXXX XXXX XXXX	0	V2	C21L	P
	44	B	0000	0000	XXXX XXXX XXXX XXXX	0	W2	C21R	P
	45	A	0000	0000	XXXX XXXX XXXX XXXX	0	0	C22L	P
	46	B	0000	0000	XXXX XXXX XXXX XXXX	0	0	C22R	P
	47	A	0000	0000	XXXX XXXX XXXX XXXX	0	0	C23L	P
	48	B	0000	0000	XXXX XXXX XXXX XXXX	0	0	C23R	P

Figure 5.15 Compact Disc subcode transmitted in user bits of serial interface.

5.6 Parallel interfacing

The AES/EBU interface and the consumer derivative are ideal for a small number of audio channels. In some professional applications, a large number of audio channels need to be conveyed together, for example between multitrack recorders and mixing consoles. The use of a parallel interface has some advantages for this application, since the distances involved are usually short, and the cost of the cable is not an issue.

In a BBC proposal[8] the 28 data-bit structure of the AES/EBU subframe has been turned sideways, with one conductor allocated to each bit. Since the maximum transition rate of the AES/EBU interface is 64 times the sampling rate it follows that, in the parallel implementation, 64 channels could be time-multiplexed into one sample period within the same bandwidth. The necessary

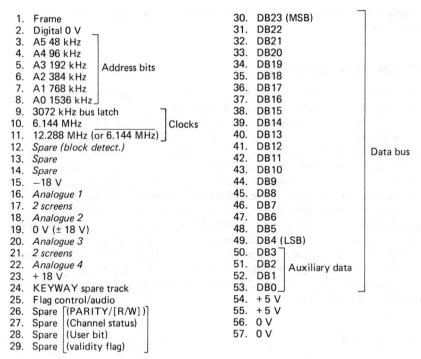

1. Frame	30. DB23 (MSB)
2. Digital 0 V	31. DB22
3. A5 48 kHz	32. DB21
4. A4 96 kHz	33. DB20
5. A3 192 kHz Address bits	34. DB19
6. A2 384 kHz	35. DB18
7. A1 768 kHz	36. DB17
8. A0 1536 kHz	37. DB16
9. 3072 kHz bus latch	38. DB15
10. 6.144 MHz Clocks	39. DB14
11. 12.288 MHz (or 6.144 MHz)	40. DB13
12. *Spare (block detect.)*	41. DB12
13. *Spare*	42. DB11 Data bus
14. *Spare*	43. DB10
15. −18 V	44. DB9
16. *Analogue 1*	45. DB8
17. *2 screens*	46. DB7
18. *Analogue 2*	47. DB6
19. *0 V (± 18 V)*	48. DB5
20. *Analogue 3*	49. DB4 (LSB)
21. *2 screens*	50. DB3
22. *Analogue 4*	51. DB2 Auxiliary data
23. + 18 V	52. DB1
24. KEYWAY spare track	53. DB0
25. Flag control/audio	54. + 5 V
26. Spare (PARITY/[R/W])	55. + 5 V
27. Spare (Channel status)	56. 0 V
28. Spare (User bit)	57. 0 V
29. Spare (validity flag)	

Figure 5.16 Time division multiplexed 64 channel audio bus proposed by BBC.

signals are illustrated in Fig.5.16. In order to separate the channels on reception, there are six address lines which convey a binary pattern corresponding to the audio channel number of the sample in that time slot. The receiver simply routes the samples according to the attached address. Such a point-to-point system does, however, neglect the potential of the system for more complex use. The bus cable can loop through several different items of equipment, each of which is programmed so that it transmits samples during a different set of time slots from the others. Since all transmissions are available at all receivers, it is only necessary to detect a given address to latch samples from any channel. If two devices decode the same address, the same audio channel will be available at two destinations.

In such a system, channel reassignment is easy. If the audio channels are transmitted in address sequence, it is only necessary to change the addresses which the receiving channels recognize, and a given input channel will emerge from a different output channel. Since the address recognition circuitry is already present in a TDM system, the functionality of a 64 × 64 point channel-assignment patchboard has been achieved with no extra hardware. The only constraint in the use of TDM systems is that all channels must have synchronized sampling rates. In multitrack recorders this occurs naturally because all of the channels are locked by the tape format.

For asynchronous systems, or where several sampling rates are found simultaneously, a cross-point type of channel-assignment matrix will be necessary, using AES/EBU signals. In such a device, the switching can be performed by logic gates at low cost, and in the digital domain there is, of course, no quality degradation.

5.7 Fibre-optic interfacing

Whereas a parallel bus is ideal for a distributed multichannel system, for a point-to-point connection the use of fibre optics is feasible, particularly as distance increases. An optical fibre is simply a glass filament which is encased in such a way that light is constrained to travel along it. Transmission is achieved by modulating the power of an LED or small laser coupled to the fibre. A phototransistor converts the received light back to an electrical signal.

Optical fibres have numerous advantages over electrical cabling. The bandwidth available is staggering. Optical fibres neither generate, nor are prone to, electromagnetic interference and, as they are insulators, ground loops cannot occur. The disadvantage of optical fibres is that the terminations of the fibre where transmitters and receivers are attached suffer optical losses, and while these can be compensated in point-to-point links, the use of a bus structure is not really feasible. Fibre-optic links are already in service in digital audio mixing consoles.[9] It is proposed to standardize a fibre-optic version of the AES/EBU/IEC interface.

5.8 Synchronizing

When digital audio signals are to be assembled from a variety of sources, either for mixing down or for transmission through a TDM system, the samples from each source must be synchronized to one another in both frequency and phase. The source of samples can often be fed with a reference sampling rate from some central generator, and will return samples at that rate. In reality, this will not always happen. In a satellite transmission, it is not really practicable to genlock a studio complex halfway round the world to another. Outside broadcasts may be required to generate their own master timing for the same reason. When genlock is not achieved, there will be a slow slippage of sample phase between source and destination due to such factors as drift in timing generators. This phase slippage will be corrected by a synchronizer, which is intended to work with frequencies which are nominally the same. It should be contrasted with the sampling-rate converter which can work at arbitrary frequency relationships. Although a sampling-rate converter can act as a synchronizer, it is a very expensive way of synchronizing. A synchronizer can be thought of as a lower-cost version of a sampling-rate converter which is constrained in the rate difference it can accept.

In one implementation of a digital audio synchronizer,[10] memory is used as a timebase corrector as was illustrated in Chapter 3. Samples are written into the memory with the frequency and phase of the source and, when the memory is half-full, samples are read out with the frequency and phase of the destination. Clearly if there is a net rate difference, the memory will either fill up or empty over a period of time, and in order to recentre the address relationship, it will be necessary to jump the read address. This will cause samples to be omitted or repeated, depending on the relationship of source rate to destination rate, and would be audible on program material. The solution is to detect pauses or

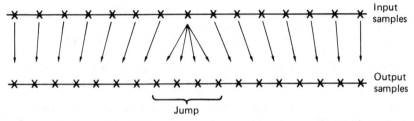

Figure 5.17 In jump-synchronizing, input samples are subjected to a varying delay to align them with output timing. Eventually the sample relationship is forced to jump to prevent delay building up. As shown here, this results in several samples being repeated, and can only be undertaken during program pauses, or at very low audio levels. If the input rate exceeds the output rate, some samples will be lost.

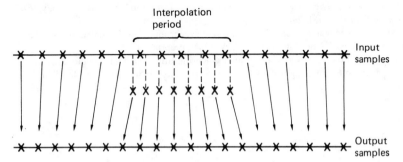

Figure 5.18 An alternative synchronizing process is to use a short period of interpolation in order to regulate the delay in the synchronizer.

low-level passages and permit jumping only at such times. The process is illustrated in Fig.5.17. Such synchronizers must have sufficient memory capacity to absorb timing differences between quiet passages where jumping is possible, and so the average delay introduced by them is quite large, typically 128 samples. They are, however, relatively inexpensive.

An alternative to address jumping is to undertake sampling-rate conversion for a short period (Fig.5.18) in order to slip the input/output relationship by one sample.[11] The delay caused by the unit can be smaller than that of a timebase corrector, because it will be determined by the window length of the digital filter, but the device is now constructionally similar to a sampling-rate converter and would be more expensive to implement. The result of interpolation is a small momentary pitch change.

The difficulty of synchronizing unlocked sources is eased when the frequency difference is small. Proposals have been made[12] for a standard of accuracy for timing generators for various purposes.

References

1. Audio Engineering Society, AES recommended practice for digital audio engineering – serial transmission format for linearly represented digital audio data. *J. Audio Eng. Soc.* **33**, 975–984 (1985)
2. Draft standard for a digital audio interface. IEC report 84/WG11
3. EIA RS-422A. Electronic Industries Association, 2001 Eye St N.W., Washington, DC 20006, USA

4. SMART, D.L., Transmission performance of digital audio serial interface on audio tie lines. *BBC Designs Dept Technical Memorandum*, 3.296/84

5. European Broadcasting Union, Specification of the digital audio interface. *EBU Doc. Tech.*, 3250

6. LAGADEC, R. and MCNALLY, G.J., Labels and their formatting in digital audio recording and transmission. Presented at 74th Audio Engineering Society Convention (New York 1983), preprint 2003

7. Digital audio taperecorder system (RDAT). Recommended design standard. DAT Conference, Part V (1986)

8. SHELTON, W.T., Interfaces for digital audio engineering. Presented at 6th International Conference on Video Audio and Data Recording, Brighton. IERE Publ. No. 67, 49–59 1986

9. LIDBETTER, P.S. and DOUGLAS, S., A fibre-optic multichannel communication link developed for remote interconnection in a digital audio console. Presented at the 80th Audio Engineering Society Convention (Montreux, 1986), preprint 2330

10. GILCHRIST, N.H.C., Digital sound: sampling-rate synchronization by variable delay. *BBC Research Dept Report*, 1979/17

11. LAGADEC, R., A new approach to sampling rate synchronisation. Presented at 76th Audio Engineering Society Convention (New York, 1984), preprint 2168

12. SHELTON, W.T., Progress towards a system of synchronization in a digital studio. Presented at the 82nd Audio Engineering Society Convention (London, 1986), preprint 2484(K7)

Chapter 6

Digital recording and channel coding

Although the physics of the record/replay process are unaffected by the meaning attributed to signals, the techniques used in digital recording are rather different from those found in analog recording, although often the same phenomenon shows up in a different guise. In this chapter the fundamentals of digital recording are treated along with the necessary coding methods.

At one time the needs of the computer industry dominated work on digital recording, but recent progress in digital audio, video and instrumentation recording has changed the emphasis. Channel coding is found in numerous audio applications, in stationary- and rotary-head digital tape recorders, in the timecode recordings on analog tape, in the rigid disk drives used for audio editing, in the Compact Disc, in floppy disk drives used for storing console set-ups and in the electrical and fibre-optic links between pieces of digital equipment. Fortunately the basic principles of coding explained here are relevant to all of these applications.

6.1 Channel SNR and tape consumption

In analog recording, the characteristics of the medium affect the signal recorded directly, whereas by expressing a signal in binary numerical form by sampling and quantizing, the quality becomes independent of the medium. The dynamic range required no longer directly decides the track width needed. In digital circuitry there is a great deal of noise immunity because the signal can only have two states, which are widely separated compared to the amplitude of noise. In digital magnetic recording there are also only two states of the medium, N–S and S–N, but paradoxically the noise immunity is much reduced. As noise immunity is a function of track width, reduction of the working SNR of a digital track allows the same information to be carried in a smaller area of the medium, improving economy of operation. It also increases the random error rate, but as an error-correction system is already necessary to deal with dropouts, it is simply made to work harder.

It is interesting to compare tape consumption between analog and digital machines where possible. A typical studio audio recorder will have 24 tracks on two-inch tape for analog recording, whereas only half-inch tape is necessary for digital recording of 24 tracks in the DASH format, and one-inch tape is used in the Mitsubishi formats to give 32 channels, the tape speed being roughly the same in each case. In digital recording narrower tracks are to be expected, and steps must be taken to register the heads accurately with the tracks by appropriate mechanical design and improved edge straightness in the tape.

6.2 Head noise and head to tape speed

There are several important sources of replay noise in a magnetic recorder, which will be examined later in this chapter. One of these is the noise from the head. All components with resistance generate noise according to their temperature, and the replay head is no exception. If a given recording exists on a tape, a better SNR will be obtained by moving the head relative to the tape at a higher speed, since the head noise is constant and the signal induced is proportional to speed. This is one reason why rotary-head recorders offer better packing density than stationary-head recorders. The other reason is much more obvious. A rotary-head machine determines track spacing by linear tape speed, whereas stationary heads are difficult to fabricate with narrow spacing between tracks. In digitizing an audio waveform, there has been an exchange in the importance of SNR and bandwidth. The bandwidth of a digital channel always exceeds the bandwidth of the original analog signal, but the extra bandwidth is only required with poor SNR. This explains the paradox that greater bandwidth is needed but less tape is used. As in analog recording, the rotating head can be used to obtain high bandwidth without excessively short tape wavelengths and at moderate linear tape speed. A further advantage of rotary-head machines is that, by changing the scanner geometry, the best compromise can be reached between bandwidth and SNR. Fig.6.1 shows that, in the same area of tape, two different recordings can be made. The first has a lower head-to-tape speed because the tracks are shorter, but better SNR because they are wider. The second has higher bandwidth due to the longer tracks, but these tracks are narrower. In the absence of head noise, the information capacity of

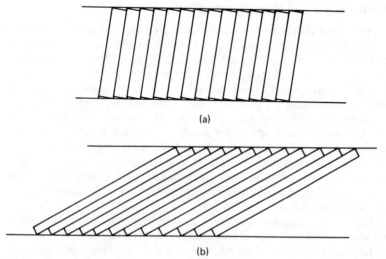

(a)

(b)

Figure 6.1 Two different rotary-head formats having the same tape consumption but different characteristics.

both formats would be the same. Where head noise is a factor, the second format will be superior. The lower limit to track width is generally set by the ability to register a head with adequate precision, and sometimes track-following servos are necessary to achieve the highest densities without sacrificing the ability to interchange a recording between machines. The comparison of tape consumption between RDAT and the Compact Cassette is even more dramatic because of the adoption of a rotary head with track following.

Whether the machine is stationary- or rotary-head, the recorded wavelengths must be kept short to conserve tape in the direction of the track. Very short wavelengths can only be replayed with consistent intimate contact between the head and the medium, so that the surface finish of the medium must be of the highest order. The roughness of the tape backcoat must be limited to prevent the back of one layer embossing an adjacent magnetic layer when the tape is wound on a spool. Digital audio tape resembles video tape in many ways. It has a thin coating, because thickness loss prevents flux from a thick coat being of much use at short wavelengths and because a thin coating is less prone to self-demagnetization. The thin coat needs high-energy particles to allow useful replay signals with reduced magnetic volume. The backing material, or substrate, is relatively thin to allow the tape to accommodate head irregularities without losing contact, but print-through is not an issue in digital recording.

6.3 Basic digital recording

The basic principle of digital recording is remarkably simple. Since the medium has only two states, the record waveform will typically be a current whose direction reverses but whose magnitude remains constant, as in Fig.6.2. To

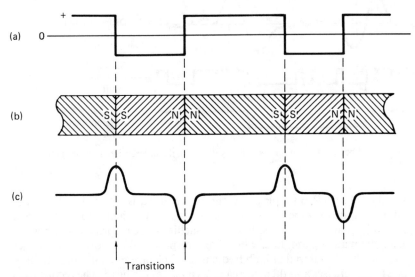

Figure 6.2 Basic digital recording. At (a) the write current in the head is reversed from time to time, leaving a binary magnetization pattern shown at (b). When replayed, the waveform at (c) results because an output is only produced when flux in the head changes. Changes are referred to as transitions.

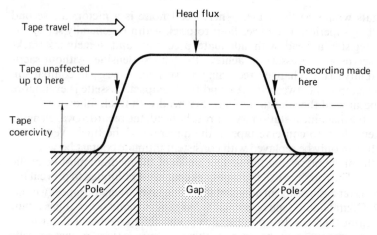

Figure 6.3 The recording is actually made near the trailing pole of the head where the head flux falls below the coercivity of the tape.

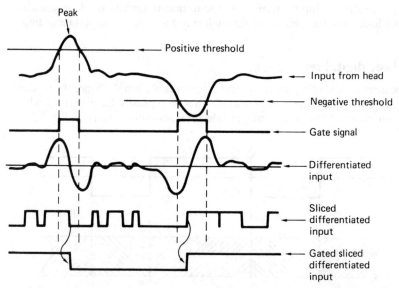

Figure 6.4 Gated peak detection rejects noise by disabling the differentiated output between transitions.

provide the best SNR on replay, the current required is a little less than that needed to saturate the tape, as saturation causes fringing fields around the head and crosstalk in adjacent tracks. In recent machines, the record current may be produced in an analog amplifier which has a response which corrects for losses in the record-head material at high frequencies. The tape encounters a strength of flux which increases and then decreases as it passes the head. The recording is actually made near the trailing pole of the head, as shown in Fig.6.3, where the flux from the head falls below the coercive force needed to change the state of the particles. The steeper the flux gradient on the trailing pole, the shorter the wavelength which can be recorded. This is generally obtained with a relatively wide gap. Bias is unnecessary in digital recording because linearity is not a goal.

When such a recording is replayed, the output of the head will be a differentiated version of the record waveform, because the head only responds to the rate of change of flux.

The initial task of the replay circuits is to reconstruct the record waveform. The amplitude of the signal is of no consequence; what matters is the time at which the write current, and hence the tape flux, reverses. This can be determined by locating the peaks of the replay impulses. At high data rates this can conveniently be done by differentiating the signal and looking for zero crossings. Fig.6.4 shows that this results in noise between the peaks. This problem is overcome by the gated peak detector, where only zero crossings from a pulse which exceeds the threshold will be counted. At the relatively low data rates of digital audio, the record waveform can also be restored by integration, which opposes the differentiation of the head as in Fig.6.5.[1]

There are a number of details which must be added to this simplistic picture in order to appreciate the real position. Fig.6.6 shows that the differentiating effect of the replay process causes the head output initially to rise at 6 dB per octave from a DC response of zero. Although a high-frequency recording can be made throughout the thickness of the medium, the flux deep within the medium cannot couple with the replay head at short wavelengths, and so as recorded wavelength falls, a thinner and thinner layer near the surface remains responsible for the replay flux.[2] This is called thickness loss, although it is a form of separation loss, and it causes a loss of 6 dB per octave, which cancels the differentiating effect to give a region of constant frequency response. The construction of the head results in the same action as that of a two-point transversal filter, as the two poles of the head see the tape with a small delay interposed due to the finite gap. As expected, the head response is like a comb filter with the well-known nulls where flux cancellation takes place across the gap. Clearly the smaller the gap the shorter the wavelength of the first null. This contradicts the requirement of the record head to have a large gap. In quality analog audio

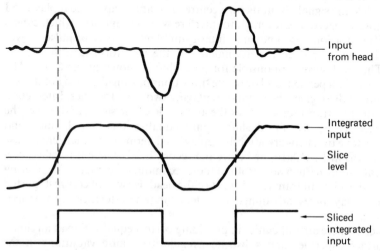

Figure 6.5 Integration method for re-creating write-current waveform.

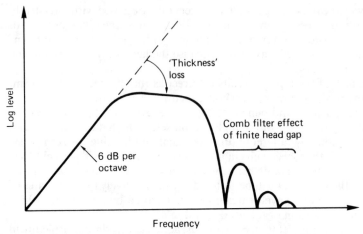

Figure 6.6 The major mechanisms defining magnetic channel bandwidth.

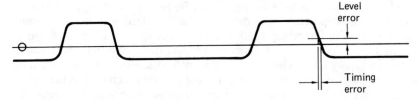

Figure 6.7 A DC offset can cause timing errors.

recorders, it is the norm to have different record and replay heads for this reason, and the same is often true in digital recording.

Fig.6.7 shows that when an uneven duty cycle is recorded, there are a number of problems. The lack of DC response causes a level shift. Combined with the finite rate of change of voltage, the shift can cause timing errors unless care is taken to slice the signal about its own centre. The finite gap in the replay head causes closely spaced flux reversals to interfere with one another, which causes peak shift distortion (also known as inter-symbol interference or pulse crowding) and tends to reduce the asymmetry of the waveform, causing timing errors. The mechanism responsible for peak shift is shown in Fig.6.8(a). The results of two independent and opposite transitions passing the head are shown, and summing these gives the result of replaying two close together. Interaction between the two transitions reduces the amplitude of the signal and moves the peaks apart. Avoidance of peak shift requires equalization of the channel,[3] and this can be done by a network after the replay head, termed an equalizer or pulse sharpener,[4] as in Fig.6.8(b), or before the record head, where it is called pre-compensation, as in Fig.6.8(c). Both of these techniques use transversal filtering to oppose the inherent transversal effect of the head. By way of contrast, partial response replay takes advantage of intersymbol interference, and indeed depends on it.

In practice there are difficulties in providing correct equalization at all times. Tape surface asperities and substrate irregularities cause variations in the intimacy of head contact, which changes the response at high frequencies much

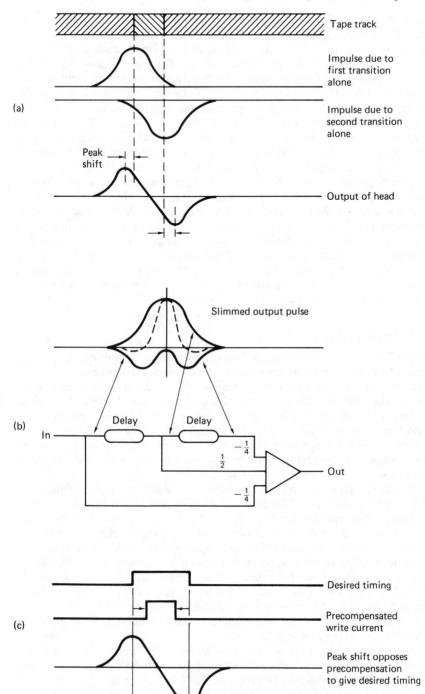

Figure 6.8 (a) Peak shift distortion can be reduced by (b) equalization in replay, or (c) precompensation.

more than at low frequencies, thereby undermining any fixed equalization. In disk drives, the varying radius of the tracks results in a linear density variation of about two to one, and the thickness of the air film, which causes severe spacing loss, is also subject to change. In the Compact Disc, spindle wobble and disk warp mean that the focal plane is continuously moving, and the spot size will vary due to the lag of the focus servo. Optimum equalization is difficult under dynamic conditions, although in principle an adaptive equalizer can be made which uses the timing errors caused by poor equalization to change the response. In most of the above, a clearer picture has been obtained by studying the impulse response of devices than from the frequency response, and this follows from the impulsive nature of digital techniques.

In laser recording, the interference readout process will respond down to DC, but usually the low-frequency portion of the channel is required by the focus and tracking mechanisms, and DC-free channel codes will still be necessary. The high frequency response is governed by the modulation transfer function of the optics, which is normally limited by the numerical aperture of the objective. The frequency response of a laser recorder falls to zero at the cutoff frequency, and unlike magnetic recording, never rises again. The reader is referred to Chapter 13 on Compact Disc and to the treatment of laser optics in Chapter 12 for a more comprehensive explanation of this subject.

6.4 Jitter windows

Fig.6.9 shows several possibilities for a complete digital recording channel. The reconstituted waveform at the output of this channel will now be a replica of the timing of the record signal, with the addition of time uncertainty in the position of the edges due to noise, jitter and dubious equalization. In the same way that binary circuits reject noise by using two voltage levels which are spaced further apart than the uncertainty due to noise, digital recording combats time uncertainty by using flux reversals, known as transitions, at multiples of some basic time period, which is larger than the typical time uncertainty. Fig.6.10 shows how this jitter-rejection mechanism works.

As digital transitions occur at multiples of a basic period, an oscilloscope, which is triggered on random data, will show an eye pattern if connected to the output of the equalizer. Study of the eye pattern reveals how well the coding used suits the channel.[5] Noise closes the eyes in a vertical direction, and jitter closes the eyes in a horizontal direction, as in Fig.6.11. In the centre of the eyes, at regular intervals, the receiver must make binary decisions about the state of the signal, high or low. If the eyes remain sensibly open, this will be possible. Clearly more jitter can be tolerated if there is less noise, and vice versa. Information theory usually only takes account of SNR and bandwidth when assessing channel capacity. Magnetic and optical recorder channels will never achieve these capacities because of jitter.

It is not possible to record data directly onto the medium, because in real data, continuous ones and continuous zeros can occur and, as shown in Fig.6.12, this is effectively a DC component of the source data. Alternate ones and zeros represent the other extreme, a frequency of half the bit rate, which is known as the Nyquist rate. Magnetic recorders will not respond to DC, nor is it possible to discriminate between successive identical bits in a channel subject to time instability.

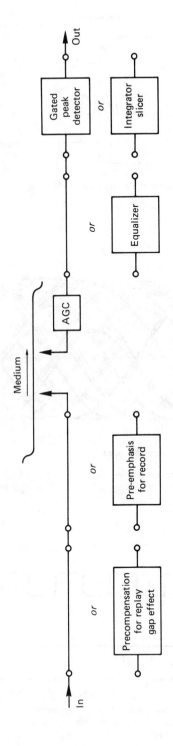

Figure 6.9 A general recording channel showing the various processes described in the text. The system shown here permits recording of a binary waveform.

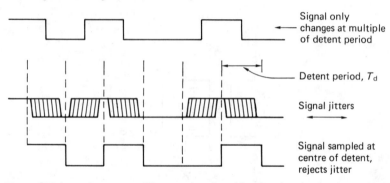

Figure 6.10 A certain amount of jitter can be rejected by changing the signal at multiples of the basic detent period T_d.

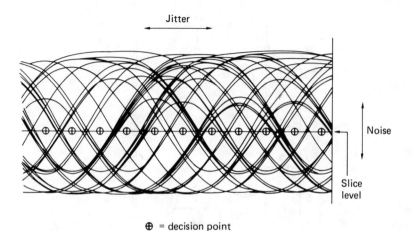

⊕ = decision point

Figure 6.11 At the decision points, the receiver must make binary decisions about the voltage of the signal, whether it is above or below the slicing level. If the eyes remain open, this will be possible in the presence of noise and jitter.

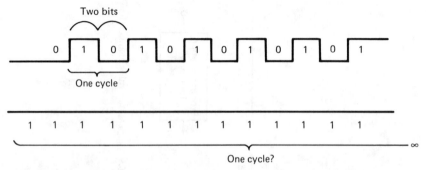

Figure 6.12 The extreme cases of real data. Alternate ones and zeros gives the highest Nyquist rate (= half bit rate). Continuous ones (or zeros) gives DC. Real data fill the spectrum from DC to Nyquist rate.

Both of these problems can be solved with a suitable channel code, which will combine a clock with the data prior to recording, in a way which reduces the DC content, and permits separation of adjacent symbols on replay. Fig.6.13 shows that a channel coder is necessary prior to the record stage, and that a decoder, known as a data separator, is necessary after the replay stage.

Some codes eliminate DC content entirely, which is advantageous for rotary-head recording. Some codes can reduce the channel bandwidth needed by lowering the upper spectrum limit. This permits higher linear density, but usually at the expense of jitter rejection. A code with a narrow spectrum has a number of advantages. The reduction in asymmetry will reduce peak shift, and data separators can lock more readily where the possible frequencies are fewer. In theory, the narrower the spectrum, the less noise, but excessive noise filtering can ruin the equalization, nullifying any gain.

A convenient definition of a channel code (for there are certainly others) is: 'A method of modulating real data such that they can be reliably received despite shortcomings of a real channel, while making maximum economic use of the channel capacity'.

The storage density of data recorders has steadily increased due to improvements in medium and transducer technology, but modern storage densities are also a function of improvements in channel coding. Fig.6.14(a) shows how linear density improvements due to channel coding alone have occurred, and introduces one of the fundamental parameters of a channel code, the density ratio (DR). One definition of density ratio is that it is the worst-case ratio of the number of data bits recorded to the number of transitions in the channel. It can also be thought of as the ratio between the Nyquist rate of the data and the frequency response of the channel. When better hardware is available to increase the capacity of a channel, the use of a higher density-ratio code multiplies the capacity further. It should be appreciated that many of the codes described in this chapter are protected by patents, and that non-optimal codes are often devised to avoid the need to pay royalties on a patented code.

The basic time periods of the recorded signal are called positions or detents, in

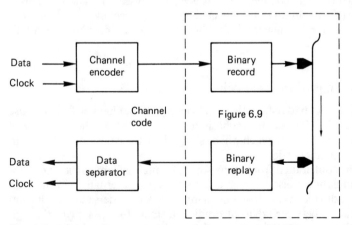

Figure 6.13 In channel coding, the input data and clock are combined into a single waveform called the channel code. On replay the channel code is restored to the original data stream by the data separator.

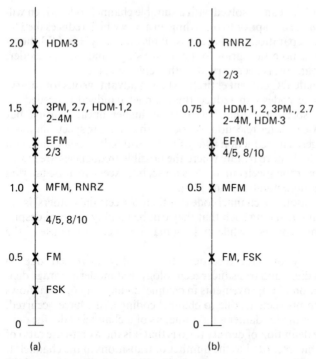

Figure 6.14 (a) Comparison of codes by density ratio; (b) comparison of codes by figure of merit. Note how 4/5, 2/3, 8/10 + RNRZ move up because of good jitter performance; HDM-3 moves down because of jitter sensitivity.

which the recorded flux will be reversed or stay the same according to the state of a channel bit which describes the detent. The symbol used for the units of channel time is T_d. Channel coding is the art of converting real data into channel bits. It is important to appreciate that the convention in coding is that a channel bit one represents a flux change, whereas a zero represents no change. This is confusing because the input data only change where successive bits differ. The differentiating action of magnetic playback has a lot to do with these conventions.

6.5 Shortcomings of the channel

It is necessary fully to understand the shortcomings of the channel if efficient use is to be made of it. Particular emphasis must be placed on the interplay of bandwidth, jitter and noise, which will be shown here to be the key to the design of a successful channel code.

Noise can be contributed from many sources, ranging from particulate, rubbing and modulation noise in magnetic recording to thermal noise in head windings and radio receivers. Crosstalk in multitrack recorders may result from mutual inductance between adjacent heads in a stack. In tapes, print-through produces further unwanted signals. In disk drives, overwrite without erasure, which is the norm, results in a previous recording becoming a source of crosstalk if there is any misregistration with the track when the head records. In laser recording, crosstalk from adjacent tracks results from the intensity function of the laser spot. Owing to all of these noises, the information capacity of the channel is reduced since the resolution of the waveform is limited. This has been defined by Shannon.

Most channels lack time stability, especially recording systems. Everyone is familiar with wow and flutter in analog audio equipment. In digital recording they are termed jitter. Time instability between channels, known as phasing in analog recording, is termed skew. In tape recording, shortcomings in the drive mechanism give rise to relatively slow-speed variations, but higher-frequency jitter is caused by the flexibility of the tape which is excited by surface irregularities at the head/tape interface. Disk drives, both magnetic and optical, have lower jitter due to the mechanism because there is no contact between the head and the medium, and the latter is rigid. Disks do, however, display a cyclic variation in track speed due to spindle runout.

In radio channels, multipath propagation can cause time-instability. This effect is also visible in multimode fibre-optic links. In both cases there can be a comb-filtering effect due to the same waveform arriving at different times. In single-mode fibres the effect is absent. As mentioned earlier, imperfect equalization also results in time-instability.

All of the defects listed reduce channel capacity. Shannon connected bandwidth and noise with information capacity, but there is a need to take into account the effect of time instability. Fig.6.15 shows that, for a signal with finite rate of change of voltage, jitter causes uncertainty about the signal voltage relative to a stable time reference, which has the same effect as noise; in fact some writers give it the name of jitter noise. As the effect is proportional to the slope of the waveform, the effect rises with frequency.[6] This introduces another

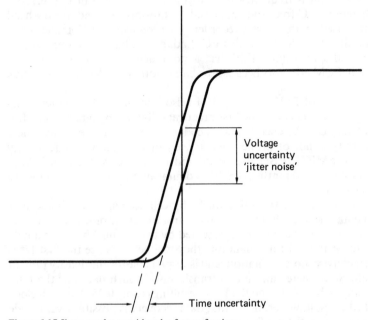

Figure 6.15 Jitter can be considered a form of noise.

important channel code parameter, the jitter margin, also known as the window margin or phase margin (T_w). It is defined as the permitted range of time over which a transition can still be recieved correctly, divided by the data bit-cell period (T).

Since equalization is often difficult in practice, a code which has a large jitter margin will sometimes be used with short recorded wavelengths because it resists the effects of peak shift distortion. Such a code may achieve a working density better than a code with a higher density-ratio but poor jitter performance.

A more realistic comparison of code performance will be obtained by taking into account both density ratio and jitter margin. This is the purpose of the figure of merit (FoM), which is defined as DR $\times T_w$. Fig.6.14(b) shows a comparison of codes by FoM.

6.6 Simple codes

Some actual codes will now be examined.

The essence of channel coding is to convert real data into channel bits. Since the time quantizing is linear, channel codes lend themselves to convenient comparison by analysis of the autocorrelation function. In autocorrelation, a signal is delayed and multiplied by itself. When the delay is swept, a graph is obtained of the product versus delay, known as the autocorrelation function. Most of the parameters of a code can be read from the autocorrelation function at a glance, whereas the more common use of the code spectrum makes this more difficult. Fig.6.16 shows the autocorrelation functions of a number of codes.

The adoption of FM in analog recorders permitted the recording of DC levels for instrumentation and video. When a binary signal is fed to a frequency modulator, the result is frequency shift keying (FSK) shown in Fig. 6.17(a). This is inherently DC-free and suits radio transmission and rotary-head recorders. It is used on the master recorders for production of Compact Disc, and indeed with any VCR used with a PCM adaptor. Chapter 8 covers rotary-head digital audio recording. FSK has a poor density ratio, but this was unimportant in PCM adaptors because the bandwidth of the VCR is more than adequate.

The limiting case of FSK is binary FM (also known as Manchester code) shown in Fig.6.17(b). This was the first practical self-clocking binary code. It is DC-free and very easy to encode and decode. It remains in use today where recording density is not of prime importance, for example in single-density floppy disks, in SMPTE/EBU time code and the reference track in DASH format. It is also specified for the AES/EBU digital audio interconnect standard described in Chapter 5.

In FM there is always a transition at the bit-cell boundary which acts as a clock. For a data one, there is an additional transition at the bit-cell centre. Fig. 6.17(c) shows that each data bit is represented by two channel bits. For a data zero, they will be 10, and for a data one they will be 11. Since the first bit is always one, it conveys no information, and is responsible for the density ratio of only one half. Since there can be two transitions for each data bit, the jitter margin can only be half a bit, and the FoM resulting is only 0.25. The high clock content of FM does, however, mean that data recovery is possible over a wide range of speeds; hence the use for timecode.

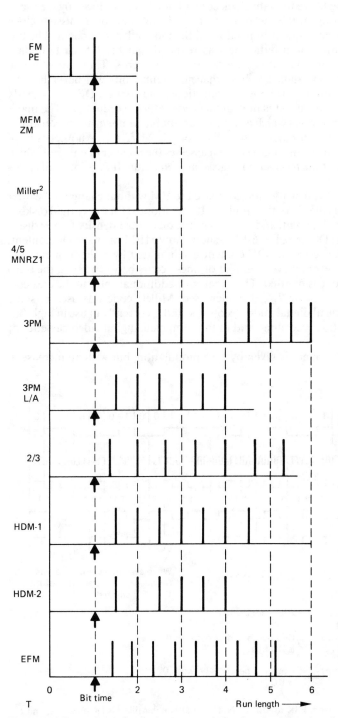

Figure 6.16 Comparison of codes by autocorrelation function of run length.

In MFM the highly redundant clock content of FM was reduced by the use of a phase-locked loop in the receiver which could flywheel over missing clock transitions. This technique is implicit in all the more advanced codes. The bit-cell centre transition on a data one was retained, but the bit-cell boundary transition is now only required between successive zeros. There are still two channel bits for every data bit, but adjacent channel bits will never be one, doubling the minimum time between transitions, and giving a DR of 1. Clearly the coding of the current bit is now influenced by the preceding bit. The maximum number of prior bits which affect the current bit is known as the constraint length L_c, measured in data-bit periods. For MFM $L_c = T$. Another way of considering the constraint length is that it assesses the number of data bits which may be corrupted if the receiver misplaces one transition. If L_c is long, all errors will be burst errors.

MFM doubled the density ratio compared to FM without changing the jitter performance; thus the FoM also doubles. It was adopted for many rigid disks at the time of its development, and remains in use on double-density floppy disks. It is not, however, DC-free. Fig.6.17(d) shows how MFM can have DC content, and that in Miller^2 code the DC content is eliminated by a slight increase in complexity. Wherever an even number of ones occurs between zeros, the transition at the last one is omitted. This creates an additional entry in the autocorrelation function because T_{max} has increased. Miller^2 code was used in some early stationary-head digital audio recorders, and is currently in use in high-bit-rate instrumentation recording, and in the composite digital video cassette for professional use.[7,8]

A similar performance is given by zero modulation, but with an increase in complexity.[9]

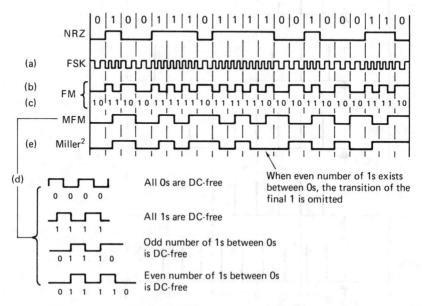

Figure 6.17 Evolution from FSK to Miller^2. Note that although Miller^2 is DC-free T_{max} and L_c are worse than MFM.

6.7 Group codes

Further improvements in coding rely on converting patterns of real data to patterns of channel bits with more desirable characteristics using a conversion table known as a codebook. If a data symbol of m bits is considered, it can have 2^m different combinations. As it is intended to discard undesirable patterns to improve the code, it follows that the number of channel bits n must be greater than m. The number of patterns which can be discarded is:

$$2^n - 2^m$$

One name for the principle is group code recording (GCR), and an important parameter is the code rate, defined as:

$$\text{Code rate, } R = \frac{m}{n}$$

It will be evident that the jitter margin T_w is numerically equal to the code rate, and so a high code rate is undesirable. The choice of patterns which are used in the codebook will be those which give the desired balance between clock content, bandwidth and DC content.

In Fig.6.18 it is shown that the upper spectral limit can be made to be some fraction of the channel bit rate according to the minimum distance between ones in the channel bits. This is known as T_{min}, also referred to as the minimum transition parameter M, and in both cases is measured in data bits T. It can be obtained by multiplying the number of channel detent periods between transitions by the code rate. Unfortunately, codes are measured by the number of consecutive zeros in the channel bits, given the symbol d, which is always one less than the number of detent periods. In fact T_{min} is numerically equal to the Density Ratio.

$$T_{min} = M = DR = \frac{(d+1) \times m}{n}$$

It will be evident that choosing a low code rate could increase the density ratio, but it will impair the jitter margin. The figure of merit is:

$$\text{FoM} = DR \times T_w = \frac{(d+1) \times m^2}{n^2}$$

since $T_w = \dfrac{m}{n}$

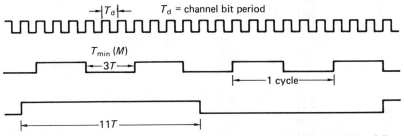

Figure 6.18 A channel code can control its spectrum by placing limits on $T_{min}(M)$ and T_{max} which define upper and lower frequencies. Ratio of T_{max}/T_{min} determines asymmetry of waveform and predicts DC content and peak shift. Example shown is EFM.

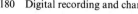

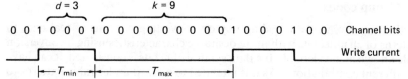

Figure 6.19 Channel-bit convention is that a 1 represents a transition. Parameters d and k are the number of zeros between ones. $d = $ min, $k = $ max. Clearly T_{min}, T_{max} are greater than d, k by one channel-bit period.

Fig.6.19 shows that the lower spectral limit is influenced by the maximum distance between transitions T_{max}. This is also obtained by multiplying the maximum number of detent periods between transitions by the code rate. Again, codes are measured by the maximum number of zeros between channel ones, k, and so:

$$T_{max} = \frac{(k+1) \times m}{n}$$

and the maximum/minimum ratio P is:

$$P = \frac{k+1}{d+1}$$

The length of time between channel transitions is known as the run length. Another name for this class is the run-length-limited (RLL) codes.[10] Since m data bits are considered as one symbol, the constraint length L_c will be increased in RLL codes to at least m. It is however possible for a code to have run-length limits without it being a group code.

In practice, the junction of two adjacent channel symbols may violate run-length limits, and it is necessary to create a further codebook of symbol size $2n$ which converts violating codes to acceptable codes. This is known as merging, and follows the golden rule that the substitute $2n$ symbol must finish with a

Table 6.1 The codebook of 4/5 code. Maximum number of zeros (k) is two; thus T_{max} is $4(k+1)/5 = 2.4$ bits. Adjacent ones are permitted: thus DR $= 4/5$.

Data Decimal	Binary	Channel bits
0	0000	11001
1	0001	11011
2	0010	10010
3	0011	10011
4	0100	11101
5	0101	10101
6	0110	10110
7	0111	10111
8	1000	11010
9	1001	01001
10	1010	01010
11	1011	01011
12	1100	11110
13	1101	01101
14	1110	01110
15	1111	01111

pattern which eliminates the possibility of a subsequent violation. These patterns must also differ from all other symbols.

Substitution may also be used to different degrees in the same nominal code, to allow a choice of maximum run length, e.g. 3PM.[11] The maximum number of symbols involved in a substitution is denoted by r.[12,13] There are many RLL codes, and the parameters d, k, m, n and r are a way of comparing them.

Sometimes the code rate forms the name of the code, as in 2/3, 8/10 and EFM; at other times the code may be named after the d, k parameters, as in 2,7 code.

Various examples will be given which illustrate the principles involved.

4/5 code uses 16 out of 32 possible channel symbols to represent the data. The criterion for 4/5 was high clock content to give immunity to jitter, without a great sacrifice of DR.[6] The codebook is shown in Table 6.1. Each one in the code represents a flux reversal, and there are never more than three channel bits (2.4 data bits) of time between clock edges ($k=2$). This permits a simple AGC system to be used in the read circuits. As codes had to be rejected to achieve the main criterion, the remaining codes have to be accepted; thus the minimum run length is only one bit, as adjacent ones are allowed in the code book ($d=0$). The code is thus described as 0,1,4,5,1. $L_c = 4T$, and the density ratio is given by:

$$DR = \frac{(d+1) \times m}{n} = 0.8$$

Data	Code
0 0	1 0 1
0 1	1 0 0
1 0	0 0 1
1 1	0 1 0

(a)

Data				Illegal code						Substitution					
0	0	0	0	1	0	1	1	0	1	1	0	1	0	0	0
0	0	0	1	1	0	1	1	0	0	1	0	0	0	0	0
1	0	0	0	0	0	1	1	0	1	0	0	1	0	0	0
1	0	0	1	0	0	1	1	0	0	0	1	0	0	0	0

(b)

Figure 6.20 2/3 code. At (a) two data bits (m) are expressed as three channel bits (n) without adjacent transitions ($d=1$). Violations are dealt with by substitution.

$$DR = \frac{(d+1)m}{n} = \frac{2 \times 2}{3} = 1.33$$

Adjacent data pairs can break the encoding rule; in these cases substitutions are made, as shown at (b).

The spectrum needed is thus 1.25 times that of the data, but there can be no merging violations, and an extremely good window margin T_w of $0.8\,T$ is obtained, giving an FoM of 0.64.

This code was used by the IBM 6250BPI tape format and represented an improvement factor of nearly four over the 1600BPI phase-encoded (PE) system which preceded it. The FoM was better than PE by a factor of more than $2\tfrac{1}{2}$, thus reducing the improvements needed to the head and tape.

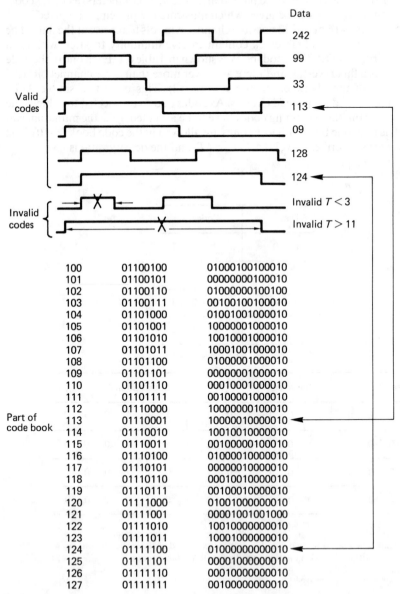

100	01100100	01000100100010
101	01100101	00000000100010
102	01100110	01000000100100
103	01100111	00100100100010
104	01101000	01001001000010
105	01101001	10000001000010
106	01101010	10010001000010
107	01101011	10001001000010
108	01101100	01000001000010
109	01101101	00000001000010
110	01101110	00010001000010
111	01101111	00100001000010
112	01110000	10000000100010
113	01110001	10000010000010
114	01110010	10010010000010
115	01110011	00100000100010
116	01110100	01000010000010
117	01110101	00000010000010
118	01110110	00010010000010
119	01110111	00100010000010
120	01111000	01001000000010
121	01111001	00001001001000
122	01111010	10010000000010
123	01111011	10001000000010
124	01111100	01000000000010
125	01111101	00001000000010
126	01111110	00010000000010
127	01111111	00100000000010

Figure 6.21 EFM code: $d=2$, $k=10$. Eight data bits produce fourteen channel bits plus three packing bits. Code rate is 8/17. $\mathrm{DR}=(3\times18)/17=1.41$.

Fig.6.20(a) shows an optimized code which also illustrates the process of merging. This is a 1,7,2,3,2 code known as 2/3. It is designed to have a large window to resist peak shift in disk drives, along with a good density ratio.[14] In 2/3 code, pairs of data bits create symbols of three adjacent channel bits. For bandwidth reduction, all codes with adjacent ones are eliminated. This halves the code spectrum, and the density ratio improves accordingly:

$$\mathrm{DR} = \frac{(d+1) \times m}{n} = \frac{2 \times 2}{3} = 1.33$$

In Fig.6.21(b), the effect of some data combinations will be code violations. Thus pairs of three channel-bit symbols are replaced with a new six channel-bit symbol. L_c is thus $4\,T$, the same as for 4/5 code. The jitter window is given by:

$$T_w = \frac{m}{n} = \frac{2}{3}T$$

and the FoM is:

$$\frac{2}{3} \times \frac{4}{3} = \frac{8}{9}$$

This an extremely good figure for an RLL code, and is some 10% better than the FoM of 3PM[15] and 2,7.

Fig.6.21 shows an 8,14 code (EFM) used in the Compact Disc. Here eight-bit symbols are represented by 14-bit channel symbols.[16] There are 256 combinations of eight data bits, whereas 14 bits have 16K combinations. Of these, only 267 satisfy the criteria that the maximum run length shall not exceed 11 channel bits ($k = 10$) nor be less than three channel bits ($d = 2$). A section of the codebook is shown in the figure. In fact 258 codes of the 267 possible codes are used, because two unique synchronizing patterns are used to denote the beginning of a subcode block (see Chapter 13). It is not possible to prevent violations between adjacent channel symbols by substitution, and three extra merging bits are necessary between symbols. These bits are used for the additional task of DC control, since the CD channel code must be DC- free. The packing bits are selected by computing the digital sum value (DSV) of the channel bits. The DSV is calculated by adding one to a count for every channel bit period the code waveform is high, and by subtracting one for every period it is low. Fig.6.22 shows that if two successive channel symbols have the same sense of DC content, they can be made to cancel one another by placing an extra transition in the packing bits, which has the effect of inverting the second pattern, and reversing its DC content. The DC-free code can be high-pass filtered on replay, and the lower-frequency signals are then used by the focus and tracking servos without noise due to the DC content of the modulation. Encoding EFM is complex, but this is acceptable because there are relatively few CD cutters made. Decoding is simpler, and can be done with a lookup table. The relationship between the data patterns and channel bits was computer-optimised to permit the implementation of a programmable logic array (PLA) decoder with minimum complexity.

Owing to the inclusion of the merging bits, the code rate becomes 8/17, and the density ratio becomes:

$$\frac{3 \times 8}{17} = 1.41$$

and the FoM is:

$$\frac{3 \times 8^2}{17^2} = 0.66$$

The code is thus a 2,10,8,17, r system, where r only has meaning in the context of DC control.[17] The constraints d and k can still be met with $r=1$ because of the merging bits. The figure of merit is less useful for optical media, because the straight-line frequency response does not produce peak shift, and the rigid, non-contact medium is largely jitter-free. The density ratio and freedom from DC are the most important factors here.

A different approach to merging is taken by the 4/6M code used in multitrack ProDigi format recorders. As will be seen from Table 6.2, the input data group will be either four bits or eight bits, depending on the data pattern, and will be encoded into six or nine channel bits. In some channel patterns, the first channel bit will be the opposite of the last channel bit of the previous group. As there are never two adjacent ones in the channel patterns, T_{min} is 1.33 T_d, and so the density ratio is also 1.33. As the code rate is 4/6, the jitter window T_w is 0.66. The FoM becomes 0.89 which is the same as that of 2/3.

The low tape consumption of RDAT is achieved by a combination of narrow track-spacing and high linear data density along the track (see Chapter 8). The latter is achieved by a combination of head design and the channel code used.[18] The head gap used is typically 0.25 μm.

The essential feature of the channel code of RDAT is that it must be able to work well in an azimuth recording system. There are many channel codes available, but few of them are suitable for azimuth recording because of the large amount of crosstalk. The crosstalk cancellation of azimuth recording fails at low frequencies, so a suitable channel code must not only be free of DC, but it must suppress low frequencies as well. A further issue is that erasure is by

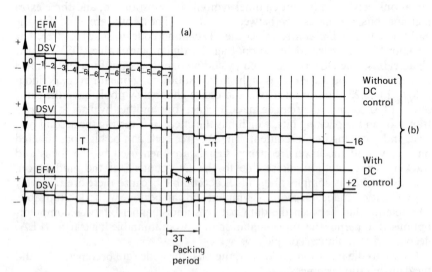

Figure 6.22 (a) Digital sum value example calculated from EFM waveform. (b) Two successive 14T symbols without DC control (upper) give DSV of -16. Additional transition (*) results in DSV of $+2$, anticipating negative content of next symbol.

overwriting, and as the heads are optimized for short-wavelength working, best erasure will be when the ratio between the longest and shortest wavelengths in the recording is small.

In Table 6.3, some examples from the 8/10 group code of RDAT are shown. Clearly a channel waveform which spends as much time high as low has no net DC content, and so all ten bit-patterns which meet this criterion of zero disparity can be found. As adjacent channel ones are permitted, the window margin and DR will be 0.8, giving an FoM of 0.64. This is the same as the IBM 4/5 code, but by using larger symbols, more combinations are available for optimization. Unfortunately there are not enough DC-free combinations in ten channel bits

Table 6.2 The 4/6M code of ProDigi multitrack recorders. Four or six data bits become six or nine channel bits. X represents 1 if the end of previous group is zero and vice versa.

Data	Channel bits
0000	010000
000100	X00010001
000101	X00100001
000110	X01000001
000111	X01010001
001000	010000001
001001	010010001
001010	010100001
001011	X00010000
001100	X01010000
001101	010010000
001110	X00100000
001111	010100000
0100	010010
0101	X00100
0110	010100
0111	X01000
1000	X01001
1001	010001
1010	X00010
1011	X01010
1100	X00000
1101	X00001
1110	X00101
1111	010101

Table 6.3 Some of the 8/10 codebook for non-zero DSV symbols (two entries) and zero DSV symbols (one entry)

Eight-bit dataword	Ten-bit codeword	DSV	Alternative codeword	DSV
00010000	1101010010	0		
00010001	0100010010	2	1100010010	−2
00010010	0101010010	0		
00010011	0101110010	0		
00010100	1101110001	2	0101110001	−2
00010101	1101110011	2	0101110011	−2
00010110	1101110110	2	0101110110	−2
00010111	1101110010	0		

$$a = A + CZ + Y\,(\overline{C} \oplus \overline{F}\,(G + H))$$

$$b = A\,(B + D\overline{E}) + \overline{A}\,(\overline{B} + \overline{C})$$

$$c = \overline{A}C + A\,(\overline{D} + E) + BDE$$

$$d = A\,(C + BD\overline{E}) + CDE + \overline{C}Z + (\overline{A}\overline{B} \oplus \overline{F}GHY)$$

$$\overline{e} = (AB + \overline{D})\,\overline{E} + \overline{A}BCDE + Y\overline{F}\,(\overline{G} + \overline{H})$$

$$f = \overline{A}\,\overline{E}\,[C + (B \oplus D)] + [(\overline{D} + C\overline{E}) \oplus F\,(\overline{G} + \overline{H})]$$

$$\overline{g} = \overline{F}\,\overline{G} + Y + (B + C)\,Z$$

$$h = FG\overline{H} + \overline{F}\,\overline{Y}$$

$$i = H + FG + \overline{F}Y \qquad \text{where } Y = \overline{A}\,(\overline{B} + C)\,D\overline{E}$$

$$j = F\overline{G} + \overline{F}\,\overline{Y} \qquad\qquad Z = \overline{A}\,\overline{D}\,\overline{E}\,F\,(\overline{G} + \overline{H})$$

(a)

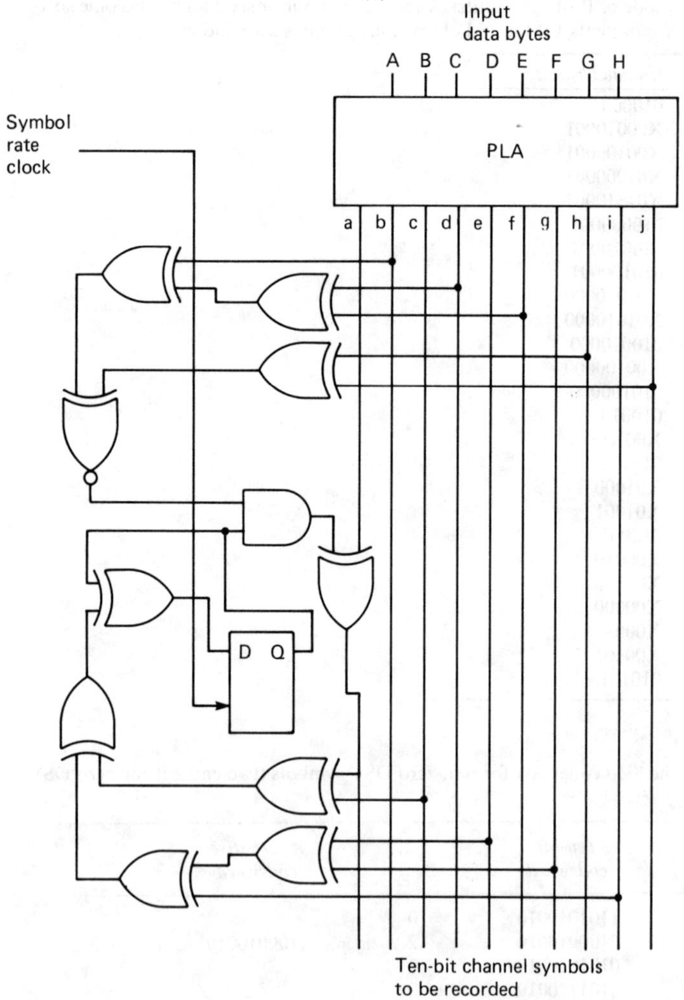

(b)

Figure 6.23 At (a) the truth table of the symbol encoding prior to DSV control. At (b) this circuit controls code disparity by remembering non-zero DSV in the latch and selecting a subsequent symbol with opposite DSV.

to provide the 256 patterns necessary to record eight data bits. A further constraint is that it is desirable to restrict the maximum run length to improve overwrite capability and reduce peak shift. In the 8/10 code of RDAT, no more than three channel zeros are permitted between channel ones, which makes T_{max} only four times T_{min}. There are only 153 ten-bit patterns which are within this maximum run length and which have a DSV of zero.

The remaining 103 data combinations are recorded using channel patterns that have non-zero DSV. Two channel patterns are allocated to each of the 103 data patterns. One of these has a DSV of $+2$, the other has a DSV of -2. For simplicity, the only difference between them is that the first channel bit is inverted. The choice of which channel-bit pattern to use is based on the DSV due to the previous code.

For example, if several bytes have been recorded with some of the 153 DC-free patterns, the DSV of the code will be zero. The first data byte is then found which has no zero disparity pattern. If the $+2$ DSV pattern is used, the code at the end of the pattern will also become $+2$ DSV. When the next pattern of this kind is found, the code having DSV of -2 will automatically be selected to return the channel DSV to zero. In this way the code is kept DC-free, but the maximum distance between transitions can be shortened. A code of this kind is known as a low disparity code.

In order to reduce the complexity of encoding logic, it is usual in GCR to computer-optimize the relationship between data patterns and code patterns. This has been done for 8/10 so that the conversion can be performed in a programmed logic array. Only DC-free or DSV $= +2$ patterns are produced by the logic, since the DSV $= -2$ pattern can be obtained by reversing the first bit. The assessment of DSV is performed in an interesting manner. If in a pair of channel bits the second bit is one, the pair must be DC-free because each detent has a different value. If the five even channel bits in a ten-bit pattern are checked for parity and the result is one, the pattern could have DSV of 0, ± 4 or ± 8. If the result is zero, the DSV could be ± 2, ± 6 or ± 10. However, the codes used are known to be either zero or $+2$ DSV, so the state of the parity bit discriminates between them.

Fig.6.23(a) shows the truth table of the PLA, and Fig.6.23(b) shows the encoding circuit. The lower set of XOR gates calculate parity on the latest pattern to be recorded, and store the DSV bit in the latch. The next data byte to be recorded is fed to the PLA, which outputs a ten-bit pattern. If this is a zero disparity code, it passes to the output unchanged. If it is a DSV $= +2$ code, this will be detected by the upper XOR gates. If the latch is set, this means that a previous pattern had been $+2$ DSV, and so the first bit of the channel pattern is inverted by the XOR gate in that line, and the latch will be cleared because the DSV of the code has been returned to zero.

Decoding is simpler, because there is a direct relationship between ten-bit codes and eight-bit data.

6.8 Convolutional RLL codes

It has been mentioned that a code can be run length limited without being a group code. An example of this is HDM-1 code which is used in DASH Format (digital audio stationary head: see Chapter 9) recorders. The coding is best

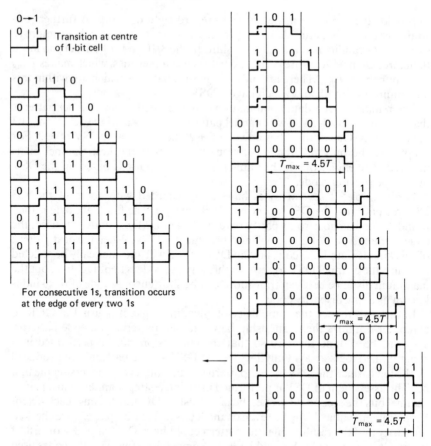

Figure 6.24 HDM-1 code of the DASH format is encoded according to the above rules. Transitions will never be closer than 1.5 bits, nor further apart than 4.5 bits.

described as convolutional, and is rather complex, as Fig.6.24 shows.[19] The DR of 1.5 is achieved by treating the input bit pattern of 0,1 as a single symbol which has a transition recorded at the centre of the one. The code then depends upon whether the code continues with ones, or reverts to zeros. The shorter run-lengths are used to describe sequential ones; the longer run-lengths describe sequential zeros, up to a maximum run-length of 4.5 T, with a constraint length of 5.5 T. In HDM-2, a derivative, the maximum run-length is reduced to 4 T with the penalty that L_c becomes 7.5 T.

The 2/4M code used by the Mitsubishi ProDigi quarter-inch format recorders[20] is also convolutional, and has an identical density ratio and window margin to HDM-1. T_{max} is eight bits. Neither HDM-1 nor 2/4M claim to be DC-free, but this is of less consequence in stationary heads, where linear density is of greater importance. Encoding of 2/4M is just as devious as HDM-1, and is shown in Fig.6.25. Two data bits form a group, and result in four channel bits where there are always two channel zeros between ones, to obtain T_{min} of 1.5. However, there are numerous exceptions to the coding to prevent run length violations, which require a running sample of ten data bits to be examined; this

X X X X E4 E3 E2 E1 D D L1 L2 L3 L4 X X X X

Running sample of
ten data bits

DD = current set of data bits
E(N) = earlier data bits
L(N) = later data bits

(a)

Data bits DD	Channel bits C_1 C_2 C_3 C_4	Exceptions and substitutions
00	0 1 0 0 0 0 0 0 0 0 0 1	E4 E3 = 10 E4 E3 ≠ 10 and E2 E2 = 10 and L1 L2 ≠ 01 E4 E3 ≠ 10 and E2 E1 = 10 and L1 L2 = 01
01	0 0 1 0	
10	Y 0 0 1 0 1 0 0 0 0 0 1 0 0 0 0	E2 E1 ≠ 10 and L1 L2 = 00 E2 E1 = 10 and L1 L2 = 10 and L3 L4 = 00 E2 E1 = 10 and L1 L2 = 00 E2 E1 = 10 and L1 L2 = 10 and L3 L4 = 00
11	Y 0 0 0	

Y = XNOR of $C_3 C_4$ of previous DD

(b)

Figure 6.25 Coding rules for 2/4 M code. At (a) a running sample is made of two data bits DD and earlier and later bits. At (b) two data bits become the four channel bits shown except when the substitutions specified are made.

is why the code has to be described as convolutional rather than a substituting group code.

6.9 Randomized NRZ

Genuine data are unsuitable for direct recording, because, as has been seen, they have an undefined maximum run-length, T_{max}, which gives severe problems with clock recovery, AGC and DC content. In other respects, however, raw data has potential because the density ratio of unity is combined with the extremely good jitter window, which is also unity, to give an FoM of 1, which is higher than the best group codes.

It is possible to convert raw data into a channel code in a nonredundant fashion by performing a modulo-2 (XOR) addition with a pseudo-random sequence. As Fig.6.26 shows, the result of this process is that T_{max} is drastically reduced. Obviously the same pseudo-random sequence must be provided on replay, synchronized to the data, if there is to be correct recovery. In practice the system cannot accept truly random data, since if by chance the data are identical to the pseudo-random sequence, the system breaks down. The probability of such an occurrence is low, and the error-correction system would deal with it.

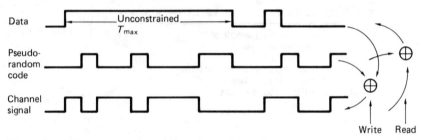

Figure 6.26 Modulo-2 addition with a pseudo-random code removes unconstrained runs in real data. Identical process must be provided on replay.

The so-called randomized NRZI coding has been used in digital video recorders (see Chapter 11), since the pseudo-random sequence reduces the DC content of the waveform, which is essential if there is a rotary transformer in the channel.

6.10 Partial response

It has been stated that the head acts as a transversal filter, because it has two poles. In addition the output is differentiated, so that the head may be thought of as a $(1-D)$ impulse response system, where D is the delay which is a function of the tape speed and gap size. It is this delay which results in intersymbol interference. Conventional equalizers attempt to oppose this effect, and succeed in raising the noise level in the process of making the frequency response linear. Fig.6.27 shows that the frequency response necessary to pass data with insignificant peak shift is a bandwidth of half the bit rate, which is the Nyquist rate. In Class IV partial response, the frequency response of the system is made to have nulls at DC and at the Nyquist rate. This is achieved by an overall impulse response of $(1-D^2)$ where D is now the bit period. There are a number of ways in which this can be done.

If the head gap is made equal to one bit, the $(1-D)$ head response may be converted to the desired response by the use of a $(1+D)$ filter, as in Fig.6.28(a).[21]

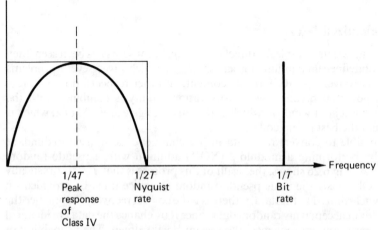

Figure 6.27 Class IV response has spectral nulls at DC and the Nyquist rate, giving a noise advantage, since magnetic replay signal is weak at both frequencies in a high-density channel.

Alternatively, a head of unspecified gapwidth may be connected to an integrator, and equalized flat to reproduce the record current waveform before being fed to a $(1 - D^2)$ filter as in Fig.6.28(b).[22]

The result of both of these techniques is a ternary signal. The eye pattern has two sets of eyes as in Fig.6.28(c).[22] When slicing such a signal, a smaller amount of noise will cause an error than in the binary case.

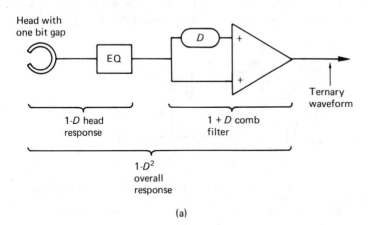

(a)

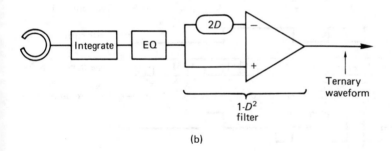

(b)

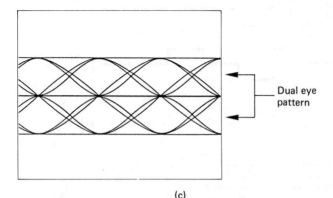

(c)

Figure 6.28 (a), (b) Two ways of obtaining partial response. (c) Characteristic eye pattern of ternary signal.

The treatment of the signal thus far represents an equalization technique, and not a channel code. However, to take full advantage of Class IV partial response, suitable precoding is necessary prior to recording, which does then constitute a channel-coding technique. This precoding is shown in Fig.6.29(a). Data are added modulo-2 to themselves with a two-bit delay. The effect of this precoding is that the outer levels of the ternary signals, which represent data ones, alternate in polarity on all odd bits and on all even bits. This is because the precoder acts like two interleaved one-bit delay circuits, as in Fig.6.29(b). As

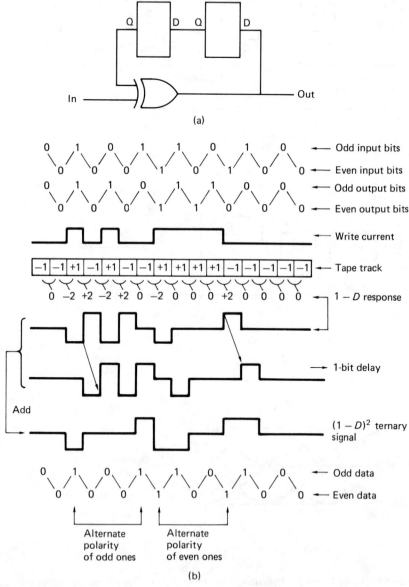

Figure 6.29 Class IV precoding at (a) causes redundancy in replay signal as derived in (b).

this alternation of polarity is a form of redundancy, it can be used to recover the 3 dB SNR loss encountered in slicing a ternary eye pattern. Viterbi decoding[24] can be used for this purpose. In Viterbi decoding, each channel bit is not sliced individually; the slicing decision is made in the context of adjacent decisions. Fig.6.30 shows a replay waveform which is so noisy that, at the decision point, the signal voltage crosses the centre of the eye, and the slicer alone cannot tell whether the correct decision is an inner or an outer level. In this case, the decoder essentially allows both decisions to stand, in order to see what happens. A symbol representing indecision is output. It will be seen from the figure that as subsequent bits are received, one of these decisions will result in an absurd situation, which indicates that the other decision was the right one. The decoder can then locate the undecided symbol and set it to the correct value.

Clearly a ternary signal having a dual eye pattern is more sensitive than a binary signal, and it is important to keep the maximum run length T_{max} small in order to have accurate AGC. The use of pseudo-random coding along with partial response equalization and precoding is a logical combination.[25]

Another way of using the information content of a ternary signal is to have the three states determine the amount by which a multilevel parameter changes from one channel bit to the next. A chart of this parameter versus channel symbols is called a trellis, as in Fig.6.31. In trellis coding, the record signal is precoded so that only certain paths through the trellis are valid, and others must represent errors, which can be corrected by deducing the most likely path from

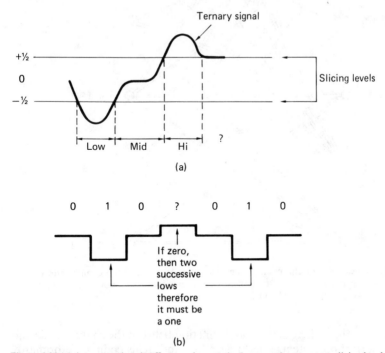

Figure 6.30 (a) A ternary signal suffers a noise penalty because there are two slicing levels. (b) The redundancy is used to determine the bit value in the presence of noise. Here the pulse height has been reduced to make it ambiguous 1/0, but only 1 is valid as zero violates the redundancy rules.

Figure 6.31 An example of trellis coding. The eight states of the trellis represent a three-bit symbol ($2^3 = 8$). From any starting state, there are four possible destinations according to a four-bit (0–15) symbol from the channel.

the received path.[26] There is then no distinction between the channel code and the error-correction system. Viterbi decoding and trellis coding are primarily applicable to channels with random errors due to Gaussian statistics, and they cannot cope with burst errors. In a head-noise- limited system, however, the use of a Viterbi detector could increase the power of an error-correction system by relieving it of the need to correct random errors due to noise. The error-correction system could then concentrate on correcting burst errors unimpaired. The significance of this statement will become clearer upon referring to Chapter 7.

6.11 Graceful degradation

In all of the channel codes described here, all the data bits have equal significance, and if the characteristics of the channel degrade, the probability of reception of all bits falls equally rapidly. In digital audio, all the bits are not of equal significance, since an error in the LSB of a sample might pass unnoticed, whereas an MSB error would be intolerable. For applications where the bandwidth of the channel is unpredictable, or where it may improve as a particular technology is mastered, a different form of channel coding has been proposed[27] where the probability of reception of bits is not equal. The channel spectrum is divided in such a way that the most significant bits of a sample occupy the lowest frequencies, and the least significant bits occupy the highest frequencies.

When the channel bandwidth of such a signal is reduced, the eye pattern is affected such that some eyes become indeterminate, but others remain sensibly open at regular intervals, guaranteeing reception of clocking and high-order bits. The effect is that low-order bits are in error. In a stream of audio samples, this means that the waveform is sensibly the same, but it suffers from an increased noise level.

The error-correction techniques needed will be different, in that codewords must be assembled from bits in different samples which have the same significance.

6.12 Synchronizing

In most of the codes described here, an improvement in some desired parameter has been obtained either by a sacrifice of some other parameter or by an increase in complexity. Often it is the clock content which suffers, so that the number of channel bits which have to be measured between transitions becomes quite large. The only way in which the channel code can be decoded is to use a phase-locked loop to regenerate the channel-bit clock. A fixed-frequency clock would be of no use, as even if the medium could be made to move at the right speed for the channel-bit rate to match the clock rate, the instantaneous errors due to jitter would be insuperable. In phase-locked loops, the voltage-controlled oscillator is driven by a phase error measured between the output and some reference, such that the oscillator eventually runs at the same frequency as the reference. If a divider is placed between the VCO and the phase comparator, as in Fig.6.32, the VCO frequency can be made to be a multiple of the reference. This also has the effect of making the loop more heavily damped. If a channel code is used as a reference to a PLL, the loop will be able to make a phase comparison whenever a transition arrives, but when there are channel zeros between transitions, the loop will flywheel at the last known frequency and phase until it can rephase at a subsequent transition. In this way, cycles of the

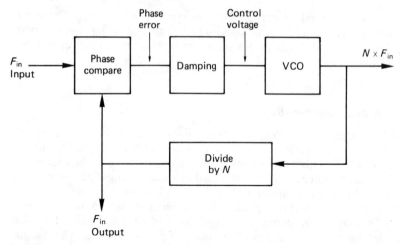

Figure 6.32 A typical phase-locked loop where the VCO is forced to run at a multiple of the input frequency. If the input ceases, the output will continue for a time at the same frequency until it drifts.

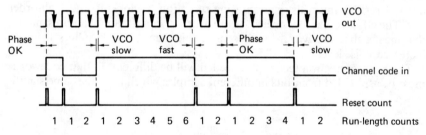

Figure 6.33 In order to reconstruct the channel patterns, a phase-locked loop is fed with the channel code, and freewheels between transitions, correcting its phase at each one. Counting the VCO edges (↓) between transitions reconstructs the channel bits. If the medium changes speed, the VCO will track. If the maximum run length is too long, the VCO will not be able to phase correct often enough, and may miscount channel bits in the presence of jitter.

VCO can be counted to measure the number of channel zeros between transitions and hence to decode the information. Fig.6.33 illustrates this mechanism.

Clearly data cannot be separated if the PLL is not locked, but it cannot be locked until it has seen transitions for a reasonable period. The solution is to precede each data block with a pattern of transitions whose sole purpose is to provide a timing reference for synchronizing the phase-locked loop. This pattern is known as a preamble. In MFM, the preamble will usually be the result of encoding all zeros, which is a square wave at the bit rate. In high-density recording, the preamble may be some simple fraction of the bit rate to avoid the attenuation of the highest frequencies when the PLL is attempting to lock. In magnetic recording there is almost always a postamble at the end of the data block. Again a few zeros are recorded after the real data. When magnetic heads are turned off at the end of a write, there is often a transient which corrupts the last bits written. The postamble can be damaged in this way without consequence. Another reason for a postamble is to enable a block to be read backwards. This is often done in computer magtapes to shorten access time. Time code has to be legible in either direction and at varying speeds. Some channel codes are designed to work backwards, such as phase encoding, 4/5GCR, zero modulation and FM. For reverse reading, the postamble will be the same length as the preamble; otherwise it will be much shorter.

Once the PLL has locked to the preamble, a data stream and a clock will emerge from the data separator. It is then vital to know at what point in the data stream the preamble finishes and the actual data commences. In serial recording, words are recorded one after the other, one bit at a time, with no spaces in between, so that although the designer knows that a block contains, say, twelve words of sixteen bits each, the medium simply holds 192 bits in a row. If the exact position of the first bit is not known, then it is not possible to put all the bits in the right places in the right words. The effect of sync slippage is devastating, because a one-bit disparity between the data-bit count and the bit stream will corrupt every word in the block, which is just as bad as a massive dropout.[28]

The synchronization of the data separator and the synchronization to the block format are two distinct problems, and they are often solved separately. At the end of the preamble, a so-called sync pattern may be inserted. This is a pattern which is identical for every block; it will be recognised by the replay circuitry and used to reset the bit count through the block. By counting bits from the sync pattern and dividing by the wordlength, the replay circuitry will be able to determine the position of the boundaries between words. The sync pattern must be chosen with care, so that a bit or bits in error does not cause sync to be recognized in the wrong place. Such a pattern is designed to be as different as possible to itself however many places it is shifted, which is the same as saying it has a low autocorrelation. A good example of a low-autocorrelation sync pattern is that used in the D-1 format DVTR, which is 0CAF hex, or

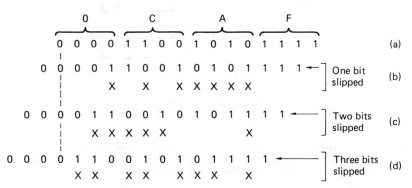

Figure 6.34 A synchronizing pattern having a low autocorrelation is shown here at (a). In (b), the pattern is one bit from synchronization, and fails to match in seven places (shown as X). In (c) the pattern is two bits away from synchronization, and fails to match in six places. At (d) the pattern is three bits away from synchronization, and fails in eight places.

Owing to the large number of differences when the pattern shifts, there is a much reduced probability of an error reading the pattern causing false synchronization. The pattern shown is used in the D-1 format DVTR for both audio and video data blocks.

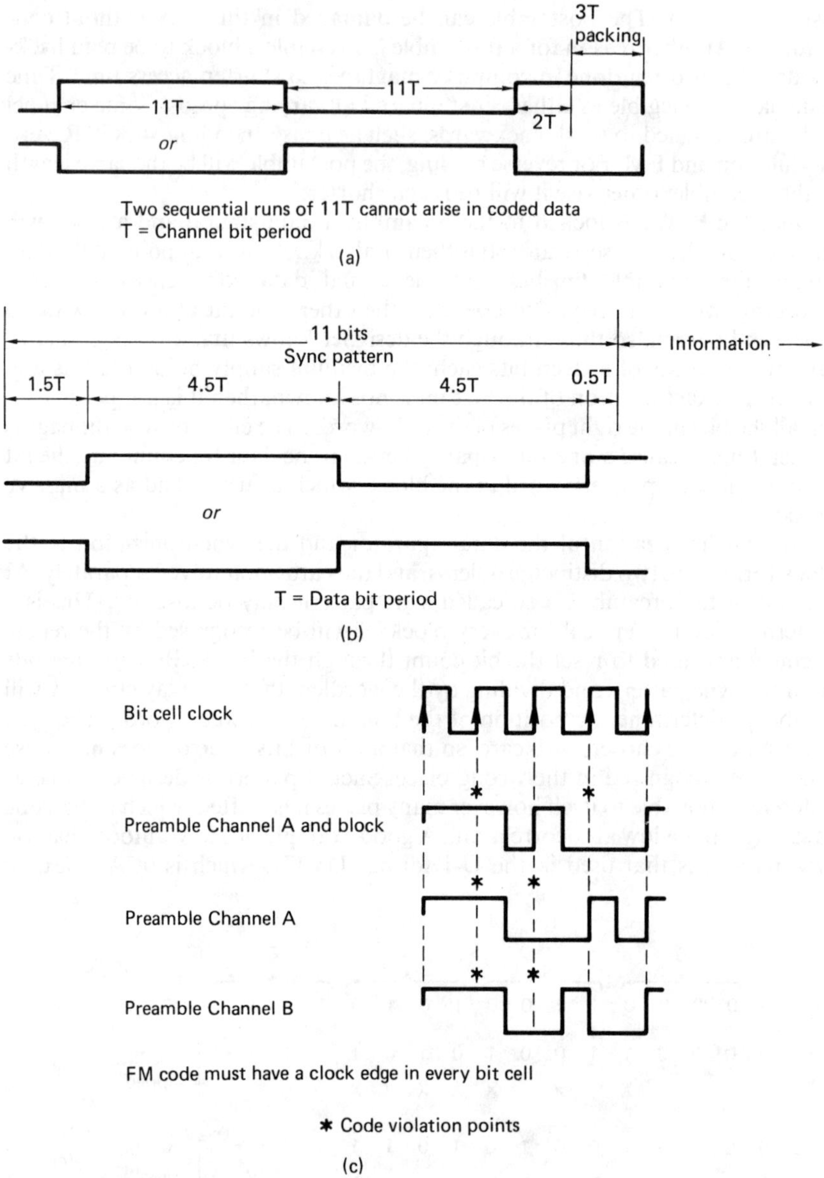

3T
packing

—11T—

—11T—

2T

or

Two sequential runs of 11T cannot arise in coded data
T = Channel bit period

(a)

11 bits
Sync pattern

Information →

1.5T

4.5T

4.5T

0.5T

or

T = Data bit period

(b)

Bit cell clock

Preamble Channel A and block

Preamble Channel A

Preamble Channel B

FM code must have a clock edge in every bit cell

✳ Code violation points

(c)

Figure 6.35 Sync patterns in various applications. At (a) the sync pattern of CD violates EFM coding rules, and is uniquely identifiable. At (b) the sync pattern of DASH stays within run length of HDM-1. At (c) the sync patterns of AES/EBU interconnect.

0000110010101111. Fig.6.34 shows how many differences are caused for different false sync states, which helps to ensure that only the correct timing is recognized. The ProDigi format uses a similar technique, except that the synchronization pattern is a pattern of channel bits not data bits.

In group codes and run length limited codes, it is possible to combine the function of preamble and sync pattern, by producing a transition pattern at the start of the block which contains timing to phase the channel bit rate PLL, but which contains run lengths which violate the limits. There is no way that these run lengths will be interpreted as data, but they can be detected by the replay circuitry. Such techniques are used in Compact Disc and the AES/EBU digital audio interconnect (see Chapter 5), and are illustrated in Fig.6.35.

Where reading in both directions is required, a reverse sync pattern will be placed between the data and the postamble. In timecode, the sync pattern is asymmetrical, so that the read circuitry can tell which way the tape is moving without any other source of information (see Fig.8.19).

References

1. DEELEY, E.M., Integrating and differentiating channels in digital tape recording. *Radio Electron. Eng.*, **56** 169–173 (1986)
2. MEE, C.D., *The Physics of Magnetic Recording.*, Amsterdam and New York: Elsevier–North Holland Publishing (1978)
3. JACOBY, G.V., Signal equalization in digital magnetic recording. *IEEE Trans. Magn.*, **11**, 302–305 (1975)
4. SCHNEIDER, R.C., An improved pulse-slimming method for magnetic recording. *IEEE Trans. Magn.*, **11**, 1240–1241 (1975)
5. NAKAJIMA, H., *et al.*, *Digital Audio Technology*, pp.150–152. Blue Ridge Summit, Pa.: TAB Books
6. TAMURA, T., *et al.*, A coding method in digital magnetic recording. *IEEE Trans. Magn.*, **8**, 612–614 (1972)
7. MALLINSON, J.C. and MILLER, J.W., Optimum codes for digital magnetic recording. *Radio and Electron. Eng.*, **47**, 172–176 (1977)
8. MILLER, J.W., DC-free encoding for data transmission system. US Patent 4 027 335, (1977)
9. PATEL, A.M., Zero-modulation encoding in magnetic recording. *IBM J. Res. Dev.*, **19**, 366–378 (1975)
10. TANG, D.T., Run-length-limited codes. IEEE International Symposium on Information Theory (1969)
11. COHN, M. and JACOBY, G., Run-length reduction of 3PM code via lookahead technique. *IEEE Trans. Magn.*, **18**, 1253–1255 (1982)
12. HORIGUCHI, T. and MORITA, K., On optimisation of modulation codes in digital recording. *IEEE Trans. Magn.*, **12**, 740–742 (1976)
13. FRANASZEK, P.A., Sequence state methods for run-length limited coding. *IBM J. Res. Dev.* **14**, 376–383 (1970)
14. JACOBY, G.V. and KOST, R., Binary two-thirds-rate code with full word lookahead. *IEEE Trans. Magn.*, **20**, 709–714 (1984)
15. JACOBY, G.V., A new lookahead code for increased data density. *IEEE Trans. Magn.*, **13**, 1202–1204 (1977)
16. OGAWA, H. and SCHOUHAMER IMMINK, K.A., EFM—the modulation method for the Compact Disc digital audio system. In *Digital Audio*, edited by B. Blesser, B. Locanthi and T.G. Stockham Jr, pp.117–124. New York: Audio Engineering Society (1982)
17. SCHOUHAMER IMMINK, K.A. and GROSS, U., Optimization of low-frequency properties of eight to fourteen modulation. *Radio Electron. Eng.*, **53**, 63–66 (1983)
18. FUKUDA, S., KOJIMA, Y., SHIMPUKU, Y. and ODAKA, K., 8/10 modulation codes for digital magnetic recording. *IEEE Trans. Magn.* **22**, 1194–1196 (1986)
19. DOI, T.T., Channel codings for digital audio recordings. *J. Audio Eng. Soc.* **31**, 224–238 (1983)
20. ANON., PD format for stationary head type 2-channel digital audio recorder. Mitsubishi (Jan. 1986)
21. YOKOYAMA, K., Digital video tape recorder. *NHK Technical Monograph*, No. 31 (Mar. 1982)

22. COLEMAN, C.H. *et al.*, High data-rate magnetic recording in a single channel. *J.IERE*, **55**, 229–236 (1985)

23. KOBAYASHI, H., Application of partial-response channel coding to magnetic recording systems. *IBM J. Res. Dev.*, **14**, 368–375 (1970)

24. FORNEY, G.D. Jr, The Viterbi algorithm. *Proc. IEEE*, **61**, 268–278 (1973)

25. WOOD, R.W. and PETERSEN, D.A., Viterbi detection of class IV partial response on a magnetic recording channel. *IEEE Trans. Commum.* **34**, 454–461 (1986)

26. WOLF, J.K. and UNGERBOECK, G., Trellis coding for partial response channels. Center for Magnetic Recording Research, University of California, San Diego.

27. SCHOUHAMER IMMINK, K.A., Graceful degradation of digital audio transmission systems. Presented at 82nd Audio Engineering Society Convention (London, 1987), preprint 2434(C-3)

28. GRIFFITHS, F.A., A digital audio recording system. Presented at 65th Audio Engineering Society Convention (London, 1980), preprint 1580(C1)

Chapter 7

Error correction

The subject of error correction is almost always described in mathematical terms by specialists for the benefit of other specialists. Such mathematical approaches are quite inappropriate for a proper understanding of the concepts of error correction, and only become necessary to analyse the quantitative behaviour of a system. The description below will use the minimum possible amount of mathematics, and it will then be seen that error correction is, in fact, quite straightforward.

7.1 Sensitivity of message to error

Before attempting to specify any piece of equipment, it is necessary to quantify the problems to be overcome and how effectively they need to be overcome. For a digital recording or transmission system the causes of errors must be studied to quantify the problem, and the sensitivity of the destination to errors must be assessed. In audio, the sensitivity to errors must be subjective. In PCM audio, the effect of a single bit in error depends upon the significance of the bit. If the least significant bit of a sample is wrong, the chances are that the effect will be lost in the noise. Conversely, if a high-order bit is in error, a massive transient will be added to the sound. The effect of uncorrected errors in PCM sounds rather like vehicle ignition interference on a radio. The effect of errors in delta modulation is much smaller, because every bit has the same significance, and the information content of each bit is low. If the error rate demanded by the destination cannot be met by the unaided channel, some form of error handling will be necessary. In some circumstances a delta-modulated system can be used with no error correction, but this is generally impossible in PCM.

7.2 Error mechanisms

Since digital data can be conveyed in many different ways, each having its own error mechanisms, it follows that there will be different approaches to protection of data. In addition, the kind of use to which a piece of equipment is put will make some error-protection schemes more practical than others.

Inside equipment, where data are conveyed in binary on wires, the noise resistance can be designed such that to all intents and purposes there will be no errors. For transmission between equipment, there will be less control of the electromagnetic environment, and interference may corrupt binary data on wires, but not in optical fibres. Such interference will generally not correlate with the data. For long-distance transmission by wire there will be the effects of lightning and switching noise in exchanges to combat.

In MOS memories the datum is stored in a tiny charge-well which acts as a capacitor (see Chapter 3), and natural radioactive decay of the chip materials can cause alpha particles which have enough energy to discharge a well, resulting in a single-bit error. This only happens once every thirty years or so in a given chip, but when a great many chips are assembled to form a large memory for a computer or a powerful audio editor, the probability rises to one error every few minutes.

In magnetic recording, there are many more mechanisms available to corrupt data, from mechanical problems such as media dropout and poor head contact, to Gaussian thermal noise in replay circuits and heads. In optical media the equivalent of dropout in manufacture is contamination of the optical layer by dust before it is sealed. In replay, surface contamination from fingerprints and birefringence in the transparent medium distort and diffuse the laser beam so that the reflected light pattern cannot be discerned.

Despite the difference in operating principle, magnetic recorders and optical media have similar effects when the corruption of data is studied. There are large isolated corruptions, called error bursts, where numerous bits are corrupted all together in an area which is otherwise error-free, and there are random errors affecting single bits or symbols. In the discussion of channel coding in Chapter 6 it was noted that, wherever group codes are used, a single corruption in a group renders meaningless all of the data bits in that group. Thus single-bit errors are much less common in group-coded data.

Whatever the mechanism, the result will be that the received data will not be exactly the same as those sent. Sometimes it is enough to know that there has been an error, if time allows a retransmission to be arranged. This is quite feasible for telex messages, but quite inappropriate for digital audio, which works in real time, with the possible exception of some operations in disk-based editors.

In computer disk drives the detection of a read error frequently results in a retry. The disk is turning at typically 3600 rev/min and repeatedly presents the same data to a fixed head, making a retry very easy. Disk drives will also verify the data integrity of a new disk, and any blocks containing dropouts will be allocated to a hypothetical file which makes them appear to be already used. The computer will never write on them. Computer magnetic tape transports read the tape as it is being written, and if an error is detected, the transport will reverse to the beginning of the block, erase a few inches of tape, and try again. These are luxuries not available to digital audio recorders. The chore of pre-formatting a tape before use would be unacceptable, and in any case there is no guarantee that new tape defects will not arise in use. The non-contact rigid disk is much more consistent in this respect. It is reasonable to expect that the error handling of digital audio equipment will be more complex than that of computer equipment.

7.3 Interpolation

Although audio recorders are at a disadvantage with respect to computer recorders in that they cannot preformat and verify the medium, and there is no time for retries, they have the advantage that there is a certain amount of redundancy in the information conveyed. If an error cannot be corrected, then it can be concealed. In audio systems, if a sample is lost, it is possible to obtain an approximation to it by interpolating between adjacent values. Momentary interpolations in music are not serious, but sustained use of interpolation restricts bandwidth and can cause aliasing if high frequencies are present. In advanced systems, a spectral analysis of the sound is made, and if sample values are not available, samples having the same spectral characteristics are inserted. This concealment method is quite successful because the spectral shape changes relatively slowly in music.

7.4 Error handling

Fig.7.1 shows the broad subdivisions of error handling. The first stage might well be called error avoidance, and includes such measures as creating bad block files in hard disks, placing digital audio blocks at the centre of the tape in D -1 format, and rewriting on a read-after-write error in computer tapes. Following these moves, the data are entrusted to the channel, which causes whatever corruptions it feels like. On receipt of the data the occurrence of errors is first detected, and this process must be extremely reliable, as it does not matter how fast the retry mechanism, or how good the concealment algorithm, if it is not known that they are necessary! The detection of an error then results in a course of action being decided. In a bidirectional link, a retransmission could be requested. In a critical financial computer, reference to the backup file may be requested. In a hard disk a retry might be issued. In audio, these options are not open, and the only course is to attempt correction. If this succeeds, the data have been restored to their original values with high probability. If correction fails or is only partly successful, then it will be necessary to use concealment. If there is too much corruption for concealment, the only course is to mute.

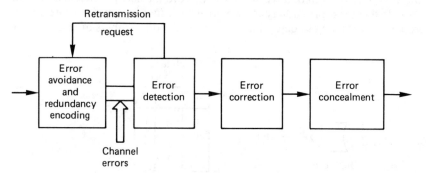

Figure 7.1 The major processes in an error-handling system.

7.5 Parity

The error detection and correction processes are closely related and will be dealt with together here. The actual correction of an error is simplified tremendously by the adoption of binary. As there are only two symbols, 0 and 1, it is enough to know that a symbol is wrong, and the correct value is obvious. Fig.7.2 shows a minimal circuit required for correction once the bit in error has been identified. The exclusive–OR gate shows up extensively in error correction and the figure also repeats the truth table from Chapter 3. One way of remembering the characteristics of this useful device is that there will be an output when the inputs are different.

The fundamental concept in error detection is known as parity. In Fig.7.3, the example is given of a four-bit data word which is to be protected. If an extra bit is added to the word which is calculated in such a way that the total number of ones in the five bit word is even, this property can be tested on receipt. Another way of looking at the XOR gate is to say that the number of ones on the three terminals is always even; it could therefore be called an even-parity gate. The generation of the parity bit in Fig.7.3 can be performed by a number of the ubiquitous XOR gates configured into what is known as a parity tree. In the figure, if a bit is corrupted, the received message will be seen to no longer have an even number of ones. If two bits are corrupted, the failure will be undetected. This example can be used to introduce much of the terminology of error correction. The extra bit added to the message carries no information of its own, since it is calculated from the other bits. It is therefore called a redundant bit. The addition of the redundant bit gives the message a special property, i.e. the number of ones is even. A message having some special property irrespective of the actual data content is called a codeword. All error correction relies on adding redundancy to real data to form codewords for transmission. If any corruption occurs, the intention is that the received message will not have the special property; in other words if the received message is not a codeword there has definitely been an error. If the received message is a codeword, there probably has not been an error. The word 'probably' must be used because the figure shows that two bits in error will cause the received message to be a codeword, which cannot be discerned from an error-free message. If it is known that generally the only failure mechanism in the channel in question is loss of a single bit, it is *assumed* that receipt of a codeword means that there has been no error. If there is a probability of two error bits, that becomes very nearly the probability of failing to detect an error, since all odd numbers of errors will be

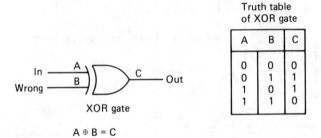

Figure 7.2 Once the position of the error is identified, the correction process in binary is easy.

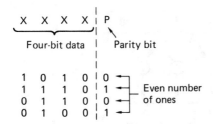

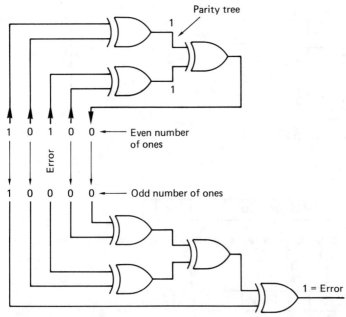

Figure 7.3 Parity checking adds up the number of ones in a word using, in this example, parity trees. One error bit and odd numbers of errors are detected. Even numbers of errors cannot be detected.

detected, and a four-bit error is much less likely. It is paramount in all error-correction systems that the protection used should be appropriate for the probability of errors to be encountered. An inadequate error-correction system is actually worse than not having any correction. Error correction works by trading probabilities. Error-free performance with a certain error rate is achieved at the expense of performance at higher error rates. If the expected error rate has been misjudged, the consequences can be disastrous. Another result demonstrated by the example is that we can only guarantee to detect the same number of bits in error as there are redundant bits.

7.6 Wyner–Ash code

Despite its extreme simplicity, the principle of parity can be used to make an effective digital-audio error correcting scheme. In the Wyner–Ash code

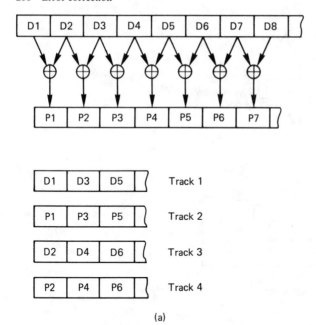

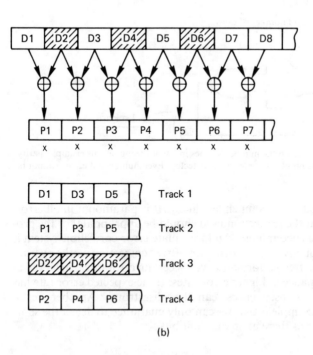

Figure 7.4 In the Wyner–Ash coding illustrated here, there is 100% overhead due to the additional parity symbols. The data and parity are distributed over the tape tracks, as shown in (a). At (b) a burst error in a data track causes continuous parity errors as shown, and correction can be performed. For example $D2 = D1 \oplus P1$ etc.

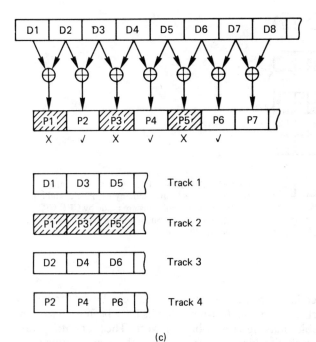

(c)

Figure 7.4 (*continued*) At (c) a burst error in a parity track causes alternate parity errors, which can be ignored.

employed in some early BBC work,[1] four tape tracks were required to convey one audio channel, which reduced the linear speed of the tape and reduced the impact of a dropout on the data. Fig.7.4(a) shows that alternate tracks carried data and parity bits computed from running pairs of data bits. With this mechanism, data-track errors always cause an even number of parity failures, and Fig.7.4(b) shows an example of how such an error can be corrected. Parity-track errors, however, cause single parity failures, which can be neglected, as in Fig.7.4(c). Whilst this technique was successful, it requires an overhead of 100 % redundancy, which implies that tape consumption must suffer. Codes which need less overhead are inevitably more complex, however.

7.7 Crossword code

In the example of Fig.7.3, the error was detected but it was not possible to say which bit was in error. Even though the code used can only detect errors, correction is still possible if a suitable strategy is used. Fig.7.5 shows the use of a crossword code, also known as a product code. The data are formed into a two-dimensional array, with parity taken on rows and columns. If a single bit fails, one row check and one column check will fail, and the failing bit can be located at the intersection of the two failing checks. Although two bits in error confuse this simple scheme, using more complex coding in a two-dimensional structure is very powerful, and further examples will be given througout this chapter.

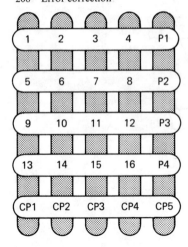

Figure 7.5 A crossword parity-check system. Horizontal checks are made by P1, P2 etc, and cross parity checks on columns are made by CP1, CP2, etc. If, for example, bit 10 were in error, it would be located by CP2 and P3 intersecting.

7.8 Hamming code

In a one-dimensional code, the position of the failing bit can be determined by using more parity checks. In Fig.7.6, the four data bits have been used to compute three redundancy bits, making a seven-bit codeword. The four data bits are examined in turn, and each bit which is a one will cause the corresponding row of a generator matrix to be added to an exclusive–OR sum. For example, if the data were 1001, the top and bottom rows of the matrix would be XORed. The matrix used is known as an identity matrix, because the data bits in the codeword are identical to the data bits to be conveyed. This is useful because the original data can be stored unmodified, and the check bits are simply attached to the end to make a so-called systematic codeword. Almost all digital audio equipment uses systematic codes. The way in which the redundancy bits are calculated is simply that they do not all use every data bit. If a data bit has not been included in a parity check, it can fail without affecting the outcome of that check. The position of the error is deduced from the pattern of successful and unsuccessful checks in the check matrix. This pattern is known as a syndrome.

In the figure the example of a failing bit is given. Bit three fails, and because this bit is included in only two of the checks, there are two ones in the failure pattern, 011. As some care was taken in designing the matrix pattern for the generation of the check bits, the syndrome, 011, is the address of the failing bit. This is the fundamental feature of the Hamming codes due to Richard Hamming.[2] The performance of this seven bit code word can be assessed. In seven bits there can be 128 combinations, but in four data bits there are only sixteen combinations. Thus out of 128 possible received messages, only sixteen will be codewords, so if the message is completely trashed by a gross corruption, it will still be possible to detect that this has happened 112 times out of 127, as in these cases the syndrome will be non-zero (the 128th case is the correct data). There is thus only a probability of detecting that all of the message is corrupt. In an idle moment it is possible to work out, in a similar way, the number of false codewords which can result from different numbers of bits being assumed to have failed. For three bits and less, the failure will always be detected, because there are three check bits. Returning to the example, if three bits or two bits fail,

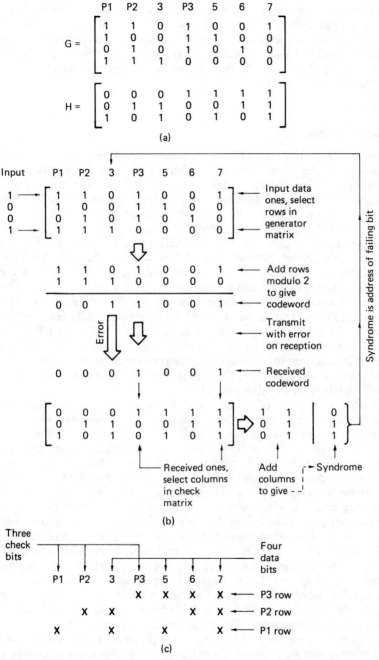

Figure 7.6 (a) The generator and check matrices of a Hamming code. The data and check bits are arranged as shown because it causes the syndrome to be the binary address of the failing bit. (b) An example of Hamming-code generation and error correction. (c) Another way of looking at Hamming code is to say that the rows of crosses in this chart are calculated to have even parity. If bit 3 fails, parity check P3 is not affected, but parity checks P1 and P2 both include bit 3 and will fail.

there will be a non-zero syndrome, but if this is used to point to a bit in error, a miscorrection will result. From these results can be deduced another important feature of error codes. The power of detection is always greater than the power of correction, which is also fortunate, since if the correcting power is exceeded by an error it will at least be a known problem, and steps can taken to prevent any undesirable consequences.

7.9 Hamming distance

It is useful at this point to introduce the concept of Hamming distance. This is the minimum number of bits that must be changed in any codeword in order to turn it into another codeword. Clearly if errors corrupt a codeword so that it is no longer a codeword, it will definitely be detectable and possibly correctable. If errors convert one codeword into another, it will not even be detected.

Fig.7.7 shows Hamming distance diagrammatically. A three-bit codeword is used with two data bits and one parity bit. With three bits, a received code could have eight combinations, but only four of these will be codewords. The valid codewords are shown in the centre of each of the disks, and at the perimeter of the disks are shown the received words which would result from a single-bit error, i.e. they have a Hamming distance of one. It will be seen that the same received word (on the vertical bars) can be obtained from a different single-bit corruption of any three codewords. It is thus not possible to tell which codeword was corrupted and so correction is not possible. Unfortunately, a more complex diagram for a longer wordlength cannot be drawn, because it exists in a vector space of more than three dimensions. It can, however, be imagined, and its characteristics studied.

The efficiency in terms of storage needed is not very good in the simple example of Fig.7.6, as three check bits are needed for only four data bits. Since the failing bit is determined using a binary split mechanism, it follows that doubling the amount of data will only require one extra check bit, provided that the number of errors to be detected remains the same. Thus for the smallest amount of redundancy, long codewords should be used. In computer memories these codewords are typically four or eight data bytes plus redundancy. A drawback of long codewords for computer memory applications is that if it is required to change only one byte in the memory, the whole word has to be read, corrected, modified, encoded and stored again —a so called read–modify–write cycle. The codes for computer memories will generally have an extra check bit which allows the occurrence of a double-bit error always to be detected but not corrected. If this happens, the syndrome will be the address of a bit which is outside the data word. Such codes are known as SECDED (single error correcting double error detecting) codes. The Hamming distance of these codes is one greater than the equivalent SEC (single error correcting) code.

The correction of one bit is of little use in the presence of burst errors, but a Hamming code can be made to correct burst errors by using interleaving. Fig.7.8 shows that if several codewords are calculated beforehand, and woven together as shown before they are sent down the channel, then a burst of errors which corrupts several bits will become a number of single-bit errors in seperate codewords upon deinterleaving. Interleaving is used extensively in digital audio, and will be discussed in greater detail later in this chapter.

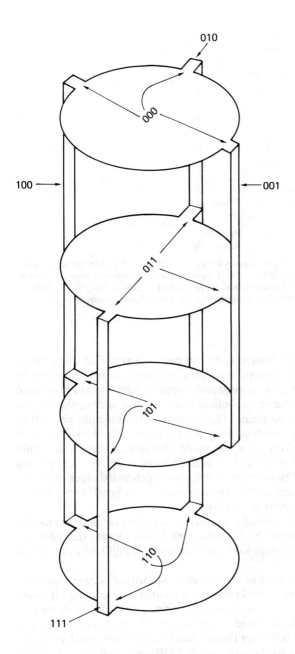

Figure 7.7 Hamming distance of two. The disk centres contain codewords. Corrupting each bit in turn produces the distance-one values on the vertical members. In order to change one codeword to another, two bits must be changed, so the code has a Hamming distance of two.

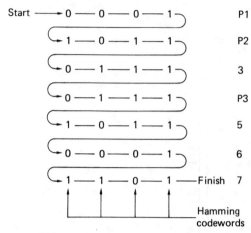

Figure 7.8 The vertical columns of this diagram are all codewords generated by the matrix of Figure 7.6, which can correct a single-bit error. If these words are recorded in the order shown, a burst error of up to four bits will result in one single-bit error in each codeword, which is correctable. Interleave requires memory, and causes delay. Deinterleave requires the same.

7.10 Cyclic codes

The implementation of a Hamming code can be made very fast using parity trees, which is ideal for memory applications where access time is increased by the correction process. However, in most audio applications, the data are stored serially, such as on a magnetic or optical track, and it is desirable to use relatively large data blocks to reduce the amount of the medium devoted to preambles, addressing and synchronizing. Where large data blocks are to be handled, the use of a lookup table has to be abandoned because it would become impossibly large. The principle of generator and check matrices will still be employed, but they will be matrices which can be generated algorithmically by an equation. The syndrome will then be converted to the bit(s) in error not by looking them up, but by solving an equation.

Where data can be accessed serially, simpler circuitry can be used because the same gate will be used for many XOR operations. Unfortunately the reduction in component count is only paralleled by an increase in the difficulty of explaining what takes place.

The circuit of Fig.7.9 is a kind of shift register, but with a peculiar feedback arrangement which leads it to be known as a twisted-ring counter. If seven message bits A–G are applied serially to this circuit, and each one of them is clocked, the outcome can be followed in the diagram. As bit A is presented and the system is clocked, bit A will enter the left-hand latch. When bits B and C are presented, A moves across to the right. Both XOR gates will have A on the upper input from the right-hand latch, the left one has D on the lower input and the right one has B on the lower input. When clocked, the left latch will thus be loaded with the XOR of A and D, and the centre one with the XOR of A and C. The remainder of the sequence can be followed, bearing in mind that when the same term appears on both inputs of an XOR gate, it goes out, as the exclusive OR of something with itself is nothing. At the end of the process, the latches contain three different expressions. Essentially, the circuit makes three parity

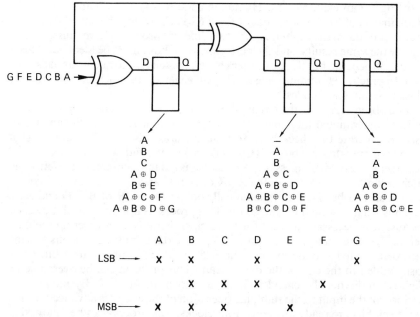

Figure 7.9 When seven successive bits A–G are clocked into this circuit, the contents of the three latches are shown for each clock. The final result is a parity-check matrix.

checks through the message, leaving the result of each in the three stages of the register. In the figure, these expressions have been used to draw up a check matrix. The significance of these steps can now be explained. The bits A B C and D are four data bits, and the bits E F and G are redundancy. When the redundancy is calculated, bit E is chosen so that there are an even number of ones in bits A B C and E; bit F is chosen such that the same applies to bits B C D and F, and similarly for bit G. Thus the four data bits and the three check bits form a seven-bit codeword. If there is no error in the codeword, when it is fed into the circuit shown, the result of each of the three parity checks will be zero and every stage of the shift register will be cleared. If a bit in the codeword is corrupted, there will be a non-zero result. For example, if bit D fails, the check on bits A B D and G will fail, and a one will appear in the left-hand latch. The check on bits B C D F will also fail, and the centre latch will set. The check on bits A B C E will not fail, because D is not involved in it, making the right-hand bit zero. There will be a syndrome of 110 in the register, and this will be seen from the check matrix to correspond to an error in bit D. Whichever bit fails, there will be a different three-bit syndrome which uniquely identifies the failed bit. As there are only three latches, there can be eight different syndromes. One of these is zero, which is the error-free condition, and so there are seven remaining error syndromes. The length of the codeword cannot exceed seven bits, or there would not be enough syndromes to correct all of the bits. This can also be made to tie in with the generation of the check matrix. If fourteen bits, A to N, were fed into the circuit shown, the result would be that the check matrix repeated twice, and if a syndrome of 101 were to result, it could not be determined whether bit D or bit K failed. Because the check repeats every seven bits, the code is said to be a cyclic redundancy check (CRC) code.

In Fig.7.6 an example of a Hamming code was given. Comparison of the check matrix of Fig.7.9 with that of Fig.7.6 will show that the only difference is the order of the matrix columns. The two different processes have thus achieved exactly the same results, and the performance of both must be identical. This is not true in general, but these examples have been selected to allow parallels to be seen. In practice Hamming code blocks will generally be much smaller than the blocks used in CRC codes.

It has been seen that the circuit shown makes a matrix check on a received word to determine if there has been an error, but the same circuit can also be used to generate the check bits. To visualize how this is done, examine what happens if only the data bits A B C and D are known, and the check bits E F and G are set to zero. If this message, ABCD000, is fed into the circuit, the left-hand latch will afterwards contain the XOR of A B C and zero, which is of course what E should be. The centre latch will contain the XOR of B C D and zero, which is what F should be and so on. This process is not quite ideal, however, because it is necessary to wait for three clock periods after entering the data before the check bits are available. Where the data are simultaneously being recorded and fed into the encoder, the delay would prevent the check bits being easily added to the end of the data stream. This problem can be overcome by slightly modifying the encoder circuit as shown in Fig.7.10. By moving the position of the input to the right, the operation of the circuit is advanced so that the check bits are ready after only four clocks. The process can be followed in the diagram for the four data bits A B C and D. On the first clock, bit A enters the left two latches, whereas on the second clock, bit B will appear on the upper input of the left XOR gate, with bit A on the lower input, causing the centre latch to load the XOR of A and B and so on.

The way in which the correction system works has been described in engineering terms, but it can be described mathematically if analysis is contemplated.

Just as the position of a decimal digit in a number determines the power of ten (whether that digit means one, ten or a hundred), the position of a binary digit determines the power of two (whether it means one, two or four). It is possible to

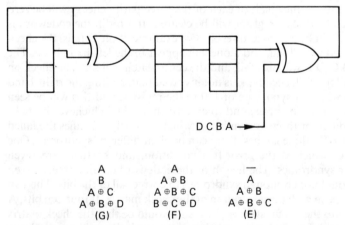

A	A	—
B	$A \oplus B$	A
$A \oplus C$	$A \oplus B \oplus C$	$A \oplus B$
$A \oplus B \oplus D$	$B \oplus C \oplus D$	$A \oplus B \oplus C$
(G)	(F)	(E)

Figure 7.10 By moving the insertion point three places to the right, the calculation of the check bits is completed in only four clock periods and they can follow the data immediately. This is equivalent to premultiplying the data by x^3.

rewrite a binary number so that it is expressed as a list of powers of two. For example, the binary number 1101 means $8 + 4 + 1$, and can be written:

$$2^3 + 2^2 + 2^0$$

In fact, much of the theory of error correction applies to symbols in number bases other than 2, so that the number can also be written more generally as:

$$x^3 + x^2 + 1 \quad (2^0 = 1)$$

which also looks much more impressive. This expression, containing as it does various powers, is of course a polynomial, and the circuit of Fig.7.9, which has

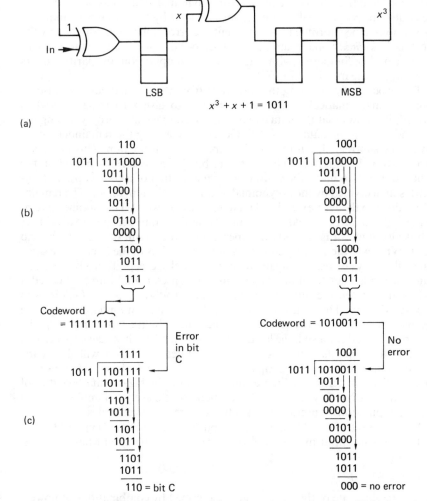

(a)

(b)

(c)

Figure 7.11 Circuit of Figure 7.9 divides by $x^3 + x + 1$ to find remainder. At (b) this is used to calculate check bits. At (c) left, there is an error, non-zero syndrome 110 points to bit C. At (c) right, zero syndrome, no error.

been seen to construct a parity-check matrix on a codeword, can also be described as calculating the remainder due to dividing the input by a polynomial using modulo-2 arithmetic. In modulo-2 there are no borrows or carries, and addition and subtraction are replaced by the XOR function, which makes hardware implementation very easy. In Fig.7.11 it will be seen that the circuit of Fig.7.9 actually divides the codeword by a polynomial which is:

$$x^3 + x + 1 \quad \text{or} \quad 1011$$

This can be deduced from the fact that the right-hand bit is fed into several lower-order stages of the register at once. Once all the bits of the message have been clocked in, the circuit contains the remainder. In mathematical terms, the special property of a codeword is that it is a polynomial which yields a remainder of zero when divided by the generating polynomial. If an error has occurred it is considered that this is due to an error polynomial which has been added to the codeword polynomial. If a codeword divided by the check polynomial is zero, a non-zero syndrome must represent the error polynomial divided by the check polynomial. Some examples of modulo-2 division are given in Fig.7.11 which can be compared with the parallel computation of parity checks according to the matrix of Fig.7.9.

The process of generating the codeword from the original data can also be described mathematically. If a codeword has to give zero remainder when divided, it follows that the data can be converted to a codeword by adding the remainder when the data is divided. Generally speaking the remainder would have to be subtracted, but in modulo-2 there is no distinction. This process is also illustrated in Fig.7.11. The four data bits have three zeros placed on the right-hand end, to make the wordlength equal to that of a codeword, and this word is then divided by the polynomial to calculate the remainder. The remainder is added to the zero-extended data to form a codeword. The modified circuit of Fig.7.10 can be described as premultiplying the data by x^3 before dividing.

It is also interesting to study the operation of the circuit of Fig.7. 9 with no input. Whatever the starting condition of the three bits in the latches, the same state will always be reached again after seven clocks, except if zero is used. The states of the latches form an endless ring of nonsequential numbers called a Galois field after the French mathematical prodigy Evariste Galois who discovered them. The states of the circuit form a maximum-length sequence because there are as many states as are permitted by the wordlength. As the all-zeros case is disallowed, the length of a maximum length sequence generated by a register of m bits cannot exceed $(2^m - 1)$ states. This figure will also be the length of the codeword in simple cyclic codes. The Galois field, however, includes the zero term. It is interesting to explore the bizarre mathematics of Galois fields which use modulo-2 arithmetic (exclusively!). Familiarity with such manipulations is useful when studying more advanced codes.

As the circuit of Fig.7.9 divides the input by the function $F(x) = x^3 + x + 1$, and there is no input in this case, the operation of the circuit has to be described by:

$$x^3 + x + 1 = 0$$

Each three-bit state of the circuit can be described by combinations of powers of x, such as:

$$x^2 = 100$$

$x = 010$

$x^2 + x = 110$, etc.

To avoid confusion, the three-bit state of the field will be called a, which is a primitive element.

Now,

$a^3 + a + 1 = 0$

In modulo 2,

$a + a = a^2 + a^2 = 0$

$a = x = 010$

$a^2 = x^2 = 100$

$a^3 = a + 1 = 011$

$a^4 = a \times a^3 = a(a+1) = a^2 + a = 110$

$a^5 = a^2 + a + 1 = 111$

$a^6 = a \times a^5 = a(a^2 + a + 1)$

$\qquad = a^3 + a^2 + a = a + 1 + a^2 + a$

$\qquad = a^2 + 1 = 101$

$a^7 = a(a^2 + 1) = a^2 + a$

$\qquad = a + 1 + a = 1 = 001$

In this way it can be seen that the complete set of elements of the Galois field can be expressed by successive powers of the primitive element. Note that the twisted-ring circuit of Fig.7.9 simply raises a to higher and higher powers as it is clocked; thus the seemingly complex multibit changes caused by a single clock of the register become simple to calculate using the correct primitive and the appropriate power.

CRC codes are of primary importance for detecting errors, and several have been standardized for use in digital communications. The most common of these are:

$x^{16} + x^{15} + x^2 + 1$ (CRC–16)

$x^{16} + x^{12} + x^5 + 1$ (CRC–CCITT)

Integrated circuits are available which contain all the necessary circuitry[3] to generate and check redundancy. A representative chip is the Fairchild 9401 which will be found in a great deal of digital audio equipment because it implements the above polynomials in addition to some others. A feature of the chip is that the feedback register can be configured to work backwards if required. The required polynomial is selected by a three-bit control code, as shown in Fig.7.12. The desired code is implemented by enabling different feedback connections kept in a ROM. The data stream to be recorded is clocked in serially, with the control signal CWE (check word enable) true. At the end of the data, this signal is made false, and it turns off the feedback, so that the device behaves as an ordinary shift register and the check bits can be clocked out of the Q output and appended to the recording. Upon playback, the entire codeword

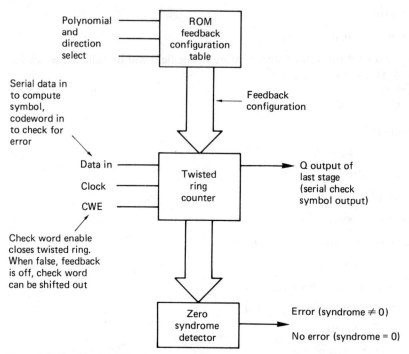

Figure 7.12 Simplified block of CRC chip which can implement several polynomials, and both generate and check redundancy.

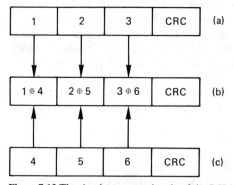

Figure 7.13 The simple crossword code of the PCM 1610/1630 format. Horizontal codewords are cyclic polynomials; vertical codewords are simple parity. Cyclic code detects errors, and acts as erasure pointer for parity correction. For example, if word 2 fails, CRC (a) fails, and 1, 2, and 3 are all erased. The correct values are computed from (b) and (c) such that :

$$1 = (1 \oplus 4) \oplus 4$$
$$2 = (2 \oplus 5) \oplus 5$$
$$3 = (3 \oplus 6) \oplus 6$$

is clocked into the device with CWE true, and at the end of the codeword, if the register contains all zeros, the error output will be false, whereas if the syndrome is non-zero, it will be true.

The output of such a chip is binary; either there was an error or (with high probability) there was not. There is no indication where the error was. Nevertheless, an effective error-correction system can be made using a product or crossword code. An example of this is the error-correction system of the Sony PCM-1610/1630 unit used for Compact Disc mastering. Fig.7.13 shows that in this system, two sets of three audio samples have a CRCC added to form codewords. Three parity words are generated by taking the exclusive–OR of the two sets of samples, and a CRCC is added to this also. If an error occurs in one sample, the CRC for the codeword containing that sample will fail, and *all* samples in the codeword are deemed to be in error. The sample can be corrected by taking the exclusive–OR of the other samples and the parity words. The error detector simply serves as a pointer to a separate correction mechanism. This technique is often referred to as correction by erasure. The error detector erases the samples which are in error, so that the corrector knows which ones to correct. If the error is in the parity words, no action need be taken. Further details of this format can be found in Chapter 8. It will be seen that there is 100 % redundancy in this simple format, but the unit is intended to operate with a standard video recorder, whose bandwidth is predefined, so there would be no saving involved in using a code with less overhead.

7.11 Burst correction

Fig.7.14 lists all the possible codewords which the circuit of Fig.7.9 can produce. If they are examined, it will be seen that it is necessary to change at least three bits in one codeword before it can be made into another; thus the code has a Hamming distance of three and will always detect three-bit errors. The single-bit error correction limit can also be deduced from this table. In the example, the codeword 0101100 suffers a single-bit error (marked *) which converts it to a non-codeword at a Hamming distance of 1. No other codeword can be turned into this code by a single-bit error; therefore the nearest codeword in Hamming

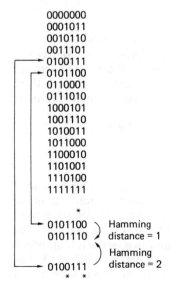

Figure 7.14 All possible codewords of $x^3 + x + 1$ are shown, and the fact that a double error in one codeword can produce the same pattern as a single error in another. Thus double errors cannot be corrected.

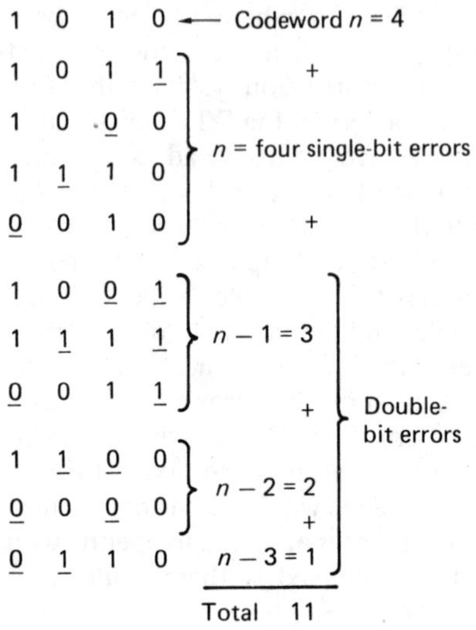

```
1   0   1   0  ◄── Codeword n = 4

1   0   1   1 ⎤         +
              ⎥
1   0  .0   0 ⎥
              ⎬  n = four single-bit errors
1   1   1   0 ⎥
              ⎥
0   0   1   0 ⎦         +

1   0   0   1 ⎤
              ⎥
1   1   1   1 ⎬  n − 1 = 3
              ⎥
0   0   1   1 ⎦
                      +

1   1   0   0 ⎤
              ⎬  n − 2 = 2
0   0   0   0 ⎦
                      +

0   1   1   0    n − 3 = 1
              ─────────────
              Total    11
```

Double-bit errors

Figure 7.15 Where double-bit errors occur, the number of patterns necessary is $(n-1)+(n-2)+(n-3)+ \ldots$ Total necessary is $1+n+(n-1)+(n-2)+(n-3)+ \ldots$ etc. Example here is of four bits, and all possible patterns up to Hamming distance of 2 are shown (errors underlined).

distance terms must be the correct one. The code can thus correct single-bit errors. However, the codeword 0100111 can be made into the same failure code by a two-bit error (also marked *) and as the original codeword can no longer be correctly deduced, a two-bit error cannot be corrected. The system will miscorrect if a two-bit error occurs. The concept of Hamming distance can be extended in this way to explain how more than one bit can be corrected. In Fig.7.15 the example of two bits in error is given. If a codeword four bits long suffers a single-bit error, it could produce one of four different words. If it suffers a two-bit error, it could produce one of $3+2+1$ different words as shown in the figure (the error bits are underlined). The total number of possible words of Hamming distance one or two from a four bit codeword is thus:

$$4+3+2+1=10$$

If the two-bit error is to be correctable, no other codeword can be allowed to become one of this number of error patterns due to a two-bit error of its own. Thus every codeword requires space for itself plus all possible error patterns of Hamming distance 2 or 1, which is eleven patterns in this example. Clearly there are only sixteen patterns available in a four bit code, and thus no data can be conveyed if two bit protection is necessary.

The number of different patterns possible in a word of n bits is:

$$1+n+(n-1)+(n-2)+(n-3)+ \ldots$$

and this pattern range has to be shared between the ranges of each codeword without overlap. For example an eight-bit codeword could result in $1+8+7+6+5+4+3+2+1=37$ patterns. As there are only 256 patterns in eight bits, it follows that only 256/37 pieces of information can be conveyed. The nearest integer below is six, and the nearest power of two below is four, which corresponds to two data bits and six check bits in the eight-bit word. The amount of redundancy necessary to correct *any* two bits in error is large, and as the number of bits to be corrected grows, the redundancy necessary becomes enormous and impractical. A further problem is that the more redundancy is added, the greater the probability of an error in a codeword. Fortunately, in practice errors occur in bursts, as has already been described, and it is a happy consequence that the number of patterns that result from the corruption of a codeword by *adjacent* two bit errors is much smaller.

It can be deduced that the number of redundant bits necessary to correct a burst error is twice the number of bits in the burst for a perfect code. This is done by working out the number of received messages which could result from corruption of the codeword by bursts of from one bit up to the largest burst size allowed, and then making sure that there are enough redundant bits to allow that number of combinations in the received message.

Some codes, such as the Fire code due to Philip Fire,[4] are designed to correct single bursts in the codeword, whereas later codes, such as the B-adjacent code due to Bossen,[5] could correct two adjacent bursts. The Reed–Solomon codes (Irving Reed and Gustave Solomon[6]) have the extremely useful feature that the number of bursts which are correctable can be chosen at the design stage by the amount of redundancy.

7.12 Fire code

The operation of a Fire code will now be illustrated. A data block has deliberately been made small for the purposes of illustration in Fig.7.16. The matrix for generating parity bits on the data is shown beneath the block. In each horizontal row of the matrix, the presence of an X means that the data bit in that column has been counted in a parity check. The five rows result in five parity bits which are appended to the data. The simple circuit needed to generate this checkword is also shown. The same codeword corrupted by three errors is

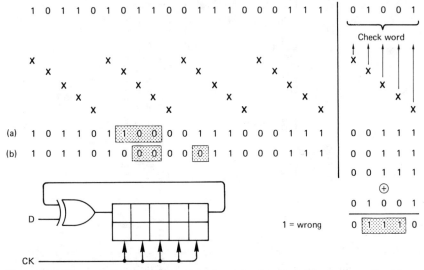

Figure 7.16 This matrix develops a burst-detecting code with circuit shown. On reading, the same encoding process is used, and the two checkwords are XOR-gated. Two examples of error bursts shown (a, b) give the same syndrome; this ambiguity is resolved by the technique of Figure 7.17.

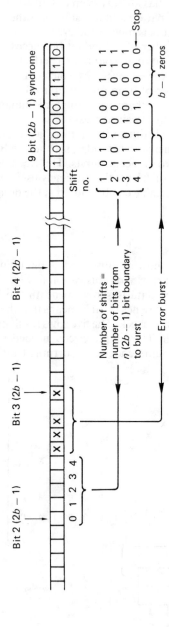

Figure 7.17 Burst of length b bits can only contain $b-2$ zeros, so $b-1$ zeros cannot be in a burst. By shifting the syndrome until $b-1$ zeros are detected, the burst is defined unambiguously. The number of shifts needed gives the position of the burst relative to the previous $n(2b-1)$th bit boundary. In this example $b=5$, hence $2b-1=9$ and the boundaries referred to will be at bits 9, 18, 27 etc. A burst of up to nine bits can be detected but not corrected. Only the nature of the burst is defined by this process; its position has to be determined independently.

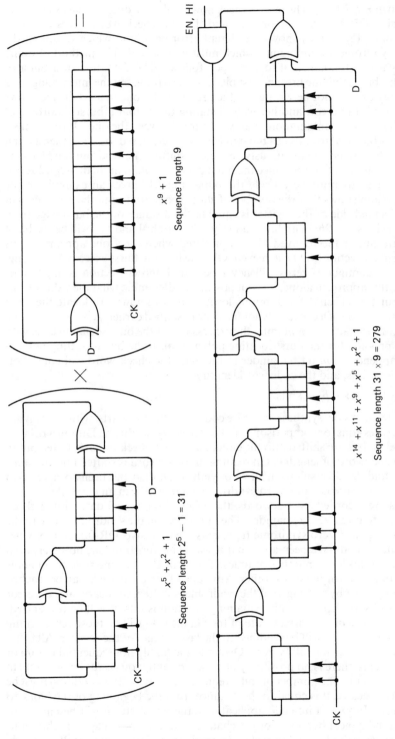

Figure 7.18 Derivation of Fire code from two fundamental expressions, together with encoding circuits. From the codeword length of 279 bits, 14 are check bits, making this a (279, 265) code.

shown in Fig.7.16(a). The matrix check now results in a different check code. An exclusive–OR between the original and the new check words gives the error syndrome. Fig.7.16(b) shows a different error condition which results in the same syndrome, an ambiguity which must be resolved. The method of doing this which is fundamental to Fire code follows. The definition of a burst of length b bits is that the first and last bits must be wrong, but the intervening $b-2$ bits may or may not be wrong. As the presence of a one in a syndrome shows there is a bit in error, another way of stating this is that a burst syndrome of length b cannot contain more than $b-2$ zeros between the ones. If the number of check bits used to correct a burst of length b is increased to $2b-1$, then a burst of length b can be unambiguously defined by shifting the syndrome and looking for $b-1$ successive zeros. Since the burst cannot contain more than $b-2$ zeros, the $b-1$ zeros must lie outside the burst. Fig.7.17 gives an example of the process and shows that the number of shifts necessary to put the $b-1$ zeros at the left-hand side of the register is equal to the distance of the burst edge from the previous $n \times (2b-1)$th bit boundary. The b right-hand bits will be the burst pattern, and if the received bits are inverted wherever a one appears in this pattern, correction will be achieved. Obviously if the burst exceeds b bits long, the $b-1$ contiguous zeros will never be found and correction is impossible. Using this approach alone, it is not possible to determine what the value of n is. The burst has been defined, but its location is not known. To locate the burst requires the use of a cyclic polynomial code described earlier. A burst-correcting Fire code is made by combining the expression for the burst-defining code with the expression for the burst-locating polynomial. If the burst-locating polynomial appends an m bit remainder to the data, the check word will consist of $m+2b-1$ bits, and the code word length n becomes:

$$n = (2^m - 1) \times (2b - 1) \text{ bits}$$

Fig.7.18 shows the synthesis of a Fire code from the two parts, with the polynomial expressions for comparison with the necessary hardware. During writing, k serial data bits are shifted into the circuit, and $n-k$ check bits are shifted out to give a codeword of length n. On reading, the codeword is shifted into the same circuit and should result in an all-zero syndrome if there has been no error, as in Fig.7.19. If there is a non-zero syndrome, there has been an error. As all data blocks are recorded as codewords, the effect of the actual data on the check circuit is to give a zero remainder. The only effect on the syndrome is due to the errors. Any non-zero syndrome represents the exclusive–OR function of what the data should have been and what it was. This function has, however, been shifted an unknown number of times. The error burst is one state of a Galois field, and the error burst is another. Any state of the Galois field can be reached from any other by shifting, so if the syndrome is shifted, sooner or later the error burst will show up. The only remaining question is how it will be recognized. The only ones in the correct state of the Galois field will be those representing the burst, and they will be confined to the last b stages of the register. All other stages of the register will be zero. Owing to the highly nonsequential nature of Galois fields, there is no possibility of $n-k-b$ contiguous zeros being found in any other state. The number of shifts required to arrive at this condition must be counted, because it is equal to the distance from the beginning of the block to the burst. In most Fire-code applications, the parameter b will be chosen to exceed the typical burst size of the channel, and the parameter m is chosen to achieve the desired probability of undetected error. This usually results in a code

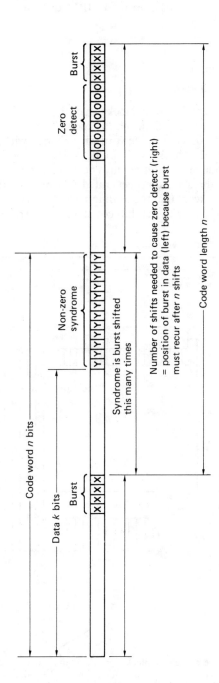

Figure 7.19 Owing to the characteristics of Galois fields, syndrome Y is simply the error burst which has been shifted a number of times equal to the number of bits from the burst to the end of the code word. As the field repeats every n shifts, it is only necessary to shift the syndrome and count the number of shifts necessary to give a zero detect condition. This number is equal to the position of the burst in the data. If no zero condition is found, then the burst is longer than b and cannot be corrected. It is, however, important to detect uncorrectable errors. The example can detect all bursts up to the length of the check word $n - k$; beyond this a statistical element is introduced.

word of enormous size, much longer than the data blocks used on most disk drives. For example, the Fire code used in many IBM disk drives uses the polynomial:

$$(x^{21} + 1)(x^{11} + x^2 + 1)$$

which gives a codeword of length:

$$(2^{11} - 1) \times 21 = 42987 \text{ bits } (42955 \text{ data bits})$$

In practice this is not a problem. The data block can be made shorter than the codeword by a technique known as puncturing the code. The actual data and the check bits represent the end of a long codeword which begins with zeros. As the effect of inputting zeros to the check-word circuit during a write is to cause no change, puncturing the code on writing requires no special action. On reading, by a similar argument, the syndrome generated will be as if the whole codeword had been recorded, except that the leading zeros are, of course, error-free, since they were not recorded. Thus the shift count which is arrived at when

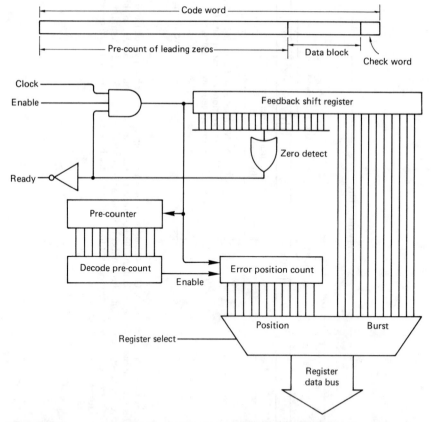

Figure 7.20 Error-correction hardware where data block is smaller than the codeword length. When a non-zero syndrome is detected after a read, the leading zeros in the codeword which precede the data are counted by the precounter. When the precount satisfies the decoder, error-position counter is enabled, which gives error position relative to the start of data when zero condition is detected. This disables the shifting and raises the ready bit.

the burst appears represents the bit count from the beginning of the codeword, not from the beginning of the real data. In practice, it is only necessary to employ an additional shift counter. This counts the number of leading zeros which were not recorded, when the syndrome is shifted. When it overflows, it enables a second shift counter, which counts shifts from the beginning of the data. The block diagram of such a system is shown in Fig.7.20. There are two outputs from the circuit, first the error-burst pattern, which will contain a one for every bit in error, and second the location of the start of the burst in bits from the beginning of the block.

An alternative is to construct a slightly different version of the twisted ring counter for syndrome shifting, which runs through the Galois field backwards. With punctured codes, this will perform correction faster. A faster correction still in Fire code can be obtained using the so called Chinese-remainder theorem. Instead of dividing the codeword by the full polynomial, it is simultaneously divided by the factors of the polynomial instead. If there is an error, the burst-pattern syndrome is shifted first to locate the burst pattern at the end of the register. The registers containing the other factors can then be shifted until their contents are the same as the burst pattern, when the number of shifts each needs can be used to find the burst position. In addition to allowing the use of conveniently sized blocks, puncturing a code can also be employed to decrease the probabilities of undetected error or miscorrection. Clearly if part of a codeword is not recorded it cannot contain errors!

Whilst Fire code was discovered at about the same time as the superior Reed–Solomon codes, it was dominant in disk drives until recently because it is so much easier to implement in circuitry. All that is needed is a handful of XOR gates, latches and counters or, more recently, one chip. Fire code is seldom used in digital audio equipment; it does, however, find an application in the subcode data structure on master U-matic cassettes used for Compact Disc cutting (see chapter 8).

7.13 B-adjacent code

In the B-adjacent code, used in consumer PCM adaptors conforming to the EIAJ format, two bursts can be corrected. The mechanism is shown in Fig.7.21, and operates as follows.

Six words of fourteen bits, A – F, are made into a codeword by the addition of two redundancy words, P and Q. The P word is a simple exclusive–OR sum of A – F, but the calculation of Q is more complex. The circuit of Fig.7.21(a) is supplied with each data word in turn and clocked, so that after six clocks the Q word has been calculated. The effect of the circuit of Fig.7.21(a) is actually to perform the matrix transform of Fig.7.21(b). If the transform is given by T, then Q will be given by:

$$Q = T^6 A \oplus T^5 B \oplus T^4 C \oplus T^3 D \oplus T^2 E \oplus TF$$

where $\oplus$ is modulo-2 addition.

The words A – F and P and Q form a codeword and are recorded. On replay, a separate mechanism determines which symbols in the codeword contain errors by the erasure method noted earlier in this chapter. For the purposes of this discussion, it is assumed that words A and C are in error. The readback

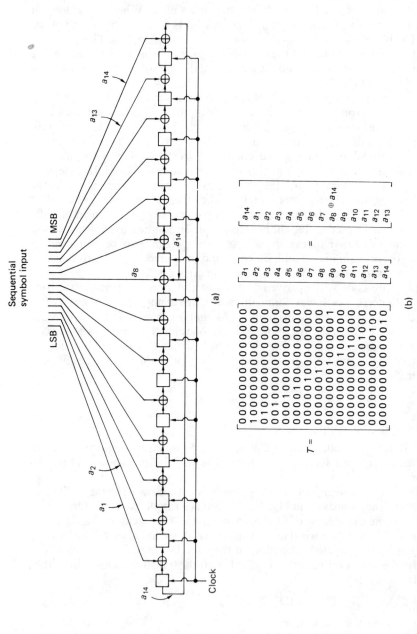

Figure 7.21 B-adjacent encoding; the circuit at (a) is presented with the input symbols sequentially, and each one is clocked. The feedback connections cause the circuit to execute the transform T shown in (b) at each clock. After several clocks, the register will contain the sum of each symbol multiplied by successively higher powers of T.

words are all fed into a similar circuit to the encoder. Since the codeword has the characteristic that it gives zero remainder when fed into the check circuit, it follows that the syndrome left in the check circuit in the case of an error is a function of the error alone. If words A and C are in error, the P section of the syndrome SP will be the exclusive–OR of the two errors, $EA \oplus EC$. The Q section of the syndrome SQ will be the exclusive–OR sum of the A word error multiplied by the sixth power of the transform T and the C word error multiplied by the fourth power of T.

$$SP = EA \oplus EC \tag{7.1}$$

$$SQ = T^6 EA \oplus T^4 EC \tag{7.2}$$

Dividing through Eqn. 7.2 by T^4 gives:

$$T^{-4} SQ = T^2 EA \oplus EC \tag{7.3}$$

Adding SP to both sides of Eqn. 7.3 gives:

$$SP \oplus T^{-4} SQ = T^2 EA \oplus EC \oplus SP$$

But $SP = EA \oplus EC$, therefore:

$$SP \oplus T^{-4} SQ = T^2 EA \oplus EC \oplus EA \oplus EC$$

$$= T^2 EA \oplus EA$$

$$= (1 + T^2) EA$$

Therefore:

$$EA = \frac{SP \oplus T^{-4} SQ}{1 + T^2}$$

and EC follows from Eqn.7.1.

It is thus only necessary to process the Q syndrome in a reverse transform according to the positions of the errors in the codeword in order to correct both errors. A more detailed description of the EIAJ format can be found in Chapter 8.

7.14 Reed–Solomon code

In the B-adjacent code, data are assembled into words for the purpose of burst correction. This is implicit in the operation of the Reed–Solomon codes.

The concept of the Galois field has been introduced earlier in this chapter in conjunction with Fire code. In Fire code, the error-burst pattern becomes one state of a Galois field, the syndrome becomes another, but the data bits are all still individually treated. In the Reed–Solomon codes, data bits are assembled into words, or symbols, which become elements of the Galois field upon which the code is based. The number of bits in the symbol determines the size of the Galois field, and hence the number of symbols in the codeword. A symbol size of eight is commonly used because it fits in conveniently with both sixteen-bit audio samples and byte-oriented computer chips. It is also highly appropriate for the Compact Disc and RDAT, since the EFM and 8/10 channel codes are group codes which can suffer up to eight bits in error if a single channel bit is corrupted. A Galois field with eight bit symbols has a maximum sequence

Table 7.1 The truth table for Galois field multiplication of GF (2^3). $F(x)=x^3+x+1$. Primitive element $a=010$.

| Element: | 0 | a | a^2 | a^3 | a^4 | a^5 | a^6 | $a^7=1$ |
Bits:	000	010	100	011	110	111	101	001
0 000	0 000	0 000	0 000	0 000	0 000	0 000	0 000	0 000
a 010	0 000	a^2 100	a^3 011	a^4 110	a^5 111	a^6 101	1 001	a 010
a^2 100	0 000	a^3 011	a^4 110	a^5 111	a^6 101	1 001	a 010	a^2 100
a^3 011	0 000	a^4 110	a^5 111	a^6 101	1 001	a 010	a^2 100	a^3 011
a^4 110	0 000	a^5 111	a^6 101	1 001	a 010	a^2 100	a^3 011	a^4 110
a^5 111	0 000	a^6 101	1 001	a 010	a^2 100	a^3 011	a^4 110	a^5 111
a^6 101	0 000	1 001	a 010	a^2 100	a^3 011	a^4 110	a^5 111	a^6 101
$a^7=1$ 001	0 000	a 010	a^2 100	a^3 011	a^4 110	a^5 111	a^6 101	1 001

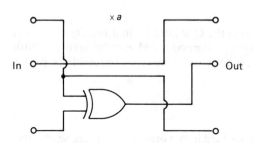

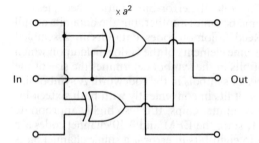

Figure 7.22 Some examples of GF multiplier circuits.

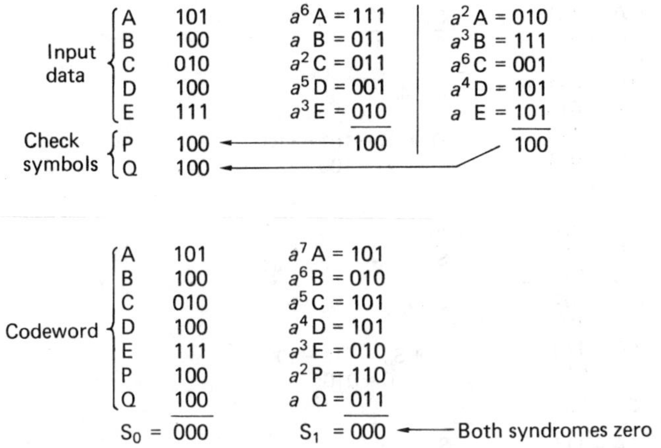

Input data	A	101	$a^6 A = 111$	$a^2 A = 010$
	B	100	$a\ B = 011$	$a^3 B = 111$
	C	010	$a^2 C = 011$	$a^6 C = 001$
	D	100	$a^5 D = 001$	$a^4 D = 101$
	E	111	$a^3 E = 010$	$a\ E = 101$
Check symbols	P	100 ← —————— 100		100
	Q	100 ←		

Codeword	A	101	$a^7 A = 101$
	B	100	$a^6 B = 010$
	C	010	$a^5 C = 101$
	D	100	$a^4 D = 101$
	E	111	$a^3 E = 010$
	P	100	$a^2 P = 110$
	Q	100	$a\ Q = 011$
		$S_0 = 000$	$S_1 = 000$ ←——— Both syndromes zero

Figure 7.23 Five data symbols A–E are used as terms in the generator polynomials derived in Appendix 7.1 to calculate two redundant symbols P and Q. An example is shown at the top. Below is the result of using the codeword symbols A–Q as terms in the checking polynomials. As there is no error, both syndromes are zero.

length of $2^8 - 1 = 255$. As each symbol contains eight bits, the codeword will be $255 \times 8 = 2040$ bits long.

As further examples, five bit symbols could be used to form a codeword 31 symbols long, and three-bit symbols would form a codeword seven symbols long. This latter size is small enough to permit some worked examples, and will be used further here.

In section 7.10 it was shown that the circuit of Fig.7.9 generated a Galois field when clocked with no input. The primitive element a will do this when raised to sequential powers. In Reed–Solomon coding, each symbol will be multiplied by some power of such a primitive element. It is necessary to construct hardware which will perform this multiplication. Table 7.1 shows that a truth table can be drawn up for a Galois field multiplier by simply adding the powers of the inputs.

For example:

$$a^2 = 100, \ a^3 = 011, \text{ so } 100 \times 011 = a^5 = 111$$

Note that the results of a Galois multiplication are quite different from binary multiplication. Because all products must be elements of the field, sums of powers which exceed seven wrap around by having seven subtracted:

$$a^5 \times a^6 = a^{11} = a^4 = 110$$

It has been stated that the effect of an error is to add an error polynomial to the message polynomial. The number of terms in the error polynomial is the same as the number of errors in the codeword. In a simple CRC system, the effect of the error is detected by ensuring that the codeword can be divided by a polynomial. In the Reed–Solomon codes, several errors can be isolated by ensuring that the codeword will divide by a number of first-order polynomials. If it is proposed to correct for a number of symbols in error given by t, the codeword must be divisible by $2t$ different polynomials of the form $(x + a^n)$ where n takes all values up to $2t$; a is the primitive element discussed earlier.

Fig.7.23, Fig.7.24 and Table 7.2 show some examples of Reed–Solomon

```
7  A    101      a⁷A = 101           S₁     a⁴
6  B    100      a⁶B = 010           ── = ── = a⁴
5  C    010      a⁵C = 101           S₀     1
4  D'   101      a⁴D' = 011  ←── k = 4
3  E    111      a³E = 010
2  P    100      a²P = 110           D' + S₀ = 101 + 001
1  Q    100      a Q = 011               D = 100
   S₀ = 001      S₁ = 110


7  A    101      a⁷A = 101           S₁    1     1    a⁵
6  B    100      a⁶B = 010           ── = ── = ── × ── = a⁵
5  C'   110      a⁵C = 100  ←        S₀    a²    a²   a⁵
4  D    100      a⁴D = 101       k = 5
3  E    111      a³E = 010
2  P    100      a²P = 110           C' + S₀ = 110 + 100
1  Q    100      a Q = 011               C = 010
   S₀ = 100      S₁ = 001


7  A'   111      a⁷A = 111           S₁    a
6  B    100      a⁶B = 010           ── = ── = 001 = a⁷
5  C    010      a⁵C = 101           S₀    a
4  D    100      a⁴D = 101       k = 7
3  E    111      a³E = 010
2  P    100      a²P = 110           A' + S₀ = 111 + 010
1  Q    100      a Q = 011               A = 101
   S₀ = 010      S₁ = 010
```

Figure 7.24 Three examples of error location and correction. The number of bits in error in a symbol is irrelevant; if all three were wrong, S_0 would be 111, but correction is still possible.

coding processes. The Galois field of Fig.7.9 has been used, and the primitive element $a = 010$ from Table 7.1 will be used. Five symbols of three bits each, A – E, are the data, and two redundant symbols, P and Q, will be used because this simple example will locate and correct only a single symbol in error. It does not matter, however, how many bits in the symbol are in error.

The two check symbols are solutions to the following equations:

$$A \oplus B \oplus C \oplus D \oplus E \oplus P \oplus Q = 0$$

$$a^7 A \oplus a^6 B \oplus a^5 C \oplus a^4 D \oplus a^3 E \oplus a^2 P \oplus a Q = 0$$

By some tedious mathematics, which are shown for reference in Appendix 7.1, it is possible to derive the following expressions which must be used to calculate P and Q from the data in order to satisfy the above equations. These are:

$$P = a^6 A \oplus a B \oplus a^2 C \oplus a^5 D \oplus a^3 E$$

$$Q = a^2 A \oplus a^3 B \oplus a^6 C \oplus a^4 D \oplus a E$$

In Fig.7.23 the redundant symbols have been calculated. In order to calculate P, the symbol A is multiplied by a^6 according to the Table 7.1, B is multiplied by a, and so on, and the products are added modulo-2. A similar process is used to calculate Q. The entire codeword now exists, and can be recorded. In Fig.7.23 it is also demonstrated that the codeword satisfies the checking equations.

Upon replaying the information, two checks must be made on the received message to see if it is a codeword. This is done by calculating syndromes using the following expressions, where the (') implies the received symbol which is not necessarily correct:

$$S_0 = A' \oplus B' \oplus C' \oplus D' \oplus E' \oplus P' \oplus Q'$$

(This is in fact a simple parity check.)

$$S_1 = a^7 A' \oplus a^6 B' \oplus a^5 C' \oplus a^4 D' \oplus a^3 E' \oplus a^2 P' \oplus a Q'$$

In Fig.7.24 three examples of errors are given, where the erroneous symbol is marked with a dash. As there has been an error, the syndromes S_0 and S_1 will not be zero. The syndrome calculation is performed with the Table 7.1 as before.

The parity syndrome S_0 determines the error bit pattern, and the syndrome S_1 is the same error bit pattern, but it has been raised to a different power of a dependent on the position of the error symbol in the block. If the position of the error is in symbol k, then:

$$S_0 \times a^k = S_1$$

Hence

$$a^k = \frac{S_1}{S_0}$$

The error symbol can be located by multiplying S_0 by various powers of a (which is the same as multiplying by successive elements of the Galois field) until the product is the same as S_1. The power of a necessary is known as the locator, because it gives the position of the error. The process of finding the error position by experiment is known as a Chien search.[7] Once the locator has identified the erroneous symbol, the correct value is obtained by adding S_0 (the corrector) to it.

In the examples of Fig.7.24, two redundant symbols have been used to locate and correct one error symbol. If the positions of errors are known by some separate mechanism (see crossinterleaving, section 7.16), the number of symbols which can be corrected is equal to the number of redundant symbols. In Table 7.2 two errors have taken place, and it is known that they are in symbols C and D. Since S_0 is a simple parity check, it will reflect the modulo-2 sum of the two errors. Hence $S_0 = EC \oplus ED$. The two errors will have been multiplied by different powers in S_1, such that:

$$S_1 = a^5 EC \oplus a^4 ED$$

It is possible to solve these two equations, as shown in the figure, to find EA and EB, and the correct value of the symbol will be obtained by adding these correctors to the erroneous values. It is, however, easier to set the values of the symbols in error to zero, and the correct values are then found more simply as shown in Table 7.2. This setting of symbols to zero gives rise to the term erasure.

The necessary circuitry for encoding the examples given is shown in Fig.7.25. The P and Q redundancy is computed using suitable Galois field multipliers to obtain the necessary powers of the primitive element according to Fig.7.21. In Fig.7.26 the circuitry for calculating the syndromes is shown. The S_0 circuit is a simple parity checker which produces the modulo-2 sum of all symbols fed to it. The S_1 circuit is more subtle, because it contains a Galois field multiplier in a feedback loop, such that early symbols fed in are raised to higher powers than later symbols because they have been recirculated through the GF multiplier more often. It is possible to compare the operation of these circuits with the examples of Fig.7.23, Fig.7.24 and Table 7.2 to confirm that the same results are obtained.

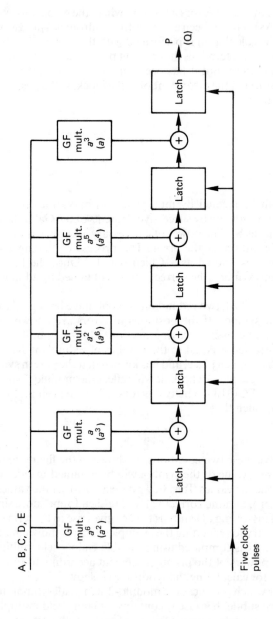

Figure 7.25 If the five data symbols of Figure 7.23, 7.24 and Table 7.2 are supplied to this circuit in sequence, after five clocks, one of the check symbols will appear at the output. Terms without brackets will calculate P, bracketed terms calculate Q.

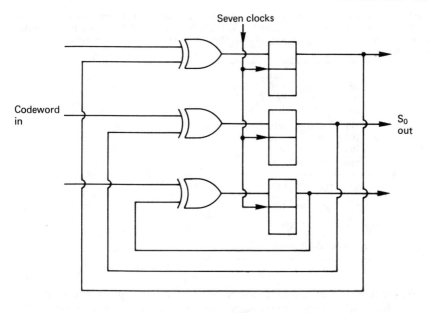

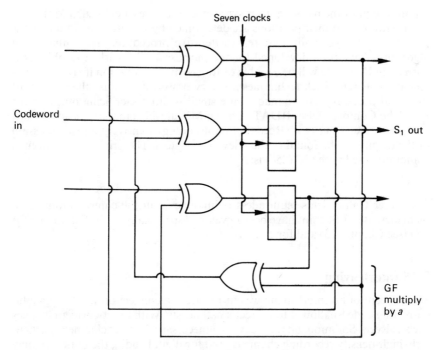

Figure 7.26 Circuits for parallel calculation of syndromes S_0, S_1. S_0 is a simple parity check. S_1 has a GF multiplication by a in the feedback, so that A is multiplied by a^7, B is multiplied by a^6 etc, and all are summed to give S_1.

Table 7.2 When the position of errors is known by some other means, two errors can be corrected for the same amount of redundancy. The technique is to set the symbols in error to zero, as shown, and calculate what they should have been. This gives the name of erasure correction to the system.

A	101	$a^7A =$	101	
B	100	$a^6B =$	010	$S_0 = C \oplus D$
C	000	$a^5C =$	000	
D	$\overline{000}$	$a^4D =$	$\overline{000}$	$S_1 = a^5\,C \oplus a^4D$
E	$\overline{111}$	$a^3E =$	$\overline{010}$	
P	100	$a^2P =$	110	
Q	100	$a\;Q =$	011	
S_0	$= 110$	$S_1\quad =$	$\overline{000}$	

$$S_1 = a^5S_0 \oplus a^5D \oplus a^4D = a^5S_0 \oplus D$$

$$\therefore D = S_1 \oplus a^5S_0 = 000 \oplus 100 = \underline{100}$$

$$S_1 = a^5C \oplus a^4C \oplus a^4S_0 = C \oplus a^4S_0$$

$$\therefore C = S_1 \oplus a^4S_0 = 000 \oplus 010 = \underline{010}$$

Where two symbols are to be corrected without the help of erasure pointers, four redundant symbols are necessary, and the codeword polynomial must then be divisible by:

$$(x + a^0)\,(x + a^1)\,(x + a^2)\,(x + a^3)$$

Upon receipt of the message, four syndromes must be calculated, and the two error patterns and their positions are determined by solving four simultaneous equations. This generally requires an iterative procedure, and a number of algorithms have been developed for the purpose.[8,9,10] Clearly a double error correcting R–S code will be capable of four-symbol correction if erasure pointers are available. Such techniques are very powerful, because the amount of overhead necessary can be made quite small without sacrificing output error rate. The Compact Disc, RDAT and the Mitsubishi stationary-head formats use erasure techniques with Reed–Solomon coding extensively, and a discussion of the details can be found in the relevant chapters. The primitive polynomial commonly used with GF (256) is:

$$x^8 + x^4 + x^3 + x^2 + 1$$

The larger Galois fields require less redundancy, but the computational problem increases. LSI chips have been developed specifically for R–S decoding for CD (see Chapter 13) and for other formats.[11]

7.15 Interleaving

The concept of bit interleaving was introduced in connection with a single-bit correcting code to allow it to correct small bursts. With burst-correcting codes such as Reed–Solomon, bit interleave is unnecessary. In most channels, particularly high-density recording channels used for digital audio, the burst size may be many bytes rather than bits, and to rely on a cyclic code alone to correct such errors would require a lot of redundancy. The solution in this case is to employ

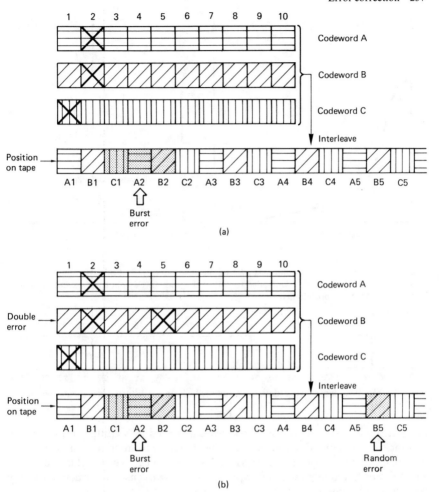

Figure 7.27 At (a), interleave controls the size of burst errors in individual code words, but at (b) the system falls down when a random error occurs adjacent to a burst.

word interleaving, as shown in Fig.7.27(a). Several codewords are encoded from input data, but these are not recorded in the order they were input, but are physically reordered in the channel, so that a real burst error is split into smaller bursts in several codewords. The size of the burst seen by each codeword is now determined primarily by the parameters of the interleave, and Fig.7.28 shows that the probability of occurrence of bursts with respect to the burst length in a given codeword is modified. The number of bits in the interleave word can be made equal to the burst-correcting ability of the code in the knowledge that it will be exceeded only very infrequently.

There are a number of different ways in which interleaving can be performed. Fig.7.29 shows that in block interleaving, words are reordered within blocks which are themselves in the correct order. This approach is attractive in PCM adaptors for use with video cassette recorders, such as the Sony PCM 1610/1630, because the blocks fit into the frame structure of the television waveform,

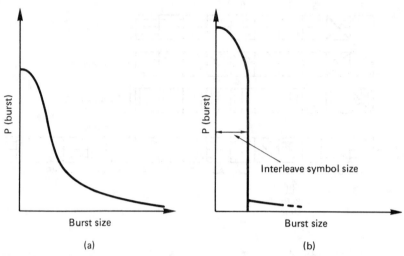

Figure 7.28 (a) The distribution of burst sizes might look like this. (b) Following interleave, the burst size within a codeword is controlled to that of the interleave symbol size, except for gross errors which have low probability.

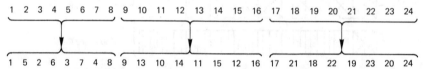

Figure 7.29 In block interleaving, data are scrambled within blocks which are themselves in the correct order.

and editing is easy. The block interleave is achieved by writing samples into a memory in sequential address locations from a counter, and reading the memory with nonsequential addresses from a sequencer. The effect is to convert a one-dimensional sequence of samples into a two-dimensional structure having rows and columns.

Fig.7.30 shows that, in convolutional interleaving, the interleave process is endless. Samples are assembled into short blocks, and then each sample is individually delayed by an amount proportional to the position in the block. Clearly rows cannot be practically assembled in an endless process, as they would be infinitely long, so convolutional interleave produces diagonal codewords. It is possible for a convolutional interleave to continue from field to field in VCR-based systems, and this is done in the EIAJ format. Convolutional interleave requires some caution in editing, and this will be discussed later in this chapter. A combination of the two techniques above is shown in Fig.7.31, where a convolutional code is made to have finite size by making it into a loop. This is known as a block-completed convolutional code, and is found in the digital audio blocks of the Video 8 format and in JVC PCM adaptors. The effect of the interleave can be maintained in block-completed interleave provided the block is large enough compared to the interleave parameters, but this requires a large interleave memory.

The above interleaves assume that a single one-dimensional channel is available for the information. In the Compact Disc this is true, as there is only one

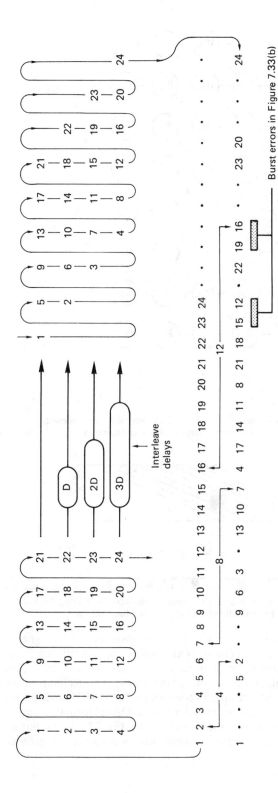

Figure 7.30 In convolutional interleaving, samples are formed into a rectangular array, which is sheared by subjecting each row to a different delay. The sheared array is read in vertical columns to provide the interleaved output. In this example, samples will be found at 4, 8 and 12 places away from their original order.

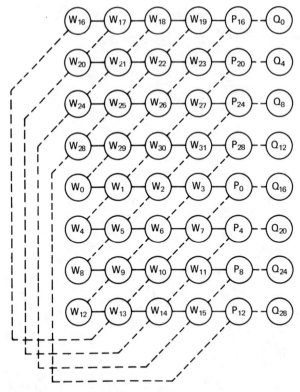

Figure 7.31 In block-completed convolutional interleave some diagonal codewords wrap around the end of the block. This requires a large memory and causes a longer deinterleaving delay.

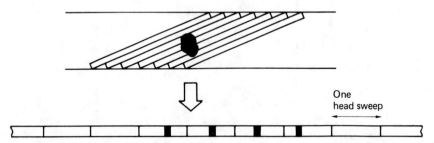

Figure 7.32 Helical-scan recorders produce a form of mechanical interleaving, because one large defect on the medium becomes distributed over several head sweeps.

laser beam and a continuous track, but in stationary-head magnetic tape recorders, there can be several channels available using a multitrack head. It is possible to interleave samples by distributing them across many tracks, because the average dropout will only affect one or two tracks. This technique is used in the Mitsubishi digital audio recorders conforming to the PD (ProDigi) format, and in the medium- and slow-speed versions of the DASH format. Rotary-head recorders naturally interleave spatially on the tape. Fig.7.32 shows that a single large tape defect becomes a series of small defects owing to the geometry of helical scanning.

7.16 Crossinterleaving

In the presence of burst errors alone, the system of interleaving works very well, but it is known that in many channels there are also uncorrelated errors of a few bits due to noise. Fig.7.27(b) shows that a noise error in the vicinity of a burst error will cause two errors in one codeword, which may not be correctable. The solution to this problem is to use a system where codewords are formed both before and after the interleave process. In block interleaving, this results in a product code, whereas in convolutional interleaving the result is known as crossinterleaving.[12] Many of the characteristics of these systems are similar. Fig.7.33(a) shows a crossinterleave system where several errors have taken place. In one row, there are two errors, which are beyond the power of the codeword to correct, and on two diagonals, the same is true. However, if a diagonal has two errors, a row will generally only have one. This one error can be corrected, which means that one of the two errors in the diagonal disappears, and so the diagonal codeword can correct it. This then means that there will be only one error in the next row and so on. Random errors in the vicinity of bursts can now be corrected.

In fact, the power of crossinterleaving and product codes goes beyond the ability to deal with real-life errors. The fact that there is a two-dimensional structure allows the position of an error to be discovered because it will be at the intersection of two codewords. If the position of the error can be established geometrically, then it is not necessary to find it by using a code which needs redundancy. The overhead required for crossinterleaving is actually less than any other system for a given performance, because the detection of an error in one codeword before deinterleave can be used to generate erasure pointers which help a further codeword after deinterleave. The combination of codewords with interleaving in several dimensions yields an error-protection strategy which is truly synergistic, in that the end result is more powerful than the sum of the parts. Needless to say, the technique is used extensively in digital audio systems.

7.17 Practical examples

Some examples of crossinterleaving and product codes will now be given to allow several different approaches to the principle to be contrasted. It should be noted that these examples are simplified to act as an introduction, and that precise details of these formats can be found in their respective chapters.

Fig.7.34 shows in a simplified form the strategy used in DASH format and in JVC PCM adaptors for Compact Disc mastering. These use an almost identical strategy, but the parameters will be different in each case. One difference is that DASH has an endless interleave, whereas the JVC unit is block-completed. Samples in correct order are assembled into short blocks, and a parity character P is calculated from the modulo-2 sum of all the samples. A convolutional interleave is then formed by delaying the symbols as a function of their position in the block. A further parity character Q is then computed in the same way. Another stage of interleave is then applied, and highly nonsequential samples from this interleave are formed into a third codeword by the calculation of a CRCC. This codeword is recorded on the tape. Clearly none of the codewords in this system has any error-locating ability. If an error occurs during replay, the

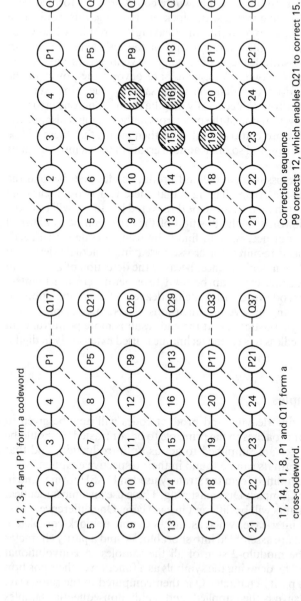

1, 2, 3, 4 and P1 form a codeword

17, 14, 11, 8, P1 and Q17 form a
cross-codeword.

(a)

Correction sequence
P9 corrects 12, which enables Q21 to correct 15.
With 15 correct, P13 corrects 16.
P17 corrects 19.

(b)

Figure 7.33 (a) In crossinterleaving, codewords are formed on data before interleaving (1, 2, 3, 4, P1), and after convolutional interleaving (21, 18, 15, 12, P5, Q21). Compare with Figure 7.30. (b) Multiple errors in one codeword will become single errors in another. If the sequence shown is followed, then all the errors can be corrected. In this example, error samples 12, 15, 16 and 19 are due to two bursts in the convolutional interleave of Figure 7.30.

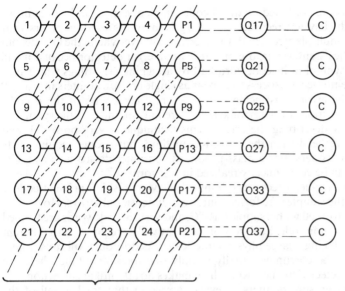

CRC codewords (error flags)

Figure 7.34 In the P, Q, CRC crossinterleave, P and Q parity codewords are formed, as in Figure 7.33(a), but then a further interleave is formed on an oblique diagonal. Data will be recorded on this diagonal, and if the CRC formed fails, all samples on the diagonal are held to be in error; upon deinterleave, the errors will become single-sample errors in many P codewords which can be corrected by erasure. If there are too many errors for P alone, the P–Q–P sequence of Figure 7.33(b) can be followed.

CRC will fail, but no other information about the error will be available. The system assumes that every sample in the CRC codeword is faulty, and attaches flags to the samples. After deinterleave to the correct sample sequence, the flagged samples will appear as single sample errors in many different P codewords, which can be corrected by taking the modulo-2 sum of the remaining samples and P. In the event of a random error occuring near a burst, some P codewords will be found after deinterleave to contain two error flags, which parity cannot correct. In this case, the samples are reinterleaved again to Q, when the two errors in P will become two single errors in two different Q codewords, which can be corrected by taking a modulo-2 sum as before. Upon deinterleaving to the correct sample sequence it is possible to allow the P codewords to correct any remaining single errors. The attraction of this strategy is that it can be implemented with a single CRC-generating chip, because the location of the errors is by geometry.

In the Compact Disc, Reed–Solomon codewords are used which can locate and correct burst errors. Fig.7.35 shows a simplified version of the crossinterleaved Reed–Solomon error-correcting strategy. Again samples in the correct order are formed into short blocks, and made into Reed–Solomon codewords by the addition of redundancy P. A convolutional interleave is then formed using delays which are a function of the position within the block. Following interleave, the symbols are used to create further Reed–Solomon codewords by the addition of further redundancy Q. These codewords are then recorded.

Random errors are corrected by the Q code which operates on the data in the order in which they are recorded, and largely prevents random errors near bursts causing multiple errors in P. Burst errors will overwhelm the Q code, but it still serves the essential purpose of acting as an error detector because it will declare every symbol in its codeword bad by attaching error flags which pass through the deinterleave process to appear as single erasure pointers in many P codewords. The error flags increase the power of correction of the P code, because if the positions of the error symbols are known, more of the syndrome can be used for describing the errors. This technique is very powerful, and requires less overhead than the P,Q,CRC method, but it does require fairly complex R–S decoders. For a mass-produced consumer device such as a CD player, these can be economically realized in LSI form.

In the stationary-head recorders designed by Mitsubishi, a product code is used whereby the samples are formed into two-dimensional arrays. Horizontal codewords are formed with a simple CRCC, and vertical codewords are formed using Reed–Solomon code. Each row of the array will be recorded on a different tape track, producing a large physical interleave. As dropouts will cause many adjacent bits to be corrupted usually in only one track at a time, these are designed to be detected by the CRC, which makes no attempt at correction, but simply attaches erasure pointers to every sample in that track in all of the Reed–Solomon column codewords of the array. The columns are then corrected using the erasure pointers and the Reed–Solomon redundancy.

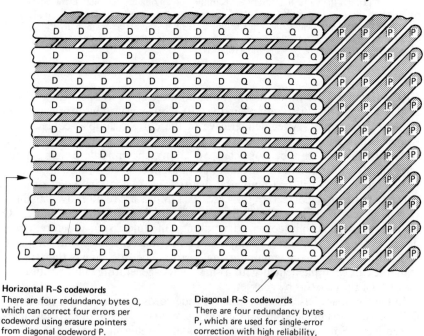

Horizontal R–S codewords
There are four redundancy bytes Q, which can correct four errors per codeword using erasure pointers from diagonal codeword P.

Diagonal R–S codewords
There are four redundancy bytes P, which are used for single-error correction with high reliability, and for multiple-error detection to generate erasure flags for the Q code.

Figure 7.35 A crossinterleaved Reed–Solomon code (CIRC). The P code corrects random errors, preventing the situation of Figure 7.27 (b) from reducing the power of the interleaving. In the presence of burst errors, P passes erasure pointers to the Q correction, which can correct up to four bytes, because the location of the errors is known (as in Table 7.2).

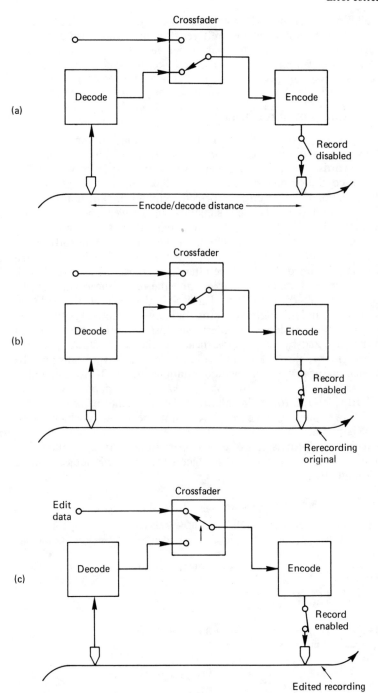

Figure 7.36 Editing a convolutionally interleaved recording. (a) Existing recording is decoded and re-encoded. After some time, record can be enabled at (b) when the existing tape pattern is being rerecorded. The crossfader can then be operated, resulting (c) in an interleaved edit on the tape.

In the audio blocks of the D-1 professional VCR and in RDAT, a product code is used where both dimensions are Reed–Solomon codewords. One is a random corrector and burst detector/erasure flag generator, whereas the other is an erasure-flag-driven burst corrector, much like the principle used in CD, although CD is crossinterleaved.

7.18 Editing interleaved recordings

The presence of a convolutional interleave means that editing has to be undertaken with care. If a new recording is joined to a previous recording, the diagonal codewords over a constraint length near the edit point will be destroyed, and the correction power of the system will be limited. There is only one way to edit a convolutional interleave correctly, and this is shown in Fig.7.36. Prior to the edit point, the replay head signal is deinterleaved, and this signal is fed to the record channel. The record channel reinterleaves the samples, and produces a signal which will, after some time, be the same as that already on the tape. By this time the original recording will have travelled some distance, and a second head is positioned that distance after the playback head. At a block boundary, the record amplifier is enabled, and the record head will then be rerecording what is already on the tape. The cross-fader can now be faded over to the new material, and the interleaved cross-fade will be recorded, followed by the new material. All recorders using interleave must adopt this technique, and it is often implemented by having extra heads as shown. In stationary-head recorders this is no problem. In rotary head recorders, the extra heads must be accommodated on the drum. This method is adopted in the D-1 format and in the PCM audio version of C-format (Chapter 11). In PCM adaptors, which use fairly standard video recorders, the additional heads are not present, and for successful editing a complex sequence of events must be followed, which will be discussed in chapter 8.

In stationary-head formats, it is often necessary to support tape-cut editing, which requires special techniques for satisfactory results. This subject will be treated in Chapter 9.

Appendix 7.1 Calculation of Reed–Solomon generator polynomials

For a Reed–Solomon codeword over $GF(2^3)$, there will be seven three-bit symbols. For location and correction of one symbol, there must be two redundant symbols P and Q, leaving A–E for data.

The following expressions must be true, where a is the primitive element of $x^3 + x + 1$ and $+$ is XOR throughout.

$$A + B + C + D + E + P + Q = 0 \tag{1}$$
$$a^7A + a^6B + a^5C + a^4D + a^3E + a^2P + aQ = 0 \tag{2}$$

Dividing eq. (2) by a:

$$a^6A + a^5B + a^4C + a^3D + a^2E + aP + Q = 0 = A + B + C + D + E + P + Q$$

Cancelling Q, and collecting terms:

$$(a^6 + 1)A + (a^5 + 1)B + (a^4 + 1)C + (a^3 + 1)D + (a^2 + 1)E = (a + 1)P$$

Using Table 7.1 to calculate $(a^n + 1)$, e.g. $a^6 + 1 = 101 + 001 = 100 = a^2$

$$a^2A + a^4B + a^5C + aD + a^6E = a^3P$$
$$a^6A + aB + a^2C + a^5D + a^3E = P \tag{3}$$

Multiply eq. (1) by a^2 and equating to eq. (2):

$$a^2A + a^2B + a^2C + a^2D + a^2E + a^2P + a^2Q = 0$$
$$= a^7A + a^6B + a^5C + a^4D + a^3E + a^2P + aQ$$

Cancelling a^2P and collecting terms (remember $a^2 + a^2 = 0$):

$(a^7 + a^2)$A $+ (a^6 + a^2)$B $+ (a^5 + a^2)$C $+ (a^4 + a^2)$D $+ (a^3 + a^2)$E $= (a^2 + a)$Q

Adding powers according to Table 7.1, e.g. $a^7 + a^2 = 001 + 100 = 101 = a^6$:

a^6A $+$ B $+ a^3$C $+ a$D $+ a^5$E $= a^4$Q

a^2A $+ a^3$B $+ a^6$C $+ a^4$D $+ a$E $=$ Q

References

1. BELLIS, F.A., A multichannel digital sound recorder. Presented at the Video and Data Recording Conference, Birmingham, England. *IERE Conf. Proc.*, No. 35 123–126 (1976)
2. HAMMING, R.W., Error-detecting and error-correcting codes. *Bell System Tech. J.*, **26**, 147–160 (1950)
3. PETERSON, W. and BROWN, D., Cyclic codes for error detection. *Proc. IRE*, 228–235 (1961)
4. FIRE, P., A class of multiple-error correcting codes for non-independent errors. *Sylvania Reconnaissance Systems Lab. Report.* RSL-E-2 (1959)
5. BOSSEN, D.C., B-adjacent error correction. *IBM J. Res. Dev.*, **14**, 402–408 (1970)
6. REED, I.S. and SOLOMON, G., Polynomial codes over certain finite fields. *J. Soc. Indust. Appl. Math.*, **8**, 300–304 (1960)
7. CHIEN, R.T., CUNNINGHAM, B.D. and OLDHAM, I.B., Hybrid methods for finding roots of a polynomial —with application to BCH decoding. *IEEE Trans. Inf. Theory.*, **IT-15**, 329–334 (1969)
8. BERLEKAMP, E.R., *Algebraic Coding Theory.* New York: McGraw-Hill (1967). Reprint edition: Laguna Hills: Aegean Park Press (1983)
9. SUGIYAMA, Y. *et al.*, An erasures and errors decoding algorithm for Goppa codes. *IEEE Trans. Inf. Theory*, **IT 22** (1976)
10. PETERSON, W.W. and WELDON, E.J., *Error Correcting Codes* 2nd.ed., MIT Press (1972)
11. ONISHI, K., SUGIYAMA, K., ISHIDA, Y., KUSUNOKI, Y. and YAMAGUCHI, T., A LSI for Reed-Solomon encoder/decoder. Presented at the 80th Audio Engineering Society Convention (Montreux, 1986) preprint 2316(A4)
12. DOI, T.T., ODAKA, K., FUKUDA, G. and FURUKAWA, S. Crossinterleave code for error correction of digital audio systems. *J. Audio Eng. Soc.*, **27**, 1028 (1979)

Chapter 8

Rotary head recorders

The rotary-head recorder has a significant part to play in digital audio because in certain applications it offers a number of advantages. The general concepts of the various kinds of rotary head machine will be explained here with particular emphasis on the equipment used for Compact Disc mastering and on the consumer RDAT recorder. The reader is referred to Chapter 7 for an explanation of the error-correction principles referred to.

8.1 Use of video recorders

Digital audio has been possible for several decades, but has only recently become economic with the development of high-density recorders. The necessary rate of about two megabits per second for a stereo signal can now be recorded with moderate tape consumption. It is not so long ago, however, that the data rate itself was a problem. When head and tape technology were less advanced than they are today, wavelengths on tape were long, and the only way that high frequencies could be accommodated was to use high speeds. High speed can be achieved in two ways. The head can remain fixed, and the tape can be transported rapidly, with obvious consequences, or the tape can travel relatively slowly, and the head can be moved. The latter is the principle of the rotary-head recorder. Fig.8.1 shows the general arrangement of the two major categories of rotary-head recorder. In transverse-scan recorders, relatively short tracks are recorded almost at right angles to the direction of tape motion by a rotating headwheel containing, typically, four heads. In helical-scan recorders, the tape is wrapped around the drum in such a way that it enters and leaves in two different planes. This causes the rotating heads to record long slanting tracks. In both approaches, the width of the space between tracks is determined by the linear tape speed. The track pitch can easily be made much smaller than in stationary-head recorders.

The use of rotary heads was instrumental in the development of the first video recorders. As video signals consist of discrete lines and frames, it was possible to conceal the interruptions in the tracks of a rotary-head machine by making them coincident with the time when the CRT was blanked during flyback. The first video recorders developed by Ampex used the transverse-scan approach, with four heads on the rotor: hence the name quadruplex which was given to this system. The tracks were a little shorter than the two-inch width of the tape,

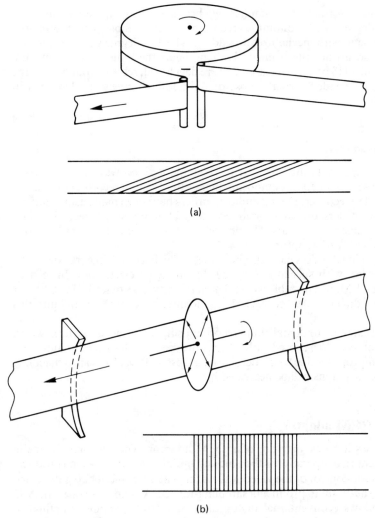

(a)

(b)

Figure 8.1 Types of rotary head recorder. (a) Helical scan records long diagonal tracks. (b) Transverse scan records short tracks across the tape.

and several sweeps were necessary to build up a video frame. The change-overs between the heads were made during the horizontal synchronizing pulses. The head contact pressure can never be made stable with rotating heads so, to this day, analog video recorders use frequency modulation which is immune to amplitude variations. The timebase stability of these machines was relatively good, but tape consumption was high, and variable-speed operation was virtually impossible. For professional use, the quadruplex format gave way to one-inch tape formats, which used helical scan and an almost total wrap to fit an entire field into a slant track about 15 in (380 mm) long. The change-over between tracks was then made in the vertical interval. The timebase stability was rather worse than quad, but the digital timebase corrector was developed to overcome this. For industrial use, the U-matic machine was developed by Sony.

In the U- matic format, the drum has two heads, so the wrap needs only to be about 180 degrees, yet a continuous recording is still possible. This allowed the use of a cassette with mechanized threading. The 180-degree wrap means that the tape passes around the drum in a U shape, hence the name. Subsequently the Betamax and VHS consumer cassettes were developed, recently followed by the 8 mm consumer video format whose digital audio channels are described in Chapter 10.

8.2 Pseudo-video

If digital sample data are encoded to resemble a video waveform, which is known as pseudo-video or composite digital, they can be recorded on a fairly standard video recorder. Digital audio recorders have been made using quadruplex video recorders, one-inch video recorders, U-matic cassette recorders, and the smaller consumer formats. The device needed to format the samples in this way is called a PCM adaptor.

Digital audio recorders have also been made which use only the transport of a video recorder, with specially designed digital signal electronics. Instead of using analog FM, it is possible to use digital recording, as described in Chapter 6, to make a direct digital recorder. The machines built by Decca fall into this category.

The final category of digital audio recorder using rotary heads is one in which direct digital recording is used with a transport specially designed for audio use with no compromises due to a video-based ancestry. RDAT is such a machine. All of these variations will be described here.

8.3 Sony PCM adaptor

Fig.8.2 shows a block diagram of a PCM adaptor. The unit has five main sections. Central to operation is the sync and timing generation, which produces sync pulses for control of the video waveform generator and locking the video recorder, in addition to producing sampling-rate clocks and timecode. An A/D converter allows a conventional analog audio signal to be recorded, but this can be bypassed if a suitable digital input is available. Similarly a D/A converter is provided to monitor recordings, and this too can be bypassed by using the direct digital output. Also visible in Fig.8.2 are the encoder and decoder stages which convert between digital sample data and the pseudo-video signal.

An example of this type of unit is the PCM-1610/1630 which was designed by Sony for use with a U-matic Video Cassette Recorder (VCR) specifically for Compact Disc mastering. A matching editor has also been designed.

Chapter 2 showed how many audio sampling rates were derived from video frequencies. The Compact Disc format is an international standard, and it was desirable for the mastering recorder to adhere to a single format. Thus the PCM- 1610 only works in conjunction with a 525/60 monochrome VCR. There is no 625/50 version. Thus even in PAL countries Compact Discs are still mastered on 60 Hz VCRs, which means that the traditional international interchange of recordings can still be achieved. The PCM-1610 was intended for professional use, and thus was not intended to be produced in volume. For this

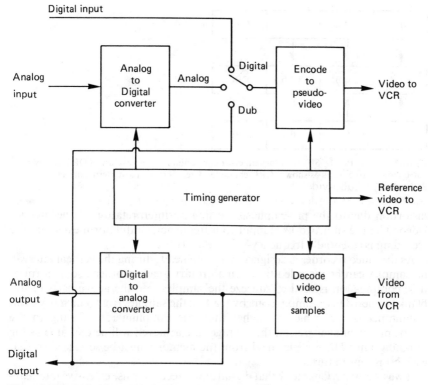

Figure 8.2 Block diagram of PCM adaptor. Note the dub connection needed for producing a digital copy between two VCRs.

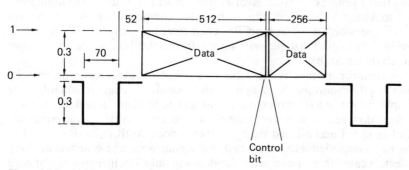

Figure 8.3 Typical line of video from PCM-1610. The control bit conveys the setting of the pre-emphasis switch or the sampling rate depending on position in the frame. The bits are separated using only the timing information in the sync pulses.

reason the format is simple, even crude, because the LSI technology needed to implement more complex formats was not available.

A typical line of pseudo-video is shown in Fig.8.3. The line is divided into bit cells and, within them, black level represents a binary zero, and about 60 % of peak white represents binary one. The reason for the restriction to 60 % is that most VCRs use nonlinear pre-emphasis and this operating level prevents any

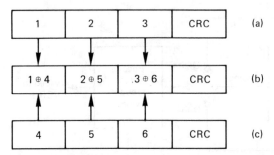

Figure 8.4 In the PCM-1610/1630 format, error correction is via an exclusive–OR term computed from two samples as shown. CRC character detects errors; parity term corrects. Redundancy is high at 100%.

distortion due to the pre-emphasis causing misinterpretation of the pseudo-video. The use of a two-level input to a frequency modulator means that the recording is essentially frequency-shift keyed (FSK).

As the video recorder is designed to switch heads during the vertical interval, no samples can be recorded there. In all rotary-head recorders, some form of time compression is used to squeeze the samples into the active parts of un-blanked lines. This is simply done by reading the samples from a memory at an instantaneous rate which is higher than the sampling rate. Owing to the interruptions of sync pulses, the average rate achieved will be the same as the sampling rate. The samples read from the memory must be serialized so that each bit is sent in turn.

It was shown in Chapter 7 that digital audio recorders use extensive interleaving to combat tape dropout. The PCM-1610 subdivides each video field into seven blocks of 35 lines each, and interleaves samples within the blocks. Fig.8.4 shows that a simple crossword error-correction scheme is used. The input samples 1 to 3 form a codeword at (a) with a CRC character. Samples 4 to 6 form another codeword at (c) with a CRC character. The exclusive–OR terms, or modulo -2 sums of the sample pairs shown, form a third codeword with its own CRC character at (b).

If an error occurs, the CRC fails, but no attempt is made to locate the error by processing the syndrome. All samples in the codeword are presumed faulty. For example, if sample 5 is corrupt, codeword (c) will be in error, and samples 4, 5 and 6 are declared to be in error. Sample 4 is obtained by taking the exclusive–OR of sample 1 and the first parity symbol, since 1 XOR (1 XOR 4) = 4. The other two sample values are obtained in a similar way. The system is not very efficient, because there is as much redundancy as data, but there is no great need to conserve bandwidth, as this is determined by the U-matic format, and is plentiful for this application.

Fig.8.5 shows that the interleave over a 35-line period includes a left/right channel interleave and an odd/even sample interleave. The reason for these is that a large burst error damages half of the samples in both audio channels instead of all of the samples in one channel. Samples to be recorded are stored in a memory, and three passes are made through the memory to encode each $11\frac{2}{3}$ line segment. The necessary time compression into the active lines is performed with the same memory. The first pass takes odd right samples and even left samples, and produces codewords as in Fig.8.5(a) for $11\frac{2}{3}$ lines. The next pass

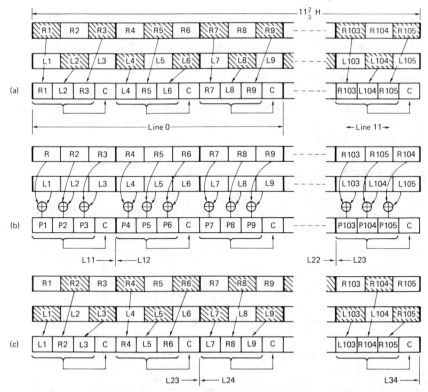

Figure 8.5 One 35-line interleave block of 1610/1630 format. The block is divided into three sections of $11\frac{2}{3}$ lines each: two data, one parity. Three passes through the interleave memory are necessary to create the signal structure (a, b, c). The large L/R interleave allows interpolation if dropout exceeds $11\frac{2}{3}$ lines.

takes both right and left samples simultaneously and computes the parity symbols and CRCs for a further $11\frac{2}{3}$ lines. Finally, on the third pass through the memory, even right and odd left samples are made into codewords.

Using this format, dropouts of up to $11\frac{2}{3}$ lines long are fully correctable, since an error of this magnitude will never corrupt more than one of the three related codewords necessary for correction. For example, if line 0 is corrupt, P1, P2 and P3 from the end of line 11, and L1, R2 and L3 from the middle of line 23 are used to correct R1, L2 and R3, and so on. If the dropout continues further, then two codewords of the related threes will be corrupted in some cases, and correction is not then possible. In this case interpolation can be used to conceal the errors. For example, if lines 0 to 12 are destroyed, L4, R5 and L6 will be uncorrectable (amongst others) but because of the interleave, in line 23, L3 and L5 can be used to re-create L4, R4 and R6 can be used to re-create R5, and L5 and L7 can be used for L6.

If the corruption is more severe, then pairs of samples either side of the wanted sample may not be available, and interpolation is impossible. The previous sample will be repeated in this case. Eventually the machine mutes the output to prevent noise. In practice dropouts are much smaller than the correctable size. The relatively large trackwidth of the U-matic gives a signal-to-noise ratio which is much higher than necessary for digital recording, so the random error rate is fairly low, and the simple format succeeds. It is not suitable for use with consumer VCRs. A further reason that the 1610 format is restricted to U-matic VCRs is that the timecode is recorded on a linear audio track. This works well with the relatively high linear tape speed of U-matic, but is not generally successful on the consumer formats.

Some VCRs have dropout compensators built in, which repeat a section of the previous line to conceal the missing picture information. Such circuits must be disabled when used with PCM adaptors because they interfere with the error-correction mechanism.

8.4 JVC PCM adaptor

A PCM adaptor for Compact Disc mastering has also been developed by JVC[1] and again an editor was designed to suit it. This format has a more powerful

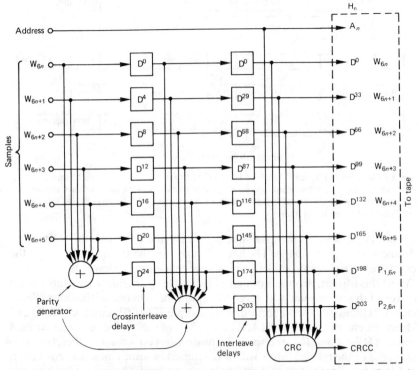

Figure 8.6 Interleave diagram of JVC format showing parity generated before and after an interleave to produce cross-interleaving. This resists a combination of burst and random errors very well. CRC character acts as error detection.

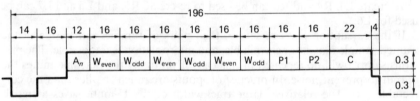

Figure 8.7 Video line of JVC system.

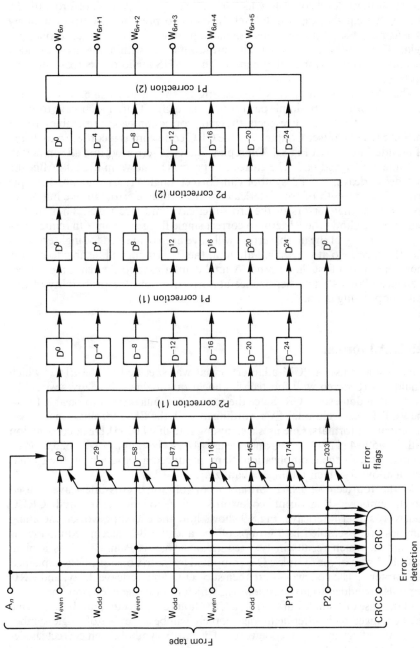

Figure 8.8 Deinterleave and correction diagram for JVC format. Depending upon distribution of errors, it may be better to correct with P1 first or P2 first. Multiple reinterleave and deinterleave allows both choices.

error-correction system, and can be used with VHS recorders; again only 525/60 machines are supported for international interchange. These recorders often have automatic level controls, which increase the video gain on record until the peak value equals peak white level. In order to prevent ALC from wrongly increasing the 0.3 V pseudo-video signal, a peak white flag is included once per field. The timecode and user bits are contained within the pseudo-video waveform, so the poor analog bandwidth of VHS audio tracks ceases to be a problem.

The JVC format uses crossinterleaving as shown in Fig.8.6. The crossinterleave is formed with simple parity only, and a CRCC after interleave to act as an error pointer. In many respects, the error-correction system resembles that of the DASH format (see Chapter 9). One CRC codeword is recorded in each line of pseudo-video as in Fig.8.7. On replay, if a CRC error occurs, all samples in that line are flagged bad. The correction process is shown in Fig.8.8. After the first deinterleave, the P2 symbol can correct single errors, but not multiple errors. The strength of crossinterleave is that multiple errors in one interleave show up as single errors in the crossinterleave and vice versa. Thus further deinterleave allows the P1 term to correct single flagged errors. On reinterleaving to P2, many of the double errors will have been converted to single errors in the P1 process, so at the second attempt, the P2 symbol will be able to correct more than it did first time round. A final deinterleave to the real-time sample sequence allows P1 another chance at correction, but the probability of this stage's operating is small.

8.5 EIAJ format

For consumer use, a PCM adapter format was specified by the EIAJ[2] which would record stereo with fourteen-bit linear quantizing. These units would be used with a domestic VCR. Since the consumer would expect to be able to use the VCR for conventional TV recording as well, the EIAJ format is in fact two incompatible formats. One uses a sampling rate of 44.0559 kHz in conjunction with 525/59.94 NTSC timing, and one uses 44.1 kHz sampling with 625/50 PAL timing. As a further complication, Sony produced a variation on the format which allowed sixteen-bit linear quantizing.

In the fourteen-bit EIAJ format, a convolutional crossinterleave is used which employs B-adjacent codewords prior to interleave, and CRCC codewords after interleave. Fig.8.9 shows how the encoding works. Incoming samples are assembled into groups of six, and the B-adjacent redundancy is calculated, which results in two redundant symbols P and Q. P is a plain modulo-2 sum of the samples; Q is computed by matrix operations as explained in Chapter 7. The codewords are then subject to an interleave delay, and CRC symbols are added to make codewords which fit into one television line.

In the case of a single burst error, a CRC failure will occur, and the entire line will be flagged bad. After deinterleave, there will be a number of single-symbol errors with flags in several codewords. The parity symbol P can correct single-symbol errors. In the case where random and burst errors occur together, then some codewords will contain double errors with pointers after deinterleave. If the location of errors is known, the B-adjacent code can correct two symbols in error, and so the error flags are used to drive the B- adjacent decoder.

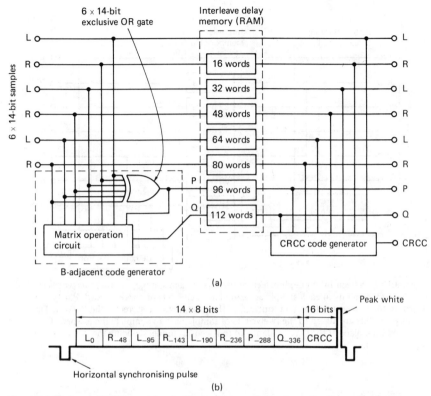

(a)

(b)

Figure 8.9 Format of EIAJ recording in fourteen-bit mode produces B-adjacent redundancy P and Q before interleave, and CRCC after as at (a). Resultant pseudo-video line shown at (b).

In this way, dropouts up to 32 lines can be corrected fully. After that it is necessary to resort to interpolation to conceal uncorrectable samples.

In the sixteen bit adaptation of the EIAJ format used by the Sony PCM- F1, the fourteen-bit structure is largely retained for replay compatibility, and the extra two bits in each of the six samples and one parity word in a line are stored as a fourteen-bit symbol which replaces the Q symbol of the B-adjacent redundancy as shown in Fig.8.10 and Fig.8.11. Owing to this reduction in redundancy, in sixteen-bit mode the error-correction mechanism is less powerful, because it is restricted to correction of single symbols after deinterleave using the CRC flags and the P redundancy. Only burst errors up to sixteen lines long can be corrected. On a given tape, more interpolations can be expected in sixteen-bit mode than in fourteen-bit mode.

The PCM-F1 was a consumer product which was built with LSI technology for low mass-production cost. Owing to the low cost of the product, it has found application in professional circles, and indeed served as the introduction to digital audio for many people. Being a consumer product, only one converter is used between digital and analog domains. This is multiplexed between the two audio channels, and results in a timeshift between samples of half the sample period, or about 11 microseconds. This is not a problem in normal use, since the opposite shift is introduced by the multiplexed converter used for replay. The standard PCM-F1 was not equipped with digital outputs or inputs, and

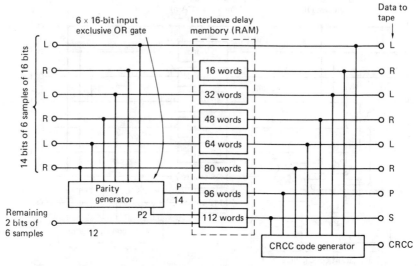

Figure 8.10 In sixteen-bit mode, fourteen of the bits of each sample are stored as words (L, R) and the extra two bits of each sample are stored as twelve bits of another word. Parity is generated on the sixteen-bit data, and fourteen of the parity bits are stored in the P word. The remaining two bits are added to the twelve bits of sample data to complete the S word. The S word takes the place of the Q redundancy of fourteen-bit mode, reducing the power of the error correction.

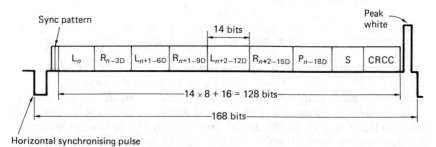

Figure 8.11 Video line of PCM-F1 in sixteen-bit mode. Q redundancy of EIAJ format is replaced by S word which contains extra bits of sixteen bit samples.

accordingly not too much trouble needed to be taken in controlling DC offsets due to converter drift. When enthusiasts began to modify the unit to fit digital connections, these problems became significant. Several companies manufacture adaptor units which incorporate digital filters to remove DC offsets and the 11 microsecond shift. The output can then be provided in the AES/EBU interconnect format, or the input standard of the PCM-1610 for dubbing to U-matic. An editor has also been developed independently. Numerous Compact Discs have been mastered on PCM-F1, and it has been claimed that these recordings sound better than those made on early PCM-1610 units, since these had instrumentation converters which were not particularly musical. Later 1610s were fitted with the same converters as the F1.

8.6 Decca rotary recorders

In contrast to the formats described above, which use the signal circuitry of video recorders virtually unmodified, the digital recorders developed by Decca[3] for vinyl and Compact Disc mastering use only the transport and servo-mechanisms of a 625/50 one-inch open-reel video recorder, and make a direct digital recording on the diagonal tracks using MFM channel code. Again an editor has been designed to complement the recorders. One of the advantages of using a one-inch transport is that confidence replay is available, because the drum carries a separate replay head which is mounted at such a height that it follows the record head along the same track. This was not available with the cassette formats until Sony produced a U-matic transport with additional heads which was designed expressly for digital audio use.

The format of the Decca recorder differs in many respects from the previously described formats. Sixteen-bit samples are split into bytes, and each is then made into an eighteen-bit codeword by the addition of a zero packing bit and nine bits of redundancy calculated according to the matrix of Fig.8.12. The redundancy used is a twin cyclic code which can correct any two bits in error, and detect three errors. By using bit-level interleaving in addition to the usual word interleaving, multiple-burst error correction becomes possible without the complexity of Reed–Solomon coding. There are several stages of interleave, the first of which is to exchange the redundancy symbols between the two audio channels, as in Fig.8.13. Following this, a large-distance interleave between the data and the redundancy is performed. 480 nine-bit redundancy symbols are assembled in time order, and then the first half and second half are exchanged to

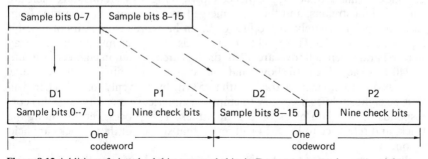

Figure 8.12 Addition of nine check bits to sample bits in Decca system produces two eighteen-bit codewords for every sample. A zero packing bit is added to make up the codeword length, so in principle the format could record eighteen-bit samples. Each codeword can correct two error bits, and so extensive interleaving is employed to handle burst errors.

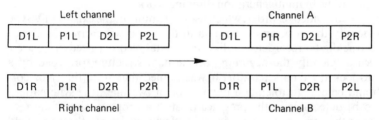

Figure 8.13 Check bits are exchanged between left and right channels to form two data channels A and B in the first stage of interleave.

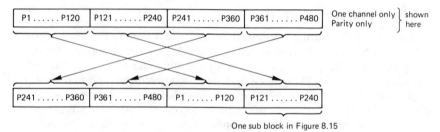

One channel only ⎫ shown
Parity only   ⎬ here

One sub block in Figure 8.15

Figure 8.14 Parity bits only are subject to a block-completed interleave, as shown here, which is the same for channel A and B. Data are unchanged.

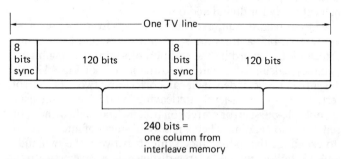

240 bits =
one column from
interleave memory

Figure 8.16 One column from the interleave memory along with two sync patterns produces one TV line. Eighteen such columns complete one interleave block.

give the data and redundancy sequence shown in Fig.8.14. At this stage there are still two data streams, and these are merged by taking one bit at a time from each channel alternately to produce eighteen-bit words from pairs of nine-bit inputs, as in Fig.8.15. These eighteen-bit words are written into a memory array in rows, and when 240 rows are filled, the bits are read out in eighteen columns of 240 bits each. Fig.8.16 shows that each of these columns occupies the same space as one TV line on the track, with two sync bytes evenly spaced. There will thus be eighteen lines necessary to empty the interleave memory, and this corresponds to one data block on the tape track. This process repeats along the track, and reference to Fig.8.17 will reveal that sixteen of these blocks are held by one track.

Burst errors of up to two TV lines can be corrected owing to the extensive bit interleave. This is more than adequate when it is realized that the raw error rate due to using a one-inch transport is lower than in cassette machines. In fact Decca prefer to work with no concealment of errors to prevent unnoticed build-up of interpolations in multigeneration dubbing work.

Unlike a pseudo-video recorder, which uses the timing of the existing TV sync pulses to identify the position of the data in the video waveform, the Decca system is a true digital recorder, and like any digital recorder needs a separate sync pattern to identify the beginning of the data structure, preceded by a preamble to lock the data separator. It was argued that since the error correction should be able to tolerate a burst error of two lines, the sync pattern should also be detectable in the presence of such a dropout, since failure to synchronize at the beginning of a field would effectively destroy the whole field of data because the bits could not be allocated to the correct places in the

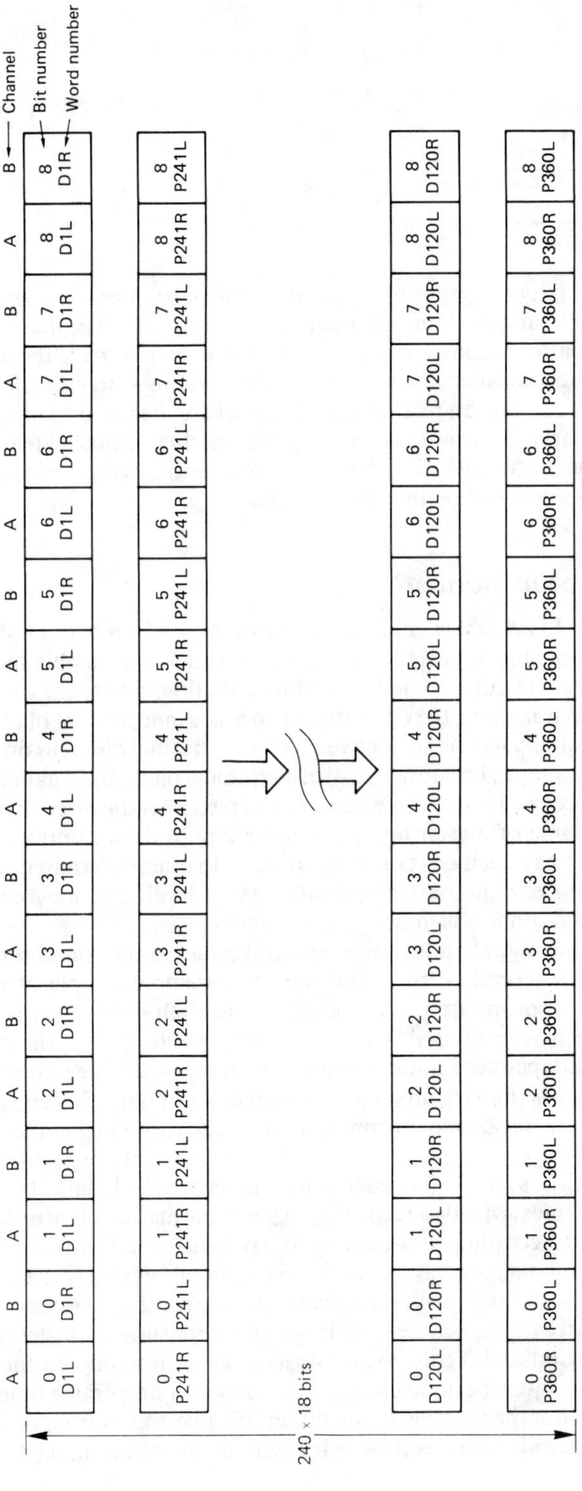

Figure 8.15 A bit interleave is produced by taking 120 Ch.A data symbols (nine-bit), 120 Ch.B data symbols, 120 Ch.A parity symbols, and 120 Ch.B parity symbols from the interleave of Figure 8.14 to produce a sub-block. Four are necessary before the full interleave repeats.

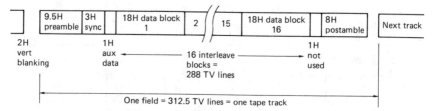

Figure 8.17 Sixteen interleave blocks complete one tape track.

samples. To permit such operation, the synchronizing pattern extends over three TV line periods, and contains numerous unique patterns. The detection of any four of these patterns consecutively is sufficient to synchronize the data in the field. This method is particularly powerful when editing is to be performed, since repeated edits can cause a tolerance build-up where the position of sync on one track differs markedly from that on the next. Another advanced feature of the machine is a means to determine the error rate quantitatively, which allows maintenance to be scheduled before failures occur.

8.7 Rotary edit point location

As the rotary-head PCM recorder is used extensively for Compact Disc mastering, it must be possible to edit the recordings in order to assemble the tape which will drive the CD cutter. Unlike vinyl disk cutting, where the operator controls the cutter parameters, the CD cutting process is independent of musical content, so responsibility for the subjective quality of the final disc falls on those who make the master tape. The duration of each musical piece, the length of any pauses between pieces and the relative levels of the pieces on the disc have to be determined at the time of mastering. The master tape will be compiled from source tapes which may each contain only some of the pieces required on the final disc, in any order. The recordings will vary in level, and may contain several retakes of a passage which was unsatisfactory.

The purpose of the digital audio editor is to take each piece, and insert sections from retakes to correct errors, and then to assemble the pieces in the correct order, with appropriate pauses between and with the correct relative levels to create the master tape. All of this is done by copying in the digital domain. The source tapes need not be changed in any way, and degradation of quality is minimal. The master tape will also have contiguous timecode, and with the addition of the subcode information, it is ready for cutting the Compact Disc.

Digital audio editors work by assembling; a term which has the same meaning as in the context of video recording, where new material is attached to the end of a previous recording without any loss of synchronization.

Fig.8.18 shows how a master tape is made up by assembly from source tapes. Clearly one recorder and one player are necessary in an editing system, but if there are many source tapes, a system with two players will work faster. As in video recording, digital audio edits are controlled using timecode on the tape cassettes. Editing per se can be done using true timecode or dropframe timecode on 60 Hz machines, but the Compact Disc cutter will reject master tapes which have dropframe timecode for reasons which are made clear in Chapter 13. The

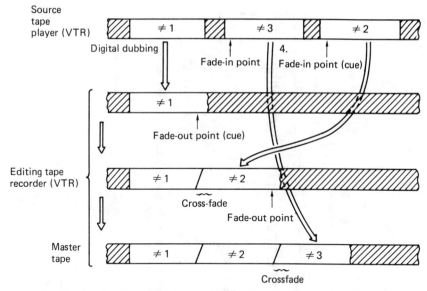

Figure 8.18 The function of an editor is to perform a series of assembles to produce a master tape from source tapes.

timecode used in the PCM-1610 is SMPTE standard for 525/60 and is shown in Fig.8.19. The JVC format stores a field address in the pseudo-video as in Fig.8.20. The Decca system uses EBU timecode which is basically similar to SMPTE. These store hours, minutes, seconds and frames as binary-coded decimal (BCD), which is serially encoded along with user bits into an FM channel code (see Chapter 6) which is recorded on one of the linear audio tracks of the video tape. The user bits are not specified in the standard, but a common use is to record the take or session number.

Editing is performed in two basic steps: edit-point location and assembling. The edit points are located under manual control to achieve the desired effect, but the assemble is completely automatic.

A digital audio editor works in conjunction with a PCM adaptor. The encode and decode sections are used for assembling, and the DAC is used for monitoring. The ADC is not normally used during editing, although in principle an analog recorder equipped with timecode could be used as a source for an assemble if connected to the ADC input. Fig.8.21 shows how the units of an edit complex interconnect. The two or three VCRs all have remote control, sync, timecode and video replay connections. The recorder has additional connections for video and timecode to be recorded. The three sections of the PCM adaptor connect to the editor separately. The timing generator in the PCM adaptor synchronizes the entire system with locked 44.1 kHz and video sync. The following description is based largely on the Sony editor,[4] but other machines are similar in principle if not in detail.

In video editing, the location of edit points is quite easy, as they will always be at a vertical interval in the video waveform, and the only care needed is with colour framing. Furthermore, most professional video recorders allow the picture to be viewed at any speed, so the editor can rock the tape back and forth to

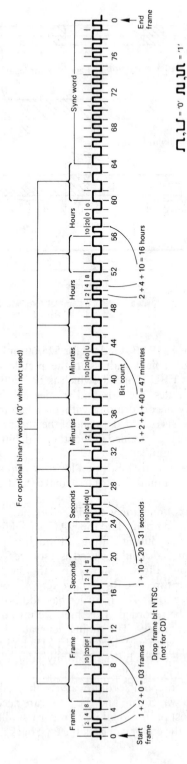

Figure 8.19 In SMPTE standard timecode, the frame number and time are stored as eight BCD symbols. There is also space for 32 user-defined bits. The code repeats every frame. Note the asymmetrical sync word which allows the direction of tape movement to be determined.

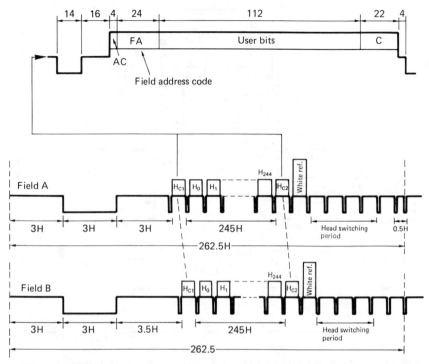

Figure 8.20 In the JVC format, two lines in each field are of the form shown here, where a field address code is stored. This address is unique for each field, and is used as a timecode for edit control.

find the precise edit point. In digital audio, the industrial VCRs do not permit variable-speed operation. A further problem in audio is that the accuracy to which the edit must be made is much greater than the frame boundary accuracy needed in video. A video frame lasts 33 ms, whereas audio needs to be edited to an accuracy of a few samples.

Digital audio editors simulate the process of edit-point location in analog audio recorders. As the VCR can only play at normal speed, the area of the edit point is transferred to memory, and the precise edit point is found by accessing the memory at any desired speed.

Fig.8.22 shows how the area of the edit point is transferred to the memory. The VCR is set to play, and the operator listens to offtape samples via the DAC in the PCM adaptor. The same samples are continuously written into a memory within the editor. This memory is addressed by a counter which repeatedly overflows to give the memory a ring-like structure rather like a timebase corrector. When the operator hears the rough area in which the edit is required, he will press a button which stops the memory writing, not immediately, but one half of the memory contents later. The effect is that the memory contains an equal number of samples before and after the rough edit point.

Typically an operator needs to be able to hear about 30 seconds of audio to be able mentally to synchronize to the rhythm and anticipate the edit point. This represents, in a stereo system, a storage requirement of at least five megabytes. This represents a significant cost, and to reduce the size of memory needed, most

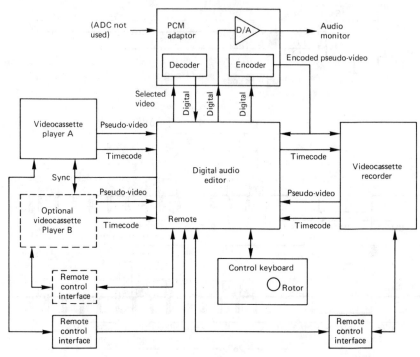

Figure 8.21 The digital audio editor for VCR-based systems uses the signal processing of the PCM adaptor.

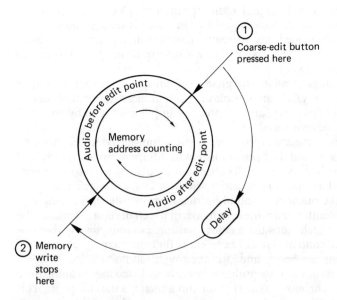

Figure 8.22 The use of a ring memory which overwrites allows storage of samples before and after the coarse edit point.

editors use some form of data reduction or companding. One obvious step is to add left and right channel samples arithmetically to give a monophonic signal with a factor of two saving. A further reduction in memory requirement can be obtained by reducing the sampling rate. It is easy to reduce the sampling rate by some power of two, since output samples will coincide in time with input samples, thus simplifying the circuitry. Typically the sampling rate will be halved, reducing the audio bandwidth to 11 kHz. As stated in Chapter 4, unwanted samples cannot just be discarded, since this causes aliasing. A suitable digital low-pass filter must be used. Further data reduction can be had by converting the linear samples to floating point notation, perhaps using floating-point block coding (see Chapter 3).

Once the recording is in the memory, it can be accessed at leisure, and the VCR plays no further part in the edit-point location. The VCR will typically perform a partial unthread so that the same part of the tape is not kept in contact with the rotating heads.

There are a number of ways in which the memory can be read. If the memory address is supplied by a counter which is clocked at the appropriate rate, the edit area can be replayed at normal speed, or at half speed repeatedly. In order to simulate the analog method of finding an edit point, the operator is provided with a handwheel or rotor, and the memory address will change at a rate proportional to the speed with which the rotor is turned, and in the same direction. Thus the sound can be heard forward or backward at any speed, and the effect is exactly that of manually rocking an analog tape past the heads of an ATR.

Fig.8.23 shows a typical rotor output. The rotor carries a grating which moves over a fixed grating with which it is not parallel. The resultant moiré patterns are picked up by two light beams positioned to produce outputs in quadrature. By comparing the phase of the two outputs, the direction of rotation can be determined.

Although this process sounds very simple, there are some difficulties to overcome. The human hand cannot turn the rotor smoothly enough to enable the rotor output to address the memory directly without flutter, and a standard 44.1 kHz sampling rate must be recreated to feed the monitor DAC. A digital phase-locked loop is generally employed to damp fluctuations in rotor speed, as in Fig.8.24, and an interpolator is necessary to restore the sampling rate to normal.

Samples which will be used to make the master tape never pass through these rate-reduction and companding processes; they are solely to assist in the location of the edit points. The sound quality in this mode is not usually very impressive.

The act of pressing the coarse edit-point button stores the timecode on the tape at that point, which is frame-accurate. As the rotor is turned, the memory address is monitored, and used to update the time-code. When the exact edit point is chosen, it will be described to great accuracy and is stored as hours, minutes, seconds, frames and position within the frame.

Before assembly can be performed, two edit points must be determined, the out point at the end of the previously recorded signal, and the in point at the beginning of the new signal. The editor's microprocessor stores these in order to control the automatic assemble process.

Edit-point location is achieved in a slightly different way in the Decca system.

The open-reel video recorders have a linear analog audio track which carries the same sound as the digital recording. This can be heard at any speed, and the edit point can be located precisely by moving the tape reels by hand if desired. Since the application of this editor is primarily to classical recordings, the operators also insert the edit points on the fly by reading the musical score as the tape plays, and pressing the edit button at the right instant.

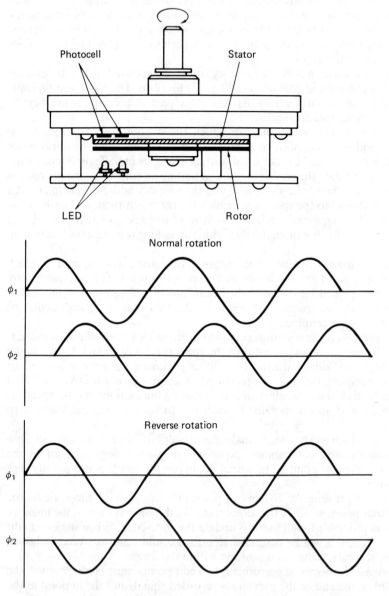

Figure 8.23 The fixed and rotating gratings produce moiré fringes which are detected by two light paths as quadrature sinusoids. The relative phase determines the direction, and the frequency is proportional to speed of rotation.

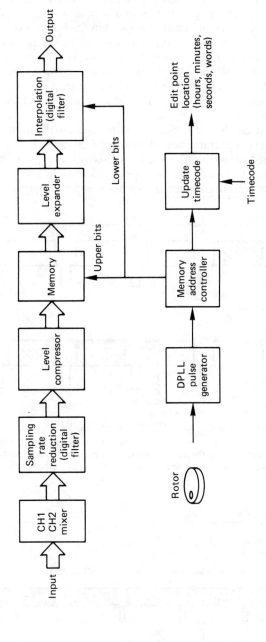

Figure 8.24 In order to simulate the edit location of analog recorders, the samples are read from memory under control of a hand-operated rotor.

8.8 Rotary editing

Samples representing the audio waveform are carried in the video-like signal recorded by the VCRs. Unlike a real video signal, which will be edited at frame boundaries, the audio samples represent a continuous stream, and it must be possible to perform an edit at any point within the frame. Fig.8.25 shows that when the assemble takes place, the out point of the old recording and the in point of the new recording are brought together. It is not possible to record a waveform with discontinuities in the sync pulses, so the solution adopted is to shift the samples in the new recording relative to the sync pulses. This can be achieved by a memory used as a delay. The sync pulses can then be continuous in the area of the edit.

The edit point may have any position with respect to the frame, but VCRs are designed to edit only at frame boundaries. Fig.8.26 shows that the desired effect may be obtained by setting the VCR into record at a frame boundary, and rerecording what is already on the tape up to the edit point, where the new recording will appear to commence. It is not possible simply to switch between

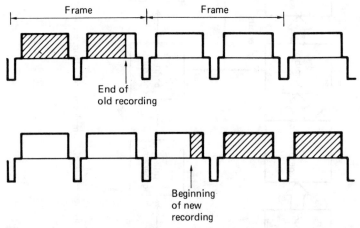

Figure 8.25 When an assemble is performed, it is necessary to bring together the end of the old recording and the beginning of the new recording. This must be achieved without making sync pulses discontinuous, which can be done by sliding the samples of the new recording with respect to sync.

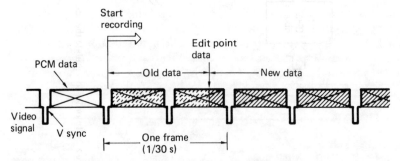

Figure 8.26 As video recorders can only start recording at the beginning of the frame, fine position of the edit point is determined by rerecording the old data up to the edit point.

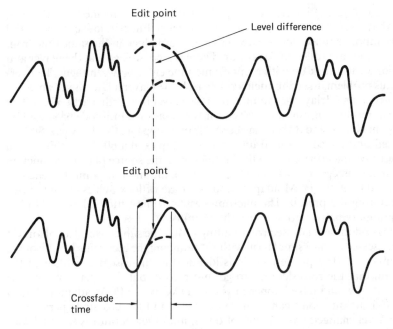

Figure 8.27 To avoid a click at the edit point due to a discontinuity in the waveform, a cross-fade takes place in the digital domain.

the old and new sample streams, since this would produce an audible click at the edit point. Fig.8.27 shows that a crossfade is carried out in the digital domain. Chapter 3 showed how this might be implemented. The operator can control the speed of the crossfade by changing the rate at which the coefficient generator ramps. To control the relative levels of the recording before and after the edit point, the new recording passed through a digital gain-control stage controlled by a manual fader before reaching the crossfade stage.

As stated, the samples on a digital audio recorder are interleaved, and this results in an unavoidable delay in both the recording and replay processes. When the recording is required to begin at a frame boundary, it is necessary to supply the samples to be recorded in advance, so that following the interleave delay they will have the correct timing relative to the tape. This advance of the samples to be rerecorded can only be achieved by playing back the end of the old recording in advance, and storing the samples in a memory. The recorder will need to roll past the edit point twice for each edit, first to load the memory, and second to perform the edit. This has the added advantage that only one PCM adaptor is necessary to decode and deinterleave the new recording, because the end of the old recording is supplied by the memory. As the crossfade period can be several frames, memory must be large enough to accommodate the old recording until it has completely faded out.

Samples in the new recording will need to slip with respect to sync but the delay needed must be modified by some detail considerations. First, the samples from the replay of the source tape supplying the new recording will be delayed by the deinterleave process, but they must be supplied in advance by an amount of time equal to the interleave delay. Thus the delay in memory needs to be reduced by one encode delay plus one decode delay. Further, low-cost industrial VCRs cannot be relied upon to accelerate to frame-lock in the same time from rest when they are rolled by the editor. There is a possibility that the player and the recorder will lock up with a one-frame time error between them. To overcome this problem, the editor deliberately rolls the player a few frames ahead of the recorder, and delays the samples from the player in a further area of memory by the corresponding amount. The editor then reads the timecode produced by the two machines, and if there has been a frame slippage, the delay can then be increased or reduced by one frame or 1470 samples in a 60 Hz machine. As a consequence, the delay given to the samples from the source player is a function of the relationship to frame timing of the in point and out point, the encode/decode delay of the PCM adaptor and the state of lock achieved by the two VCRs during the preroll. The microprocessor in the editor takes care of the calculations, which do not concern the operator.

A tremendous asset of electronic editing is that the subjective effect of an edit can be assessed using a simulation without changing the recording on any of the tapes involved. The preview mode is identical to the assemble edit, with the exception that the recorder fails to go into record, but the operator can hear exactly what would have happened via the DAC in the PCM adaptor. The in point and the out point can then be trimmed, and the crossfade period and relative level changed any number of times, until the operator is satisfied with the edit, which can then be recorded. Editors differ in the way in which preview is performed. Some machines only store the area of the out point in memory, and the player has to roll to preview, whereas others, with larger memory, store both areas in memory, and the preview does not involve the VCRs.

In order to permit correct monitoring of the preview or of the actual assemble, there is an additional complication. During the preroll prior to the edit point, the PCM adaptor supplies samples from the recorder which are delayed by the deinterleave process. When the samples from the recorder which were previously loaded into the memory are reached, there is a sudden time jump, because these must be supplied to the PCM adaptor one encode delay ahead of real time. To allow continuous monitoring through this transition, the samples from the preloaded memory are subjected to a delay equal to one encode delay plus one decode delay, so that they will be time-aligned with the samples from the recorder during preroll and from the source player even though they are supplied in advance to the encoder. There are thus three areas of memory required: the preloaded recorder sample memory, the player timebase corrector memory and the monitor delay memory. These memory areas are obtained by reassigning the edit- point location memory, since it has no further purpose once the points are found.

8.9 Assembly

The complete sequence of events in an assemble edit can now be described, with reference to Fig.8.28. The in and out points are located as described, and the edit process is enabled by the operator. The first step is to preload the memory with samples from the area of the recorder out point. The recorder is reversed away from the edit point, and put into play. When the appropriate frame is reached

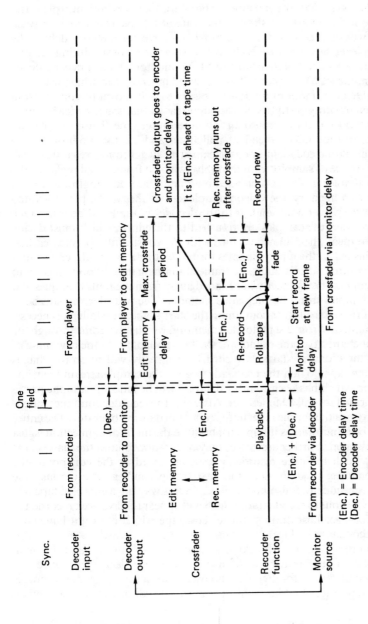

Figure 8.28 Timing of an assemble sequence in a digital audio editor. There is only one decoder so this must be handed over from the replay function of the recorder to the replay function of the player. The remainder of the recorder data come from the record memory. Crossfade output goes to the encoder which must be supplied one encode period in advance. A monitor delay is necessary so that the advanced crossfader output can be time-aligned with the delayed decoder output at the time the monitor switches sources. Edit delay slides the player data along the video timing to close any gaps and compensate for frame slips in machine synchronization. Edit delay output feeds the crossfader and must also be one encode period ahead of tape time.

according to the timecode reader, samples are stored in the memory. There will be no audible monitoring at this stage, which can be disconcerting if the reason for tape movement is not appreciated. Following the preload, the recorder and player reverse away from the edit point. The editor then sets both into play, and reads timecode from both to establish the state of relative frame lock between them. This will be used to adjust the timebase-corrector memory delay. The video multiplexer switches to pseudo-video from the recorder during the pre-roll, and sends it to the decoder of the PCM adaptor. After a decode delay, samples from the PCM adaptor will be returned to the editor, which will route them to the DAC for monitoring. It is necessary to switch over to samples from the preloaded memory just prior to the edit area, so that the decoder becomes available to decode the new recording from the source tape. These samples are accessed one encode delay ahead of real time, and so, for monitoring, the monitor delay of one encode/decode time must be switched in so that the DAC will have its source of samples imperceptibly switched from actual replay of the recorder to samples from the preloaded memory. Once the monitor output is established from memory, the video multiplexer switches to the pseudo- video from the source player, and sends it to the decoder in the PCM adaptor. One decode delay later, the samples are returned to the editor, which must decide how much to delay them in accordance with the constraints specified earlier. Following this delay, the replay samples form the other input to the cross-fader via the gain control. At this stage, the frame containing the edit point has yet to be reached, and the cross-fader will be faded away from the replay samples and toward the samples from the preloaded memory. The recorder will still be in play mode. Prior to the frame containing the start of the crossfade, it is necess-ary to route samples from the preloaded memory, which have come through the crossfader unchanged, to the encoder of the PCM adaptor. At the beginning of that frame, the recorder starts to record, and initially will rerecord what is already on the tape. When the crossfade begins, the sample stream from the source player, which has been suitably delayed, will be faded in, and the prere-corded memory data will be faded out. After this the recorder continues indefi-nitely to dub from the source tape, until it is stopped by the operator. The entire process can be monitored as it happens, because the monitor connection is just after the crossfader. Further assembles may be performed until the master tape is complete. Each time the recorder goes into record at the edit point, the timecode generator is jammed to the next frame number after the last one played, and timecode will also be recorded. In this way the assembled tape will contain a contiguous timecode track which will appear to have been recorded at one time. Compact Disc cutters will reject a tape which does not have con-tiguous timecode.

   The action of an editor of this kind is unavoidably complex, and the main reason for that is the restriction of using video recorders which were not designed from the outset for digital audio use. When a rotary-head transport is designed to have digital audio from the outset, the editor can be made much simpler.

8.10 Introduction to RDAT

When a video recorder is used as a basis for a digital audio recorder, the video bandwidth is already defined, and in most cases is much greater than necessary.

Table 8.1 The significance of the recognition holes on the RDAT cassette. Holes 1, 2 and 3 form a coded pattern; whereas hole 4 is independent.

Hole 1	Hole 2	Hole 3	Function
0	0	0	Metal powder tape or equivalent/13 μm thick
0	1	0	MP tape or equivalent/thin tape
0	0	1	1.5 TP/13 μm thick
0	1	1	1.5 TP/thin tape
1	×	×	(Reserved)

Hole 4		
0	Non-prerecorded tape	
1	Prerecorded tape	

1 = Hole present
0 = Hole blanked off

Furthermore, the signal-to-noise ratio of video recorders is much too high for the purposes of storing binary. The result of these factors is that the tape consumption of such a machine will be far higher than necessary. Now that digital audio is becoming established, and markets are seen to exist for large numbers of machines, it is no longer necessary to borrow technology from other disciplines, because it is economically viable to design a purpose-built product. The first of this generation of machines is RDAT (rotary head digital audio tape). By designing for a specific purpose, the tape consumption can be made very much smaller than that of a converted video machine. In fact the RDAT format achieves more bits per square inch than any other form of magnetic recorder at the time of writing. The origins of RDAT are in an experimental machine built by Sony,[5] but the RDAT format has grown out of that through a process of standardization involving some eighty companies.

The general appearance of the RDAT cassette is shown in Fig.8.29. The overall dimensions are only 73 mm × 54 mm × 10.5 mm which is rather smaller than the Compact Cassette. The design of the cassette incorporates some improvements over its analog ancestor.[6] As shown in Fig.8.30, the apertures through which the heads access the tape are closed by a hinged door, and the hub drive openings are covered by a sliding panel which also locks the door when the cassette is not in the transport. The act of closing the door operates brakes which act on the reel hubs. This results in a cassette which is well sealed against contamination due to handling or storage. The short wavelengths used in digital recording make it more sensitive to spacing loss caused by contamination. As in the Compact Cassette, the tape hubs are flangeless, and the edge guidance of the tape pack is achieved by liner sheets. The flangeless approach allows the hub centres to be closer together for a given length of tape. The cassette has recognition holes in four standard places so that players can automatically determine what type of cassette has been inserted. In addition there is a write-protect (record-lockout) mechanism which is actuated by a small plastic plug sliding between the cassette halves. The end-of-tape condition is detected optically and the leader tape is transparent. There is some freedom in the design of the EOT sensor. As can be seen in Fig.8.31, transmitted-light sensing can be used across the corner of the cassette, or reflected-light sensing can be used, because the cassette incorporates a prism which reflects light around the back of the tape. Study of Fig.8.30 will reveal that the prisms are moulded integrally with the corners of the transparent insert used for the cassette window.

The high coercivity (typically 1480 oersteds) metal powder tape is 3.81 mm wide, the same width as Compact Cassette tape. The standard overall thickness is 13 μm. A striking feature of the metal tape is that the magnetic coating is so thin, at about 3μm, that the tape appears translucent. The maximum capacity of the cassette is about 60 m.

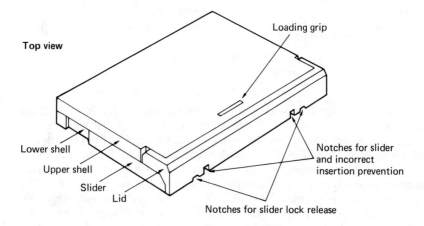

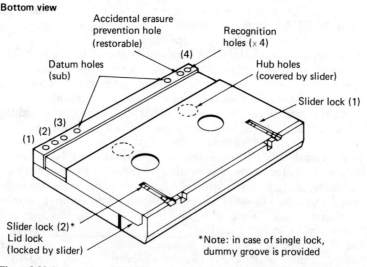

Figure 8.29 Appearance of RDAT cassette. Access to the tape is via a hinged lid, and the hub-drive holes are covered by a sliding panel, affording maximum protection to the tape. Further details of the recognition holes are given in Table 8.1. (Courtesy TDK)

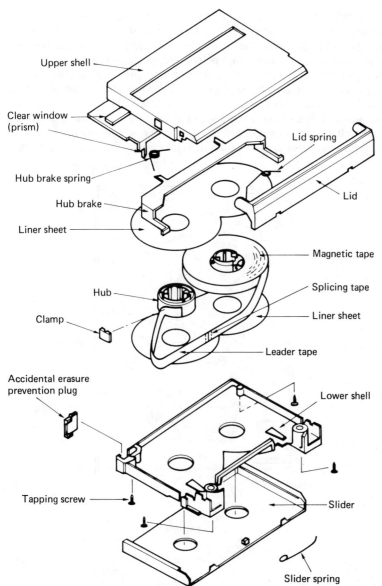

Upper shell

Clear window (prism)

Lid spring

Hub brake spring

Hub brake

Liner sheet

Lid

Magnetic tape

Hub

Splicing tape

Clamp

Liner sheet

Leader tape

Accidental erasure prevention plug

Lower shell

Tapping screw

Slider

Slider spring

Figure 8.30 Exploded view of RDAT cassette showing intricate construction. When the lid opens, it pulls the ears on the brake plate, releasing the hubs. Note the EOT/BOT sensor prism moulded into the corners of the clear window. (Courtesy TDK)

When the cassette is placed in the transport, the slider is moved back as it engages. This releases the lid lock. Continued movement into the transport pushes the slider right back, revealing the hub openings. The cassette is then lowered onto the hub drive spindles and tape guides, and the door is fully opened to allow access to the tape.

As its name suggests, the system uses rotary heads, but there is only limited similarity to video recorders. In video recorders, each diagonal tape track stores one television field, and the switch from one track to the next takes place during the vertical interval. In a recorder with two heads, one at each side of the drum, it is necessary to wrap the tape rather more than 180 degrees around the drum so that one head begins a new track just before the previous head finishes. This constraint means that the threading mechanism of VCRs is quite complex. In RDAT, threading is simplified because the digital recording does not need to be continuous. RDAT extends the technique of time compression used to squeeze continuous samples into intermittent video lines. Blocks of samples to be recorded are written into a memory at the sampling rate, and are read out at a much faster rate when they are to be recorded. In this way the memory contents

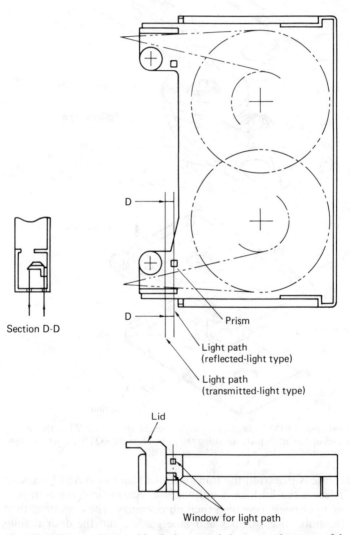

Section D-D

Prism

Light path
(reflected-light type)

Light path
(transmitted-light type)

Lid

Window for light path

Figure 8.31 Tape sensing can either be by transmission across the corner of the cassette, or by reflection through an integral prism. In both cases, the apertures are sealed when the lid closes. (Courtesy TDK)

can be recorded in less time. Fig.8.32 shows that when the samples are time-compressed, recording is no longer continuous, but is interrupted by long pauses. During the pauses in recording, it is not actually necessary for the head to be in contact with the tape, and so the angle of wrap of the tape around the drum can be reduced, which makes threading easier. In RDAT the wrap angle is only 90 degrees on the commonest drum size. As the heads are 180 degrees apart, this means that for half the time neither head is in contact with the tape. Fig.8.33 shows that the partial-wrap concept allows the threading mechanism to be very simple indeed. As the cassette is lowered into the transport, the pinch roller and several guide pins pass behind the tape. These then simply move toward the capstan and drum and threading is complete. A further advantage of partial wrap is that the friction between the tape and drum is reduced, allowing power saving in portable applications, and allowing the tape to be shuttled at high speed without the partial unthreading needed by videocassettes. In this way the player can read subcode during shuttle to facilitate rapid track access.

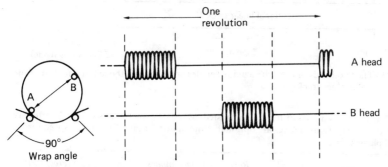

Figure 8.32 The use of time compression reduces the wrap angle necessary, at the expense of raising the frequencies in the channel.

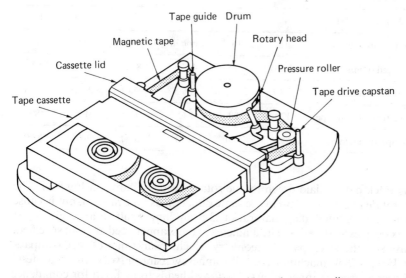

Figure 8.33 The simple mechanism of RDAT. The guides and pressure roller move towards the drum and capstan and threading is complete.

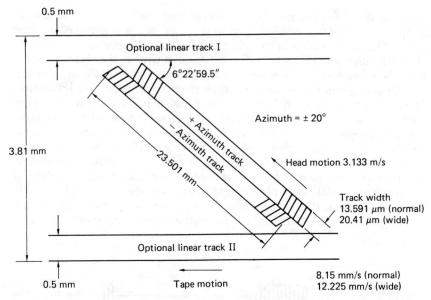

Figure 8.34 The two heads of opposite azimuth angles lay down the above track format. Tape linear speed determines track pitch.

Table 8.2 The various modes of RDAT contrasted. Mandatory modes are 48 kHz record/play and 44.1 kHz replay. Other modes are optional. Note option 2 runs drum at half-speed for extended playing time.

	Record/playback modes				*Prerecorded tape playback*	
	Mandatory	*Option 1*	*Option 2*	*Option 3*		
Number of channels	2	2	2	4	2	2
Sampling rate (kHz)	48	32	32	32	44.1	44.1
Quantization (bits)	16	16	12 non lin.	12 non lin.	16	16
Tape speed (mm/s)	8.15	8.15	4.075	8.15	8.15	12.225
Subcode rate (kbit/s)	273.1	273.1	136.5	273.1	273.1	273.1
Playing time (13 µm tape)	120	120	240	120	120	80
Drum speed (rev/min)	2000	2000	1000	2000	2000	2000

The track pattern laid down by the rotary heads is shown in Fig.8.34. The heads rotate at 2000 rev/min in the same direction as tape motion, but because the drum axis is tilted, diagonal tracks 23.5 mm long result, at an angle of just over six degrees to the edge. The diameter of the scanner needed is not specified, because it is the track pattern geometry which ensures interchange compatibility. For portable machines, a small scanner is desirable, whereas for professional use, a larger scanner allows additional heads to be fitted for confidence replay and editing.

There are two linear tracks, one at each edge of the tape, where they act as protection for the diagonal tracks against edge damage. Owing to the low linear tape speed the use of these edge tracks is somewhat limited.

Within the standard cassette, several related modes of operation are available. These are compared in Table 8.2. One of the most important modes uses a sampling rate of 48 kHz, with sixteen-bit two's complement linear quantization. Alongside the audio samples can be carried 273 kilobits/s of subcode (about four times that of Compact Disc) and 68.3 kilobits/s of ID coding, whose purpose will be explained in due course. With a linear tape speed of 8.15 mm/s, the standard cassette offers 120 min unbroken playing time. All RDAT machines can record and play at 48 kHz. For consumer machines, playback only of prerecorded media is proposed at 44.1 kHz sixteen-bit two's complement linear quantization. For reasons which will be explained later, prerecorded tapes run at 12.225 mm/s to offer playing time of 80 min. The same subcode and ID rate is offered. The above two modes are mandatory if a machine is to be considered to meet the format. A professional RDAT machine used for CD or prerecorded RDAT mastering, will record at 44.1 kHz.

Option 1 is identical to 48 kHz mode except that the sampling rate is 32 kHz.

Option 2 is an extra-long-play mode. In order to reduce the data rate, the sampling rate is 32 kHz and the samples change to twelve bit two's complement with nonlinear quantizing. Halving the subcode rate allows the overall data rate necessary to be halved. The linear tape speed and the drum speed are both halved to give a playing time of four hours. All of the above modes are stereo, but option 3 uses the sampling parameters of option 2 with four audio channels. This doubles the data rate with respect to option 2, so the standard tape speed of 8.15 mm/s is used.

Fig.8.35 shows a block diagram of a typical RDAT recorder, which will be used to introduce the basic concept of the machine and the major topics to be described. In order to make a recording, an analog signal is fed to an input ADC, or a direct digital input is taken from an AES/EBU interface. The incoming samples are subject to interleaving to reduce the effects of error bursts. Reading the memory at a higher rate than it was written performs the necessary time compression. Additional bytes of redundancy computed from the samples are added to the data stream to permit subsequent error correction. Subcode information is added, and the parallel byte structure is converted to serial form and fed to the channel encoder, which combines a bit clock with the data, and produces a recording signal known as a 10/8 code which is free of DC (see Chapter 6). This signal is fed to the heads via a rotary transformer to make the binary recording, which leaves the tape track with a pattern of transitions between the two magnetic states.

On replay, the transitions on the tape track induce pulses in the head, which are used to re-create the record current waveform. This is fed to the 10/8 decoder which converts it to a serial bit stream and a separate clock. The subcode data are routed to the subcode output, and the audio samples are fed into a de-interleave memory which, in addition to time-expanding the recording, functions to remove any wow or flutter due to head-to-tape speed variations. Error correction is performed partially before and partially after deinterleave. The corrected output samples can be fed to DACs or to a direct digital output.

In order to keep the rotary heads following the very narrow slant tracks, alignment patterns are recorded as well as the data. The automatic track-

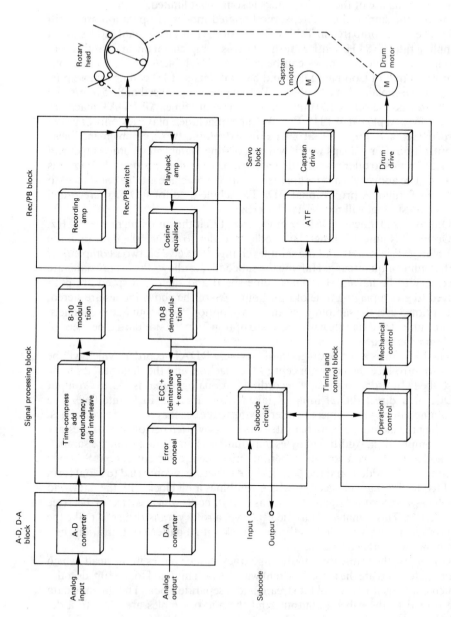

Figure 8.35 Block diagram of RDAT.

following system processes the playback signals from these patterns to control the drum and capstan motors. The subcode and ID information can be used by the control logic to drive the tape to any desired location specified by the user.

8.11 Track following in RDAT

The track structure and track-following system of RDAT will now be described in detail.

As with any recorder intended for consumer use, economy of tape consumption is paramount, and this involves numerous steps to use the tape area as efficiently as possible. As magnetic tape is flexible and is manufactured to finite tolerances, there will always be some error between the path of the replay head and the recorded track. In the relatively wide tracks of analog audio recorders this is seldom a problem. The high-output metal tape used in RDAT allows an adequate signal-to-noise ratio to be obtained with very narrow tracks on the tape. This reduces tape consumption and allows a small cassette, but it becomes necessary actively to control the relative position of the head and the track in order to maximize the replay signal and minimize the error rate.

Conventional magnetic recorders record the transitions on the tape track at

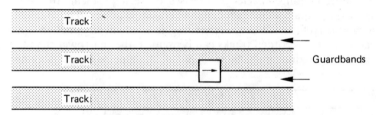

Figure 8.36 In conventional recording, a space or guard band must be left between tracks so that if a head is misaligned, the output signal simply reduces instead of becoming a composite signal from two tracks. The guard bands represent unused tape.

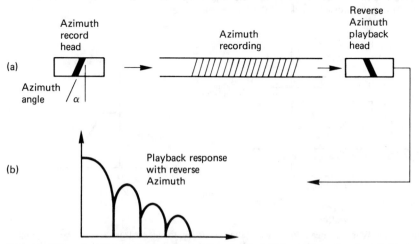

Figure 8.37 In azimuth recording (a), the head gap is tilted. If the track is played with the same head, playback is normal, but the response of the reverse azimuth head is attenuated (b).

right angles to the edge of the track, and Fig.8.36 shows that it is necessary to leave so-called guard bands between tracks to allow some tracking error without causing crosstalk from adjacent tracks. These guard bands represent wasted tape.

Fig.8.37(a) shows that in azimuth recording, the transitions are laid down at an angle to the track by using a head which is tilted. Machines using azimuth recording must always have an even number of heads, so that adjacent tracks can be recorded with opposite azimuth angle. The two track types are usually referred to as A and B. Fig.8.37(b) shows the effect of playing a track with the wrong type of head. The playback process suffers from an enormous azimuth error. The effect of azimuth error can be understood by imagining the tape track to be made from many identical parallel strips. In the presence of azimuth error, the strips at one edge of the track are played back with a phase shift relative to strips at the other side. At some wavelengths, the phase shift will be 180 degrees, and there will be no output; at other wavelengths, especially long wavelengths, some output will reappear. The effect is rather like that of a comb filter, and serves to attenuate crosstalk due to adjacent tracks. Since no tape is wasted between the tracks, efficient use is made of the tape. The term guard-band-less recording is often used instead of, or in addition to, the term azimuth recording. If a channel code is used which has a small low-frequency content, the failure of the azimuth effect at long wavelengths ceases to be a problem. In digital recording there is no separate erase process, and erasure is achieved by overwriting with a new waveform. When overwriting is used in conjunction with azimuth recording, the recorded tracks can be made rather narrower than the head pole simply by reducing the linear speed of the tape so that it does not

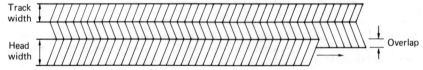

Figure 8.38 In azimuth recording, the tracks can be made narrower than the head pole by overwriting the previous track.

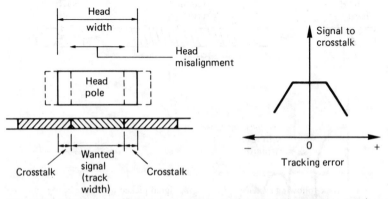

Figure 8.39 When the head pole is wider than the track, the wanted signal is picked up along with crosstalk from the adjacent tracks. If the head is misaligned, the signal-to-crosstalk ratio remains the same until the head fails to register with the whole of the wanted track.

advance so far between sweeps of the rotary heads. In RDAT, the head pole is 20.4 μm wide, but the tracks it records are only 13.59 μm wide. The same head can be used for replay, even though it is 50% wider than the tracks. It can be seen from Fig.8.38 that there will be crosstalk from tracks at both sides of the home track, but this crosstalk is attenuated by azimuth effect. The amount by which the head overlaps the adjacent track determines the spectrum of the crosstalk, since it changes the delay in the azimuth comb-filtering effect. More importantly, the signal-to-crosstalk ratio becomes independent of tracking error over a small range (Fig.8.39), because as the head moves to one side, the loss of crosstalk from one adjacent track is balanced by the increase of crosstalk from the track on the opposite side. This phenomenon allows for some loss of track straightness and for the residual error which is present in all track-following servo systems.[7]

The azimuth angle used has to be chosen with some care. The greater the azimuth angle, the less will be the crosstalk, but the effective writing speed is the head-to-tape speed multiplied by the cosine of the azimuth angle. A further smaller effect is that the tape is anisotropic because of particle orientation. Noise due to the medium, head or amplifier is virtually unaffected by the azimuth angle, and there is no point in reducing crosstalk below the noise. The chosen value of ± 20 degrees reduces crosstalk to the same order as the noise, with a loss of only 1 dB due to the apparent reduction in writing speed.

The track width and the coercivity of the tape largely define the signal-to-noise ratio. A track width has been chosen which makes the signal-to- crosstalk ratio dominant in cassettes which are intended for user recording.

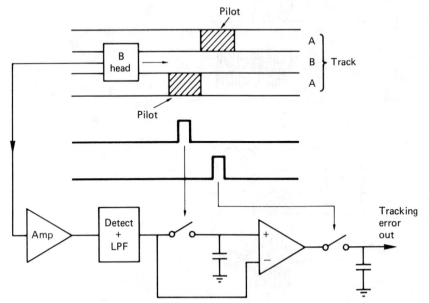

Figure 8.40 In the track-following system of RDAT, the signal picked up by the head comes from pilot tones recorded in adjacent tracks at different positions. These pilot tones have low frequency, and are unaffected by azimuth error. The system samples the amplitude of the pilot tones, and subtracts them.

Prerecorded tapes are made by contact duplication, and this process only works if the coercivity of the copy is less than that of the master. The output from prerecorded tapes at the track width of $13.59\,\mu m$ would be too low, and would be noise-dominated, which would cause the error rate to rise. The solution to this problem is that in prerecorded tapes the track width is increased to be the same as the head pole. The noise and crosstalk are both reduced in proportion to the reduced output of the medium, and the same error rate is achieved as for normal high-coercivity tape.

The 50 % increase in track width is achieved by raising the linear tape speed from 8.15 to 12.225 mm/s, and so the playing time of a prerecorded cassette falls to 80 min as opposed to the 120 min of the normal tape. This is not a real restriction since most consumers would not want to purchase so much copyright material at once. Whereas the 20 min playing time per side of vinyl disks was often bemoaned, very few Compact Discs have been released which contain the full 75 min programme.

The track-following principles are the same for prerecorded and normal cassettes, but there are detail differences which will be noted. Tracking is achieved in conventional video recorders by the use of a linear control track which contains one pulse for every diagonal track. The phase of the pulses picked up by a fixed head is compared with the phase of pulses generated by the drum, and the error is used to drive the capstan. This method is adequate for the wide tracks of

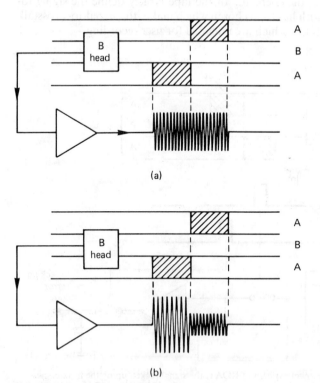

(a)

(b)

Figure 8.41 (a) A correctly tracking head produces pilot-tone bursts of identical amplitude. (b) The head is off-track, and the first pilot burst becomes larger, whereas the second becomes smaller. This produces the tracking error in the circuit of Figure 8.40.

analog video recorders, but errors in the mounting of the fixed head and variations in tape tension rule it out for high-density use. In any case the control-track head adds undesirable mechanical complexity. In RDAT, the tracking is achieved by reading special alignment patterns on the tape tracks themselves, and using the information contained in them to control the capstan.

RDAT uses a technique called area-divided track following (ATF) in which separate parts of the track are set aside for track-following purposes. Fig.8.40 shows the basic way in which a tracking error is derived. The tracks at each side of the home track have bursts of pilot tone recorded in two different places. The frequency of the pilot tone is 130 kHz, which has been chosen to be relatively low so that it is not affected by azimuth loss. In this way a B head following a B track will be able to detect the pilot tone from the adjacent A tracks.

In Fig.8.41(a) the case of a correctly tracking head is shown. The amount of side-reading pilot tone from the two adjacent B tracks is identical. If the head is off track for some reason, as shown in Fig.8.41(b), the amplitude of the pilot tone from one of the adjacent tracks will increase, and the other will decrease. The tracking error is derived by sampling the amplitude of each pilot-tone burst as it occurs, and holding the result so the relative amplitudes can be compared.

There are some practical considerations to be overcome in implementing this simple system, which result in some added complication. The pattern of pilot tones must be such that they occur at different times on each side of every track. To achieve this there must be a burst of pilot tone in every track, although the pilot tone in the home track does not contribute to the development of the tracking error. Additionally there must be some timing signals in the tracks to determine when the samples of pilot tone should be made. The final issue is to prevent the false locking which could occur if the tape happened to run at twice normal speed.

Fig.8.42 shows how the actual track-following pattern of RDAT is laid out.[8] The pilot burst is early on A tracks and late on B tracks. Although the pilot bursts have a two-track cycle, the pattern is made to repeat over four tracks by changing the period of the sync patterns which control the pilot sampling. This can be used to prevent false locking. When an A head enters the track, it finds the home pilot-burst first, followed by pilot from the B track above, then pilot from the B track below. The tracking error is derived from the latter two. When a B head enters the track, it sees pilot from the A track above first, A track below next, and finally home pilot. The tracking error in this case is derived from the former two. The machine can easily tell which processing mode to use because the sync signals have a different frequency depending on whether they are in A tracks (522 kHz) or B tracks (784 kHz). The remaining areas are recorded with the interblock gap frequency of 1.56 MHz which serves no purpose except to erase earlier recordings. Although these pilot and synchronizing frequencies appear strange, they are chosen so that they can be simply obtained by dividing down the master channel-bit-rate clock by simple factors. The channel-bit-rate clock, F_{ch}, is 9.408 MHz; pilot, the two sync frequencies and erase are obtained by dividing it by 72, 18, 12 and 6 respectively. The time at which the pilot amplitude in adjacent tracks should be sampled is determined by the detection of the synchronizing frequencies. As the head sees part of three tracks at all times, the sync detection in the home track has to take place in the presence of unwanted signals. On one side of the home sync signal will be the interblock gap frequency, which is high enough to be attenuated by azimuth. On the other side

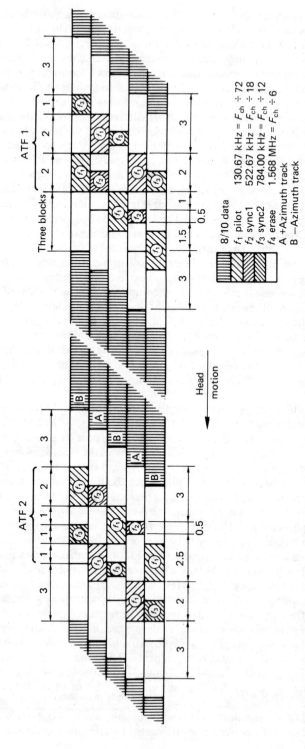

Figure 8.42 The area-divided track-following (ATF) patterns of RDAT. To ease generation of patterns on recording, the pattern lengths are related to the data-block dimensions and the frequencies used are obtained by dividing down the channel bit clock F_{ch}. The sync signals are used to control the timing with which the pilot amplitude is sampled.

is pilot, which is unaffected by azimuth. This means that sync detection is easier in the tracking-error direction away from pilot than in the direction towards it. There is an effective working range of about $+4$ and $-5\,\mu m$ due to this asymmetry, with a dead band of $4\,\mu m$ between tracks. Since the track-following servo is designed to minimize the tracking error, once lock is achieved the presence of the dead zone becomes academic. The differential amplitude of the pilot tones produces the tracking error, and so the gain of the servo loop is proportional to the playback gain, which can fluctuate due to head contact variations and head tolerance. This problem is overcome by using AGC in the servo system. In addition to subtracting the pilot amplitudes to develop tracking error, the circuitry also adds them to develop an AGC voltage. Two sample and hold stages are provided which store the AGC parameter for each head separately. The heads can thus be of different sensitivities without upsetting the servo. This condition could arise from manufacturing tolerances, or if one of the heads became contaminated.

8.12 Recording in RDAT

The channel code used in RDAT is designed to function well in the presence of crosstalk, to have zero DC component to allow the use of a rotary transformer, and to have a small ratio of maximum and minimum run lengths to ease over-write erasure. The code used is a group code where eight data bits are represented by ten channel bits, hence the name 8/10. The details of the code are given in Chapter 6.

The basic unit of recording is the sync block shown in Fig.8.43. This consists of the sync pattern, a three-byte header and 32 bytes of data, making 36 bytes in total, or 360 channel bits. The subcode areas each consist of eight of these blocks, and the PCM audio area consists of 128 of them. Note that a preamble is

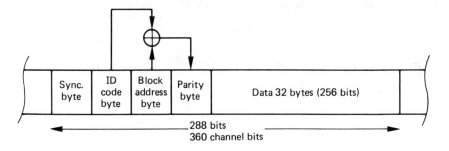

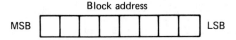

MSB = 0 → PCM audio block; remaining seven bits = block address
MSB = 1 → subcode block; 4 LSBs = subcode block address

Figure 8.43 One sync block of RDAT. 128 of these are assembled in an unbroken sequence to form the audio segment of a track, with a preamble at the beginning and a postamble after the last block. The seven-bit block address is sufficient to uniquely label the 128 blocks. The block structure of the subcode area is identical, but only eight blocks make a subcode segment.

only necessary at the beginning of each area to allow the data separator to phase-lock before the first sync block arrives. Synchronism should be maintained throughout the area, but the sync pattern is repeated at the beginning of each sync block in case sync is lost due to dropout.

The first byte of the header contains an ID code which in the PCM audio blocks specifies the sampling rate in use, the number of audio channels, and whether there is a copy-prohibit in the recording. The second byte of the header specifies whether the block is subcode or PCM audio with the first bit. If set, the least significant four bits specify the subcode block address in the track, whereas if it is reset, the remaining seven bits specify the PCM audio block address in the track. The final header byte is a parity check and is the exclusive–OR sum of header bytes one and two.

The data format within the tracks can now be explained. The information on the track has three main purposes, PCM audio, subcode data and ATF patterns. It is necessary to be able to record subcode at a different time from PCM audio in professional machines in order to make mastering tapes for Compact Discs or prerecorded RDAT cassettes. The subcode is placed in separate areas at the beginning and end of the tracks. When subcode is recorded on a tape with an existing PCM audio recording, the heads have to go into record at just the right time to drop a new subcode area onto the track. This timing is subject to some tolerance, and so some leeway is provided by the margin area which precedes the subcode area and the interblock gap (IBG) which follows. Each area has its own preamble and sync pattern so the data separator can lock to each area individually even though they were recorded at different times or on different machines.

The track-following system will control the capstan so that the heads pass precisely through the centre of the ATF area. Fig.8.44 shows that, in the presence of track curvature, the tracking error will be smaller overall if the ATF pattern is placed part-way down the tracks. This explains why the ATF patterns are between the subcode areas and the central PCM audio area.

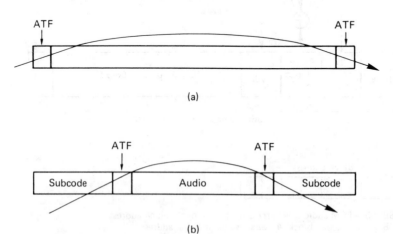

Figure 8.44 (a) The ATF patterns are at the ends of the track, and in the presence of track curvature the tracking error is exaggerated. (b) The ATF patterns are part-way down the track, minimizing mistracking due to curvature, and allowing a neat separation between subcode and audio blocks.

The data interleave is not convolutional, but is block-structured. One pair of tape tracks (one + azimuth and one − azimuth) corresponding to one drum revolution make up an interleave block. Since the drum turns at 2000 rev/ min, one revolution takes 30 ms and, in this time, 1440 samples must be stored for each channel for 48 kHz working.

The first interleave performed is to separate both left- and right-channel samples into odd and even. The right-channel odd samples followed by the left even samples are recorded in the + azimuth track, and the left odd samples followed by the right even samples are recorded in the − azimuth track. Fig.8.45 shows that this interleave allows uncorrectable errors to be concealed by interpolation. At (b) a head becomes clogged and results in every other track having severe errors. The split between right and left samples means that half of the samples in each channel are destroyed instead of every sample in one channel. The missing right even samples can be interpolated from the right odd samples, and the missing left odd samples are interpolated from the left even samples. Fig.8.45(c) shows the effect of a longitudinal tape scratch. A large error burst occurs at the same place in each head sweep. As the positions of left- and right-channel samples are reversed from one track to the next, the errors are again spread between the two channels and interpolation can be used in this case also.

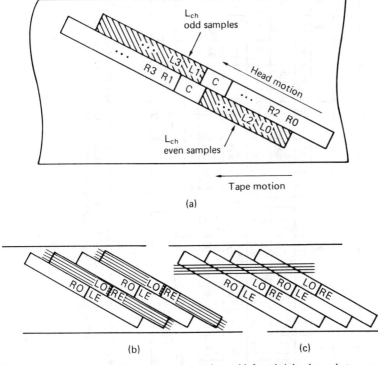

Figure 8.45 (a) Interleave of odd and even samples and left and right channels to permit concealment in case of gross errors. (b) Clogged head loses every other track. Half of the samples of each channel are still available, and interpolation is possible. (c) A linear tape scratch destroys odd samples in both channels. Interpolation is again possible.

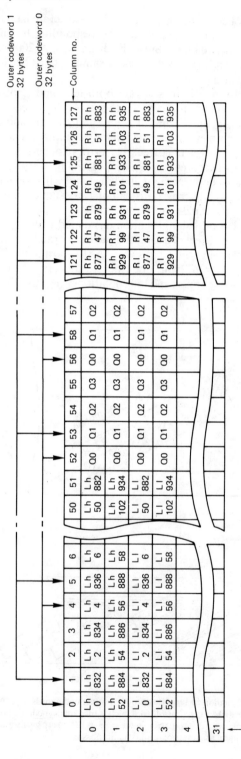

Figure 8.46 (a) Left Even/Right Odd Interleave Memory. Incoming samples are split into high byte (h) and low byte (l), and written across the memory rows using first the even columns for L 0–830 and R 1–831, then the odd columns for L 832–1438 and R 833–1439. For 44.1 kHz working, the number of samples is reduced from 1440 to 1323, and fewer locations are filled.

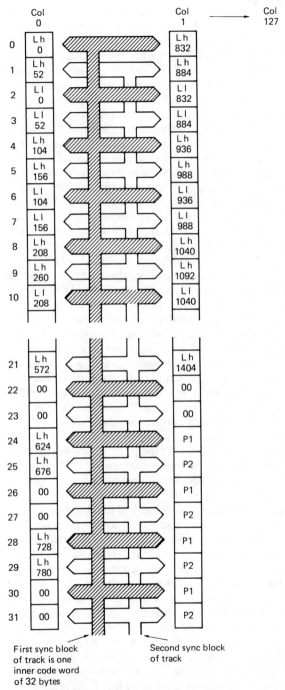

Figure 8.46 (b) The columns of memory are read out to form inner codewords. First, even bytes from the first two columns make one codeword, which is also one sync block; then odd bytes from the first two columns. As there are 128 columns, there will be 128 sync blocks in one audio segment.

The incoming samples for one head revolution are routed to a pair of memory areas of 4 kbytes capacity, one for each track. These memories are structured as 128 columns of 32 bytes each. The error correction works with eight-bit symbols, and so each sample is divided into high byte and low byte and occupies two locations in memory. Fig.8.46 shows one of the two memories. Incoming samples are written across the memory in rows, with the exception of an area in the centre, 24 bytes wide. Each row of data in the RAM is used as the input to the Reed–Solomon encoder for the outer code. The encoder starts at the left-hand column, and then takes a byte from every fourth column, finishing at column 124 with a total of 26 bytes. Six bytes of redundancy are calculated to make a 32-byte outer codeword. The redundant bytes are placed at the top of columns 52, 56, 60 etc. The encoder then makes a second pass through the memory, starting in the second column and taking a byte from every fourth column finishing at column 125. A further six bytes of redundancy are calculated and put into the top of columns 53, 57, 61 and so on. This process is performed four times for each row in the memory, except for the last eight rows where only two passes are necessary because odd-numbered columns have sample bytes only down to row 23. The total number of outer codewords produced is 112.

In order to assemble the data blocks to be recorded, the memory is read in columns. Starting at top left, bytes from the sixteen even-numbered rows of the first column, and from the first twelve even-numbered rows of the second column, are assembled and fed to the inner encoder. This produces four bytes of redundancy which when added to the 28 bytes of data makes an inner codeword of 32 bytes long. Reference to Fig.8.43 will show that this codeword can be accommodated in one sync block. The second sync block is assembled by making a second pass through the first two columns of the memory to read the samples on odd-numbered rows. Four bytes of redundancy are added to these data also. The process then repeats down the next two columns in the memory and so on until 128 blocks have been written to the tape.

Upon replay, the sync blocks will suffer from a combination of random errors and burst errors. The effect of interleaving is that the burst errors will be converted to many single-symbol errors in different outer codewords. As there are four bytes of redundancy in each inner codeword, one or two bytes due to random error can be corrected, which prevents random errors impairing the burst-error correction of the outer code. The probability of miscorrection in the inner code is minute for a single-byte error, because all four syndromes will agree on the nature of the error, but the probability of miscorrection on a double-byte error is higher. If more than two bytes are in error in a sync block, the inner code will be overwhelmed and can only declare all bytes bad by attaching flags to them as they enter the deinterleave memory. After deinterleave, these flags will show up as single-byte errors in many different outer codewords accompanied by error flags. To guard against miscorrections in the inner code, the outer code will calculate syndromes even if no error flags are received from the inner code. If two or less bytes in error are detected, the outer code will correct them even though they were due to inner code miscorrections. This can be done with high reliability because the outer code has three-byte detecting and correcting power which is never used to the full. If more than two bytes are in error in the outer codeword, the correction process uses the error flags from the inner code to correct up to six bytes in error.

The reasons behind the devious interleaving process now become clearer.

Because of the four-way interleave of the outer code, four entire sync blocks can be destroyed, but only one byte will be corrupted in a given outer codeword. As an outer codeword can correct up to six bytes in error by erasure, it follows that a burst error of up to 24 sync blocks could be corrected. This corresponds to a length of track of just over 2.5 mm, and is more than enough to cover the tenting effect due to a particle of debris lifting the tape away from the head.

8.13 Editing in RDAT

In order to edit an RDAT tape, many of the constraints of pseudo-video editing apply. Editing can only take place at the the beginning of an interleave block which is contained in two diagonal tracks. The transport would need to perform a preroll, starting before the edit point, so that the drum and capstan servos would be synchronized to the tape tracks before the edit was reached. Fortunately, the very small drum means that mechanical inertia is minute by the standards of video recorders, and lock-up can be very rapid. One way in which an edit could be performed would be to use an editor of the type designed for PCM adaptors. This would permit editing on an RDAT machine which could only record or play.

A better solution in professional machines would be to fit two sets of heads in the drum. The standard permits the drum size to be increased and the wrap angle to be reduced provided that the tape tracks are recorded to the same dimensions. In normal recording, the first heads to reach the tape tracks would make the recording, and the second set of heads would be able to replay the recording immediately afterwards for confidence monitoring. For editing, the situation would be reversed. The first heads to meet a given tape track would play back the existing recording, and this would be deinterleaved and corrected, and presented as a sample stream to the record circuitry. The record circuitry would then interleave the samples ready for recording. If the heads are mounted a suitable distance apart in the scanner along the axis of rotation, the time taken for tape to travel from the first set of heads to the second will be equal to the decode/encode delay. If this process goes on for a few blocks, the signal going to the record head will be exactly the same as the pattern already on the tape, so the record head can be switched on at the beginning of an interleave block. Once

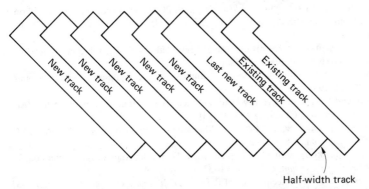

Half-width track

Figure 8.47 When editing a small track-pitch recording, the last track written will be 1.5 times the normal track width, since that is the width of the head. This erases half of the next track of the existing recording.

this has been done, new material can be crossfaded into the sample stream from the advanced replay head, and an edit will be performed.

If insert editing is contemplated, following the above process, it will be necessary to cross-fade back to the advanced replay samples before ceasing rerecording at an interleave block boundary. The use of overwrite to produce narrow tracks causes a problem at the end of such an insert. Fig.8.47 shows that this produces a track which is half the width it should be. Normally the error-correction system would take care of the consequences, but if a series of inserts were made at the same point in an attempt to make fine changes to an edit, the result could be an extremely weak signal for one track duration. One solution would be to use the track-pitch of prerecorded tapes for editing applications; another would be to incorporate a randomizing algorithm into the editor so that following the cross-fade back to samples from the replay head at the end of the insert the recorder continued to rerecord the original samples for a different length of time on each attempted edit.

8.14 Quarter-inch rotary

Following work which suggests that a rotary-head machine can accept spliced tape, Kudelski[9] has proposed a format for $\frac{1}{4}$-inch tape using a rotary head. The block structure is that of the audio channels of the D-1 DVTR (see Chapter 11) which would allow the chips developed for that purpose to be used. It is proposed that the format should allow low-density recording on open reels to support manual-splice editing, and high-density recording on cassette for tape protection and ease of storage, which would support electronic editing. A common transport would accept both tapes. Many of the proposals and features of stationary-head recorders are included, such as control-track-commanded jump editing, using internal memory, and double recording to increase splice tolerance. These topics are detailed in Chapter 9.

References

1. .YAMADA, Y., FUJII, Y., MORIYAMA, M. and SAITOH, S., Professional use PCM audio processor with a high efficiency error-correction system. Presented at 66th Audio Engineering Society Convention (Los Angeles, 1980), preprint 1628 (G7)
2. ISHIDA, Y., NISHI, S., KUNII, S., SATOH, T. and UETAKE, K., A PCM digital audio processor for home use VTRs. Presented at 64th Audio Engineering Society Convention (New York, 1979), preprint 1528
3. GRIFFITHS, F.A., A digital audio recording system. Presented at 65th Audio Engineering Society Convention (London, 1980), preprint 1580(C1)
4. OHTSUKI, T., KAZAMI, S., WAIARI, M., TANAKA, M. and DOI, T.T., A digital audio editor. *J. Audio Eng. Soc.*, **29**, 358 (1981)
5. NAKAJIMA, H. and ODAKA, K., A rotary-head high-density digital audio tape recorder. *IEEE Trans. Consum. Electron.*, **CE-29**, 430-437 (1983)
6. ITOH, F., SHIBA, H., HAYAMA, M. and SATOH, T., Magnetic tape and cartridge of R-DAT. *IEEE Trans. Consum. Electron.*, **CE-32**, 442-452 (1986)
7. ARAI, T., NOGUCHI, T., KOBAYASHI, M. and OKAMOTO, H., Digital signal processing technology for R-DAT. *IEEE Trans. Consum. Electron.*, **CE-32**, 416-424 (1986)
8. HITOMI, A. and TAKI, T., Servo technology of R-DAT. *IEEE Trans. Consum. Electron.*, **CE-32**, 425-432 (1986)
9. KUDELSKI, S., *et al.*, Digital audio recording format offering extensive editing capabilities. Presented at 82nd. Audio Engineering Society Convention (London, 1987), preprint 2481(H-7)

Chapter 9

Stationary head recorders

Digital audio recorders having fixed heads like an analog recorder have been developed because rotary-head recorders could not overcome certain operational requirements. The two types have coexisted, each supreme for its own intended purpose. In this chapter, stationary-head recorders for multitrack studio use, two-track recorders for general stereo recording, and the proposed SDAT consumer recorder will be discussed.

9.1 Requirements of audio production

Professional stationary-head recorders are specifically designed for record production and mastering, and have to be able to offer all the features of an analog multitrack. It could be said that many digital multitracks mimic analog machines so exactly that they can be installed in otherwise analog studios with the minimum of fuss. The necessary functions of a professional machine are: independent control of which tracks record and play, synchronous recording, punch-in/punch-out editing, tape-cut editing, variable-speed playback, offtape monitoring in record, various tape speeds and bandwidths, autolocation and the facilities to synchronize several machines.

This is a much more rigorous set of constraints than those for a digital computer or instrumentation recorder, and they largely determine the formats used.

9.2 Why stationary head?

In both theory and practice a rotary-head recorder can achieve a higher storage density than a stationary-head recorder, thus using less tape. When multitrack digital audio recorders were first proposed, the adaptation of a video-recorder transport had to be ruled out because it lacked the necessary bandwidth. For example, a 24-track machine requires about 24 megabits per second. A further difficulty is that helical-scan recorders do not take kindly to tape-cut edits. Accordingly, multitrack digital audio recorders have evolved with stationary heads and open reels; they look like analog recorders, but offer sufficient bandwidth and support splicing, although some early multitrack machines were built which did not support tape-cut editing. These had to be supplied in pairs so that editing could be performed by assembling from one machine to the other.

Now that the digital video recorder has arrived, with a prodigious bit-rate which may be put to other purposes, the situation may change.

9.3 Introduction

A stationary-head recorder is basically quite simple, as the block diagram of Fig.9.1 shows. The transport is not dissimilar to that of an analog recorder. The tape substrate used in professional analog recording is quite thick to reduce print-through, whereas in digital recording the tape is very thin, rather like videotape, to allow it to conform closely to the heads for short-wavelength working. Print-through is not an issue in digital recording. The roughness of the backcoat has to be restricted in digital tape to prevent it embossing the magnetic layer of the adjacent turn when on the reel, since this would nullify the efforts made to provide a smooth surface finish for good head contact. The roughness of the backcoat allows the boundary layer to bleed away between turns when the tape is spooled, and so digital recorders do not spool as quickly as analog recorders. They cannot afford to risk the edge damage which results from storing a poor tape pack. The digital transport has rather better tension and reel-speed control than an analog machine. Some transports offer a slow-wind mode to achieve an excellent pack on a tape prior to storage.

Control of the capstan is rather different too, being more like that of a video recorder. The capstan turns at constant speed when a virgin tape is being recorded, but for replay, it will be controlled to run at whatever speed is necessary to make the offtape sample rate equal to the reference rate. In this way, several machines can be kept in exact synchronism by feeding them with a common reference. Variable-speed replay can be achieved by changing the reference frequency. It should be emphasized that, when variable speed is used, the output sampling rate changes. This may not be of any consequence if the samples are returned to the analog domain, but it causes enormous problems if an attempt is made to connect to a digital mixer, since these usually have fixed sampling rates.

The major items in the block diagram have been discussed in the relevant chapters. Samples are interleaved, redundancy is added, and the bits are converted into a suitable channel code. In stationary-head recorders, the frequencies in each head are low, and complex coding is not difficult. The lack of the rotary transformer of the rotary-head machine means that DC content is a less important issue. The codes used generally try to emphasize density ratio, which keeps down the linear tape speed, and the jitter window, since this helps to reject the inevitable crosstalk between the closely spaced heads.

On replay there are the usual data separators, timebase correctors and error-correction circuits. Fortunately for the task of this chapter, the general layout of a stationary-head machine does not vary that much from one format to the next. The DASH format will be treated in detail and will be contrasted with the ProDigi formats as both have a substantial amount of equipment in service. Finally the proposed SDAT consumer stationary-head cassette recorder will be examined.

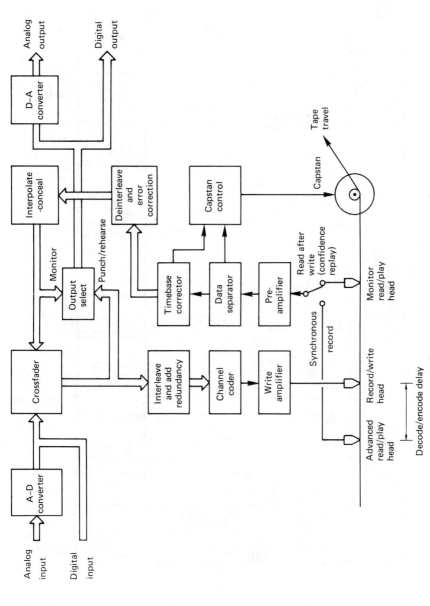

Figure 9.1 Block diagram of typical open-reel digital audio recorder. Note advanced head for synchronous recording, and capstan controlled by replay circuits.

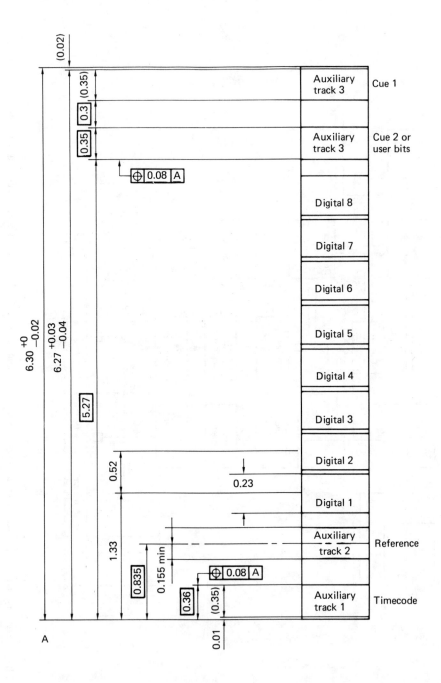

Figure 9.2 Track dimensions for DASH I Q (quarter-inch) above, and DASH 1 H (half-inch) on facing page.

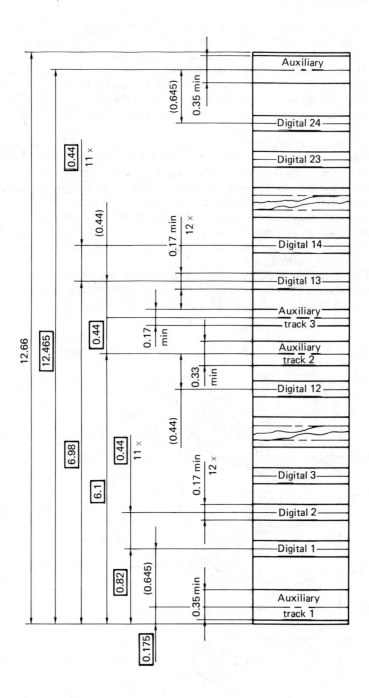

9.4 DASH format

The DASH[1] format is not one format as such, but a family of like formats, and thus supports a number of different track layouts. With current ferrite-head technology, it is possible to obtain adequate channel SNR with 24 tracks on $\frac{1}{2}$ in tape (H) and eight tracks on $\frac{1}{4}$ in tape (Q). The reason that these numbers are not pro-rata is that the same number of analog and control tracks are necessary for both, and take up proportionately more space on the narrower tape. This gave rise to the single-density family of formats known as DASH I. The track layouts are shown in Fig.9.2.

Note that the analog tracks are placed at the edges where they act as guard bands for the digital tracks, protecting them from edge lifting. Additionally there is a large separation between the analog tracks and the digital tracks. This prevents the bias from the analog heads from having an excessive erasing effect on the adjacent digital tracks. For the same reason AC erase may have to be ruled out. One alternative mechanism for erasure of the analog tracks is to use two DC heads in tandem. The first erases the tape by saturating it, and the second is wound in the opposite sense, and carries less current, to return the tape to a near-demagnetized state.

In the $\frac{1}{2}$ in format, the timecode and control tracks are placed at the centre of the tape, where they suffer no more skew with respect to the digital tracks than those at the edge of $\frac{1}{4}$ in tape in the presence of tape weave.

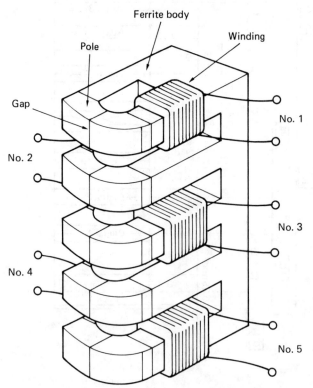

Figure 9.3 A typical ferrite head used for DASH I. Windings are placed on alternate sides to save space, but parallel magnetic circuits have high crosstalk.

The construction of a bulk ferrite multitrack head is shown in Fig.9.3, where it will be seen that space must be left between the magnetic circuits to accommodate the windings. Track spacing is improved by putting the windings on alternate sides of the gap. The parallel close-spaced magnetic circuits have considerable mutual inductance, and suffer from crosstalk. This can be compensated when several adjacent tracks record together by cross-connecting antiphase feeds to the record amplifiers.

Using thin-film heads, the magnetic circuits and windings are produced by deposition on a substrate at right angles to the tape plane, and as seen in Fig.9.4 they can be made very accurately at small track spacings. Perhaps more importantly, because the magnetic circuits do not have such large parallel areas, mutual inductance and crosstalk are smaller allowing a higher practical track density.

The so-called double-density version, known as DASH II, uses such thin-film heads to obtain 48 digital tracks on $\frac{1}{2}$ in tape and sixteen tracks on $\frac{1}{4}$ in tape. The track layouts of DASH II are shown in Fig.9.5 where it will be seen that the dimensions allow a DASH II machine to play tapes recorded on a DASH I machine.

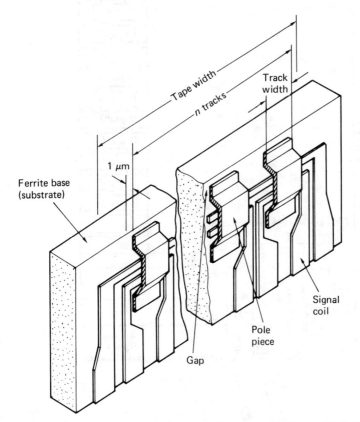

Figure 9.4 The thin-film head shown here can be produced photographically with very small dimensions. Flat structure reduces crosstalk. This type of head is suitable for DASH II which has twice as many tracks as DASH I.

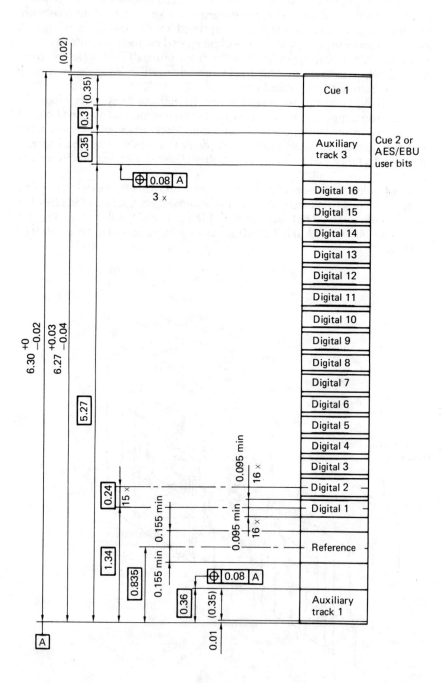

Figure 9.5 Track dimensions for DASH II Q (above) and DASH II H (facing page). Half the double-density tracks align with DASH I, so a DASH II machine can play a DASH I Tape.

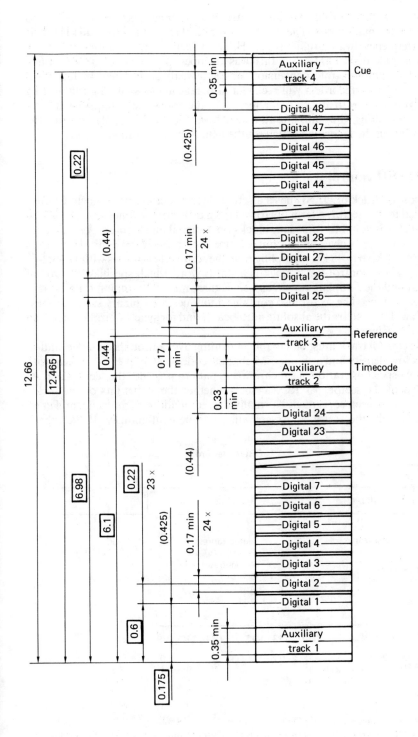

DASH supports three sampling rates and the tape speed is normalized to 30 in/s at the highest rate. The three rates are 32 kHz, 44.1 kHz and 48 kHz. This last frequency was originally 50.4 kHz, which had a simple fractional relationship to 44.1 kHz, but this was dropped in favour of 48 kHz when arbitrary sampling rate conversion was shown to be feasible. In fact most stationary-head recorders will record at any reasonable sampling rate just by supplying them with an external reference at the appropriate frequency. Under these conditions, the sampling-rate switch on the machine only controls the status bits in the recording which set the default playback rate.

9.5 DASH control track

The control track of DASH has a discrete block structure, where each record is referred to as a sector, a term borrowed from disk-drive technology. The length of a sector is equal to four data blocks on a digital audio track. As each data block contains twelve audio samples, one sector corresponds to 48 samples along a track, so at 48 kHz sampling rate, the sector will last 1 ms with DASH-F.

Part of the control-track block is a status word which specifies the type of format and the sampling rate in use, since these must be common for all tracks across the tape. The sector also contains a unique 28-bit binary sector address which will be used by the absolute autolocator and for synchronization between several machines.

The control track must be capable of reading over a wide speed range, and so it uses low density and a simple FM channel code (see Chapter 6). To help with variable-speed operation, a synchronizing pattern precedes the sector data. At the end of the sector, a CRCC detects whether the status bits or the sector address have been corrupted. Normally the sector address counts up, and at an assemble edit the sector addresses will continue contiguously. If the tape is

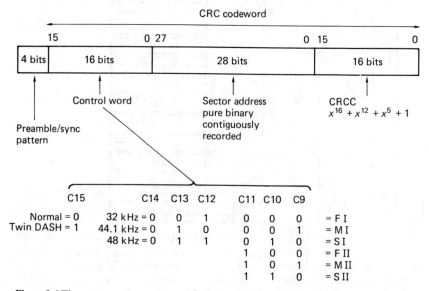

Figure 9.6 The contents of one sector of the control track. Note the Twin DASH status bit.

spliced, there will be a sector address jump. The structure of the control track is detailed in Fig.9.6.

The presence of the sampling-rate and track-allocation data in the control track means that a suitable machine could automatically drive the capstan at the right speed and demultiplex the tape tracks whatever type of tape is loaded. Thus a multiformat DASH recorder is feasible.

9.6 Versions of DASH

In the digital domain it is quite easy to distribute samples from one audio channel over a number of tape tracks. In DASH-F, the fast version, one audio track requires one tape track, and the tape moves at its greatest speed. In DASH-M, the medium version, one audio channel is spread over two tape tracks, and the tape runs at half speed. In DASH-S, the slow version, one audio channel is spread over four tape tracks, and the tape runs at one quarter speed. In twin DASH, the data corresponding to one audio channel are recorded twice, giving advantages in splice tolerance. Clearly the number of audio channels must be halved in twin DASH-F, but in DASH-M and DASH-S the tape speed could be doubled instead.

By way of example, the well-known PCM-3324 is a DASH-FIH machine:

F = Fast format, one channel per track
I = Single density
H = Half-inch tape, hence 24 tape tracks and 24 audio channels

The PCM-3102 is a DASH-SIQ machine:

S = Slow format, four tracks per channel
I = Single density
Q = Quarter-inch tape, hence eight tape tracks and two audio channels

The PCM-3202 is a twin DASH-MIQ machine:

M = Medium format, two tracks per channel
I = Single density
Q = Quarter-inch tape, hence eight tape tracks, and two audio channels double-recorded

The track allocation mechanisms for S, M and F are shown in Fig.9.7 which also depicts the relationship with the control track.

9.7 Block contents

The digital audio tracks have an identical structure in all DASH formats. Once the physical dimensions of the tape track are defined, it remains to determine the kind of channel code to be used, a block structure and an error correction strategy.

The channel code of DASH is known as HDM-1 (see Chapter 6 for detailed explanation) which is a run-length-limited code with a high density-ratio to minimize the linear tape speed necessary. The contents of a block are shown in Fig.9.8. There is a sync word necessary to synchronize the phase-locked loop in the data separators, some control bits, twelve samples, four parity words and a

(a) Fast version ($C_{11} = C_{10} = C_9 = 0$)

Data block sequence	n	$n+1$	$n+2$	$n+3$	$n+4$	$n+5$	$n+6$	$n+7$	$n+8$	$n+9$	$n+10$	$n+11$	$n+12$	$n+13$	$n+14$	$n+15$
Block address	0	1	2	3	0	1	2	3	0	1	2	3	0	1	2	3
Control track (sector address)	$4m + 0$				$4m + 1$				$4m + 2$				$4m + 3$			

Track A o→ Encoder

Word sequence 1, 2, 3, 4, ...

(b) Medium version ($C_{11} = C_{10} = 0, C_9 = 1$)

	Data block sequence	n	$n+1$	$n+2$	$n+3$	$n+4$	$n+5$	$n+6$	$n+7$	$n+8$	$n+9$	$n+10$	$n+11$	$n+12$	$n+13$	$n+14$	$n+15$
A	Block address	0	1	2	3	0	1	2	3	0	1	2	3	0	1	2	3
B	Block address	0	1	2	3	0	1	2	3	0	1	2	3	0	1	2	3
	Control track (sector address)	$4m + 0$				$4m + 1$				$4m + 2$				$4m + 3$			

Track (A and B)

Track A o→ Encoder — Word sequence 1, 2, 5, 6

Track B o→ Encoder — 3, 4, 7, 8

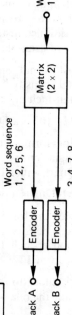

Matrix (2 × 2) o→ Word sequence 1, 2, 3, 4, ···

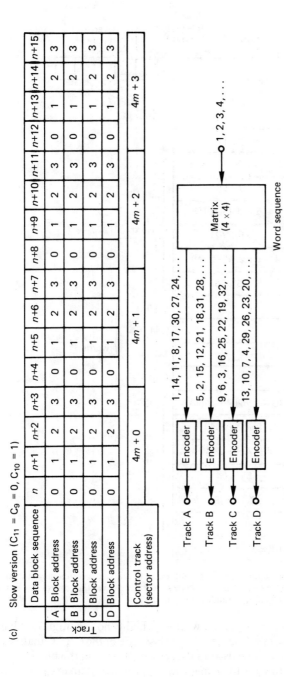

Figure 9.7 Relationships of blocks to control-track sectors. At (a), there are four blocks in one track, representing one audio channel (fast version). At (b) there are eight blocks in two tracks, representing one audio channel. The tape speed can be halved to give the medium version. At (c) there are sixteen blocks in four tracks representing one audio channel. In this, the slow version, speed can be 0.25 of fast version.

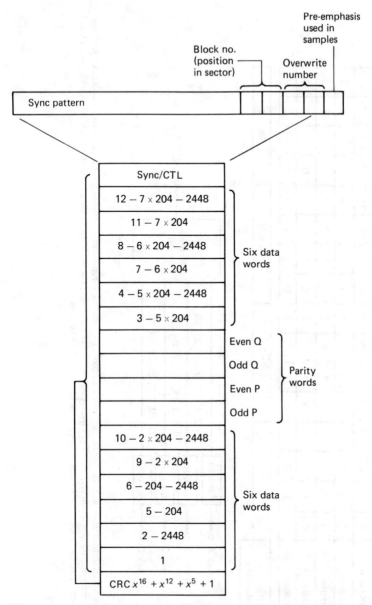

Figure 9.8 Contents of one data block. The samples are highly non-contiguous according to the interleave expressions shown. The CRC codeword extends over the control bits but not the sync pattern. If the check fails, all samples are assumed bad.

CRCC. The samples and the parity words are highly non-contiguous, due to the use of crossinterleave (see Chapter 7). The presence of the CRCC makes a block into a codeword and can be used to detect a read error in the block.

When a new recording is to be made in the presence of an existing recording, the new recording will begin at a block boundary. In practice it is difficult physically to position the tape, and the last block of the previous recording may be corrupted by the beginning of the new one. The error-correction system is designed to cope with this.

The control bits identify the use of pre-emphasis prior to the ADC, and there is a sector-position count. Since there are four data blocks to every sector, a two-bit binary code is sufficient to identify the block within the sector.

9.8 Redundancy in DASH

The error-correction strategy of DASH is to form codewords which are confined to single tape tracks. This should be contrasted with the approach of ProDigi, which forms codewords across the tape tracks as well. DASH uses crossinterleaving, which was described in principle in Chapter 7. The principles will not be repeated here, but the details relating to the application in DASH will be given. In all practical recorders measures have to be taken for the rare cases when the error correction is overwhelmed by gross corruption. In open-reel stationary-head recorders, one obvious mechanism is the act of splicing the tape and the resultant contamination due to fingerprints.

A large interleave is created between odd and even samples. In the case of a severe dropout, after deinterleave, the effect will be to cause two separate error bursts, first in the odd samples, then in the even samples. The odd samples can be interpolated from the even and vice versa. The interpolation causes a momentary reduction in frequency response which may result in aliasing if there is significant audio energy above one quarter of the sampling rate. This interpolation will not take place in twin DASH, as will be seen. The interleave structure of DASH will now be described, based on the above principles.

Samples from the converter or direct digital input are first sorted into odd and even. They will then be time-displaced by 2448 samples to permit interpolation on replay. The magnitude of this displacement will be justified in the section on splice handling. As there are twelve samples in each block, the odd and even samples are assembled into groups of six each, and reordered. Thus samples 1, 3, 5, 7, 9 and 11 become 1, 5, 9, 3, 7 and 11. This reordering produces the maximum distance between adjacent samples. After interleave they will be widely separated on tape. For example, samples 1 and 3 will be three times further apart on tape than they would be without reordering. In the case of gross error, samples 1 and 3 will be used to interpolate sample 2. The wide separation between them increases the probability that both will be correct or correctable.

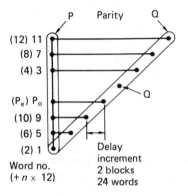

Figure 9.9 The crossinterleave of DASH is achieved with a system of different delays. Data are formed into two arrays of six samples each, one odd numbered and one even numbered. The odd samples are shifted relative to even by 2448. Parity P is generated, followed by the delays shown here to produce parity Q. The remaining interleave is shown in Figure 9.11.

P codeword

Q codeword

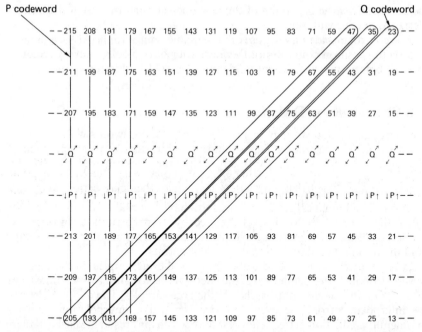

Figure 9.10 The system of Figure 9.9 results in P and Q codewords passing in two directions through the array. The CRC codeword passes in a third direction, and will be recorded in that sequence. This example shows only odd samples.

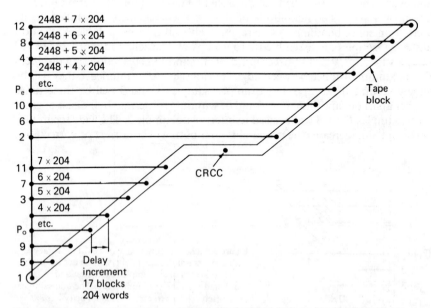

Figure 9.11 Following the interleave of Figure 9.9, further delays produce the final data block and its CRCC.

The six odd samples and the six even samples produce redundancy words P_o and P_e by simple parity. Placing the parity symbols in the centre of the reordered samples further increases the distance between adjacent samples on tape. Fig.9.9 shows that the samples and P words are then interleaved so that adjacent symbols appear two blocks apart. This is achieved by inserting delays which are a function of the position in the block. Following this interleave, Q parity words are generated.

Fig.9.10 shows the resultant structure for odd samples for the DASH cross-interleave. The P redundancy is on vertical columns, the Q redundancy is on diagonals. The data cannot be recorded in the Q diagonal sequence, since bursts would damage multiple symbols, and parity has no way of determining the position of random errors. A further interleave is necessary. Fig.9.11 shows that this is achieved by further stages of delay, where the delay period is again a function of position in the block. Note the difference of 2448 words between odd and even samples. A CRCC is calculated from the ouput of the final interleave, and this covers the samples, and P and Q words, as well as the status word in the block. This is the only polynomial calculation in DASH since all other redundancy is simple parity.

Twin DASH differs from the original DASH format in the following way. All incoming samples will be recorded twice which means twice as many tape tracks or twice the linear speed is necessary. The interleave structure of one of the tracks will be identical to the interleave already described, whereas on the second recording, the odd even sample interleave is reversed. When a gross error occurs in twin DASH, it will be seen from Fig.9.12 that the result after deinterleave is that when odd samples are destroyed in one channel, even samples

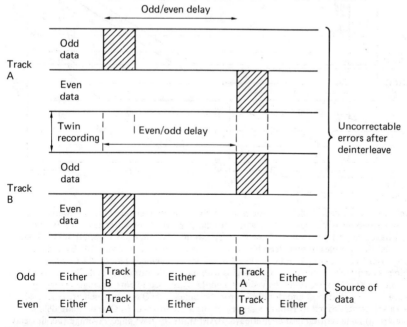

Figure 9.12 In twin DASH, the reversed interleave on the twin recordings means that correct data are always available. This makes twin DASH much more resistant to mishandling.

are destroyed in the other. By selecting valid data from both channels, a full bandwidth signal can be obtained and no interpolation is necessary. The only other difference in twin DASH is that the status bits in the control track reflect the use of twin recording.

9.9 How error correction works in DASH

The error correction mechanism works as follows. If a block CRC check fails, then the error could be in any or all of the samples in the block. No attempt is made to determine which, because the simple CRCC used has no locating power. All the samples in the block are declared bad by attaching an error flag to them. After deinterleave, single-error-flagged samples will be found in several different P codewords, and these can be corrected by erasure using the parity symbols and the flags, which are then reset.

The presence of a random error in the vicinity of a burst can result in two error flags appearing in one P codeword, which the simple parity system cannot correct. Samples are then reinterleaved to time-align symbols in a Q codeword. As stated in Chapter 7, if two samples are in error in a P word then, in most cases, only one will be in error in two different Q words and vice versa. The Q parity symbol and the error flags will again correct single faulty samples, and the error flags will again be reset. Samples must be deinterleaved again following

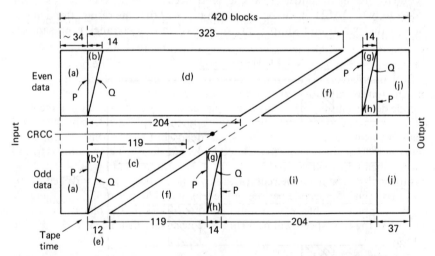

Figure 9.13 Encode/decode delays through PCM-3324 (all numbers are blocks = twelve words). (a) Data written into interleave RAM waits for read page. (b) Cross interleave of P (vertical) and Q (diagonal) parity is formed. Note this step has no effect on encode period. (c) Odd data are delayed by multiples of seventeen blocks up to maximum of 119 blocks. (d) Even data are delayed from 204 blocks up to 323 blocks by multiples of seventeen blocks. CRC is formed and block is written. (e) Replay process begins with data separator delay and TBC delay of twelve blocks. (f) Data are reinterleaved to P and flags are used to correct single errors. (g) Data are reinterleaved to Q and double P errors become single Q errors which are corrected. (h) Data are deinterleaved to P and remaining errors are corrected. (i) Odd data are delayed 204 blocks. (j) Data written into deinterleave. RAM waits for read page. Average encode delay is 34 + 323/2 = approx. 196 blocks. Average decode delay is 12 + 37 + 14 + 323/2 = approx. 224 blocks.

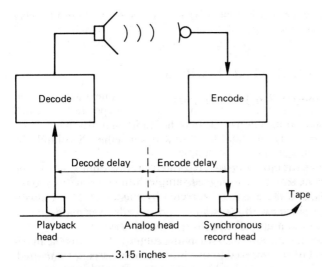

Figure 9.14 Synchronous recording requires displaced heads, separated by the decode/encode delay. In DASH this is about 3.15 in or 420 blocks.

this stage. A final stage of correction is then possible using P parity, but this is often omitted and interpolation is used to conceal samples which leave the deinterleave process with error flags still set.

Fig.9.13 shows the total interleave timing through a DASH machine. The apparently complex interleaving process is achieved using a RAM. Samples are written into the RAM in sequence, but are read out using a sequencer. De-interleave on playback is achieved using an equal and opposite process.

Both interleave and deinterleave processes cause a delay in the sample stream, but the reinterleave on replay means that the decode delay is longer than the encode delay. This is only of any consequence when using a multitrack recorder to perform synchronous recording. Analog machines play back using the record head in this mode to eliminate tape-path delay, but clearly this will not work with digital machines owing to the encode/decode delays. The solution is to add another head downstream for synchronous recording, as in Fig.9.14. The head has to be displaced from the replay head by exactly the distance travelled by the tape in one encode/decode period, or the length of 420 tape blocks. As there are twelve samples in a block, at a sampling rate of 48 kHz the block rate will be 4 kHz. As the tape speed will be 30 in/s, the necessary distance will be:

$$\frac{30}{4000} \times 420 \text{ in} = 3.15 \text{ in}$$

If a synchronous record head has to be replaced on a stationary-head machine, an adjustment will be necessary to set this distance accurately. When DASH was normalized to 30 in/s at 48 kHz instead of 50.4 kHz, the head blocks of DASH machines had to be replaced to get the head spacing correct.

The original sampling frequency of 50.4 kHz resulted in an elegant encode/decode delay of exactly:

$$\frac{50\,400}{420 \times 12} \text{s} = 0.1 \text{ s}$$

with a head spacing of exactly 3 in. In 48 kHz DASH the encode/decode delay becomes 105 ms.

9.10 Interleave in DASH-M and DASH-S

The discussion so far has assumed the use of DASH-F, with one track per audio channel. In the M and S versions, more than one track is used per audio channel and this has additional implications. Clearly the audio samples have to be distributed around the tracks, but the question arises whether this should be done before or after interleaving.

If multiplexing takes place after interleaving, then the constraint length of the interleave which governs the burst-error-correcting ability exists over a shorter length of tape track, and so the resistance to dropout is reduced. The contamination due to fingerprints is two-dimensional, and spreads over many tracks, which would badly affect a multiplex-after-interleave system.

Where multiplexing is done before interleaving, each track retains the maximum constraint length of the interleave, and burst correction is not impaired. Fingerprint-induced errors are corrected on a track-by-track basis, since codewords do not then cross between tracks. The tracks which result from one audio channel are distributed throughout the width of the tape, further reducing the effect of fingerprint-induced errors.

9.11 Punching and editing

The operating modes of a DASH machine will now be discussed with reference to the necessary features of the format.

On many occasions it is necessary to replace a short section of a long recording, because a wrong note was played or something fell over and made a noise. The tape is played back to the musicians before the bad section, and they play along with it. At a musically acceptable point prior to the error, the tape machine passes into record, a process known as punch-in, and the offending section is rerecorded. At another suitable time, the machine ceases recording at the punch-out point, and the musicians can subsequently stop playing.

The problem with an interleaved recording is that it is not possible to point to a specific place on the tape and say that it represents the recording at a particular instant. It is not possible just to begin recording at some arbitrary place, as the interleave structure would be destroyed. The mechanism necessary is shown in Fig.9.15. Prior to the punch-in point, the replay-head signal is deinterleaved, and this signal is fed to the record channel. The record channel reinterleaves the samples, and after some time will produce a signal which is identical to what is already on the tape. At a block boundary the record current can be turned on, when the existing recording will be rerecorded. At the punch-in point, the samples fed to the record encoder will be crossfaded to samples from the ADC. The crossfade takes place in the noninterleaved domain. The new recording is made to replace the unsatisfactory section, and at the end, punch-out is commenced by returning the crossfader to the samples from the replay head. After some time, the record head will once more be rerecording what is already on the tape, and at a block boundary the record current can be switched off. The crossfade duration can be chosen according to the nature of the recorded material. If a

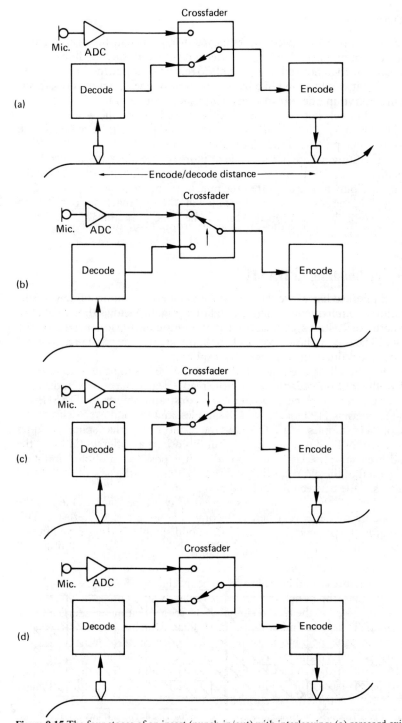

Figure 9.15 The four stages of an insert (punch-in/out) with interleaving: (a) rerecord existing samples for at least one constraint length; (b) crossfade to incoming samples (punch-in point); (c) crossfade to existing replay samples (punch-out point); (d) rerecord existing samples for at least one constraint length. An assemble edit consists of steps (a) and (b) only.

genuine silence appears between notes played in a dead acoustic, a rapid cross-fade may be optimum. With a large chorus in reverberant surroundings, a long crossfade might go unnoticed. It is possible to rehearse the punch-in process and monitor what it would sound like by feeding headphones from the crossfader, and doing everything described except that the record head is disabled. The punch-in and punch-out points can then be moved to give the best subjective result. The machine can learn the sector addresses at which the punches take place, so the final punch is fully automatic.

Assemble editing, where parts of one or more source tapes are dubbed from one machine to another to produce a continuous recording, is performed in the same way as a punch-in, except that the punch-out never comes. After the new recording from the source machine is faded in, the two machines continue to dub until one of them is stopped. This will be done some time after the next assembly point is reached.

9.12 Splice handling in DASH

The use of interleaving is essential to handle burst errors; unfortunately it con-flicts with the requirements of tape-cut editing. Fig.9.16 shows that a splice in cross-interleave destroys codewords for the entire constraint length of the interleave. The longer the constraint length, the greater the resistance to burst errors, but the more damage is done by a splice.

In order to handle splices, the odd/even interleave has to be used to interpo-late when the P/Q redundancy is overwhelmed. Clearly the odd/even distance has to be greater than the crossinterleave constraint length. In DASH, the constraint length is 119 blocks, or 1428 samples, and the odd/even delay is 204 blocks, or 2448 samples. Fig.9.17 shows the results of a perfect splice. Samples are destroyed for the constraint length, but this occurs at different times for the odd and even samples. Using interpolation, it is possible to obtain simultan-eously the end of the old recording and the beginning of the new one. A digital crossfade is made between the old and new recordings.

In twin DASH, the same samples are fed to two tape tracks. One has the normal odd/even interleave, whereas the other has an opposite interleave. This means that in the presence of a splice, when odd samples are destroyed in one track, even samples will be destroyed in the other track. Thus at all times, all

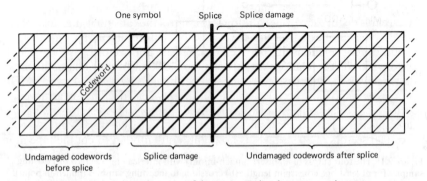

Figure 9.16 Although interleave is a powerful weapon against burst errors, it causes greater data loss when tape is spliced because many codewords are replayed in two unrelated halves.

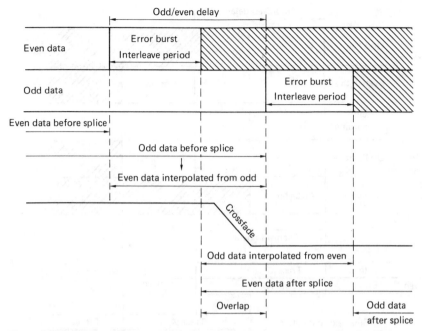

Figure 9.17 Following deinterleave, the effect of a splice is to cause odd and even data to be lost at different times. Interpolation is used to provide the missing samples, and a crossfade is made when both recordings are available in the central overlap.

samples will be available without interpolation, and full bandwidth can be maintained across splices. Fig.9.18 shows the results of a splice in twin DASH.

For splice handling, the crossfader can be the same physical unit as that used for punch-in/punch-out, but the crossfade time will need to be fixed so that it can complete during the time for which both old and new recordings are available. The crossfade is triggered by the jump in sector address in the control track.

A tape splice will result in a random jump of control track phase of $\pm\frac{1}{2}$ sector. In replay, the capstan is controlled by comparing the data rate offtape with a reference, and this is sometimes done by a phase comparison between sector sync from tape and a reference-derived sector-rate signal. The effect of a splice will be to cause a sudden phase step which disturbs the capstan. In order to reduce this disturbance, one solution is to control the capstan using block phase, since a block is one quarter the size of a sector. This results in rapid locking, but produces four relationships between block phase and sector phase. In order to restore the correct relationship between the block and sector phase, the replay data delay in the timebase corrector will be changed by 12 or 24 samples. This process is important because synchronism between machines is achieved by sector lock; thus samples must have a fixed relationship to sector timing, and tape splicing always operates in sector steps, however the tape is cut. As there are 1000 sectors in 30 in, there is no point in attempting to cut the tape more accurately than 0.03 in. This represents 1 ms in DASH-F, 2 ms in DASH-M and 4 ms in DASH-S.

When a synchronous recording is made over a splice, it is necessary to duplicate exactly the change in block to sector phase. Thus a timebase corrector is

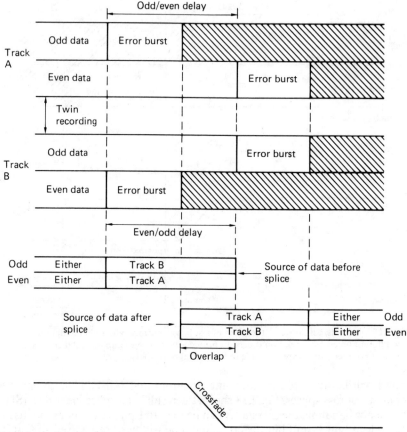

Figure 9.18 In twin DASH, two recordings are made of the same data, but with a reversed interleave. In the area of a splice, when one recording loses odd samples, the other will lose even samples, and vice versa. By selecting samples as above, full bandwidth is maintained through the splice, since no interpolation is necessary.

necessary in the record channel also, which will experience a timing change of 12 or 24 samples at the instant the splice passes the record head. When a synchronous recording is made, the recording takes place 420 blocks after the replay. The replay-TBC delay change is made the instant the splice passes the playback head, whereas the record-TBC must change its delay by the same amount when the splice passes the synchronous record head. The delay change parameter must be stored for 420 blocks to ensure that this is so.[2]

Clearly a crossfade is neither necessary nor desirable in a synchronous recording made over a splice. Thus the decision to operate the crossfade mechanism must be made on a channel-by-channel basis. The presence of a splice causes a sector-address jump in the control track. There can be no other cause, since an assemble results in sector addresses which are contiguous.

A synchronous recording made over a splice will suffer a relatively small number of errors which will be correctable. A splice between two different recordings will result in uncorrectable errors and cause interpolation. Accordingly, any track which is not interpolating continuously in the presence of a sector

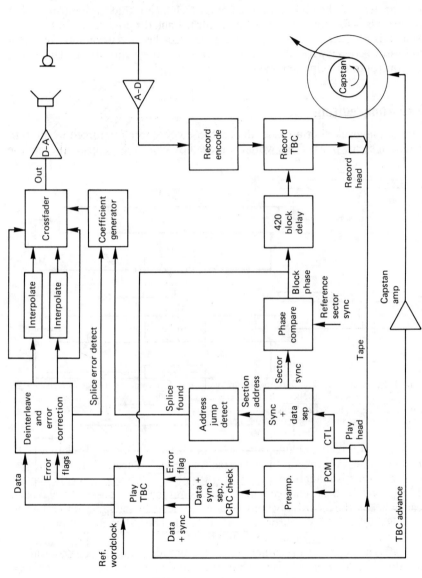

Figure 9.19 Splicehandling DASH recorder requires interpolators and a crossfader after error-correction unit, and a block-phase delay for synchronous recording over an earlier splice. In twin DASH, the interpolators would not be necessary, and would be replaced by a multiplexer selecting correct data from the two recordings.

address jump will not need to crossfade. Fig.9.19 shows the essentials of a DASH splice handling system, which supports synchronous recording over splices.

Some DASH recorders control the capstan in replay by examining the average delay in the timebase correctors, which means that the control track is not necessary for normal replay, and control-track dropout ceases to be a problem. It is still necessary to retain the control track because it contains the sector addresses necessary for absolute autolocation and synchronizing. This led to the control track being renamed the reference track.

9.13 Jump editing

During playback over a splice, the timebase correctors are forced to jump to maintain sector phase. This would cause a TBC-controlled capstan to rephase

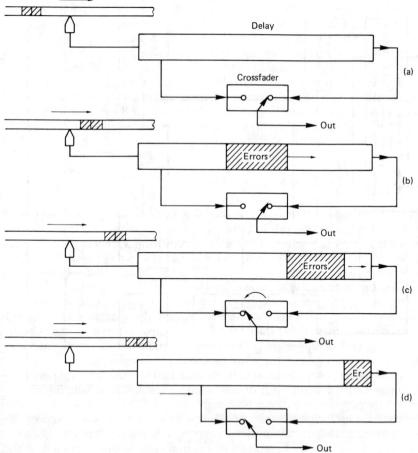

Figure 9.20 Jump editing. At (a) splice approaches, capstan is advanced, and audio is delayed. (b) Splice passes head, and error burst travels down delay. (c) Crossfader fades to signal after splice. (d) Capstan accelerates, and delay increases. When the delay tap reaches the end, the crossfader can switch back ready for the next splice.

automatically. An extension to the TBC jumping principle has been suggested by Lagadec[3] so that the jump can be externally controlled.

In this system, a tape splice is made physically with excess tape adjacent to the intended edit points. The timebase corrector has two read-address generators which can access the memory independently. It will be seen in Fig.9.20 that when the machine plays the tape, the capstan is phase-advanced so that the timebase corrector is causing a long delay to compensate. As the splice is detected, the corruption due to the splice enters the TBC memory and travels towards the output. As the splice nears the end of the memory, the machine output crossfades to a signal from the second TBC output which has been delayed much less. The data in the area of the tape splice are thus omitted. The capstan will now be effectively lagging because the delay has been shortened, and it will speed up slightly for a short period until the lead condition is re-established. This can be done without ill effect since the sample rate from the memory remains constant throughout. Although the splice is an irrevocable mechanical act, the precise edit timing can be changed at will by controlling the sector address at which the TBC jumps, which determines the out point, and the address difference, which determines the length of tape omitted, and thus controls the in point. The size of the jump is limited by the available memory. Such a system would be excellent for news broadcasts where it is often necessary to remove many short sections of tape to eliminate hesitations and unwanted pauses from interviews. Control of the jumping could be by programming a CPU to recognise timecode or sector addresses and insert the commands, or, as suggested by Lagadec, inserting the jump distance in the reference track prior to the splice. In either case machines not equipped to jump would handle the splice with mechanically determined timing.

9.14 Timecode

The standardization of timecode for digital audio recorders has been hampered by the diversity of standards in video. Synchronization between timecode and the sampling rate is desirable. The EBU timecode format relates easily to digital audio sampling rates of 48 kHz, 44.1 kHz and 32 kHz, but this is not true of the dropframe SMPTE timecode necessary for NTSC recording due to the 0.1 % slip between the actual field rate and 60 Hz.

One use of timecode is synchronization between several different machines. One of the machines must be the master, and the synchronizer will read timecode from master and slave, and will slip capstan phase on the slave to achieve the correct time relationship. If a digital audio recorder is the slave, and the timecode on the recording is not locked to the sampling rate, the synchronizer will force the sampling rate to be nonstandard in order to lock timecode to the master. If the master is a digital video recorder, whose sampling rate is locked to field rate, it will not be possible to synchronize the samples. Conversely if sample lock is achieved, timecode will slip. In this case it is necessary to revert to the analog domain or use a sampling-rate converter to time-align the two recordings. Chapter 11 explains how digital video recorders can unlock the digital audio sampling rate from video frequencies to make a nonstandard recording in such circumstances.

A further problem with the use of synchronizers is that if they attempt to slew the capstan too fast, the data separators may lose lock and mute the machine output.

9.15 Cue tracks

The cue tracks of DASH are at the extreme edges of the tape in the H format, and together at the top edge in Q format. As most digital audio recorders mute if the speed is more than 25 % out, the cue tracks are important to locate edit points over a wide speed range.

Sony use biased analog recording for the cue tracks. As the digital headstacks are optimized for short-wavelength recording, their analog performance is poor, and separate heads are used for the analog tracks. These are placed one decode delay downtape from the digital replay head, and one encode delay uptape from the synchronous record head in order to maintain sync. This head also records timecode.

Studer take the view that the cue tracks should use a form of modulation suited to short wavelengths which operates over a wide speed range, so that the digital headstacks can be used.[3] Fig.9.21 shows how a three-head DASH machine could be constructed using CCD delays to time-align the cue and timecode signals with the digital audio channels which are subject to interleave delays.

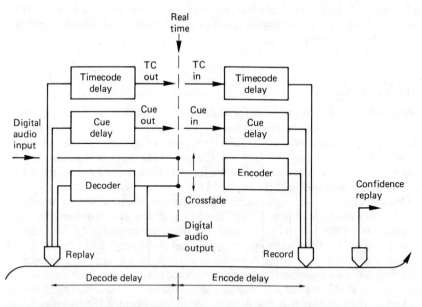

Figure 9.21 Three-head DASH machine with synchronous record capability and time-aligned cue and timecode using CCD delays. The same delay circuits could be used for record or reproduce. Similarly, decoder stages could be shared between replay and confidence.

9.16 Mitsubishi formats

In the Mitsubishi formats, there are three tape widths supported, $\frac{1}{4}$ in stereo recording, $\frac{1}{2}$ in sixteen-channel and 1 in 32-channel multitrack. The $\frac{1}{4}$ in ProDigi format is a more sophisticated version of an earlier format designed by Mitsubishi, which was not given a title. Both variations will be described here, so that the evolution can be seen. Since the time the ProDigi name came into existence, it has also been applied to the multitrack formats.

A fundamental difference between DASH and the Mitsubishi formats is that the latter produce codewords across the tape as well as along the tracks. This means that there must be redundant tracks to carry the check symbols which are part of the transverse code words.

The stereo format of the Mitsubishi X-80 will be discussed first.[4] It is a true stereo format in that samples for both audio channels are combined into a single data structure which is then distributed over all the digital tracks. It is not possible to record one channel only without recording the other, therefore if only one audio channel is to be rerecorded, it is necessary to play back the existing recording, change half of the samples to those of the input channel, and rerecord every digital track. Fig.9.22 shows how this can be done with an advanced playback head. A further consequence of combining the channels into all tracks is that the channels cannot lose relative synchronization, so no control track is necessary. None of the Mitsubishi formats uses a control track.

In the X-80 format, there are eight digital tracks, so that one codeword can be formed across the tape. As Fig.9.23 shows, there are also two auxiliary tracks, one for timecode, and one analog audio track for cueing and to assist the location of edit points.

Incoming sixteen-bit samples from the left and right audio channels are assembled into a rectangular block 14×6 as in Fig.9.24. Samples are written into the block such that odd-numbered samples and even-numbered samples are always on different rows. The number of samples in the block was chosen to give a block rate of 1200 Hz with a sampling rate of 50.4 kHz.

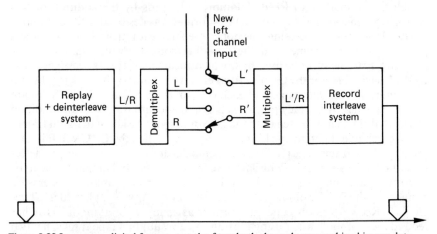

Figure 9.22 In a stereo digital format, samples from both channels are combined in one data structure. The only way that one channel can be updated without changing the other is fully to decode and demultiplex the recording, substitute the new recording (L') and rerecord the entire tape data structure.

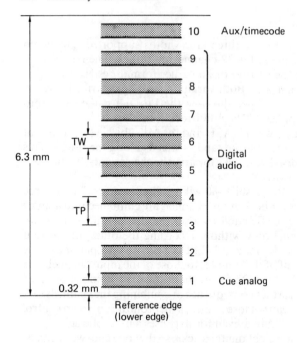

TP = 0.625 mm   TW = 0.305 mm

Figure 9.23 Track dimensions of X-80 stereo format.

The error-correction mechanism uses a product code, where detection of the errors and correction are two separate processes. Fig.9.25 shows that the rows of the sample block are made into codewords by the addition of a sixteen-bit CRCC at the end of each. These codewords are known as frames. Columns of the block are made into Reed–Solomon codewords by the addition of two symbols of redundancy. At the time this format was designed, LSI technology for Reed–Solomon processing was not cost-effective for professional recorders produced in low volume, and the decoding complexity was minimized by adopting symbols of only four bits, which meant that it was feasible to use ROM-based tables for the Galois arithmetic. As a result, each block is split into 56 columns of four bits each, and each column is made into a Reed–Solomon codeword. The redundancy produced is also made into frames by the addition of a CRCC. Data are written onto the tape by assigning each of the eight frames of the block to a different track. If an error occurs, then the CRC will fail for a given track, or frame. The CRC is not intended to locate the error, only to detect it, so the CRC failure simply declares every four-bit symbol in that frame to be in error by attaching an error flag to it. These error flags are used as erasure pointers by the Reed–Solomon code in the columns. As was explained in Chapter 7, a Reed–Solomon code can correct as many error symbols as it has redundancy symbols when using erasure. As a result, two tape tracks, i.e. two rows of the block, can be in error, and correction is still possible.

Actual measurements of tape performance revealed that in general, if an error was present in one track, there was only a minute probability that an error

L1	R1	L7	R7	L13	R13	L19	R19	L25	R25	L31	R31	L37	R37
L2	R2	L8	R8	L14	R14	L20	R20	L26	R26	L32	R32	L38	R38
L3	R3	L9	R9	L15	R15	L21	R21	L27	R27	L33	R33	L39	R39
L4	R4	L10	R10	L16	R16	L22	R22	L28	R28	L34	R34	L40	R40
L5	R5	L11	R11	L17	R17	L23	R23	L29	R29	L35	R35	L41	R41
L6	R6	L12	R12	L18	R18	L24	R24	L30	R30	L36	R36	L42	R42

Figure 9.24 A stereo sample block from X-80 format. There are 42 left-channel and 42 right-channel samples, which gives a block rate of 1200 Hz with a sampling rate of 50.4 kHz.

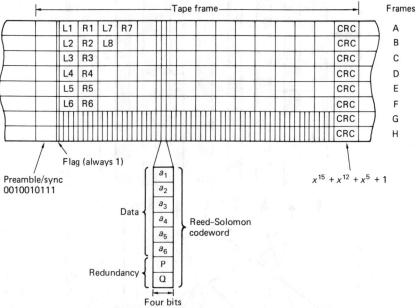

Figure 9.25 The sample block of Figure 9.24 is made into a product code by the addition of redundancy in two dimensions. Horizontally, a CRCC is added for error detection; vertically, two Reed–Solomon symbols are used per column. The R–S symbols are only from bits to simplify processing, and four R–S codewords are needed for one column of samples.

would also be present in an adjacent track.[5] The error-correction system is thus adequate to deal with random errors.

There are two eventualities which cause exceptions to these measurements. When the tape is handled, fingerprints cause two-dimensional dropouts due to spacing loss which affect all tracks simultaneously. Similarly, when the tape is spliced, all tracks are affected at once.

In order to overcome these problems, interleave is used. The interleave is specified in Fig.9.26, where it will be seen that each tape track records data that have been subjected to different delays. The samples which have been heavily delayed on record will receive less delay on replay, and vice versa. It will also be clear from Fig.9.26 that the odd samples are given rather less delay than the even samples.

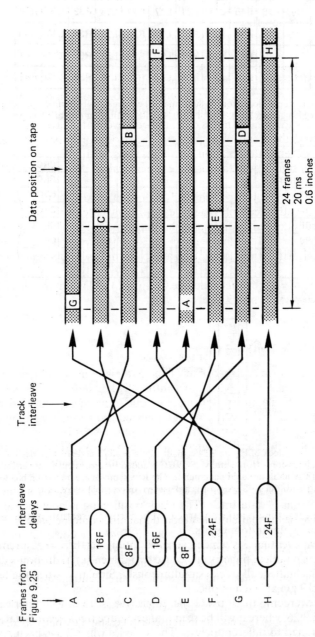

Figure 9.26 The product block of Figure 9.25 is interleaved for recording on tape by the delay system shown here. Further physical interleave is obtained by rearranging the tracks used to record the frames.

The effect of this interleave is that on replay, errors which affect all tracks simultaneously will affect different rows of the array at different times after deinterleave. The effect of fingerprints will thus be to cause a few rows of the array to be corrupted in many different tape frames, rather than many rows being corrupted in a few frames.

When the tape is spliced, errors will occur due to three mechanisms. First, there will be surface contamination due to handling. Secondly, the beginning and end of the adhesive tape will cause separation-loss errors where the flexibility of the tape changes. These two will be dealt with as described. Thirdly, the actual splice results in a massive error-burst due to distortion of the tape by cutting and the temporary loss of synchronization caused by the arbitrary frame phase jump across the splice. In this case, the odd/even interleave will be used. After deinterleave, the result of a splice will be two error bursts, first in odd samples, then in even. Interpolation can be used as for the DASH format in Fig.9.17, and in a similar way, a crossfade is made when both the old and new recordings are available.

Punch-in and punch-out are achieved in the same way as in the DASH format, using the advanced playback head to provide early replay samples which can be deinterleaved for fading to new material. The result of the fade will then be reinterleaved and fed to the record head. The advanced replay head is the same one needed for recording one audio channel without changing the other.

The X-80 used MFM channel code (see Chapter 6) and was normalized for a linear tape speed of 15 in/s at 50.4 kHz.

9.17 Quarter-inch ProDigi format

In the $\frac{1}{4}$ in ProDigi format, the format of the X-80 is refined and available in three different modes.[6,7] In mode 1, sixteen-bit 48 kHz stereo at 15 in/s is suggested for maximum tolerance to splicing. In mode 2, the tape speed is halved by increasing the packing density, for applications requiring long recording time. Mode 3 uses twenty-bit samples at 15 in/s, so that the entire contents of the AES/EBU digital audio interface signal can be recorded. As usual in stationary-head machines, the use of 44.1 kHz or 32 kHz sampling results in a pro-rata reduction in tape speed.

Reference to Fig.9.27 will reveal that there are two analog tracks, a timecode track, and an auxiliary data track. The track positioning is now the same as DASH-Q, which means that a dual-standard machine could be built.

The channel code used in ProDigi is known as 2/4M,[8] a convolutional run-length-limited code, which was described in Chapter 6. This has a higher density ratio than MFM, and contributes to the higher packing density needed. Interestingly, the density ratio and jitter window are identical to those of the HDM-1 code of DASH.

As LSI circuitry for Galois arithmetic was developed for this machine, the error-correction strategy reflects the increased processing flexibility available.[9] The symbol size in the Reed–Solomon coding is now eight bits and the codewords are now sixteen symbols long. The data structure is changed to a convolutional crossinterleave.

Fig.9.28 shows that for sixteen-bit working (modes 1 and 2) the samples from

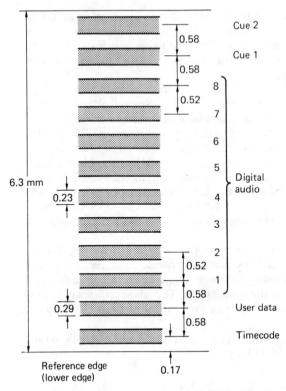

Figure 9.27 Dimensions of quarter-inch ProDigi tracks. Note auxiliary tracks are wider than digital tracks. Track positions are identical to DASH Q.

both audio channels are formed into a four-symbol word, whereas for twenty-bit working the word will be five symbols long, and one symbol contains four bits from each channel.

These words form the input to the interleave system of Fig.9.29. Odd-numbered samples and even-numbered samples enter the interleave on alternate rows, and so the first set of delays cause an odd/even interleave. Following these, twelve symbols are used to compute four redundant Reed–Solomon symbols, making a sixteen-symbol codeword. A further large odd/even delay is now inserted, which is intended to allow interpolation during splices and gross errors. Following this, the convolutional interleave is implemented with delays which increase proportionately to the symbol position in the codeword, resulting in sets of sixteen interleaved symbols. These symbols are then multiplexed into the eight digital tracks on tape. The manner in which this is done is most important. The redundancy symbols are fed to tracks 1 and 8 which are at opposite edges of the tape. If the tape is damaged, the most corruption is likely at the edges of the tape, because they will lose contact with the head if the substrate is distorted. Since the Reed–Solomon redundancy is only necessary if errors are detected in the other tracks, it is recorded nearer the edge of the tape, so that the actual samples can be put in the most secure area near the centre.

The remaining twelve output channels of the interleave are multiplexed into

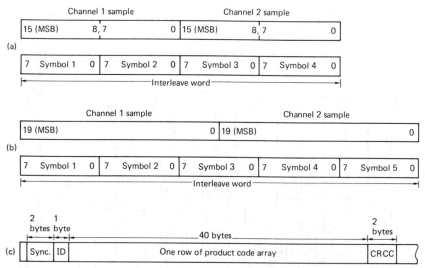

Figure 9.28 (a) In modes 1 and 3, two sixteen-bit samples from left and right channels are formatted into four bytes for the eight-bit error-correction system. At (b) in mode 2, two twenty-bit samples are formatted into five bytes. At (c) one tape frame commences with a sync pattern and ID byte, and contains forty bytes, which are one row of the product-code array. This can be ten words in sixteen-bit mode; eight words in twenty-bit mode; or forty bytes of R–S redundancy in the check rows. Frame rate at 48 kHz sampling rate is 800 Hz (modes 1, 2) or 1000 Hz (mode 3).

six digital tracks in accordance with Fig.9.30. It will be noted that pairs of symbols which are separated in the interleave by constant distance are combined into one track. The distance chosen is odd so that each track contains an equal number of odd and even samples which increases the probability that interpolation will be possible. It also means that there is actually an interleave along each track. As an example, if a given even sample enters the first row, it is undelayed, and fed to track 2. Seven samples later, an odd sample passes through the eighth row of the interleave delay, and is also fed to track 2. Track 2 thus contains odd and even samples with an interleave between them. Data on each track are assembled into blocks of forty bytes, which represent ten stereo samples of sixteen bits or eight stereo samples of twenty bits. An ID or address code is added, and the whole is made into a codeword by the addition of a CRCC. This is recorded as a frame on the tape track. In the event of an error, the CRC will fail, and add error flags to all the symbols in the frame. These will act as erasure pointers for the Reed–Solomon code working after deinterleave. As there are four redundancy symbols in the Reed–Solomon code, four errors in each codeword can be corrected by erasure. The interleave ensures that errors occurring in one place across the tape, such as the end of the splicing tape, are distributed throughout widely spaced frames. In twenty bit mode, the recording density has to be raised to contain the additional data with the same tape speed, and this has the effect of making the physical interleave slightly smaller. Fig.9.31 shows the resulting interleave distances on tape for modes 1 and 3.

The format must support punch-in/out, which requires read and write heads working together as has been described. There are three modes of operation, which must all be available with a common head block. The interleave/

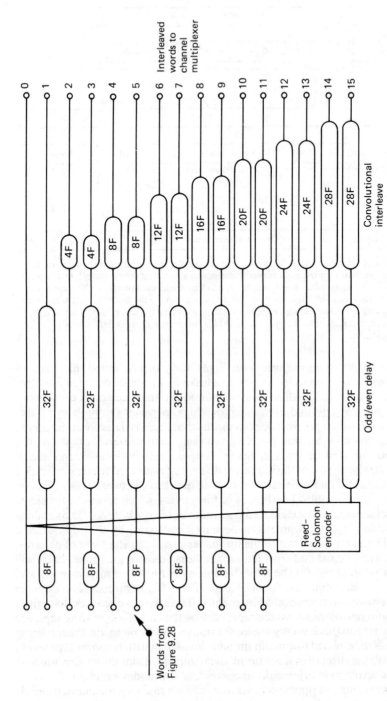

Figure 9.29 Interleave system of ProDigi takes successive words from Figure 9.28 and passes them down twelve different paths. The R–S encoder increases this to sixteen paths. The odd/even delay (forty frames total) is for error concealment and splice handling. Convolutional interleave helps error correction of bursts. Delays shown are in frames for modes 1 and 3. For mode 2, double all numbers.

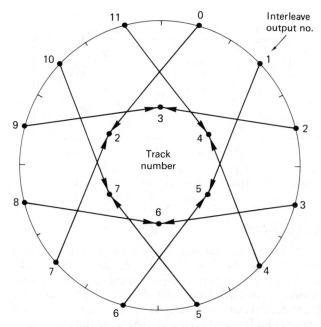

Figure 9.30 The sixteen paths of Figure 9.29 are combined into eight tape tracks. The redundancy (12–15) is combined into the outer tracks (1 and 8), and the data (0–11) are multiplexed into the remaining six digital tracks as shown here. By combining odd and even interleave outputs into one tape track, each track is made to have an equal number of odd and even samples.

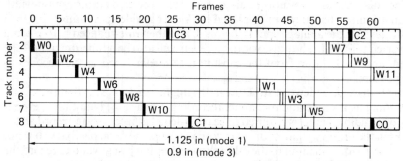

Figure 9.31 Interleave patterns for modes 1 and 3. In mode 3 there are fewer samples in a frame, and interleave becomes physically shorter because the packing density is increased.

deinterleave distance (constraint length) on the tape must be made to appear identical if the same head spacing is to be used.

The slow-speed option results in the data density along the tracks being doubled. This would result in the physical interleave distance being halved. It would leave the format twice as prone to damage by dropouts of given dimensions, and extra memory would be needed to delay signals to suit the head spacing. It is more intelligent use of the necessary memory to restore the physical interleave distance by doubling the delays. The resulting interleave is shown in Fig.9.32.

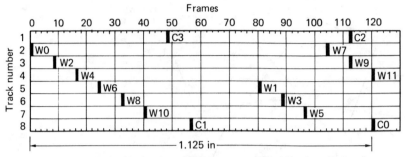

Figure 9.32 In mode 2 (double-density mode) the tape speed is halved, so the interleave extends over twice as many blocks to make the physical interleave of the same size as in mode 1.

9.18 One-inch ProDigi format

In the multitrack Mitsubishi formats, the principle of transverse codewords is retained. In the one-inch format there are 32 audio channels of sixteen-bit resolution, and these are divided into four groups of eight channels. In each group, the eight channels are recorded on eight different tape tracks, but transverse codewords are constructed from samples in all eight channels, and the redundancy is recorded in a further two tracks. There are thus forty main digital tracks. In addition there are two cue tracks, a timecode track and two auxiliary digital data tracks, making 45 tracks in all. Note that there is no control track. The track dimensions are shown in Fig.9.33. In the half-inch format, two of the track groups of the one-inch format are used to offer sixteen audio channels, as shown in Fig.9.34.

The cue tracks are not analog, but are recorded using pulse-width modulation, so that they can be played back over a wide speed range. Fig.9.35 illustrates that the analog input is digitized, and then rate-reduced before being converted to PWM. The pulse width on replay will also be a function of the tape speed, and so an input from the capstan tachometer is fed to the decoder to compensate.

The transverse codeword structure in the digital tracks means that there is no such thing as a single-audio-channel recording. On a new, blank tape, even if only one audio channel is required to be recorded, it is necessary to record all ten tracks in the group so that error correction will be possible on playback. It is not necessary to have an input to the other channels, as it is just as valid to record the zeros of a muted input. It is the format on the tape which is most important. Most users of the system format new tapes by switching on the timecode generator, and setting the machine into record on all channels with or without audio inputs until the whole area of the tape is recorded. Recording one or more sets of eight channels is straightforward, but there is a complication if it is required to rerecord less than that number. The necessary mechanism is illustrated in Fig.9.36. An advanced replay head is used to play back the relevant set of ten digital tracks. The error-correction process acts normally to provide eight corrected sample streams. The replay samples from the channels which are to be recorded are then discarded, and the input samples are substituted. New codewords are produced across the eight channels and the new check symbols are recorded in the two redundant tracks at the same time that the required

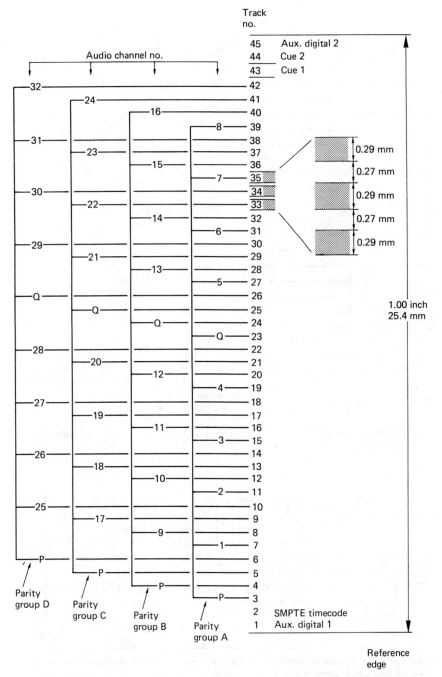

Figure 9.33 Track layout of one-inch Mitsubishi format. Each group of eight audio channels requires ten tracks, and the four groups are interleaved as shown. All tracks are of identical width.

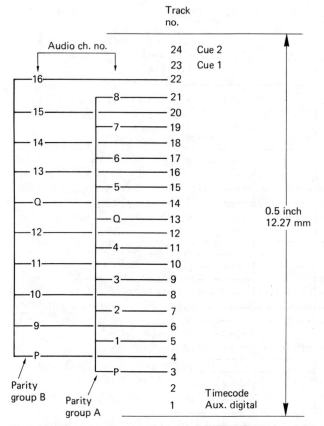

Figure 9.34 Track layout of half-inch Mitsubishi format, showing resemblance to one-inch format in Figure 9.33.

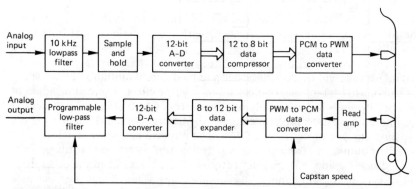

Figure 9.35 The cue audio channels of 32-track ProDigi use a digital recording system which will work over a wide speed range.

audio tracks are recorded. The audio tracks which are not to be changed are not rerecorded; they are left as originally recorded.

The error correction is again by a product code which is similar in principle to that of the X-80 format. A data block consists of rows of twelve samples from each of eight audio channels. The samples are split into four-bit symbols, and two Reed–Solomon symbols are added to make codewords from each column. The samples and redundancy rows are made into horizontal codewords by the addition of a CRCC. The CRCC is used to detect errors, and if the check fails, all 48 symbols in that codeword are declared to be in error. The error flags are then transmitted to the Reed–Solomon decoder, which can use them to correct up to two symbols in error in each column of the array. In theory two tape tracks out of the group of ten could fail to produce any signal at all, and all audio channels would still be recoverable. In practice dropouts on the remaining tracks could then only be concealed by interpolation.

Unlike the $\frac{1}{4}$ in format, which spreads samples from one audio channel over many tape tracks, the 32-channel format dedicates one tape track to the samples from one audio channel, and so an extensive interleave is necessary along the track in order to cope with contamination and splices.

The interleave is a combination of block and convolutional processes, and is shown at block level in Fig.9.37. The first stage of interleave is performed on the data block of 192 samples in Fig.9.38. These samples are written into columns of the block, but the addresses are modified by exchanging the bits as indicated. This has the effect of interleaving the input into two sets of even-numbered samples and two sets of odd. Once twelve columns of the block have been written, the block is read in rows of twelve samples. Odd rows are delayed by four blocks or 768 samples relative to even rows. This produces a large odd/even displacement which will be used to allow interpolation concealment in the case of contamination or tape-cut editing.[10,11]

This process will have been taking place simultaneously in eight associated audio channels, and the output of these eight interleaves must be combined to generate the contents of the two redundancy tracks, which can be seen toward the right of Fig.9.37.

In order to increase the resistance of the transverse Reed–Solomon codewords to contamination, a further interleave is made to distribute them physically over a large tape area. The first stage of this process is electronic, and it will be seen in Fig.9.37 that prior to the production of transverse codewords, the data for different tracks will be delayed by different amounts. These delays are from one to four interleave blocks, and have the effect of spreading adjacent codeword symbols longitudinally on tape. Errors which affect many tracks at the same time, such as fingerprints, will then cause limited damage to many codewords instead of destroying a few. The physical interleave is achieved by track distribution, as the ten tracks carrying transverse codewords are not recorded side by side, but are interleaved with the tracks from the other three groups of eight audio channels. It should be appreciated that the electronic interleave affects the position of codeword symbols only; it does not change the position of recorded samples. The resultant track layout of transverse codewords is shown in Fig.9.39.

R–S encoding is done by the system shown in Fig.9.40 where it will be seen that the audio-channel data are taken four bits at a time, and used to produce two four-bit check symbols, P and Q. Each check-symbol stream has the same

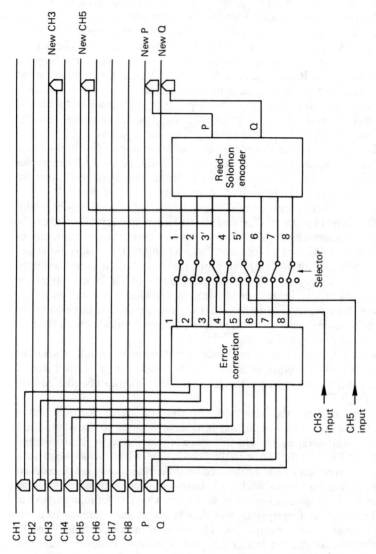

Figure 9.36 If fewer than eight channels in a group are to be recorded, the process shown here is necessary. All tracks in the group are replayed, and error correction is used to give eight corrected channels. Some of these channels are exchanged for new data (here channels 3 and 5), and all channels go to the encoder to produce new redundancy tracks. Only the new data tracks are recorded, however.

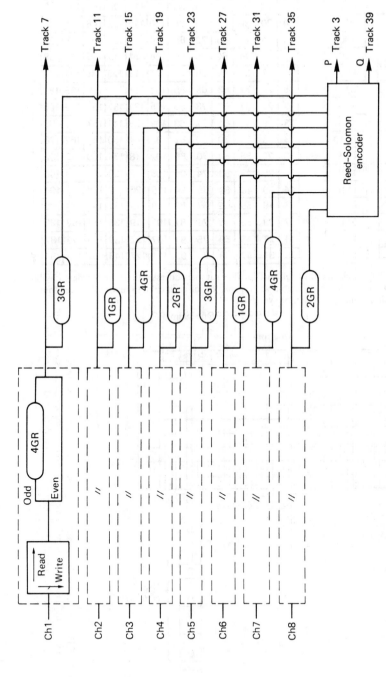

Figure 9.37 The interleave of multitrack ProDigi. Samples are block-interleaved in each channel, then subject to an odd/even delay before recording. Redundancy is calculated across eight channels, but after a further interleave which distributes codewords over a large tape area.

				Readout sequence

0	0000	0000
1	0001	0100
2	0010	1000
3	0011	1100
4	0100	0001
5	0101	0101
6	0110	1001
7	0111	1101
8	1000	0010
9	1001	0110
10	1010	1010
11	1011	1110
12	1100	0011
13	1101	0111
14	1110	1011
15	1111	1111

0	16	32	48	64	80	96	112	128	144	160	176
4	20	36	52	68	84	100	116	132	148	164	180
8	24	40	56	72	88	104	120	136	152	168	184
12	28	44	60	76	92	108	124	140	156	172	188
1	17	33	49	65	81	97	113	129	145	161	177
5	21	37	53	69	85	101	117	133	149	165	181
9	25	41	57	73	89	105	121	137	153	169	185
13	29	45	61	77	93	109	125	141	157	173	189
3	18	34	50	66	82	98	114	130	146	162	178
6	22	38	54	70	86	102	118	134	150	166	182
10	26	42	58	74	90	106	122	138	154	170	186
14	30	46	62	78	94	110	126	142	158	174	190
3	19	35	51	67	83	99	115	131	147	163	179
7	23	39	55	71	87	103	119	135	151	167	183
11	27	43	59	75	91	107	123	139	155	171	187
15	31	47	63	79	95	111	127	143	159	175	191

Write sequence

Figure 9.38 The block-interleave of ProDigi. The sample addresses (left) are reordered by bit exchange to produce a nonsequential write sequence for each column of samples. Readout is in rows, each of which forms a tape sync block.

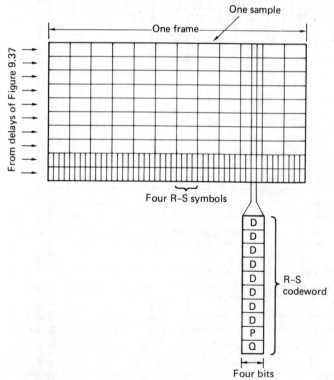

One sample

One frame

From delays of Figure 9.37

Four R–S symbols

D
D
D
D
D
D
D
D
P
Q

R–S codeword

Four bits

Figure 9.40 Reed–Solomon codewords are produced vertically using four-bit symbols. Four codewords are necessary for each column of samples.

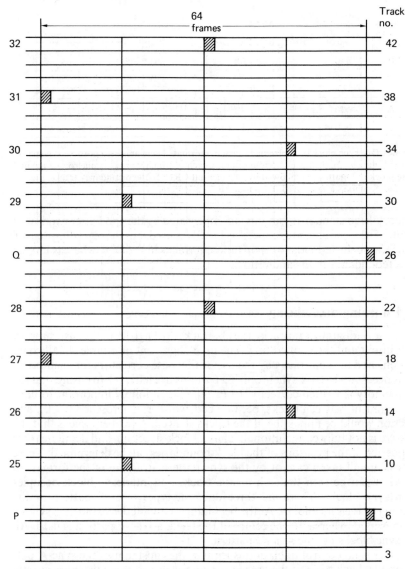

Figure 9.39 Physical position of transverse codeword in Mitsubishi format. The wide physical separation of symbols gives immunity to contamination. Example here is of parity group D.

symbol rate as one audio channel, and can be recorded with the same block structure. There are now ten parallel data streams which are to be recorded on ten different tracks.

As each data stream leaves the encoder, it is used to produce one tape sync block or, in Mitsubishi terminology, one subframe. A subframe is shown in Fig.9.41; it consists of a synchronizing pattern, twelve audio samples and a sixteen-bit CRCC. In the P and Q tracks a subframe contains 48 four-bit redundancy symbols. The sync blocks are recorded using 4/6M channel code, described in Chapter 6. This has a density ratio of 1.33, which is not high by

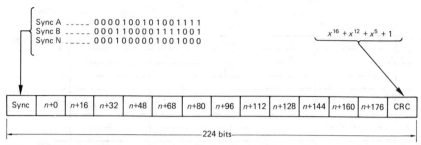

Figure 9.41 One sync block or subframe in ProDigi format. There are three possible sync patterns (see Figure 9.42); then twelve audio samples, each of which represents one row of the interleave block in Figure 9.38; followed by a sixteen-bit CRC. In the redundancy tracks, the twelve audio samples are replaced by 48 four-bit R–S symbols.

stationary-head standards, but this is compensated by the good jitter window of 0.66 bits. The same linear tape speed as DASH is used, but the recording density is less because the redundancy is on different tracks in ProDigi, whereas DASH carries redundancy in the audio tracks.

9.19 Punching and editing

As with any digital multitrack, the 32-track ProDigi format must support punch-in/out and tape-cut editing. The time-alignment of samples in all channels is ensured in multitracks by the use of timebase correctors for each track, but it is necessary to have synchronizing patterns in each track to ensure that the TBC memory is written correctly. In ProDigi, it is doubly important to have time-alignment between tracks, because codewords run across ten tracks, and correction would be impossible if the tracks skewed. A further issue is that the interleave is not fully convolutional; it has a block structure, and deinterleave is only possible if the positions of the block boundaries can be determined. These concerns are all taken care of by the sync pattern structure of the format. In Fig.9.42 it can be seen that, on a tape track, one interleave block occupies sixteen sync blocks. There are three different types of sync pattern at the beginning of the sync blocks. At the beginning of an interleave block, a sync-A pattern is used, whereas at the centre of the block a sync-B pattern is used. All other sync blocks use the sync-N pattern.

As there is no control track in this format, the capstan uses the sync-A patterns on playback to drive the tape at the correct speed. Since there are exactly 192 samples in an interleave block, at 48 kHz the sync-A rate will be 250Hz.

If a punch-in is to be performed, it is necessary to play back all of the tracks in the group which contains the track to be punched. The playback signals pass through the crossfader, and to the interleave and record circuits. After some time, during the preroll, the record circuits will be producing a signal which is identical to what is already recorded, not only on the target track, but on the redundancy tracks. At an interleave block boundary before the punch point, the machine turns on record current on the target track and the associated redundancy tracks, and begins to rerecord what was already there. At the punch-in point, the crossfader swings to the incoming signal in the noninterleaved domain, and the target track and the redundancy tracks gradually start

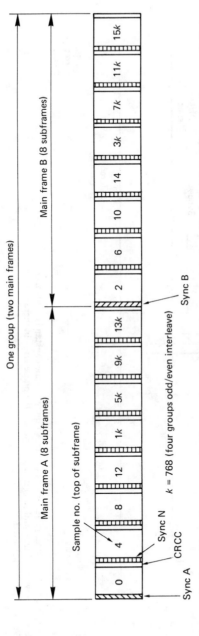

Figure 9.42 One group of sync blocks on tape contains the same number of samples as one interleave block, but the odd/even interleave means that samples in one group have come from two interleave blocks four groups apart. To ensure correct deinterleave, and synchronizing between tracks, the beginning and centre of the group are denoted by different sync patterns, as shown in Figure 9.41.

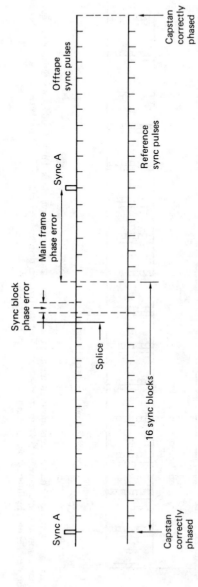

Figure 9.43 A splice causes a large phase error in Sync A timing. As the capstan is controlled by the phase error between offtape and reference sync pulses, the phase error in there is much smaller, and lock is quickly achieved.

to differ from the original tracks as the changed samples begin to pass through the interleave. After a constraint length, the target track and the redundancy tracks are recording normally. At the end of the punch-in, the crossfader moves back to the offtape samples, and the recording gradually becomes more like the original as the offtape samples pass through the reinterleave process. Once this has taken place for a constraint length, the machine will again be rerecording what was already there, and at an interleave block boundary the record current can be switched off. As the record head is displaced from the replay head, and is mounted with finite accuracy, a punched track may be skewed with respect to its neighbours, but this is of no consequence as the sync patterns can be used to recover the correct relationships with other tracks so that the transverse codewords are still intact. At the points where the record current turns on and off, it is possible that adjacent sync blocks will be corrupted, but this will be handled by the error-correction system as if it were a burst error due to contamination.

When the tape is spliced, it must be at right angles to the tape edge as with all digital machines. As there is no control track, the machine detects the splice by loss of signal in all tracks, and it is necessary to leave a gap of about 1 mm between the two halves of the tape to ensure that this happens. The splice causes an arbitrary jump in sync-A phase, and steps have to be taken to prevent this upsetting the capstan servo. For normal play, it is sufficient for the reference sampling rate to be divided by 192 to obtain 250 Hz, which is then phase-compared with sync-A to develop a capstan error. In fact the capstan divides the sampling rate reference by twelve, and phase-compares that with sync-A. Only one comparison out of sixteen will produce a phase error, and this drives the capstan. When a splice passes the heads, the phase of sync-A can change by $\pm$ 180 degrees, but by making the comparison with sixteen times the frequency of sync-A, the largest phase error the capstan sees is $\pm$ 11 degrees. This process is illustrated in Fig.9.43, and should be compared with the broadly similar process in DASH. Because the capstan phases at one-twelfth of the sampling rate, the splice causes a phase jump which is an integer multiple of a sync block.

Depending on the position of the splice, the effect is irrecoverably to damage about two interleave blocks in each track. Owing to the interleave along the tape which is used when forming transverse codewords, error correction is not possible for a constraint length either side of the splice, because part of those codewords will be removed with the piece of tape which has been cut off. The only solution is to take advantage of the large odd/even delay of four interleave blocks. After deinterleave, the error burst due to the splice turns into two bursts in odd and even samples at different times. Interpolation and a crossfade are used to conceal the splice exactly as described for the normal DASH format system.

9.20 SDAT consumer digital cassette

The SDAT format uses tape which is 3.81 mm wide and 10 μm thick in a cassette, roughly the size of a Compact Cassette, which holds some 130 m. There are many similarities between RDAT (see Chapter 8) and SDAT, which is not surprising as they were both the result of the DAT Conference which was set up to explore consumer digital recording technology.[12] As with RDAT, there are

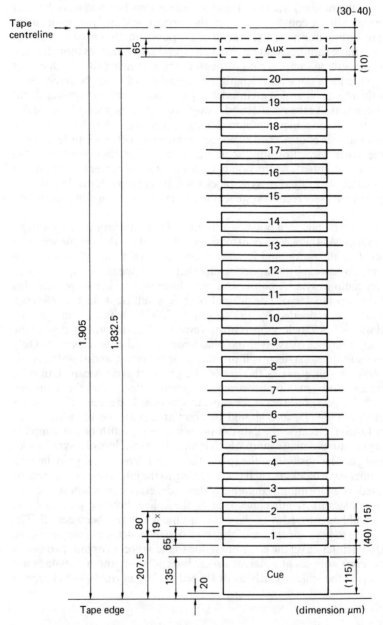

Figure 9.44 Dimensions of S-DAT tape tracks. Note that only one side is shown here. Turning over the cassette reveals the same structure on the other side of the tape.

Table 9.1 The operating modes of the SDAT format consumer stationary-head cassette recorder.

	Mandatory	*Option 1*	*Option 2*	*Option 3*	*Prerecorded*
Number of channels	2	2	2	4	2
Sampling frequency (kHz)	48	32	32	32	44.1
Quantization	16	16	12 nonlin.	12 nonlin.	16
Tape speed (mm/s)	47.6	31.7	23.8	47.6	43.7
Subcode rate (kbit/s)	128	85.3	64	128	117.6
Play time (10 μm tape)	90	135	180	90	98

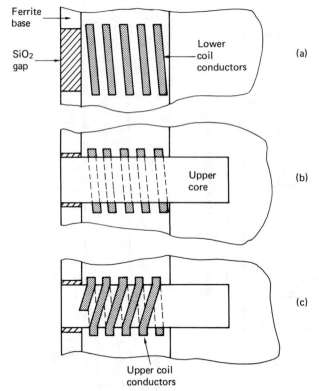

Figure 9.45 In a multitrack thin-film head, the individual magnetic circuits must be close together, and a compact method of construction is needed. The coil is deposited in two halves, with the upper core of the head between, so that the halves link up to form a continuous winding.

several modes of operation, with consumers being able to record at 48 kHz and 32 kHz, and prerecorded tapes being recorded at 44.1 kHz. These modes are shown in Table 9.1, where it will be seen that a four-channel mode is also offered. It will be seen that the linear tape speed is incredibly low by stationary-head digital standards in order to obtain the desired playing time. The only way

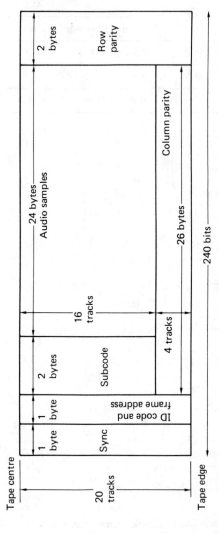

Figure 9.46 SDAT uses a product code similar to the Mitsubishi format, with row and column codewords, using erasure correction.

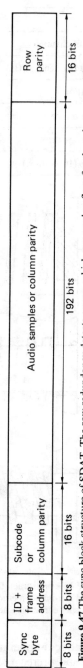

Figure 9.47 The sync block structure of SDAT. The row redundancy detects errors, which are used as flags for the column-correction process.

in which the bit rate of a stereo digital recording can be accommodated is to use many tracks in parallel. In SDAT, the tape has two sides, or running directions, like the Compact Cassette. There are twenty digital tracks on each side of the tape, each of which is only 65 μm wide, roughly the diameter of a human hair. The track dimensions are illustrated in Fig.9.44. Small as these dimensions are, they are still enormous compared to those of RDAT. The secret of making such a recording is the thin-film head which contains all the parallel magnetic circuits. This is made by the same photographic techniques needed to fabricate integrated circuits. Fig.9.45 shows how strips of conductor are laid down on a ferrite substrate, followed by a flat magnetic pole. Further strips are then laid down at a slightly different angle, which connect to the first set to make a coil. The rate of change of flux in the replay head is very small due to the low tape speed, and conventional generator-type heads are at a severe disadvantage because their self-noise drowns the signal. Magnetoresistive heads are necessary because they do not have a derivative action, and so the signal is independent of speed. A magnetoresistive head uses an element whose resistance is influenced by the strength of flux from the tape. This would tend to cause a frequency doubling or rectifying effect if a bias current were not provided to make all flux from the head appear unidirectional. The replay signals from such tiny tracks are so small that integrated-circuit amplifiers need to be incorporated into the head in order to prevent noise pickup. The head circuitry also acts as a parallel-to-serial converter to reduce the number of head connections needed.

The format of SDAT uses Reed–Solomon product codes, and is similar in concept to the ProDigi format, where codewords along the tracks act as error detectors for codewords across the tracks. Fig.9.46 shows the product block, where it will be seen that there are sixteen data tracks and four redundancy tracks, which are placed nearest the edge of the tape. Using erasure correction, the system could work with four tracks out of action. Each row of the product block becomes a sync block on tape as shown in Fig.9.47. Unlike RDAT, subcode is recorded within the audio data blocks, and cannot be recorded at a different time. The channel code used is the same 8/10 code used for RDAT (see Chapter 6).

References

1. DOI, T.T., TSUCHIYA, Y., TANAKA, M. and WATANABE, N., A format of stationary-head digital audio recorder covering wide range of applications. Presented at 67th Audio Engineering Society Convention (New York, 1980), preprint 1677(H6)
2. WATKINSON, J.R., Splice-handling mechanisms in DASH format. Presented at 77th Audio Engineering Society Convention (Hamburg, 1985) preprint 2199(A-2)
3. LAGADEC, R., Current status in digital audio. Presented at IERE Video and Data Recording Conf. (Southampton, 1984)
4. TANAKA, K., YAMAGUCHI, T. and SUGIYAMA, Y., Improved two-channel PCM tape recorder for professional use. Presented at 64th Audio Engineering Society Convention (New York, 1979), preprint 1533(G-3)
5. TANAKA, K., OZAKI, M., INOUE, T. and FURUKAWA, T., Application of generalized product code for stationary-head-type professional digital audio recorder. *Trans. IECE Japan*, **E 69**, 740–749 (1986)
6. ISHIDA, Y., *et. al.*, A professional use 2-channel digital audio recorder adopting an improved signal format. Presented at 80th Audio Engineering Society Convention (Montreux, 1986) preprint 2322(B-3)

7. ISHIDA, Y., ONISHI, K., SUGIYAMA, K., INOUE, T. and TANAKA, K., On the signal format for the improved professional use 2-channel digital audio recorder. Presented at 79th Audio Engineering Society Convention (New York, 1985) preprint 2270(A-4)

8. FURUKAWA, T. and TANAKA, K., A new run-length-limited code. Presented at 70th Audio Engineering Society Convention (New York, 1981) preprint 1839(I-2)

9. ONISHI, K., SUGIYAMA, K., ISHIDA, Y., KUSONOKI, Y. and YAMAGUCHI, T., An LSI for Reed–Solomon encoder/decoder. Presented at 80th Audio Engineering Society Convention (Montreux, 1986) preprint 2316(A-4)

10. ONISHI, K., OZAKI, M., KAWABATA, M. and TANAKA, K., Tape-cut editing of stereo PCM tape deck employing stationary head. Presented at 60th Audio Engineering Society Convention (Los Angeles, 1978) preprint 1343(E-6)

11. TANAKA, K., ONISHI, K., OZAKI, M. and KAWABATA, M., On tape-cut editing with a fixed-head-type PCM tape recorder. *IEEE Trans. Acoust. Speech Signal Process.*, **ASSP-27** 739–745 (1979)

12. KOSAKA, M., Report of the DAT Conference. *J. Audio Eng. Soc.*, **34**, 570–576 (1986)

Chapter 10

Digital audio in 8 mm video

The impact of digital audio techniques on consumer products goes beyond the Compact Disc and RDAT, to embrace high-quality sound recording in the 8 mm VCR format which is the subject of this chapter.

10.1 Introduction

In consumer recorders, both audio and video, economy of tape consumption is paramount. In videocassette recorders such as VHS and Betamax, the rotary head combined with azimuth recording (see Chapter 8) allowed extremely narrow tape tracks, with the result that linear tape speed was very low. The analog audio tracks of these systems gave marginal performance, especially when the azimuth recording process was really pushed to offer LP mode. One solution to the audio quality issue was to frequency-modulate the audio onto a carrier which was incorporated in the spectrum of the signals recorded by the rotary heads. The audio quality of such systems was impressive, but there was a tremendous drawback for certain applications that the audio could not be recorded independently of the video, or vice versa, as they were both combined into one signal.

The Video-8 format uses high-coercivity tape which allows an even narrower track pitch of 34.4 μm or 17.2 μm in LP mode. In order accurately to follow such narrow tracks, a track-following system is essential to the standard. The linear tape speeds in the two modes of operation are 20.05 and 10.06 mm/s. These linear speeds are even less suitable for quality analog recording, and so in addition to two narrow linear tracks for audio, Video-8 also supports the FM carrier audio in the video waveform. This is monophonic.

For applications where the audio needs to be recorded at a different time to the video, Video-8 also offers PCM audio recording, this time in stereo.[1]

The PCM audio shares the rotary heads with the video, but on a track-segmentation basis, so that each can be recorded independently. The use of the rotary heads for audio also minimizes tape consumption. The high recording density of Video-8 allows the use of a cassette which is only 95 × 62.5 × 15 mm. This is about 20 % of the volume of a VHS cassette. The cassette is designed to protect the tape well, and to this end has a double door which encloses the front and the back of the tape when the cassette is out of the machine. There are identification holes on the shell to allow the VCR to detect the use of metal powder or evaporated tape, and to denote the thickness of the tape.

10.2 Relationship to video

A video recording needs to be almost continuous, and this is achieved by having two heads in the drum so that one of them is always in contact with the tape. The change-over between heads takes place during the vertical interval of the video waveform. Space is found for the PCM audio by wrapping the tape a further 31 degrees around the drum as shown in Fig.10.1. This extends the diagonal tracks, and the tape is made about 1.25 mm wider to accommodate the extension.[2] Each head is now active for 221 degrees of rotation, which implies that, for some of the time, both will be active. Reference to Fig.10.2 will confirm that this is indeed the case, because when one head is playing video in the last 31 degrees of a field, the other head will be playing the PCM audio at the beginning of the next

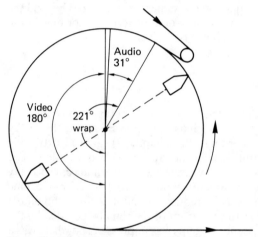

Figure 10.1 The 180° wrap necessary for video recording is extended by more than 30° to accommodate a time-compressed digital audio recording.

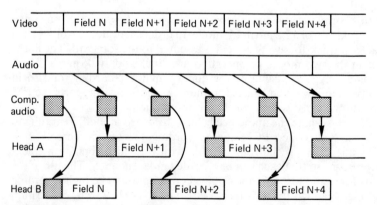

Figure 10.2 The audio corresponding to one field-period is time-compressed and recorded prior to each video field. This means that for part of the time both heads are active simultaneously.

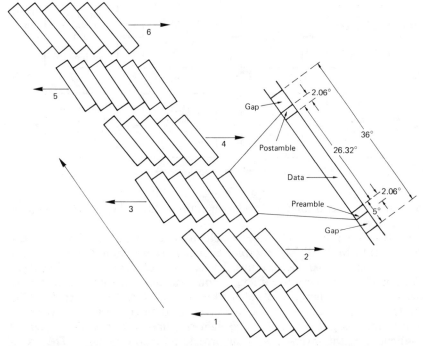

Figure 10.3 In audio-only mode, six recordings are made in alternate directions. As the tape reverses, the head-to-tape speed will change, and the track angle in reverse is shallower. Note that, as the six recordings are made at different times, they do not line up with each other.

track. The PCM audio information must be time- compressed into the 31-degree segments in the same way as for RDAT. This gives the potential for an audio-only mode, where six different time-compressed audio segments, of 36 degrees each, are placed in one tape track. As shown in Fig.10.3, the tape travels forward, recording only one audio segment in each track, until the end of the tape is reached. The tape then reverses, and recording then continues in the next audio segment. As the drum continues to turn in the same direction when the tape reverses, the track angle will be different in the reverse recorded segments, and the head-to-tape speed will be slightly different also. The tape can thus make six passes through the machine before all the audio segments are filled. The Video-8 format has no control track, and head tracking is achieved by control of the capstan by automatic track-following signals buried in the recording. When the machine records, it simply drives the tape at constant speed. As a result, recordings made in the multiple PCM mode will have arbitrary physical relationships between different segments due to speed tolerance and tape slip. This means that it is not possible to play back several segments simultaneously to make a multitrack machine. This was never intended.

10.3 Need for data reduction

The PCM audio signal in Video-8 suffers from a bandwidth restriction in order

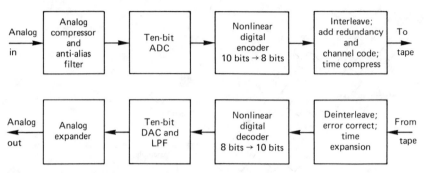

Figure 10.4 Overall block diagram of 8 mm PCM audio processing.

to minimize tape consumption, and to limit the additional wrap needed around the drum.

Fig.10.4 illustrates the processes which take place in the recording and play-back of the PCM signal. The incoming analog signal is compressed as a function of level to reduce its dynamic range. The compressed signal is fed to the ADC which produces a ten-bit linear conversion. The sampling rate is twice the line rate of the TV standard in use, i.e. 31.5 kHz for NTSC and 31.25 kHz for PAL. The ten-bit linear samples are then converted to an eight-bit nonlinear code prior to recording. Upon replay, the eight-bit samples are extended to ten-bit wordlength by the inverse nonlinear process prior to expansion. The use of digital recording overcomes most of the objections to companding, specifically that there can be no level errors to upset the tracking between the expander and the compressor. This is important in a consumer product where user adjustments should not be necessary, and yet compatibility must be assured between machines of different manufacture.

10.4 Compression

The layout of a typical compression/expansion unit is shown in Fig.10.5. When the switch at the left is closed, the output signal is detected to control a VCA in the feedback loop of an amplifier, which results in a compressed signal being available at the right-hand side. On replay, the switch is opened, and the expanded output is available on the left.

The digital compression is illustrated in Fig.10.6. To obtain the most transparent performance, the smallest signals are left unchanged. In a ten-bit system, there are 1024 quantizing intervals, but these are symmetrical about the centre of the range; therefore there are only 512 levels in the system, an equal number positive and negative. The ten-bit samples are expressed as signed binary, and only the nine-bit magnitude is compressed to seven bits, following which the sign bit is added on.

The first sixteen input levels (0–15) pass unchanged, except that the most significant two bits below the sign bit are removed. The next 48 input levels (16–63) are given a gain of one half, so that they produce 24 output levels from 16 to 39. The next 256 input levels (64–319) have a gain of one quarter, so that they produce 64 output levels from 40 to 103. Finally, the remaining 208 levels (320–511) have a gain of one eighth, so they occupy the remaining output levels

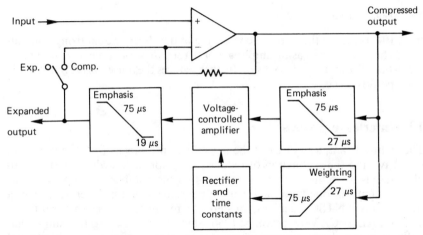

Figure 10.5 Analog compressor/expander for 8 mm video audio channels. Mode is changed by enabling or disabling feedback with the switch.

Input X	Conversion	Output Y
0–15	$Y = X$	0–15
16–63	$Y = \dfrac{X}{2} + 8$	16–39
64–319	$Y = \dfrac{X}{4} + 24$	40–103
320–511	$Y = \dfrac{X}{8} + 44$	104–127

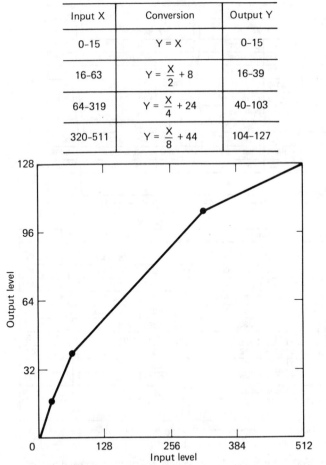

Figure 10.6 The digital compression of PCM samples in 8 mm video. Note that there are only 512 levels in a ten-bit signal, since positive and negative samples can have the same level.

from 104 to 127. In this way the coarsening of the effective quantizing intervals is matched by the increasing amplitude of the signal, so that the increased noise is masked. The analog compansion further reduces the noise to give remarkably good performance.

10.5 Interleave process

The eight-bit samples must next be assembled into blocks for the purpose of interleave and the calculation of redundancy prior to recording. As the sampling rate is twice the line rate, it follows that the number of samples for one audio channel in one tape track will be the same as the number of lines in a frame. Thus in NTSC machines, for stereo there will be 1050 samples per track, and for PAL/SECAM there will be 1250 samples per track. Fig.10.7 shows that right- and left-channel samples are written into an array in a horizontal direction in such a way that adjacent samples are separated by one third of the

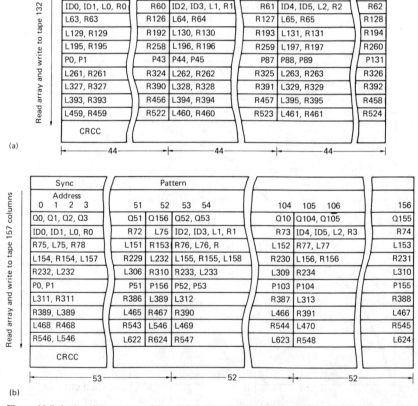

Figure 10.7 the interleave array of 8 mm digital audio samples is written in rows and read in columns. (a) For NSTC, 132 columns are necessary, interleaved in three blocks of 44. (b) For PAL, 157 columns are necessary, and an odd column is added to the triple 52-block interleave.

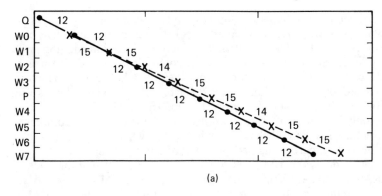

(a)

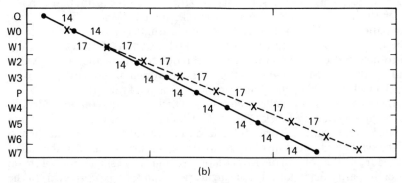

(b)

Figure 10.8 (a) In NTSC the block-completed cross-interleave uses one straight diagonal for Q parity with a spacing of twelve columns per row, and a bent diagonal P codeword due to the change from fifteen to fourteen columns per row. (b) In PAL, the cross-interleave uses two straight diagonals with slopes of fourteen and seventeen columns per row.

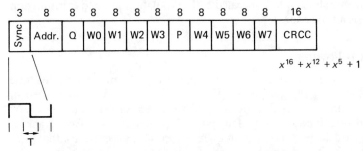

$$x^{16} + x^{12} + x^5 + 1$$

Figure 10.9 One sync block in the PCM audio recording of 8 mm video. The sync pattern violates the run-length limits of FM by having $1\frac{1}{2}T$ between transitions. There are 132 of these blocks in a field for NTSC and 157 for PAL.

width of the array. The samples occupy eight rows in the array when six ID bytes are added. In NTSC, there will be 132 columns, and in PAL/SECAM there will be 157 columns. Two parity symbols P and Q are then calculated on two different diagonals through the array as in Fig.10.8. The remaining parity symbols are calculated by moving the diagonals one column to the right, when the extreme right-hand end will wrap around to the left-hand side of the array.

In PAL, the dimensions of the array allow constant slopes on the diagonals of 14 and 17 columns between rows, whereas in NTSC one of the diagonals has distances of 14 and 15. There will now be ten rows of information and redundancy in the array. At the top of each column a byte is added which contains the column number or address, and then the whole column is made into a codeword by the addition of a sixteen bit CRCC. The columns are sequentially recorded as data blocks on the tape track. The duration of the recording is only 31 degrees of drum rotation owing to the use of time compression. The structure of a data block is shown in Fig.10.9 where it will be seen that there is a three-bit synchronizing pattern at the beginning of the block.

The channel code used is FM (see Chapter 6). The advantage of this code is that it is DC-free, and has a similar spectrum to the analog FM video signal, so that the same circuitry can be used to drive the heads whether video or PCM is being recorded. This spectral similarity also means that the azimuth difference between the heads continues to reject crosstalk in the PCM area. The synchronizing pattern is of the type that violates the run-length constraints of the code, and in this case consists of three transitions $1\frac{1}{2}$ bits apart. As the track width and head-to-tape speed are determined by the requirements of the analog video recording, the signal-to-noise ratio is quite good by digital standards, and with the high clock content of the channel code gives a good raw-error rate.

Upon replay, the array is filled a column at a time, using the column addresses at the beginning of each block. The CRC will fail if one or more symbols in a tape block are corrupted. The CRC failure causes error flags to be attached to all of the symbols in a column of the array. When the array is filled at the end of the PCM track, the column of errors becomes a number of single-symbol errors in different parity diagonals. These single errors can then be corrected. In the case where there is more than one error in a P codeword, the Q codeword can be used for correction and vice versa. The principle of crossinterleaving was explained in Chapter 7. The corrected symbols can then be read out of the array in real time. Since odd and even samples are separated by the interleave process, uncorrectable samples can be concealed by interpolation prior to transmission to the expansion processor.

10.6 Track following

The track following system of Video-8 is based on the embedded pilot-tone system developed by Philips for the Video-2000 system. As can be seen in Fig.10.10, an additional frequency outside the range of the video or PCM signals is added to the recording. This pilot frequency changes from track to track in a four-track cycle. The four frequencies are all sufficiently low that head azimuth does not affect them. A correctly tracking head will replay the sum of three pilot tones, the frequency from the home track, and the frequencies from the adjacent tracks due to the overlap of the head. Difference or beat frequencies can be detected between these three. The four pilot frequencies are chosen so that there are only two difference frequencies, approximately 45 kHz and 16 kHz. A correctly tracking head will produce these frequencies with equal amplitude, but if the head moves off centre, one pilot signal will increase whilst the other will reduce, thus imbalancing the relative level of the difference frequencies. This imbalance can be used to develop a tracking error which drives the capstan. As a result, no control track is needed.

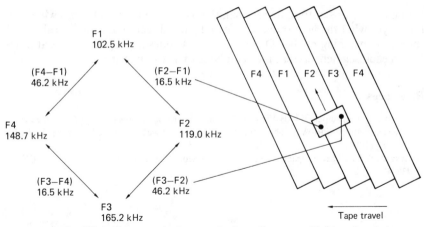

Figure 10.10 The difference frequencies between the four pilot tones will change in relative amplitude according to the state of tracking.

During recording, the pilot tones are added into the waveform being fed to the head, during both the video segment and the PCM audio segment. The difference-tone detectors will be permanently active during replay. When the tape is used for the audio-only multiple-PCM option, only one PCM segment is recorded at a time and, as noted, segments recorded at different times do not necessarily align. In order to play correctly the audio segment of interest, the difference-tone detectors are only enabled for that segment, and switched off for the remainder of the drum rotation. The tracking error is held between active segments.

10.7 Audio-only mode

When in audio-only mode[3], a machine can automatically reverse at each end of the tape, and switch to replaying a different segment of the recording. In order

Table 10.1 The ID codes used by the 8 mm format to co-ordinate auto-reverse in multiple-audio mode.

B7	0			1			
B6	1 = cue flag			0 = forward 1 = reverse			
B5	B4	B5		Position of recording on next track 0 = same as current 1 = beginning of track			
	1	0	Valid audio				
B4	1	1	Mute	Always 1			
B3	Always 1			B1	B2	B3	Next track no.
				0	0	0	—
B2	B1	B2		0	0	1	3
	0	0	Standard speed	0	1	0	5
B1	0	1	Reserved	0	1	1	1
	1	0	Half speed	1	0	0	6
	1	1	Reserved	1	0	1	2
				1	1	0	4
				1	1	1	Increment
B0	0 = forward 1 = reverse			0 = forward 1 = reverse			

to coordinate this automatic reversal, the format contains ID codes which tell the player what the next track will be and what direction it runs in. Table 10.1 shows the meaning of the ID codes. The ID codes are repeated several times within each segment so that they can be read at winding speed.

References

1. RUMSEY, F., Did somebody say Eight bit? *Broadcast Systems Engineering*, Feb. 1986, 52–55
2. SHIBATA, Y. and MACHIDA, Y., The 8mm format and how it was established. *J. Imag. Tech.*, **12,** 280–287 (1986)
3. ITOH, S. *et al.* PCM Multitrack format on 8 mm video. *IEEE Trans. Consum. Electron.*, **CE-31,** 438–446 (1985)

Chapter 11

Digital audio in professional VTR

This chapter concentrates specifically on the digital audio systems of professional VTRs, including the EBU/SMPTE D-1 component format, the Ampex/Sony composite digital format, and the Sony PCM audio derivative of the C-format.

11.1 Requirements of production VTRs

Digital audio recording with video is rather more difficult than in an audio-only environment. It will be shown here how the special requirements of video recording have determined many of the parameters of these formats, and have resulted in techniques not found in audio-only recorders. Professional video formats must permit different degrees of flexibility in audio editing, allowing at one extreme simple circuits for portable recorders and at the other extreme complex post-production recorders. These will perform track bouncing, synchronous recording and split audio edits with variable crossfade times. A further requirement is the ability to unlock the audio sampling rate from the television frequencies.

11.2 Problems of analog audio in VTRs

The audio performance of video recorders has traditionally lagged behind that of audio-only recorders. In video recorders, the use of rotary heads to obtain sufficient bandwidth results in a wide tape which travels relatively slowly by professional audio standards. The most common professional video recorders today adhere to the C-format, where the audio tracks are longitudinal. The audio performance is limited by the format itself and by the nature of video recording. From an audio viewpoint there are really two C-formats. In NTSC, there are three audio tracks, two of which are on the same edge of the tape. In PAL/SECAM, there can be an additional audio track if the vertical interval of the video is not recorded. In all rotary-head recorders, the intermittent head contact causes shock-wave patterns to propagate down the tape, making low flutter figures difficult to achieve. This is compounded by the action of the capstan servo which has to change tape speed to maintain control-track phase if the video heads are to track properly.

The requirements of lip-sync dictate that the same head must be used for both recording and playback, when the optimum head design for these two functions is different. When dubbing from one track to the next, one head gap will be recording the signal played back by the adjacent magnetic circuit in the head, and mutual inductance can cause an oscillatory loop if extensive antiphase crosstalk cancelling is not employed. Placing the tracks on opposite sides of the tape would help this problem, but phase errors between the channels can then be introduced by tape weave. This can mean the difference between a two-channel recorder and a stereo recorder. Crosstalk between the timecode and audio tracks can also restrict performance. Whilst the number of C-format machines in use speaks for the current adequacy of performance, the modern trend is toward extensive post-production where multigeneration work is essential.

The adoption of digital techniques essentially removes these problems for the audio in VTRs just as it does for audio-only recorders. Once the audio is in numerical form, wow, flutter and channel-phase errors can be eliminated by timebase correction; crosstalk ceases to occur and, provided a suitable error correction strategy is employed, the only degradation of the signal will be due to quantizing. The most significant advantages of digital recording are that there is essentially no restriction on the number of generations of rerecording which can be used and that proper crossfades can be made in the audio at edit points, following a rehearsal if necessary.

11.3 Digital audio in C-format

The above considerations led Sony to modify the C-format to allow digital audio to be recorded.[1] It was desirable to make the modification in such a way that a normal C-format recorder would still be able to play the tape. In order to do this, the existing analog audio tracks must be retained. The only remaining area of tape suitable was that used by the optional vertical interval or fourth audio track. There was the possibility of using several narrow longitudinal tracks with stationary digital heads, but this would have caused congestion in the already restricted fixed-head area, as at least three heads would have been necessary for reasons explained in Chapter 9.

The approach adopted is to install digital heads in the rotating drum which use the area of tape previously recorded by the video sync heads. The tracks are only accessible to the head for 22 degrees of drum rotation, so that time compression is necessary to squeeze the recording of all the audio samples in a field period into the available space. Digital tracks can be much narrower than analog tracks, as a smaller signal-to-noise ratio is acceptable. Multiple heads record three digital tracks in the same space as one analog sync track, as shown in Fig.11.1. This combination of track length and bandwidth allows two digital audio channels to be recorded along with necessary redundancy.

The use of three heads has an additional practical benefit. In the C- format, the record head is displaced by $\frac{1}{3}$ revolution from the playback head in the drum. When a machine is playing, the drum phase is 120 degrees shifted relative to when it is recording. This causes a one-third track displacement in the position of the audio heads relative to the tape. As there are three audio tracks for every video track, changing drum phase simply causes the audio tracks to be registered with different audio heads.

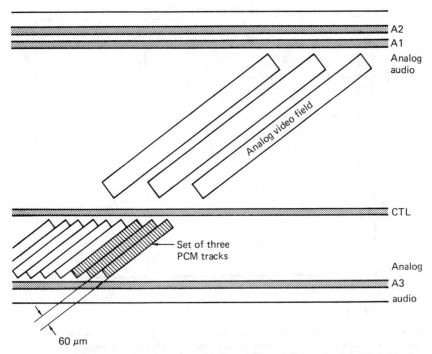

A2
A1
Analog
audio

Analog video field

CTL

Set of three
PCM tracks

Analog
A3
audio

60 μm

Figure 11.1 In the PCM audio adaptation of C-format, three PCM tracks are recorded in the sync/A4 area of the tape within one video track pitch. The use of an azimuth offset at 15° on the PCM heads means that a conventional video recorder will fail to replay it, and assume a sync-less recording is being played.

The block structure of the digital format is flexible to enable sampling rates of 48 kHz and 44.1 kHz to be supported. This is done by part-filling the blocks when using the lower rate. Sixteen-bit samples to be recorded are split into bytes which are the symbol size of the Reed–Solomon error-correction system. The two channels are merged into one data stream, which is extensively interleaved. In order to simplify editing, the interleave is restricted to samples associated with one drum revolution. A block-completed crossinterleave is used, as shown in Fig.11.2 where data are written into an array in rows, and codewords are formed on a diagonal which wraps around. Further codewords are then formed on columns of the array, which correspond to the order in which the data are sent to the heads. One third of the memory columns are sent to each head, which has the effect of distributing adjacent samples over all three heads and thus assists the use of interpolation in the presence of uncorrectable errors.

The channel code used is the same 8/10 code as used by RDAT (see Chapters 6 and 8). The use of time compression and rotary heads gives the two applications a great deal in common.

The C-format uses three video heads on the drum in order to erase, record and confidence-monitor the picture tracks. The format also calls for three sync heads to perform the same functions if the vertical interval is to be recorded. In the digital audio machine, three sets of digital heads take the place of the sync heads in order to allow digital audio confidence-replay and editing. The digital heads all have the same azimuth angle, but it is different to the perpendicular

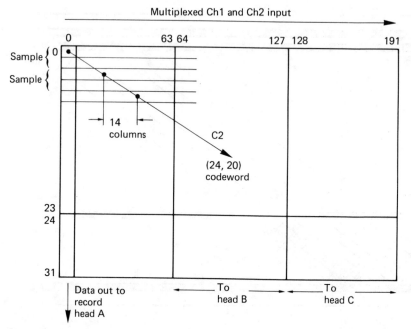

Figure 11.2 In the C-format PCM audio interleave, an array 192 × 32 bytes is used. Samples from both channels are written into the array in rows. C2 codewords are produced on diagonals with a slope of fourteen columns per two rows (2 bytes = 1 sample). C1 codewords are produced from columns of the array by adding eight bytes of redundancy. These produce sync blocks on tape, 64 columns are recorded by each head.

azimuth of the video heads. When a tape with digital audio is played on a machine with sync replay heads, three uncorrelated digital tracks are played in parallel by one sync head, which attenuates the signal, and the azimuth error causes the digital recording to be further attenuated such that the tape appears to have been recorded without sync.

The three sets of digital heads are, in the order in which they pass the tape, the advanced playback heads, the record heads and the confidence/normal replay heads. As the two audio channels are multiplexed into one data stream, the recording of one channel leaving the other unchanged requires replay with the advanced head, and replacement of the samples in one channel followed by rerecording all digital data which can be checked by the confidence heads. Owing to interleave, editing can only be performed using the advanced replay heads, as in stationary-head machines (see Chapter 9).

If such a machine is operated at nonstandard speed, the rotating heads will no longer be able to read the digital tracks, so the replay must revert to the analog tracks.

11.4 Digital VCRs

Technology has permitted the digital recording of a television programme for some time, but there is a great deal more to professional video recording than just recording and playing back.

A digital machine must offer the same features which users have come to expect from the C-format, such as still frame, slow motion, timecode, editing, pictures in shuttle and so on as well as the further features needed in the digital audio tracks, such as the ability to record the user data in the AES/EBU digital audio interconnect standard. It must be possible to edit the video and each of the audio channels independently, whilst maintaining lip-sync. There is also a great deal of difference between a laboratory machine built for research or to prove a point, and an affordable machine which is reasonable in its tape consumption whilst allowing interchange. These were the goals of the DVTR formats.

Digital tape tracks are always narrower than analog tracks, since they carry binary data, and a large signal-to-noise ratio is not required. This helps to balance the greater bandwidth required by a digitized video signal, but it does put extra demands on the mechanical accuracy of the transport in order to register the heads with the tracks. The prodigious data rate requires high-frequency circuitry, which causes headaches when complex processing such as error correction is contemplated. There is an immediate contradiction in digital video error correction, because the amount of redundancy has to be kept down so it does not increase the already high channel data rate. This can only be achieved using sophisticated codes, such as the Reed–Solomon codes, which require complex decoding. Such decoding schemes are difficult to implement at high speeds. As in most design processes, compromise is necessary.

11.5 The D-1 cassette: composite and component

At the moment there are two digital video recording formats, the 4:2:2 colour-difference or D-1 format,[2] and the composite-digital format.[3] These will be contrasted presently, but as they share the same standard cassette, this will be introduced first. The D-1 tape is conventional oxide, whereas the composite-digital format requires metal powder tape similar to that used in 8 mm video and RDAT. The higher coercivity of this tape contributes to the increased recording density of the composite format.

In the digital domain, samples can be recorded in any structure whatsoever without penalty provided they are output in the correct order on replay. This means that a segmented scan is acceptable without performance penalty in a digital video recorder. A segmented scan permits a less than complete wrap of the scanner, which eases the design of the cassette-threading mechanism. The use of very short recorded wavelengths in digital recording makes the effect of spacing loss due to contamination worse, and so a cassette system is an ideal way of keeping the medium clean.

The so-called D-1 cassette is a significant advance in cassette design and incorporates a number of useful features. It is in fact a family of cassettes since it comes in three sizes: small, medium and large. Two tape thicknesses, 13 and 16 μm, are supported in the colour different format, whereas the composite digital format uses only 13 μm tape. Table 11.1 shows a comparison of playing times for each size.

The use of three cassette sizes was decided upon to satisfy the contradicting demands of a portable machine which must be small and a studio machine which must give good playing time. Unlike the U-matic cassette, the hubs are at different spacings in the different sizes, so a machine built to play more than one

Table 11.1 High-coercivity tape and the use of azimuth recording give the composite digital recorder a playing-time advantage.

Cassette	D–1 16 μm	D–1 13 μm	Composite digital 13 μm
Small	11 min	13 min	32 min
Medium	34 min	41 min	99 min
Large	76 min	94 min	221 min

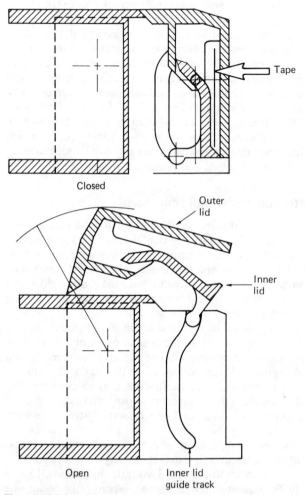

Figure 11.3 When the cassette lid is closed, both sides of the tape are protected by covers. As the outer lid swings up on a pivot, the inner lid is guided around the back of the tape by a curved track.

size would need swinging reel-motors. The two smaller cassettes are centralized in the aperture of a player built for large cassettes by a deep central slot.

The cassette lid locks in the closed position until part of the player engages the release. Fig.11.3 shows that the lid is in fact in two parts, which totally enclose the tape when it is closed.

The hubs which hold the tape are locked against rotation when the cassette is outside the machine. The brake mechanism is released by a projection in the centre of the cassette slot in the small cassette, and by the act of opening the door in the medium and large cassettes. Fig.11.4 contrasts the interior of the small and medium cassettes, and makes clear the reason for the different hub-locking arrangements. There is no room for a door-operated mechanism in the small cassette because it would interfere with the tape exit.

The cassette shell contains patterns of holes which can be read by sensors in

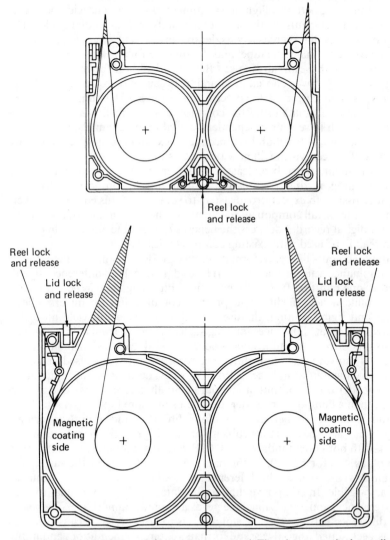

Figure 11.4 The small and medium cassettes contrasted. There is no room in the small cassette for the reel locks to be operated by the lid, so the locks are centrally placed, and released by a post in the transport.

the player. One set of these can be used to allow tapes of different coercivity to change the write current automatically. The other set is intended for the user, and one of these causes total record-lockout, or write-protect, when a plug is removed.

There is a certain amount of compromise necessary in the choice of tape width. The wider the tape for a given recording density, the slower it needs to move and the shorter it needs to be for the same recording time. This means that spooling through a given recorded period becomes faster. The outline of the cassette becomes smaller, but it becomes thicker. However, the stiffness of tape in its own plane rises disproportionately with increasing width, since it is pro-portional to the moment of inertia of the cross-section. Accordingly narrower tapes accommodate better to slight misalignment of guides. The wider a tape is, the larger and heavier must be the scanner assembly and associated guides. The final major point is that there is a considerable investment around the world in plant for producing magnetic tape, and it would be folly to choose a different width from one of those already in use.[4] Bearing all of these factors in mind, the existing width of $\frac{3}{4}$ in was chosen, although it is generally expressed as 19 mm which is not strictly correct as the precise dimension is 19.01 mm.

The two digital formats using the common cassette shell offer similar fea-tures, in that both have four independent digital audio channels, a linear cue audio track, a control track and a timecode track. In other respects there are significant differences which will now be contrasted.

At the moment, most broadcasters have enormous investments in the recording, editing, mixing, routing and transmitting of composite video. It is simply not possible to expect broadcasters to scrap all of this equipment over-night in order to install component machines. In the short to medium term, the composite-digital recorder delivers the benefits of digital technology in a form that can readily be used with existing composite installations.

The digital colour-difference format accepts CCIR-601[5] digital video, that is to say luminance sampled at 13.5 MHz and two colour-difference signals sampled at one half that frequency with eight-bit quantizing. Where it is pro-posed to build a new facility, and provide colour-difference mixers, effects machines and signal routing, the use of such a machine will yield all of the advantages of colour-difference working, such as freedom from colour-framing problems and from the additional codecs needed to pass through effects machines. If, however, a colour difference recorder were to be used in a com-posite environment, it would need a PAL or NTSC decoder on the input, and a suitable encoder on the output, and would actually deliver worse overall per-formance than a composite recorder, despite using more tape.

The radical differences between the colour-difference and composite formats can largely be traced back to the problems of building practical machines which will work with both line standards. In CCIR-601, the sampling rate is the same for 525/60 as it is for 625/50, so the data rates are also about the same. It is relevant in this case to make the different line-standard versions of the format as similar as possible. In composite digital, the data rate is proportional to sub-carrier frequency, and a PAL machine needs a data rate almost 25 % higher. A greater difference between the line standards is to be expected because of this.

As has been stated, digital cassette formats require segmentation, and imply multiple heads on the scanner, not only to give continuous data with less than complete scanner wrap, but also to reduce the data rate of individual heads.

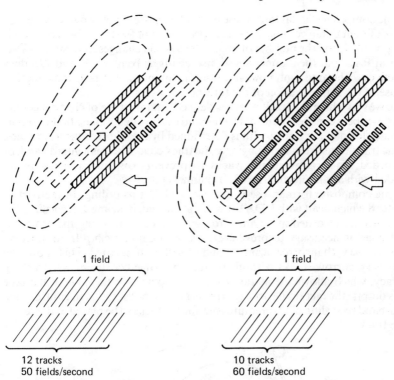

1 field

1 field

12 tracks
50 fields/second

10 tracks
60 fields/second

Figure 11.5 One field segment consists of two tracks. The segment rate is 300 Hz, and six seg-ments are necessary for one field in 50 Hz systems. Five segments are on field in 60 Hz systems. The audio is central in the track, and a logical segment begins after the audio blocks, finishing in the next head sweep. Only the track geometry is defined; shown here is one way in which the scanner may have four heads and yet still record a standard format.

With modern technology, four heads is a reasonable number to manage the throughput. In the colour-difference format, it was proposed to segment the recording such that, within a standard segment rate of 600 Hz, fields containing ten segments could be recorded at 60 Hz and fields containing twelve segments could be recorded at 50 Hz This works well except that, with a four headed machine, in 60 Hz mode the relationship between which head is playing which segment of the field changes from field to field. To overcome this problem, each segment was split into two segments on the tape track, such that the segment rate became 1200 Hz. The 60 Hz mode then had twenty segments per field, a number which was divisible by four, so there would always be the same relationship between head number and segment number. The gap between the segments was made large enough to insert the digital audio blocks. Fig.11.5 shows the principle of the track layout in the two line standards. Note that, because the segment rate is constant, the scanner speed is the same in 50 Hz or 60 Hz systems, except for the 0.1 % difference due to the fact that 60 Hz is actually 59.94 Hz. The D-1 standard does not compel the manufacturer to adopt specific scanner dimensions, provided the track dimensions are to the standard. This permits various numbers of heads to be used, and various scan-ner diameters can be adopted depending on the degree of time compression performed on the signal.

In the composite-digital format the data rates between the two line standards are so different that a common scanner speed was not feasible. The recording is still segmented, and the number of segments in a field changes from six in NTSC to ten in PAL, but the scanner speed also changes, being 89.91 and 125 rev/s respectively. This does not, however, result in an increase in tape consumption because of the sophistication of the format.

The way in which the track width is defined, and the type of channel coding used, differ between the colour-difference and composite formats. In the colour-difference format, the track width is determined by the width of the head poles, and the transitions are at right angles to the track edge. There is a guard band, or unrecorded space, between the tracks to prevent crosstalk. The tracks are recorded with a randomized (RNRZ) channel code.

In the composite format, use is made of azimuth recording. In the part of Chapter 8 which dealt with RDAT it was shown that, in azimuth recording, the transitions are recorded at an angle to the track edge by tilting the head. No guard band is necessary to prevent crosstalk, because pickup from adjacent tracks will be with incorrect azimuth and so will be attenuated. This allows the use of very narrow tracks without putting excessive constraints on tracking accuracy, which allows the audio blocks to be placed at the ends of the tape tracks despite the fact that tracking error is usually worst there. In contrast, the guard-band recording of D-1 requires the audio blocks to be placed in the centre of the tracks.

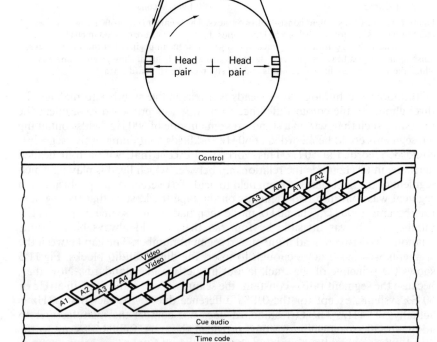

Figure 11.6 The twin head pairs of the composite digital format produce a staggered track pattern. The overlap due to azimuth recording can be seen clearly here.

The crosstalk in azimuth recording has effectively passed through a comb filter due to the geometry of the replay mechanism, so that it will be rather poor at low frequencies. This will not be a problem if the digital recording uses a channel code which reduces spectral energy at the frequencies where crosstalk is worst. RNRZ is not suitable for azimuth recording because it has too much LF content even though randomizing makes it DC-free. The composite digital recorder uses the Miller[2] code (see Chapter 6) which performs very well in azimuth recording. It has been shown to be very nearly as good as the 8/ 10 code of RDAT in an azimuth recording application,[6] but has the necessary simplicity of implementation which is important at the kind of data rates used in digital video.

The use of azimuth recording with track overlap in the composite digital format allows the track width to be changed simply by changing the speed of the drum. As drum speed is raised, the tape moves a shorter linear distance in each drum revolution, and the amount by which the next track overlaps the current track is increased. There is no need to change the heads when the standard is changed, the same drum assembly is used in both standards.

Fig.11.6 shows the drum arrangement in a composite digital recorder, where it will be seen that there are two head pairs at opposite sides of the drum. In each pair, one head has positive azimuth and the other has negative azimuth. The physical displacement between the heads causes the tape pattern to have a staggered appearance, but this causes no ill effect.

The use of a narrower track in PAL must reduce the signal-to-crosstalk ratio, but it should be remembered that the drum speed is raised in PAL, and this permits the recorded wavelength to be increased, reducing gap and spacing losses; the increased head-to-tape speed raises the replay signals further above head noise. The net result is adequate performance in both line-scan standards with a common mechanism, although achieved in a different way from D-1. The main difference between the two is storage efficiency. With a 13 μm thick tape in the small cassette, composite digital offers a playing time of 32 min, which is nearly $2\frac{1}{2}$ times the playing time of D-1 at 13 min, although the data rate of colour-difference recording is only $1\frac{1}{2}$ times that of composite digital PAL.

It is important to remember that, although both composite and colour difference-formats are dual standard, a dual-standard player can only produce signals to the standard recorded on the cassette. In other words a 525/60 D-1 cassette cannot be played back as a 625/50 signal. The DVTR is not a standards converter.

11.6 Track sectoring

The audio samples in a DVTR are binary numbers just like the video samples, and although there is an obvious difference in sampling rate and wordlength, this only affects the relative areas of tape devoted to the audio and video samples. The most important difference between audio and video samples is the tolerance to errors. The acuity of the ear means that uncorrected audio samples must not occur more than once every few hours. There is little redundancy in sound, and concealment of errors is not desirable on a routine basis. In video, the samples are highly redundant, and concealment can be effected using samples from previous or subsequent lines or, with care, from the previous frame. No analog VTR corrects dropouts. All dropout compensation in analog

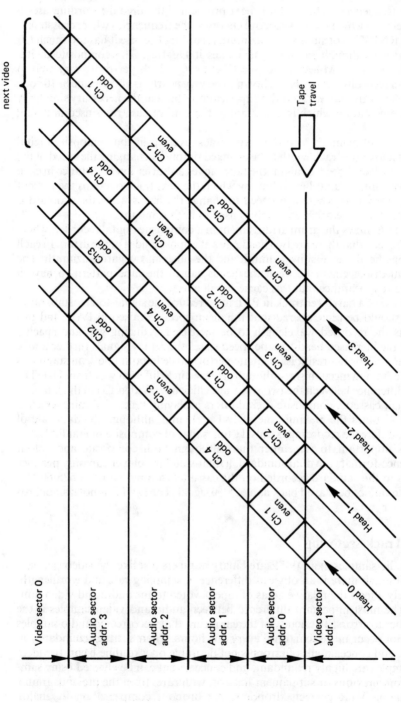

Figure 11.7 The structure of the audio blocks in D-1 format showing the double recording, the odd/even interleave, the sector addresses, and the distribution of audio channels over all heads. The audio samples recorded in this area represent 6.666 ms timeslot in the audio recording.

recording is by concealment; a section of a previous line is typically substituted for the dropout. Major differences can be expected between the ways that audio and video samples are handled in a DVTR. One such difference is that the audio samples have 100 % redundancy: every one is recorded twice with a physical separation. Apart from data-integrity considerations, this double recording is also necessary to support simple audio editing, as will be discussed later. In both formats the audio samples are carried by the same channel as the video samples. The audio could have used separate stationary heads, but this would have increased tape consumption and machine complexity. The use of the same rotary heads for video and audio reduces the number of preamplifiers and data separators needed in the system, whilst increasing the bandwidth requirement by only a few percent even with double recording. In order to permit independent audio and video editing, the tape tracks are given a block structure. Editing will require the heads momentarily to go into record as the appropriate audio block is reached. Accurate synchronization is necessary if the other parts of the recording are to remain uncorrupted. The concept of a head which momentarily records in the centre of a track which it is reading is the normal operating procedure for all computer disk drives, which are described in Chapter 12. There are in fact many parallels between digital helical recorders and disk drives. Perhaps the only major difference is that in one the heads move slowly and the medium revolves, whereas in the other, the medium moves slowly and the heads revolve. Disk drives support their heads on an air bearing, achieving indefinite head life at the expense of linear density. Helical digital machines must use high-density recording and so there will be head contact and a wear mechanism. With these exceptions, the principles of disk recording apply to DVTRs, and some of the terminology has migrated.

One of these terms is the sector. In moving-head disk drives, the sector address is a measure of the angle through which the disk has rotated. This translates to the phase of the scanner in a rotary-head machine. The part of a track which is in one sector is called a block. The word 'sector' is often used instead of 'block' in casual parlance when it is clear that only one head is involved. However, as this format has two heads in action at any one time, it is necessary to be quite clear which one is involved, and the use of the word 'sector' in the SMPTE/EBU D-1 documents unfortunately reflects the casual definition. Fig.11.7 and Fig.11.8 show the structure of the tape tracks. As there are four independent audio channels, there are four audio sectors, since for reasons which will become clear, it is only possible to edit complete blocks. In D-1 (Fig.11.7), the audio is in the centre of the track, so there must be two video sectors and four audio sectors in one head sweep, and since there are two active heads, in one sweep there will be four video blocks written and eight audio blocks. In composite digital (Fig.11.8) there are also two active heads in each sweep, but the audio blocks are at the ends of the tracks, so that there are only two video blocks in the centre.

There is a requirement for the DVTR to produce pictures in shuttle. In this case, the heads cross tracks randomly, and it is most unlikely that complete video blocks can be recovered. To provide pictures in shuttle, each block is broken down into smaller components called sync blocks. These contain their own error checking and an address, which in disk terminology would be called a header, which specifies where in the picture the samples in the sync block belong. In shuttle, if a sync block is read properly, the address can be used to

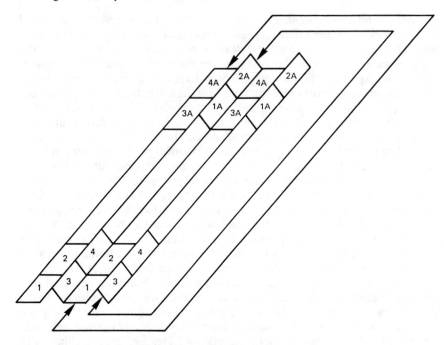

Figure 11.8 In the composite digital format, data from each audio channel are recorded twice, so that the copy is at the opposite edge of the tape, and read by a different head. This gives immunity to head clogs and linear tape scratches.

update a frame store. Thus it can be said that a write block is the smallest amount of data which can be written and is that part of a track within the same sector address, whereas a sync block is the smallest amount of data which can be read. Clearly there are many sync blocks in a write block. In D-1, one video-write block contains 160 sync blocks, and one audio-write block contains five sync blocks. The sync block structure continues in the audio because the same read/write circuitry is used for audio and video data. Clearly the address structure must also continue through the audio. To prevent audio samples from arriving in the frame store in shuttle, the audio addresses are different from the video addresses. In both formats, the arrangement of the audio blocks is designed to maximize data integrity in the presence of tape defects and head clogs. In D-1, the audio is separated into odd and even samples, which are recorded in physically different places. If uncorrectable errors occur, interpolation can be used to conceal the errors. As stated, every sample is recorded twice at different sector addresses. If, for example, a linear tape scratch damages the data in audio-sector zero, the data can be found in sector two, albeit in a different order. It will also be seen that the relationship of the audio channels to the physical tracks rotates by one track against the direction of tape movement from one audio sector to the next. The effect of this is that, if a head becomes clogged, the errors will be distributed through all audio channels, instead of causing severe damage in one channel. In a four-headed machine, one head can fail completely, and all channels are fully recoverable owing to the distribution strategy and the double recording. There are sixteen audio-write blocks in one sequence, which requires two segment periods to complete. As the segment rate is 300 Hz in D-1 the audio sequence will have a rate of 150 Hz or a period 6.6666...ms.

In composite digital the audio blocks are at the ends of the head sweeps; the double recording ensures that the second copy of an audio block is at the opposite edge of the tape, and that it will be played with a different head.

11.7 Channel coding and addressing

The channel coding of the two formats is different, as has been stated. A full description of the principles of channel coding can be found in Chapter 6. In the RNRZ code of D-1, the data to be recorded are added modulo-2 (exclusive–OR) to a pseudo-random sequence. The frequent transitions in the sequence break up long runs to ensure clock content and, by definition, a pseudo-random sequence is virtually DC-free. Upon reading, it is necessary to provide a bit-rate clock which flywheels through the run lengths of the code. This is the function of the phase-locked loop in the data separator. Clearly the PLL must be synchronized to the offtape bit rate before reading can commence, and therefore it is necessary to provide a preamble before the block. This is recorded at one half of the highest frequency in the system, which is given by alternate pairs of ones and zeros (CC hex = 11001100). There must be at least twenty bytes of this pattern. At the end of the preamble, the PLO frequency will be synchronized, but it will not be known where the data block proper begins, or where the boundaries between bytes are. It is important to establish this, not least because the same pseudo-random sequence must be supplied on replay, synchronized to bit accuracy, to recover the data. This is the function of the sync pattern which follows the preamble. The sync pattern is designed to be as different as possible both from the preamble and from itself shifted. The pattern chosen is 0CAF hex. In order to allow the reading of less than one write block, the sync pattern is repeated at the beginning of every sync block: hence the name. Each sync block contains 128 bytes of data and redundancy. As all the sync blocks in a write block are written at the same time, there is continuity of bit phase from one to the next, and the preamble is only needed before the first one. Immediately following the sync pattern is the header containing the sync-block address. For hardware simplicity, there is also a block address after the sync pattern in the preamble, but this contains a unique address allocated to preambles so that the read sequencer can distinguish it from the beginning of a genuine sync block. In addition, there are four bytes of CC hex fill between the address and the first full sync block. There are enough addresses in the system to define every sync block in four fields individually. The consequences of an error in the sync block address are that audio and video data could be interchanged or replayed out of sequence. Even worse, an edit could be commenced at the wrong place. It is necessary to provide protection against error on reading the address. The address consists of four nibbles, each of which is a base 14 symbol, i.e. it can have a value 0–D hex. Using a distance 4 BCH code, each of these nibbles becomes an eight-bit codeword, which is checked on replay. This is similar to

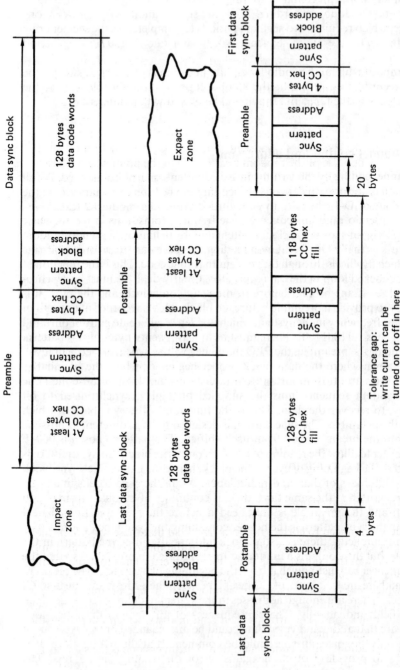

Figure 11.9 The preamble and postamble in D-1 format are shown here to be the same as the ends of the tolerance gap. The tolerance gap allows writing to begin with a physical position error without corrupting adjacent data. It is intended that the address in the centre of the tolerance gap can be destroyed by an edit. This is no problem, provided that the preamble and postamble remain intact.

the use of cyclic polynomials for header-address protection in disk drives, but the codeword generation is via lookup table for reasons of speed.

At the end of a write block, it is not possible simply to turn off the write current after the last bit, as the turnoff transient would cause data corruption. It is necessary to provide a postamble such that current can be turned off away from the data. Again, for hardware simplicity, the postamble is identical to the start of a sync block, and again the header address identifies it. The sync block contains CC hex fill, and current can be turned off after at least four bytes have been written. It should now be evident that any editing has to take place a sector at a time. Any attempt to rewrite one sync block would result in damage to the previous block owing to the physical inaccuracy of replacement, damage to the next block due to the turnoff transient, and inability to synchronize to the replaced block because of the random phase jump at the point where it began. Owing to the difficulty of writing in exactly the same place as a previous recording, it is necessary to leave tolerance gaps between sectors where the write current can turn on and off to edit individual write blocks. Again, for hardware simplicity, the tolerance gaps have exactly the same length as two sync blocks, and they will be written as such when a blank tape is first recorded. The first sync block of the tolerance gap is the postamble of the previous block, and after the sync pattern and address, there is CC hex fill as before. The end of the second sync block of the tolerance gap acts as the preamble for the next block; thus the sync block contains a second sync pattern and address just before the end. The tolerance gap following editing will contain, somewhere in the centre, an arbitrary jump in bit phase, and a certain amount of corruption due to turnoff transients. Provided that the postamble and preamble remain intact, this is of no consequence. The sync pattern at the centre of the tolerance gap will probably be destroyed by editing, and strictly speaking might as well not be recorded, but it is much easier to let the system record it than to attempt to inhibit it. Fig.11.9 shows the structure of the preamble, postamble and the tolerance gap.

11.8 D-1 error correction

The error-correction system of D-1 uses product codes as described in Chapter 7. Codewords are formed prior to interleaving — the so called outer code — and further codewords are formed after interleaving, known as the inner code. The inner code is optimized to correct random errors, so that these will not be seen by the outer code. Burst errors will overwhelm the inner code; it will simply declare all data in the codeword as bad, and attach error flags to it. Following deinterleave, the outer code can use the error flags to perform erasure correction, which will not be impaired by random errors. The product coding is done by writing data into an array in columns, and adding column redundancy to form the outer code. The array is then read in rows, which interleaves the data, and row redundancy is added to form the inner code. Fig.11.10 shows the details of the audio product-code generation. The inner code is the same as for video, because common circuitry can then be used, but the outer code is different from the video outer code which is not discussed here. The audio data are contained in twenty-bit words, and 168 of these form one audio-write block. Most of these are audio samples, but there are also control words and

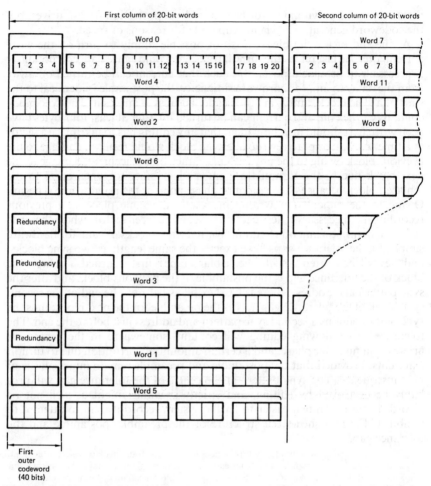

First
outer
codeword
(40 bits)

Figure 11.10 (a) Data are written into an array as twenty-bit columns, and read out as rows. The column redundancy is produced in four-bit wide columns, and forms the outer codewords of 40 bits each.

housekeeping data which will be detailed later. The data are written into columns which are seven words high. The columns are written nonsequentially to produce the maximum distance between adjacent samples after interleave. 24 columns are necessary. Each column is then treated as five columns of four bits each, and three nibbles of redundancy are added to each column, so that there are now ten rows. Redundancy is now produced along each row, and four bytes are added, making the total length of a row 64 bytes. One sync block holds 128 bytes; thus the rows are written sequentially, and can be accomodated in five sync blocks, which is one audio-write block. Although it is common to use a further interleave between the inner code and the actual recording stage in digital audio-only recording, this is not practicable in the DVTR because it contradicts the requirement for blocks to be read randomly in shuttle. The use of four-bit symbols in the error correction resembles the approach of the Mitsubishi multitrack formats described in Chapter 9. The advantage is the same, in

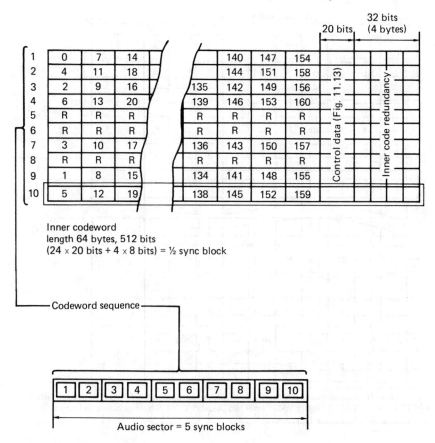

Figure 11.10 (b) The row redundancy forms the inner code, as four check bytes are added to the data to produce ten codewords of 64 bytes each. The relationship to the tape track is such that two inner codewords occupy one sync block. Five sync blocks can hold the entire interleave block.

that PROM decoders can be used with short symbol lengths, but in this case the simplicity is used to allow operation at high speed.

11.9 Composite error correction

In the composite-digital format, each audio channel is recorded independently as in D-1. A product code is used, and the interleave is generated by the usual memory array, as Fig.11.11 illustrates. The twenty-bit audio samples are written into the array in rows, where $2\frac{1}{2}$ rows of bytes are needed for one row of samples. Each row of the array is loaded with eight samples, and then four bytes of Reed–Solomon redundancy are added to form an outer code. Reading the array in rows and adding eight bytes of R–S redundancy produces inner codewords. Two of these inner codewords can be accommodated in one sync block as shown in Fig.11.12. Accordingly six sync blocks are necessary to record one audio block.

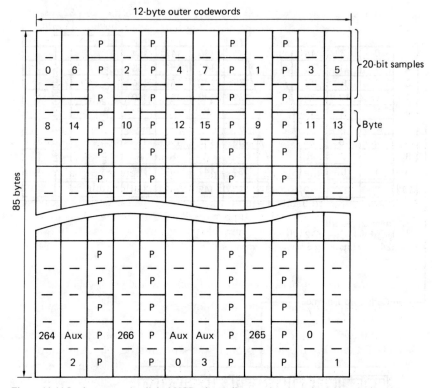

Figure 11.11 In the composite digital VCR, the audio samples are written into the interleave array in rows to produce outer codewords, and read out in 8 5-byte columns to form sync blocks as shown in Figure 11.12.

Sync	1 D	Data	Inner check	Data	Inner check
2 bytes	2 bytes	85 bytes	8 bytes	85 bytes	8 bytes

Inner codeword (95 bytes)   Inner codeword (93 bytes)

Figure 11.12 One sync block of the composite digital format contains two inner codewords formed from columns of Figure 11.11. Six sync blocks are necessary to hold the entire interleave block, and form one audio sector.

11.10 Audio functions in DVCR

The contents of the audio blocks of the D-1 format can now be detailed in relation to the various audio functions. For most purposes the following description is relevant to the composite digital format since it also supports these functions.

11.10.1 AES/EBU compatibility

In order to comply with the AES/EBU digital audio interconnect, wordlengths between sixteen and twenty bits can be supported, but it is necessary to record a code in the sync block to specify the wordlength in use. Pre-emphasis may have been used prior to conversion, and this status is also to be conveyed, along with the four channel-use bits. The AES/EBU digital interconnect (see Chapter 5) uses a block-sync pattern which repeats after 192 sample periods corresponding to 4 ms at 48 kHz. He who confuses block sync with sync block is lost. Since the block size is different to that of the DVTR interleave block, there can be any phase relationship between interleave-block boundaries and the AES/EBU block-sync pattern. In order to re-create the same phase relationship between block sync and sample data on replay, it is necessary to record the position of block sync within the interleave block. It is the function of the interface control word in the audio data to convey these parameters. There is no guarantee that the 192-sample block-sync sequence will remain intact after audio editing; most likely there will be an arbitrary jump in block-sync phase. Strictly speaking a DVTR playing back an edited tape would have to ignore the block-sync positions on the tape, and create new block sync at the standard 192-sample spacing.

11.10.2 Synchronization between audio sampling rate and video field rate

Clearly the number of audio sync blocks in a given time is determined by the number of video fields in that time. It is only possible to have a fixed tape structure if the audio sampling rate is locked to video. This is the preferred mode of the DVTR, and results, for 625/50, in the same number of audio samples in every write block. At a sampling rate of 48 kHz there will be 48 samples per millisecond. There will thus be 24 odd and 24 even samples per millisecond. As it has been shown that the interleave period is 6.666...ms, the number of samples in an interleave array must be $24 \times 6.666 = 160$.

For use on 525/60, it must be recalled that the 60 Hz is actually 59.94 Hz. As this is slightly slow, it will be found that in sixty fields, exactly 48048 audio samples will be necessary. Unfortunately 60 will not divide into 48048 without a remainder. The largest number which will divide 60 and 48048 is 12; thus in $60/12 = 5$ fields there will be $48048/12 = 4004$ samples. This five-field sequence conflicts with the fact that the audio block structure spreads over four associated tracks; thus the repeat rate becomes ten fields or five frames. This five-frame sequence is one of the items carried in the linear control track. Clearly the fields are not all the same. The 8008 samples corresponding to that period represent 4004 odd and 4004 even samples. Thus in four odd and four even audio blocks every five frames, an extra sample is recorded. A code is present in each block which denotes the number of useful samples in the block, and this will be read on replay to synchronize the audio correctly. There will be either 160 or 161 samples per block. In either of the above modes, the audio is synchronous, and there is one status bit in the block to denote that fact. A further bit conveys the line standard in use.

Although only the use of synchronous audio is deemed to meet the format standard for interchange, the format permits nonsynchronous operation. There will be cases where it is not possible to make a synchronous recording, for example where a digital-audio mixing desk is responsible for the audio sampling rate, but the recorder cannot genlock to the desk because it has to lock to network for a simultaneous broadcast. In these cases, the variable-size block concept is extended. A further code pattern allows the use of 159 samples per block in addition to the use of 160 and 161, and the synchronous status bit is changed. The DVTR locks to its video reference, and simply varies the block content according to how many audio samples are received. In 625/50, if every block has 159 samples, this corresponds to the audio sampling rate being about 0.6 % slow, whereas if every block has 161 samples, the sampling rate is 0.6 % fast. In 525/60, the sampling rate is already 0.1% fast relative to the 59.94 Hz field rate, so the speed range will be $+0.5$ % to -0.7 %. These ranges are adequate to provide recordings which are not synchronized, where only a slow phase drift takes place. It is not intended to support the use of a nonstandard sampling rate.

11.10.3 Variable speed replay

At nonstandard speeds, the recovery of audio data is assisted by a parameter known as the sector sequence count which is present in all interleave blocks. Variable-speed operation really falls into two categories: speeds close to normal, and more extreme speeds. At extreme speeds, the digital audio system is overwhelmed by errors and lack of data and gives up. If audio is required, the analog linear track at the edge of the tape must be used.

At speeds close to normal, used for example to squeeze the length of a program to insert a newsflash, the highest possible video and audio quality are required. This will be obtained by changing capstan and scanner speed by the same amount, to allow the heads to follow the tape tracks correctly. The incorrect video field rate will be corrected by a suitable frame store. Clearly if the head-to-tape speed is changed, the audio sampling rate will change also. If the audio samples are simply being fed to a DAC for immediate conversion to the analog domain, this is of no consequence, but if the samples have to be fed at standard rate into a fully digital studio, a sampling-rate converter will be necessary to avoid the degradation due to reverting to analog.

11.10.4 Editing

It has been explained that the audio-write blocks can be individually written with the use of tolerance gaps to protect adjacent data. There is, however, rather more to editing than that. The format supports three levels of audio editing, all of which leave a standard formatted tape, but which deliver different performance according to the complexity of the recorder. Assemble editing, insert editing and split audio/video editing are all supported to achieve maximum flexibility; however, a machine which can only record audio and video together is still capable of meeting the format. In other words a machine can still achieve interchange without supporting every possible edit feature. These features will be described in turn.

(1) Split audio/video editing is achieved in the overall control system of the DVTR. As video and audio data occupy different sync block addresses on tape, they can be written quite independently, and it is only a matter of supplying different timecodes to the video and audio record enables and the split edit will be performed automatically.

(2) Assemble and insert recording of audio are a little more complex because the tape tracks are shared between audio and video. The block structure of the

tracks must always be maintained; therefore it is not possible to record only video or only audio on a blank tape. When an assemble is made, the tape beyond the assemble point is assumed to be blank, and a new control track will be written. If only video is supplied to the machine after an assemble, the audio blocks will still be written, filled, most likely, with zero samples, and including the content count which allows the sampling rate to be established. If only audio is supplied after an assemble point, the video blocks will still be written, filled with black. The major difference between assemble and insert is that the control track is read in insert, such that at the end of the insert, the original recording carries on without loss of synchronism. During an insert any or all of the audio channels may be changed, by having the heads record during audio sectors, and/or video may be changed, by having the heads record during the video sectors. In practice, once a tape has been recorded, all future work on that tape can be in insert mode as, in digital recording, the format of the tape has a separate existence to the programme material.

(3) The actual mechanism of video editing is simply to start recording the new data at a field boundary, the result appearing as a cut in the picture. This is also the most basic way of editing the audio; at an interleave block boundary the new recording is substituted for the old. It is to be expected that this will result in step discontinuities of the audio waveform, audible as clicks, but this may well be acceptable in a portable machine whose tapes will be the raw material for post-production. As all audio data are recorded twice in different blocks, there is a possibility of performing a more satisfactory edit by initially updating only half of the blocks with new data. During this overlap period, the end of the previous recording and the beginning of the new will both be present, and the DVTR can perform a crossfade in the digital domain between the two sample streams. At the end of an insert, the reverse crossfade would take place. The overlap period is flexible, because the best crossfade time varies subjectively with the material recorded. Clearly on performing the edit, the crossfade period is simply the time for which only half of the sample blocks are recorded. On replay, the crossfader needs to know how its coefficients should vary with time to match what has been recorded. This is neatly solved by incorporating a gain parameter in the audio blocks, which will change during the overlap period, and control the replay crossfader. The format is such that machines which do not support this mode record zeros in the parameter position, and this code results in no action in any player. There is an imperfection in this simple crossfading approach because the 100 % redundancy is absent during the overlap period, and large dropouts during crossfades could cause the machine to interpolate using the odd/even interleave. At first sight, the accuracy to which an audio edit can be made appears subject to the position of the nearest block boundary, causing an error of ±3.3 ms. However, the actual state of the crossfade is determined by the crossfade code carried in the sync blocks, and this can be used to position the crossover point anywhere. The restrictions on this mode are thus not severe, and it is anticipated that this mode will be used by most general-purpose machines. The AES/EBU user bits complete the necessary audio block contents, and a diagram of the block content in excess of the sample data appears in Fig.11.13.

(4) For post-production, it will be seen that audio editing can be carried out to the same standards of accuracy and fidelity as in the best digital audio-only recorders, albeit with some hardware complexity. The use of interleaving is a

powerful tool against dropouts, but it makes editing to sample accuracy much more difficult. The principles involved are exactly those of a digital audio-only machine. Because of the structure of the codewords, only entire blocks can be recorded without error, whereas crossfades need to be performed on deinterleaved data. In order to perform a true crossfade edit with sample accuracy and 100% redundancy, the existing recording in the area of the edit must first be

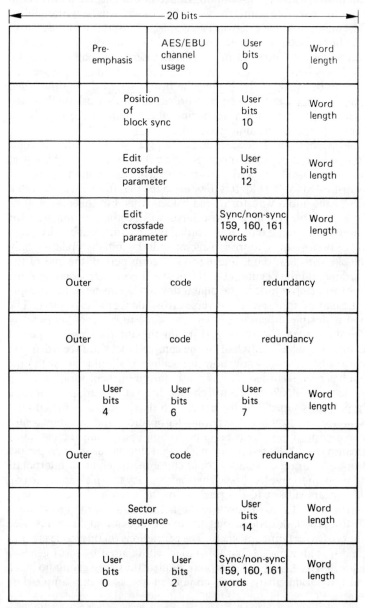

|← — — — — — — — — — 20 bits — — — — — — — — — →|

	Pre-emphasis	AES/EBU channel usage	User bits 0	Word length
	Position of block sync		User bits 10	Word length
	Edit crossfade parameter		User bits 12	Word length
	Edit crossfade parameter		Sync/non-sync 159, 160, 161 words	Word length
Outer	code		redundancy	
Outer	code		redundancy	
	User bits 4	User bits 6	User bits 7	Word length
Outer	code		redundancy	
	Sector sequence		User bits 14	Word length
	User bits 0	User bits 2	Sync/non-sync 159, 160, 161 words	Word length

Figure 11.13 The audio block also contains various user and control bits, with positions as shown here. Note that many of them are repeated. This diagram is an enlargement of the rightmost column of data in Figure 11.10 (b).

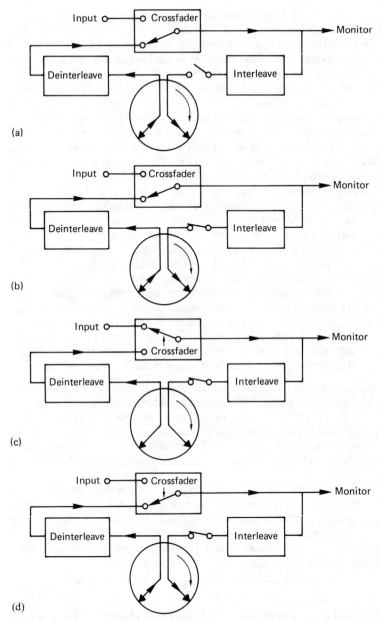

(a)

(b)

(c)

(d)

Figure 11.14 In the most sophisticated version of audio editing, there are advanced replay heads on the scanner, which allow editing to be performed on deinterleaved data. An insert sequence is shown.

At (a) the replay head signal is decoded, and fed to the encoder which, after some time, will produce an output representing what is already on the tape. In (b), at a sector boundary, the write circuits are turned on, and the machine begins to rerecord. In (c) the crossfade is made to the insert material. At (d) the insert ends with a crossfade back to the signal from the advanced replay heads. After this, the write heads will once again be recording what is already on the tape, and the write circuits can be disabled at a sector boundary. An assemble edit consists of the first three of these steps only.

played back, deinterleaved and corrected, and then digitally crossfaded at any point with the insert/assemble audio. The output of the crossfader has then to be reinterleaved, and the result has to be recorded in the blocks which were played back earlier to update them. The problem is that, until the block has been played, the contents cannot be deinterleaved, and by the time the correction, crossfading and reinterleave have been performed, the block has long gone. There are two solutions to this. The first is the solution adopted by Compact Disc mastering editors (see Chapter 8). The area of the edit point is played into a memory on a first pass of the tape; then the machine is backed up, and the crossfade to new material and the rerecording takes place on a second pass. This is slow, but allows the use of a simple DVTR. The second method is that of stationary-head multitrack digital audio recorders (see Chapter 9) which use an advanced replay head, or a delayed record head , separated by the decode/correction–encode delay period. In the DVTR this would require extra heads on the scanner, and an additional amount of memory to delay the data from the advanced replay head, or a delayed record head, separated by the decode/ This system is shown in Fig.11.14. As the complete audio structure of the channel to be edited is rewritten, there is no loss of redundancy at the edit crossfade point, and the resistance to corruption will be the same as elsewhere.

(5) In order to dub one channel to another (track bouncing), the deinterleave and correction process must precede the record interleave and, clearly, to avoid loss of lip-sync, an advanced playback head is necessary as for the most sophisticated edit technique. Synchronous recording is similar in principle to track bouncing, except that a performer can listen to the playback of an existing recording, and play along to it to record another track in synchronism.

There are some further possibilities with such a multiheaded post- production machine. In conjunction with a digital sampling-rate converter, such a machine could convert a nonsynchronous recording to a synchronous recording. The advanced replay heads would play back into the rate converter, which would be fed with a synchronous output reference. The output could then be recorded on the same tape before it left the scanner. The use of the advanced head ensures the preservation of lip-sync.

As a DVTR can individually edit audio channels, it does not require a great leap of the imagination to see that a multitrack audio-only machine could be made by filling the tape tracks with audio sectors. The number of channels this would permit is staggering and it may be more useful to incorporate a reduced-resolution or monochrome video channel. It should be pointed out that such a machine is outside the intentions of the formats described here.

References

1. TAKAYAMA, J. and BURGESS, S.P., Enhancement to one-inch VTRs. Presented at 11th International Broadcasting Convention (Brighton, 1986). IEE Conference Pub. 268 66–70
2. Proposed American National Standard for component digital video recording. *Soc. Motion Picture Television Eng. J.*, **95** 359–400 (1986)
3. Draft proposal D-X. Private Committee Document (Jan. 1987)
4. BALDWIN, J.L.E., The Evolution of the digital television recording format. Presented at 11th International Broadcasting Convention (Brighton, 1986). IEE Conference Pub. 268 47–56
5. Encoding parameters of digital television for studios. CCIR Recommendation 601 (1982)
6. FUKUDA, S., *et al.* 8/10 modulation codes for digital magnetic recording *IEEE Trans. Magn.* **22**, 1194–1196 (1986)

Chapter 12

Disk drives in digital audio

Disk drives came into being as random-access file-storage devices for digital computers. They were prominent in early experiments with digital audio, but were soon abandoned in favour of digital tape. Now that high-density techno-logy in disk drives has advanced, the rapid access of disk drives is finding applications in digital audio editing.

12.1 Types of disk drive

Once the operating speed of computers began to take strides forward, it became evident that a single processor could be made to jump between several different programs so fast that they all appeared to be executing simultaneously, a process known as multiprogramming. Computer memory remains more expensive than other types of mass storage, and so it has never been practicable to store every program or data file necessary within the computer memory. In practice some kind of storage medium is necessary where only programs which are running or are about to run are in the memory, and the remainder are stored on the medium. Punched cards, paper tape and magnetic tape are all computer media, but suffer from the same disadvantage of slow access. The disk drive was developed specifically to offer rapid random access to stored data. Fig.12.1 shows that, in a disk drive, the data are recorded on a circular track. In floppy disks, the magnetic medium is flexible, and the head touches it. This restricts the rotational speed. In hard-disk drives, the disk rotates at several thousand rev/min so that the head-to-disk speed is of the order of one hundred miles per hour. At this speed no contact can be tolerated, and the head flies on a boundary layer of air turning with the disk at a height measured in microinches. The longest time it is necessary to wait to access a given data block is a few milliseconds. To

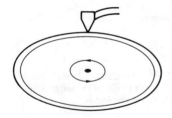

Figure 12.1 The rotating store concept. Data on the rotating circular track are repeatedly presented to the head.

387

increase the storage capacity of the drive without a proportional increase in cost, many concentric tracks are recorded on the disk surface, and the head is mounted on a positioner which can rapidly bring the head to any desired track. Such a machine is termed a moving-head disk drive. The positioner was usually designed so that it could remove the heads away from the disk completely, which could thus be exchanged. The exchangeable-pack moving-head disk drive became the standard for mainframe and minicomputers for a long time, and usually at least two were furnished so that important data could be 'backed up' or copied to a second disk for safe keeping.

Later came the so-called Winchester technology disks, where the disk and positioner formed a sealed unit which allowed increased storage capacity but precluded exchange of the disk pack. This led to the development of high-speed tape drives which could be used as security backup storage.

Optical-disk storage has also emerged in computer peripherals, with earlier devices offering enormous capacity by magnetic disk standards, but being

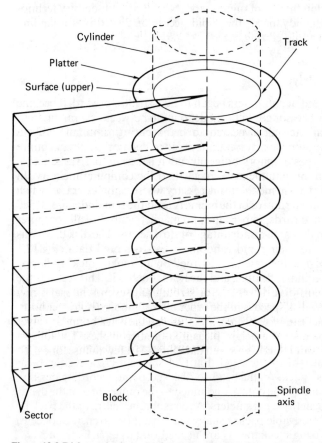

Figure 12.2 Disk terminology. Surface: one side of a platter. Track: path described on a surface by a fixed head. Cylinder: imaginary shape intersecting all surfaces at tracks of the same radius. Sector: angular subdivision of pack. Block: that part of a track within one sector. Each block has a unique cylinder, head and sector address.

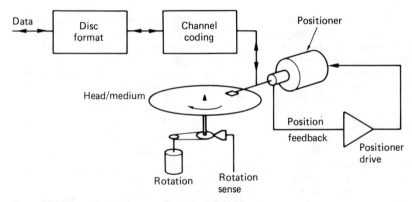

Figure 12.3 The main subsystems of a typical disk drive.

unable to erase or alter a recording once made. These are known as write once read many (WORM) devices. Later disks offered the ability to erase through the adoption of thermomagneto-optic technology. The positioners of optical disks are still rather slow when compared to those of magnetic drives.

These technologies will all be explained in this chapter, followed by a treatment of the applications of disks to digital audio.

12.2 Disk terminology

In all technologies there are specialist terms, and those relating to disks will be explained here. Fig.12.2 shows a typical multiplatter disk pack in conceptual form. Given a particular set of coordinates (cylinder, head, sector), known as a disk physical address, one unique data block is defined. A common block capacity is 512 bytes. The subdivision into sectors is sometimes omitted for special applications. Fig.12.3 introduces the essential subsystems of a disk drive which will be discussed.

12.3 Structure of disk

The floppy disk is actually made using tape technology, and will be discussed later. Rigid disks are made from aluminium alloy. Magnetic-oxide types use an aluminium oxide substrate, or undercoat, giving a flat surface to which the oxide binder can adhere. Later metallic disks are electroplated with the magnetic medium. In both cases the surface finish must be extremely good owing to the very small flying height of the head. Fig.12.4 shows a cross-section of a typical multiplatter disk pack. As the head-to-disk speed and recording density are functions of track radius, the data are confined to the outer areas of the disks to minimize the change in these parameters. As a result, the centre of the pack is often an empty well. Removable packs usually seat on a taper to ensure concentricity and elaborate fixing mechanisms are needed on large packs to prevent the pack from working loose in operation. Smaller packs are held to the spindle by a permanent magnet, and a lever mechanism is incorporated in the cartridge to assist their removal.

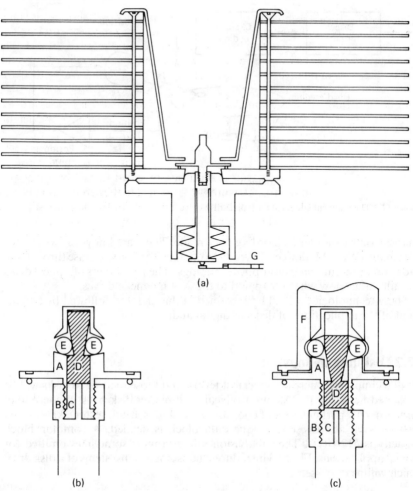

Figure 12.4 (a) Typical construction of multiplatter exchangeable pack. The pack weighs about 20 lb (9 kg) and turns at up to 3600 rev/min. The hold-down mechanism must be faultlessly reliable, to resist the forces involved, and must centre the pack precisely to allow proper track alignment and balance. In (b), the hold-down screw A is fully engaged with the lockshaft B, and the pin C lifts the ramp D, retracting the balls E. In (c), the hold-down screw is withdrawn from the lockshaft, which retracts, causing the ramp to force the balls into engagement with the cover F. The lockshaft often operates a switch to inform the logic that a pack is present (G).

12.4 Principle of flying head

Disk drives permanently sacrifice storage density in order to offer rapid access. The use of a flying head with a deliberate air gap between it and the medium is necessary because of the high medium speed, but this causes a severe separation loss which restricts the linear density available. The air gap must be accurately maintained, and consequently the head is of low mass and is mounted flexibly.

The aerohydrodynamic part of the head is known as the slipper; it is designed to provide lift from the boundary layer which changes rapidly with changes in flying height. It is not initially obvious that the difficulty with disk heads is not making them fly, but making them fly close enough to the disk surface. The boundary layer travelling at the disk surface has the same speed as the disk, but as height increases, it slows down due to drag from the surrounding air. As the lift is a function of relative air speed, the closer the slipper comes to the disk, the greater the lift will be. The slipper is therefore mounted at the end of a rigid cantilever sprung towards the medium. The force with which the head is pressed towards the disk by the spring is equal to the lift at the designed flying height. Because of the spring, the head may rise and fall over small warps in the disk. It would be virtually impossible to manufacture disks flat enough to dispense with this feature. As the slipper negotiates a warp it will pitch and roll in addition to rising and falling, but it must be prevented from yawing, as this would cause an azimuth error. Downthrust is applied to the aerodynamic centre by a spherical thrust button, and the required degrees of freedom are supplied by a thin flexible gimbal. The slipper has to bleed away surplus air in order to approach close enough to the disk, and holes or grooves are usually provided for this purpose in the same way that tyres have grooves to take away water on wet roads.

In exchangeable-pack drives, there will be a ramp on the side of the cantilever which engages a fixed block when the heads are retracted in order to lift them away from the disk surface.

12.5 Reading and writing

Fig.12.5 shows how disk heads are made. The magnetic circuit of disk heads was originally assembled from discrete magnetic elements. As the gap and flying height became smaller to increase linear recording density, the slipper was made from ferrite, and became part of the magnetic circuit. This was completed by a small C-shaped ferrite piece which carried the coil. In thin-film heads, the magnetic circuit and coil are both formed by deposition on a substrate which becomes the rear of the slipper.

In a moving-head device it is not practicable to position separate erase, record and playback heads accurately. Erase is by overwriting, and reading and writing are carried out by the same head. The presence of the air film causes severe separation loss, and peak shift distortion is a major problem. The flying height of the head varies with the radius of the disk track, and it is difficult to provide accurate equalization of the replay channel because of this. The write current is often controlled as a function of track radius so that the changing reluctance of the air gap does not change the resulting record flux. Equalization is used on recording in the form of precompensation, which moves recorded transitions in such a way as to oppose the effects of peak shift. This was discussed in Chapter 6, which also introduced digital channel coding.

Early disks used FM coding, which was easy to decode, but had a poor density ratio. The invention of MFM revolutionized hard disks, and was at one time universal. Further progress led to run-length-limited codes such as 2/3 and 2/7 which had a high density ratio without sacrificing the large jitter window necessary to reject peak shift distortion. Partial response is also suited to disks, but is not yet in common use.

Typical drives have several heads, but with the exception of special- purpose

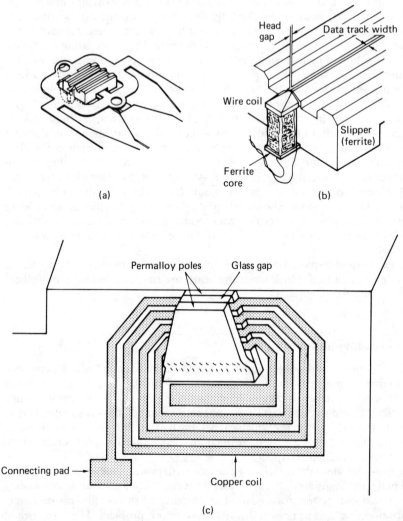

Figure 12.5 (a) Winchester head construction showing large air bleed grooves. (b) Close-up of slipper showing magnetic circuit on trailing edge. (c) Thin-film head is fabricated on the end of the slipper using microcircuit technology.

parallel-transfer machines for digital video or instrumentation work, only one head will be active at any one time, which means that the read and write circuitry can be shared between the heads. It can be seen from Fig.12.6 that the centre-tapped heads are isolated by connecting the centre tap to a negative voltage, which reverse-biases the matrix diodes. The centre tap of the selected head is made positive. When reading, a small current flows through both halves of the head winding, as the diodes are forward-biased. Opposing currents in the head cancel, but read signals due to transitions on the medium can pass through the forward biased diodes to become differential signals on the matrix bus. During writing, the current from the write generator passes alternately through the two

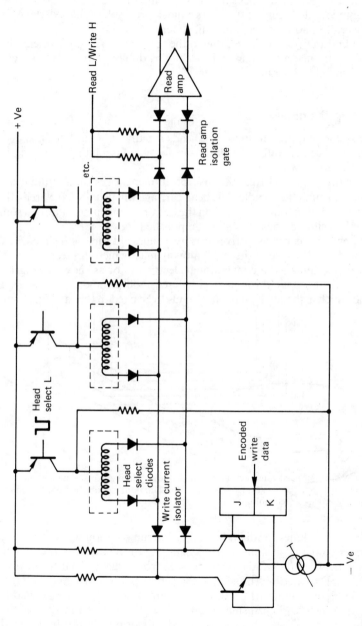

Figure 12.6 Representative head matrix.

halves of the head coil. Further isolation is necessary to prevent the write-current-induced voltages from destroying the read preamplifier input.

The read channel usually incorporates AGC, which will be overridden by the control logic between data blocks in order to search for address marks, which are short unmodulated areas of track. As a block preamble is entered, the AGC will be enabled to allow a rapid gain adjustment.

The high bit rates of disk drives, due to the speed of the medium, mean that peak detection in the replay channel is usually by differentiation. The detected peaks are then fed to the data separator.

12.6 Moving the heads

The servo system required to move the heads rapidly between tracks, and yet hold them in place accurately for data transfer, is a fascinating and complex piece of engineering.

In exchangeable pack drives, the disk positioner moves on a straight axis which passes through the spindle. The head carriage will usually have preloaded ball races which run on rails mounted on the bed of the machine, although some drives use plain sintered bushes sliding on polished rods.

Motive power on early disk drives was hydraulic, but this soon gave way to moving-coil drive, because of the small moving mass which this technique permits. Lower-cost units use a conventional electric motor as shown in Fig.12.7 which drives the carriage through steel wires wound around it, or via a split metal band which is shaped to allow both ends to be fixed to the carriage despite

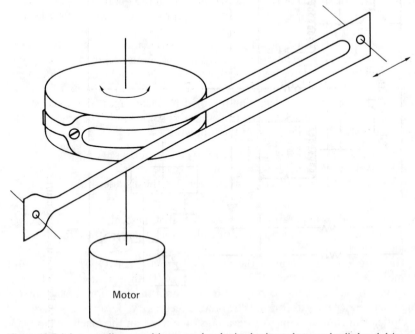

Motor

Figure 12.7 A low-cost linear positioner can be obtained using a drum and split-band drive, shown here, or with flexible wire. The ends of the band are fixed to the carriage.

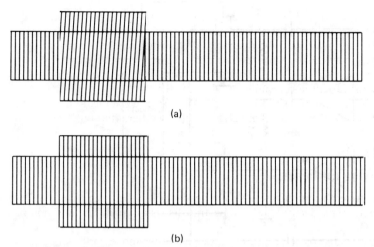

(a)

(b)

Figure 12.8 Glass-grating transducers work by modulating a light beam with the interaction of moving and stationary bars. It is vital that these units are correctly adjusted both mechanically and electrically, and this is often a time consuming process. (a) Moiré-grating transducer has non-parallel bars, and the resulting fringe patterns generate a sinusoidal output. (b) Parallel-bar grating transducer generates triangular waveform.

the centre making a full turn around the motor shaft. The final possibility is a coarse threaded shaft or leadscrew which engages with a nut on the carriage. In very low-cost drives, the motor will be a stepping motor, and the positions of the tracks will be determined by the natural detents of the stepping motor. This has an advantage for portable drives, because a stepping motor will remain detented without power. Moving-coil actuators require power to stay on track.

When a drive is track-following, it is said to be detented, in fine mode or linear mode depending on the manufacturer. When a drive is seeking from one track to another, it can be described as being in coarse mode or velocity mode. These are the two major operating modes of the servo.

With the exception of stepping-motor-driven carriages, the servo system needs positional feedback from a transducer of some kind. The purpose of the transducer will be one or more of the following:

(1) to count the number of cylinders crossed during a seek
(2) to generate a signal proportional to carriage velocity
(3) to generate a position error proportional to the distance from the centre of the desired track

Sometimes the same transducer is used for all of these, and so transducers are best classified by their operating principle rather than by their function in a particular drive.

The simplest transducer is the magnetic moving-coil type, with its complementary equivalent the moving-magnet type. Both generate a voltage proportional to velocity, and can give no positional information, but no precise alignment other than a working clearance is necessary.

Optical transducers consist of gratings, one fixed on the machine base, and one on the carriage. The relative position of the two controls the amount of light which can shine through onto a sensor. Reference to Fig.12.8 will show that

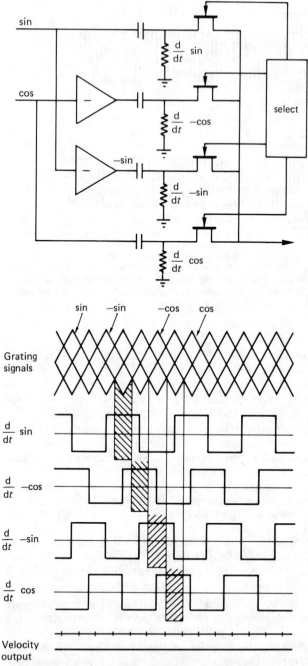

Figure 12.9 Optical-velocity transducer. Four quadrature signals are produced from the two-phase transducer. Each of these is differentiated, and the four derivatives are selected one at a time by analog switches. This process results in a continuous analog output voltage proportional to the slope of the transducer waveform, which is itself proportional to carriage velocity. In some drives one of the transducer signals may also be used to count cylinder crossings during a seek and to provide a position error for detenting.

there are basically two categories of grating transducer, the moiré-fringe device and the parallel-bar type.

In a moiré-fringe transducer, the two sets of bars are not parallel, and relative movement causes a fringe pattern which travels at right angles to the direction of carriage motion. This results in sinusoidal modulation of the light beam. In the parallel-bar type, the moving grating acts as a simple shutter, and the output is a triangle wave. In both types, the spacing between the two parts of the grating is critical. Both types give the same performance for counting cylinder crossings, as the waveform is not of any consequence for that application. The choice of which type to use is determined by whether positional information for track following or velocity feedback for seeking is needed. The slope of a sine wave is steeper in the zero region than an equivalent triangle wave, and so the moiré type is preferable for position sensing. Conversely, the constant slope of the triangle wave is easier to differentiate to give a velocity signal.

As the differential of a triangle wave changes sign twice per cycle, a two-phase optical system is often used to give a continuous output. The stationary grating has two sets of bars with a 90 degree phase relationship, and the resultant two output signals are invariably called sin and cos even if they are triangular waves. Fig.12.9 shows that the two waveforms and their complements are differentiated, and then the four differentials are selected at times when they have no sign change. This process of commutation is achieved by analog switches controlled by comparators looking for points where the input waveforms cross. The result is a clean signal proportional to carriage velocity.

Where one transducer has to generate all three signals, the moiré type is better as the position sensing is more important, and ripple on the velocity signal has to be accepted.

Optical transducers usually contain additional light paths to aid carriage-travel limit detection and to provide an absolute reference to the incremental counting.

12.7 Controlling a seek

A seek is a process where the positioner moves from one cylinder to another. The speed with which a seek can be completed is a major factor in determining the access time of the drive. The main parameter controlling the carriage during a seek is the cylinder difference, which is obtained by subtracting the current cylinder address from the desired cylinder address. The cylinder difference will be a signed binary number representing the number of cylinders to be crossed to reach the target, direction being indicated by the sign. The cylinder difference is loaded into a counter which is decremented each time a cylinder is crossed. The counter drives a DAC which generates an analog voltage proportional to the cylinder difference. As Fig.12.10 shows, this voltage, known as the scheduled velocity, is compared with the output of the carriage-velocity transducer. Any difference between the two results in a velocity error which drives the carriage to cancel the error. As the carriage approaches the target cylinder, the cylinder difference becomes smaller, with the result that the run-in to the target is critically damped to eliminate overshoot.

Fig.12.11(a) shows graphs of scheduled velocity, actual velocity and motor current with respect to cylinder difference during a seek. In the first half of the

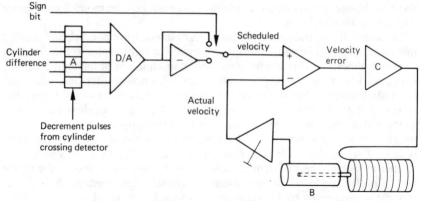

Figure 12.10 Control of carriage velocity by cylinder difference. The cylinder difference is loaded into the difference counter A. A digital-to-analog converter generates an analog voltage from the cylinder difference, known as the scheduled velocity. This is compared with the actual velocity from the transducer B in order to generate the velocity error which drives the servo amplifier C.

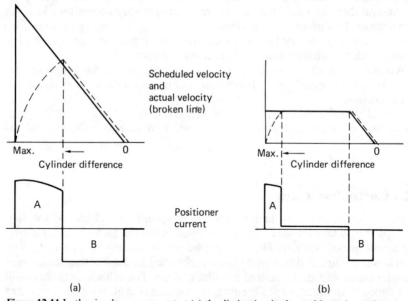

Figure 12.11 In the simple arrangement at (a) the dissipation in the positioner is continuous, causing a heating problem. The effect of limiting the scheduled velocity above a certain cylinder difference is apparent in (b) where heavy positioner current only flows during acceleration and deceleration. During the plateau of the velocity profile, only enough current to overcome friction is necessary. The curvature of the acceleration slope is due to the back EMF of the positioner motor.

seek, the actual velocity is less than the scheduled velocity, causing a large velocity error which saturates the amplifier and provides maximum carriage acceleration. In the second half of the graphs, the scheduled velocity is falling below the actual velocity, generating a negative velocity error which drives a reverse current through the motor to slow the carriage down. The scheduled deceleration slope can clearly not be steeper than the saturated acceleration slope. Areas A and B on the graph will be about equal, as the kinetic energy put into the carriage has to be taken out. The current through the motor is continuous, and would result in a heating problem, so to counter this, the DAC is made nonlinear so that above a certain cylinder difference no increase in scheduled velocity will occur. This results in the graph of Fig.12.11(b). The actual velocity graph is called a velocity profile. It consists of three regions: acceleration, where the system is saturated; a constant velocity plateau, where

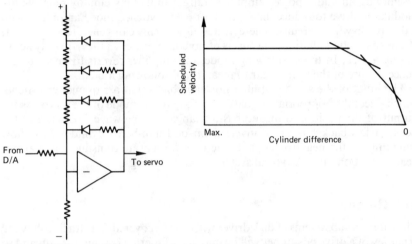

Figure 12.12 The use of voltage-dependent feedback around an operational amplifier permits a piecewise-linear approximation to a curved velocity profile. This has the effect of speeding up short seeks without causing a dissipation problem on long seeks. The circuit is referred to as a shaper.

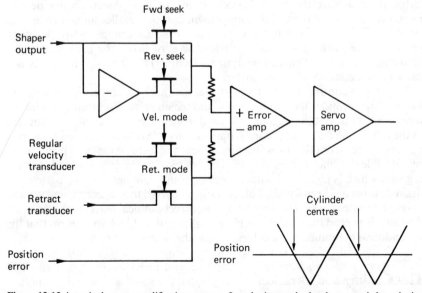

Figure 12.13 A typical servo-amplifier input stage. In velocity mode the shaper and the velocity transducer drive the error amp. In track-following mode the position error is the only input.

the only power needed is to overcome friction; and the scheduled run-in to the desired cylinder. Dissipation is only significant in the first and last regions.

A consequence of the critically damped run-in to the target cylinder is that short seeks are slow. Sometimes further nonlinearity is introduced into the velocity scheduler to speed up short seeks. The velocity profile becomes a piecewise linear approximation to a curve by using nonlinear feedback. Fig.12.12 shows the principle of the shaper or profile generator.

In small disk drives the amplifier may be linear in all modes of operation, resembling an audio power amplifier. Larger units may employ pulse-width-modulated drive to reduce dissipation, or even switched-mode amplifiers with inductive flywheel circuits. These switching systems can generate appreciable electromagnetic radiation, but this is of no consequence as they are only active during a seek. In track-following mode, the amplifier reverts to linear mode; hence the use of the term linear to mean track-following mode.

The input of the servo amplifier normally has a number of analog switches which select the appropriate signals according to the mode of the servo. As the output of the position transducer is a triangle or sine wave, the sense of the position feedback has to be inverted on odd-numbered cylinders, to allow detenting on the negative slope. Sometimes a separate transducer is used for head retraction only. A typical system is shown in Fig.12.13.

12.8 Rotation

The rotation subsystems of disk drives will now be covered. The track-following accuracy of a drive positioner will be impaired if there is bearing runout, and so the spindle bearings are made to a high degree of precision. On larger drives, squirrel-cage induction motors are used, to drive the spindle through a belt. The different motor speeds resulting from 50 Hz and 60 Hz supplies are accommodated by changing the relative sizes of the pulleys. As recording density increases, the size of drives has come down, and the smaller units incorporate brushless DC motors with integral speed control. In exchangeable-pack drives, some form of braking is usually provided to slow down the pack rapidly for convenient removal. This can be done by feeding DC to an AC motor, which causes it to act as an eddy-current brake.

In order to control reading and writing, the drive control circuitry needs to know which cylinder the heads are on, and which sector is currently under the head. Sector information is often obtained from a sensor which detects slots cut in the hub of the disk. These can be optical, variable reluctance or eddy current devices. Pulses from the transducer increment the sector counter, which is reset by a double slot once per revolution. The desired sector address is loaded into a register, which is compared with the sector counter. When the two match, the desired sector has been found. This process is referred to as a search, and usually takes place after a seek. Having found the correct physical place on the disk, the next step is to read the header associated with the data block to confirm that the disk address contained there is the same as the desired address.

12.9 Cooling and filtration

Rotation of a disk pack at speed results in heat build-up through air resistance.

This heat must be carried away. A further important factor with exchangeable pack drives is to keep the disk area free from contaminants which might lodge between the head and the disk and cause the destructive phenomenon known as a head crash, where debris builds up on the head until it ploughs the disk surface.

The cooling and filtration systems are usually combined. Air is drawn through an absolute filter, passed around the disk, and exhausted, sometimes cooling the positioner motor and circuitry on the way. This full-flow system is fine for environmentally controlled computer rooms, but for the office or studio environment, a closed-circuit filtration system can be used, where the same air goes round the pack and through the blower and filter endlessly. This results in extended filter life in adverse environments, but requires a heat exchanger in the loop to carry away the heat developed by disk rotation.

12.10 Servo-surface disks

One of the major problems to be overcome in the development of high-density disk drives was that of keeping the heads on track despite changes of temperature. The very narrow tracks used in digital recording have similar dimensions to the amount a disk will expand as it warms up. The cantilevers and the drive base all expand and contract, conspiring with thermal drift in the cylinder transducer to limit track pitch. The breakthrough in disk density came with the introduction of the servo-surface drive. The position error in a servo-surface drive is derived from a head reading the disk itself. This virtually eliminates thermal effects on head positioning and allows great increases in storage density.

In a multiplatter drive, one surface of the pack holds servo information which is read by the servo head. In a ten-platter pack this means that 5 % of the medium area is lost, but this is unimportant since the increase in density allowed is enormous. Using one side of a single-platter cartridge for servo information would be unacceptable as it represents 50 % of the medium area, so in this case the servo information can be interleaved with sectors on the data surfaces. This is known as an embedded-servo technique. These two approaches are contrasted in Fig.12.14.

The servo surface is written at the time of disk pack manufacture, and the disk drive can only read it.

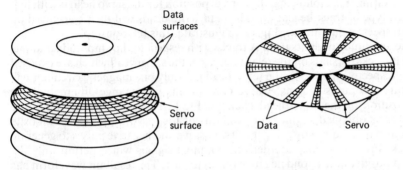

Figure 12.14 In a multiplatter disk pack, one surface is dedicated to servo information. In a single platter, the servo information is embedded in the data on the same surfaces.

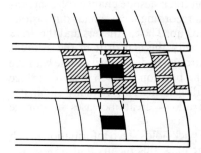

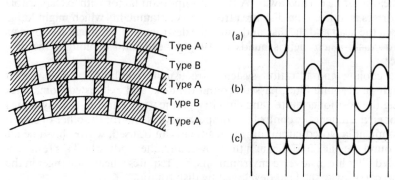

Figure 12.15 The servo surface is divided into two types of track, A and B, which are out of phase by 180° and are recorded with reverse polarity with respect to one another. Waveform (a) results when the servo head is entirely above a type A track, and waveform (b) results from reading solely a type B track. When the servo head is correctly positioned with one half of its magnetic circuit over each track, the waveform of (c) results.

Figure 12.16 When the servo head is straddling two servo tracks, the data heads are correctly aligned with their respective tracks.

The key to the operation of the servo surface is the special magnetic pattern recorded on it. In a typical servo surface, recorded pairs of transitions, known as dibits, are separated by a space. Fig.12.15 shows that there are two kinds of track. On an A track, the first transition of the pair will cause a positive pulse on reading, whereas on a B track, the first pulse will be negative. In addition the A-track dibits are shifted by one half cycle with respect to the B-track dibits. The width of the magnetic circuit in the servo head is equal to the width of a servo track. During track following, the correct position for the servo head is with half of each type of track beneath it. The read/write heads will then be centred on their respective data tracks. Fig.12.16 illustrates this relationship.

The amplitude of dibits from A tracks with respect to the amplitude of dibits from B tracks depends on the relative areas of the servo head which are exposed to the respective tracks. As the servo head has only one magnetic circuit, it will generate a composite signal whose components will change differentially as the position of the servo head changes. Fig.12.17 shows several composite waveforms obtained at different positions of the servo head. The composite waveform is processed by using the first positive and negative pulses to generate a clock. From this clock are derived sampling signals which permit only the second positive and second negative pulses to pass. The resultant waveform has a DC component which after filtering gives a voltage proportional to the distance from the centre of the data tracks. The position error reaches a maximum

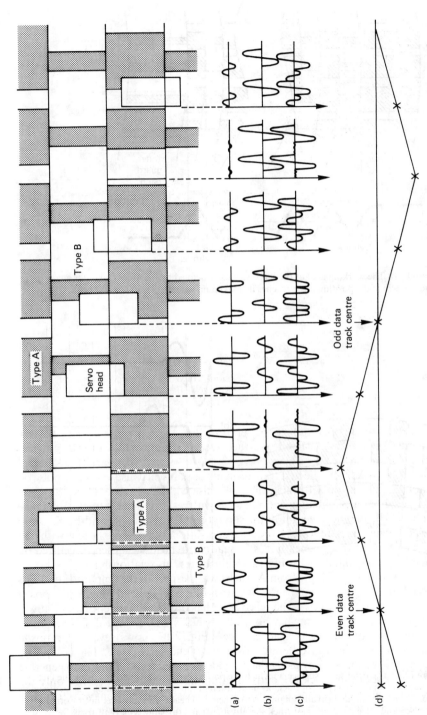

Figure 12.17 Waveforms resulting from several positions of the servo head with respect to the disk. At (a) and (b) are the two components of the waveforms, whose relative amplitudes are controlled by the relative areas of the servo head exposed to the two types of servo track. Because the servo head has only one magnetic circuit, these waveforms are not observed in practice, but are summed together, resulting in the composite waveforms shown at (c). By comparing the magnitudes of the second positive and second negative peaks in the composite waveforms, a position error signal is generated, as shown at (d).

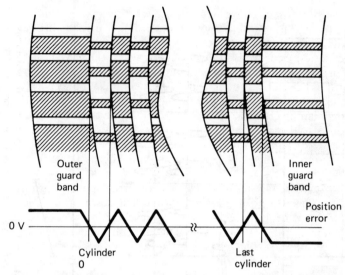

Figure 12.18 The working area of the servo surface is defined by the inner and outer guard bands, in which the position error reaches its maximum value.

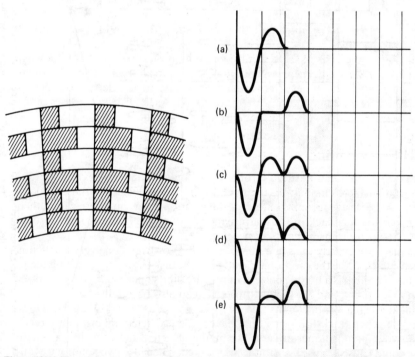

Figure 12.19 The tribit servo surface, in which the position error is extracted by using the fact that pulses from the two types of track occur at different times after the common negative sync pulse. Waveforms (a) and (b) are obtained when the servo head is entirely over one or other of the tracks, and (c) is the correct on-track waveform. (d) and (e) show typical off-track waveforms.

when the servo head is entirely above one type of servo track, and further movement causes it to fall. The next time the position error falls to zero will be at the centre line of the adjacent cylinder.

Cylinders with even addresses (LSB = 0) will be those where the servo head is detented between an A track and a B track. Cylinders with odd addresses will be those where the head is between a B track and an A track. It can be seen from Fig.12.17 that the sense of the position error becomes reversed on every other cylinder. Accordingly, an inverter has to be switched into the track-following feedback loop in order to detent on odd cylinders. This inversion is controlled by the LSB of the desired cylinder address supplied at the beginning of a seek, such that the sense of the feedback will be correct when the heads arrive at the target cylinder.

Seeking across the servo surface results in the position-error signal rising and falling in a sawtooth. This waveform can be used to count down the cylinder difference counter which controls the seek. As with any cyclic transducer there is the problem of finding the absolute position. This difficulty is overcome by making all servo tracks outside cylinder 0 type A, and all servo tracks inside the innermost cylinder type B. These areas of identical track are called guard bands, and Fig.12.18 shows the relationship between the position error and the guard bands. During a head load, the servo head generates a constant maximum positive position error in the outer guard band. This drives the carriage forward until the position error first falls to zero. This, by definition, is cylinder zero. Some drives, however, load by driving the heads across the surface until the inner guard band is found, and then perform a full-length reverse seek to cylinder zero.

An alternative form of servo surface for exchangeable pack drives is shown in Fig.12.19. In this type, there is a common sync bit in all tracks, and subsequent servo bits at different times afterwards. The position error is derived by opening sampling gates at different times after the sync bit. As three distinct pulses can be seen in the waveform, the result is called a tribit signal.

12.11 Soft sectoring

It has been seen that a position error and a cylinder count can be derived from the servo surface, eliminating the cylinder transducer. The carriage velocity could also be derived from the slope of the position error, but there would then be no velocity feedback in the guard bands or during retraction, and so some form of velocity transducer is still necessary.

As there are exactly the same number of dibits or tribits on every track, it is possible to describe the rotational position of the disk simply by counting them. All that is needed is a unique pattern of missing dibits once per revolution to act as an index point, and the sector transducer can also be eliminated.

Unlike the read-data circuits, the servo-head circuits are active during a seek as well as when track-following, and have to be protected against interference from switching positioner drivers. The main problem is detecting index, where noise could cause a 'missing' dibit to be masked. There are two solutions available: a preamplifier can be built into the servo-head cantilever, or driver switching can be inhibited when index is expected.

The advantage of deriving the sector count from the servo surface is that the number of sectors on the disk can be varied. Any number of sectors can be accommodated by feeding the dibit-rate signal through a programmable divider, so the same disk and drive can be used in numerous different applications.

In a non-servo-surface disk, the write clock is usually derived from a crystal oscillator. As the disk speed can vary owing to supply fluctuations, a tolerance gap has to be left at the end of each block to cater for the highest anticipated speed, to prevent overrun into the next block on a write. In a servo-surface drive, the write clock is obtained by multiplying the dibit-rate signal with a phase-locked loop. The write clock is then always proportional to disk speed, and recording density will be constant.

Most servo-surface drives have an offset facility, where a register written by the controller drives a DAC which injects a small voltage into the track-following loop. The action of the servo is such that the heads move off track until the position error is equal and opposite to the injected voltage. The position of the heads above the track can thus be program-controlled. Offset is only employed on reading if it is suspected that the pack in the drive has been written by a different drive with nonstandard alignment. A write function will cancel the offset.

12.12 Embedded servo drives

In drives with a small number of platters, the use of an entire surface for servo information gives an excessive loss of data-recording area. In the embedded-servo drive, servo information is interleaved with data on the same surface, causing a smaller loss of storage area.

The embedded-servo drive heads will be reading data at some times and alignment information at others as the disk rotates. A sector transducer is required to generate a pulse which is true when the head is over servo information. Fig.12.20 and Fig.12.21 show the principle. On all disk drives, the width of the head pole is less than the track pitch to prevent crosstalk. As the servo head is also the read/write head in an embedded-servo drive, it is slightly narrower than the servo-information pitch. This has the harmless effect of rounding off the peaks of the position-error waveform. During the pulse from the sector transducer, the head sees alignment information, and develops a position

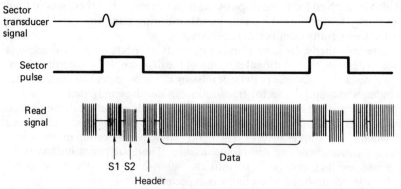

Figure 12.20 The same head is used on the embedded servo drive for both servo information and read/write data. During a sector pulse, the read signal is treated as servo information.

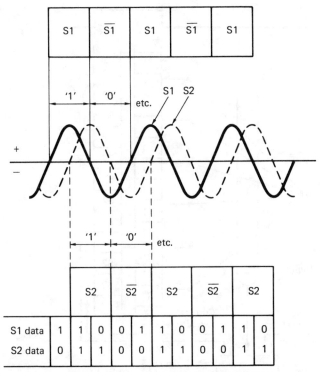

| S1 data | 1 | 1 | 0 | 0 | 1 | 1 | 0 | 0 | 1 | 1 | 0 |
| S2 data | 0 | 1 | 1 | 0 | 0 | 1 | 1 | 0 | 0 | 1 | 1 |

Figure 12.21 There are two basic types of servo track, S_1 and S_2, but these are recorded at two different places, in a staggered fashion. During S1 time, a position error is generated from the relative areas of the two types of track under the head as in the conventional servo-surface drive. This position error is maintained with sample-and-hold circuitry. For track counting, the position error is compared with 0 V to generate a data bit. At S2 time another position error and another data bit are generated. The four possible combinations of the two bits are shown here in relation to the two position errors.

error in much the same way as any servo drive. Within the servo area are two sets of patterns, the second giving a position error of zero when the first is a maximum, i.e. there is a 90-degree phase shift between them. The two bursts of information are known as S1 and S2. Sample-and-hold circuitry is used to carry over the position errors whilst the head is reading and writing in the data area.

The discontinuous nature of the servo information means that cylinder crossings cannot be counted directly during a seek as the positioner is fast enough to cross several tracks between bursts. With reference to Fig.12.22, this problem is overcome as follows. During the S1 period, the position error is compared with zero volts to produce a single data bit, whose state depends upon whether the head was inside or outside the track centre. A similar process takes place for the S2 period, and the position of the head relative to the track centre is then described to the accuracy of one fourth of the track pitch by the two bits. These bits are stored, and at the next servo burst, two further bits are computed, describing the new position of the head. Fig.12.22 shows that there can be many cases which can satisfy the same initial and final conditions. The only difference between the cases is the carriage velocity, so the output of the velocity transducer is digitized and used to resolve the ambiguity. At every sector pulse,

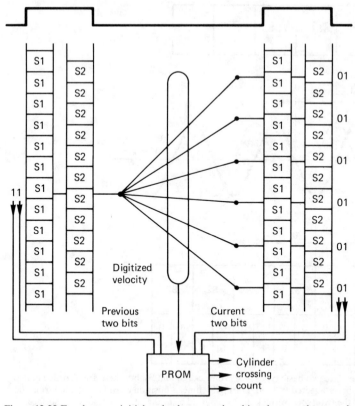

Figure 12.22 For the same initial and subsequent data bits, there can be several possible head trajectories. The ambiguity is resolved by using the carriage velocity in digital form.

two bits from the previous burst, two bits from the current burst and the digitized velocity are fed into a ROM which is preprogrammed to return the number of cylinders which must have been crossed for all combinations of inputs. This number is then subtracted from the cylinder-difference counter which is controlling the seek. The calculation will only be valid for one disk rotational speed, and so the disk motor requires close control. This is conveniently done by counting cycles of a reference clock between sector pulses to produce a speed error. As the cylinder count is deductive, there will be the odd occasion where the count is in error and the positioner comes to the wrong cylinder. In a conventional disk drive this would result in a mispositioning error which would warrant maintenance. In the embedded-servo drive, however, the condition is handled differently. Fig.12.23 shows a flowchart for control of the drive, which has no absolute cylinder-address register, and in which all seeks are relative. The system only knows where the heads are by reading headers. In order to reach a particular cylinder, the program has to read the first header it sees on the current cylinder, and calculate the cylinder difference needed. This is used to perform a deductive seek. When this is complete, a further header will be read. Most of the time this will indicate the correct cylinder, but in the occasional condition where the positioning was in error, the program simply loops and calculates a new cylinder difference until the correct cylinder is finally reached.

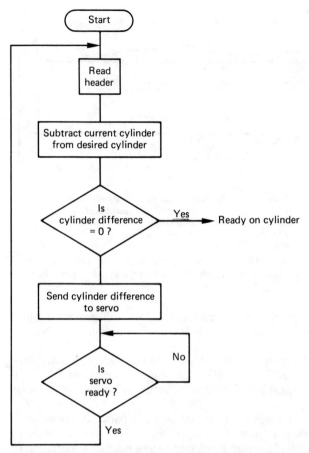

Figure 12.23 Flowchart for the control of an embedded-servo positioner. All seeks are relative, and seek errors are transparent, as they simply cause an extra execution of the loop.

Since each surface has its own alignment information, some exchangeable-pack drives using this principle need no head alignment during manufacture at all. When switching between heads, a repositioning cycle will be necessary because all of the heads will not necessarily be on the same cylinder. In fact the definition of a cylinder is indistinct in such drives.

12.13 Winchester technology

In order to offer extremely high capacity per spindle, which reduces the cost per bit, a disk drive must have very narrow tracks placed close together, and must use very short recorded wavelengths, which implies that the flying height of the heads must be small. The so-called Winchester technology is one approach to high storage density. The technology was developed by IBM, and the name came about because the model number of the development drive was the same as that of the famous rifle.

Reduction in flying height magnifies the problem of providing a

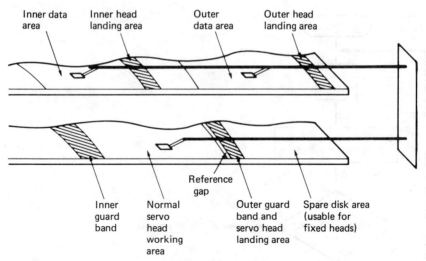

Inner data area   Inner head landing area   Outer data area   Outer head landing area

Reference gap

Inner guard band   Normal servo head working area   Outer guard band and servo head landing area   Spare disk area (usable for fixed heads)

Figure 12.24 When more than one head is used per surface, the positioner still only requires one servo head. This is often arranged to be equidistant from the read/write heads for thermal stability.

contaminant-free environment. A conventional disk is well protected whilst inside the drive, but outside the drive the effects of contamination become intolerable.

In exchangeable-pack drives, there is a real limit to the track pitch that can be achieved because of the impossibility of engineering head-alignment mechanisms to make the necessary minute adjustments to give interchange compatibility.

The essence of Winchester technology is that each disk pack has its own set of read/write and servo heads, with an integral positioner. The whole is protected by a dust-free enclosure, and the unit is referred to as a head disk assembly, or HDA.

As the HDA contains its own heads, compatibility problems do not exist, and no head alignment is necessary or provided for. It is thus possible to reduce track pitch considerably compared with exchangeable pack drives. The sealed environment ensures complete cleanliness which permits a reduction in flying height without loss of reliability, and hence leads to an increased linear density. If the rotational speed is maintained, this can also result in an increase in data transfer rate.

The HDA is completely sealed, but some have a small filtered port to equalize pressure. Into this sealed volume of air, the drive motor delivers the majority of its power output. The resulting heat is dissipated by fins on the HDA casing. Some HDAs are filled with helium which significantly reduces drag and heat build-up.

An exchangeable-pack drive must retract the heads to facilitate pack removal. With Winchester technology this is not necessary. An area of the disk surface is reserved as a landing strip for the heads. The disc surface is lubricated, and the heads are designed to withstand landing and take-off without damage. Winchester heads have very large air-bleed grooves to allow low flying height with a much smaller downthrust from the cantilever, and so they exert less force on the disk surface during contact. When the term retraction is used in the context of Winchester technology, it refers to the positioning of the heads over the landing area.

Disk rotation must be started and stopped quickly to minimize the length of time the heads slide over the medium. A powerful motor will accelerate the pack quickly. Eddy-current braking cannot be used, since a power failure would allow the unbraked disk to stop only after a prolonged head-contact period. A failsafe mechanical brake is used, which is applied by a spring and released with a solenoid.

A major advantage of contact start/stop is that more than one head can be used on each surface if retraction is not needed. This leads to two gains: first, the travel of the positioner is reduced in proportion to the number of heads per surface, reducing access time; and, second, more data can be transferred at a given detented carriage position before a seek to the next cylinder becomes necessary. This increases the speed of long transfers. Fig.12.24 illustrates the relationships of the heads in such a system.

12.14 Servo-surface Winchester drives

With contact start/stop, the servo head is always on the servo surface, and it can be used for all of the transducer functions needed by the drive. Fig.12.25 shows the position-error signal during a seek. The signal rises and falls as servo tracks are crossed, and the slope of the signal is proportional to positioner velocity. The position-error signal is differentiated and rectified to give a velocity feedback signal. Owing to the cyclic nature of the position-error signal, the velocity signal derived from it has troughs where the derivative becomes zero at the peaks. These cannot be filtered out, as the signal is in a servo loop, and the filter would introduce an additional lag. The troughs would, however, be interpreted by the servo driver as massive momentary velocity errors which might overload the amplifier. The solution which can be adopted is to use a signal obtained by integrating the positioner-motor current which is selected when there is a trough in the differentiated position-error signal.

In order to make velocity feedback available over the entire servo surface, the conventional guard-band approach cannot be used since it results in steady

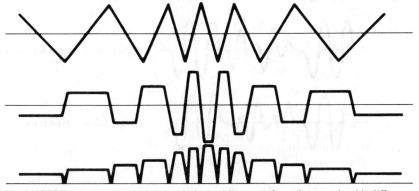

Figure 12.25 To generate a velocity signal, the position error from the servo head is differentiated and rectified.

position errors in the guard bands. In contact start/stop drives, the servo head must be capable of detenting in a guard band for the purpose of landing on shutdown.

A modification to the usual servo surface is used in Winchester drives, one implementation of which is shown in Fig.12.26, where it will be seen that there are extra transitions, identical in both types of track, along with the familiar dibits. The repeating set of transitions is known as a frame, in which the first dibit is used for synchronization, and a phase-locked oscillator is made to run at a multiple of the sync signal rate. The PLO is used as a reference for the write clock, as well as to generate sampling pulses to extract a position error from the composite waveform and to provide a window for the second dibit in the frame, which may or may not be present. Each frame thus contains one data bit, and successive frames are read to build up a pattern in a shift register. The parallel output of the shift register is examined by a decoder which recognizes a number of unique patterns. In the guard bands, the decoder will repeatedly recognize the guard band code as the disk revolves. An index is generated in the same way, by recognizing a different pattern. In a contact start/stop drive, the frequency of

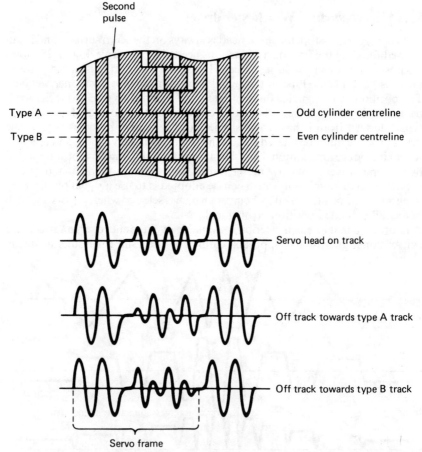

Figure 12.26 This type of servo surface pattern has a second pulse which may be omitted to act as a data bit. This is used to detect the guard bands and index.

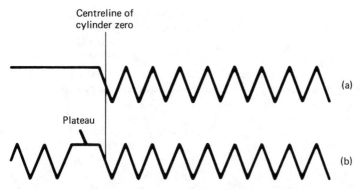

Centreline of
cylinder zero

Plateau

(a)

(b)

Figure 12.27 (a) Conventional guard band. (b) Winchester guard band, showing the plateau in the position error, known as the reference gap, which is used to locate cylinder zero.

index detection is used to monitor pack speed in order to dispense with a separate transducer. This does mean, however, that it must be possible to detect index everywhere, and for this reason, index is still recorded in the guard bands by replacing the guard-band code with index code once per revolution.

A consequence of deriving velocity information from the servo surface is that the location of cylinder zero is made more difficult, as there is no longer a continuous maximum position error in the guard band. A common solution is to adopt a much smaller area of continuous position error known as a reference gap; this is typically three servo tracks wide. In the reference gap and for several tracks outside it, there is a unique reference gap code recorded in the frame-data bits. Fig.12.27 shows the position error which is generated as the positioner crosses this area of the disk, and shows the plateau in the position-error signal due to the reference gap. During head loading, which in this context means positioning to cylinder zero, the heads move slowly inwards away from the head landing area. When the reference code is detected, positioner velocity is reduced, and the position error is sampled. When successive position-error samples are the same, the head must be on the position-error plateau, and if the servo is put into track-following mode, it will automatically detent on cylinder zero, since this is the first place that the position error falls to zero.

12.15 Rotary positioners

Fig.12.28 shows that rotary positioners are feasible in Winchester drives; they cannot be used in exchangeable-pack drives because of interchange problems. There are some advantages to a rotary positioner. It can be placed in the corner of a compact HDA allowing smaller overall size. The manufacturing cost will be less than a linear positioner because fewer bearings and precision bars are needed. Significantly, a rotary positioner can be made faster since its inertia is smaller. With a linear positioner all parts move at the same speed. In a rotary positioner, only the heads move at full speed, as the parts closer to the shaft must move more slowly. Fig.12.29 shows a typical HDA with a rotary positioner. The principle of a rotary positioner is exactly that of a moving- coil ammeter, where current is converted directly into torque.

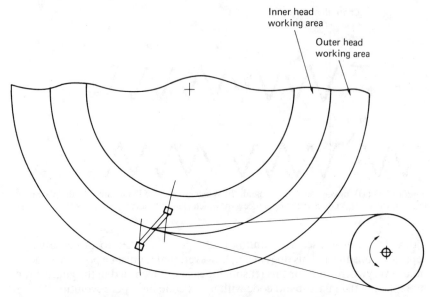

Figure 12.28 A rotary positioner with two heads per surface. The tolerances involved in the spacing between the heads and the axis of rotation mean that each arm records data in a unique position. Those data can only be read back by the same heads, which rules out the use of a rotary positioner in exchangeable-pack drives. In a head disk assembly the problem of compatibility does not arise.

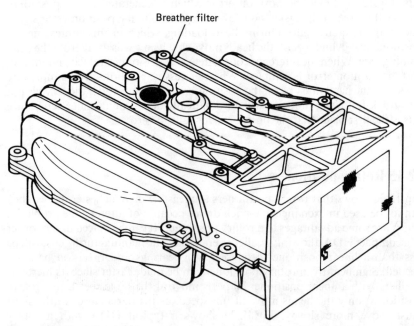

Figure 12.29 Head disk assembly with a rotary positioner. The adoption of this technique allows a very compact structure.

One disadvantage of rotary positioners is that there is a component of windage on the heads which tends to pull the positioner in towards the spindle. In linear positioners windage is at right angles to motion and can be neglected. Windage is overcome in rotary positioners by feeding the current cylinder address to a ROM which sends a code to a DAC. This produces an offset voltage which is fed to the positioner driver to generate a torque which balances the windage whatever the position of the heads.

When extremely small track spacing is contemplated, it cannot be assumed that all the heads will track the servo head due to temperature gradients. In this case the embedded-servo approach must be used, where each head has its own alignment patterns. The servo surface is often retained in such drives to allow coarse positioning, velocity feedback and index and write-clock generation, in addition to locating the guard bands for landing the heads.

Winchester drives have been made with massive capacity, but the problem of backup is then magnified, and the general trend has been for the physical size of the drive to come down as the storage density increases. Early drives used 14 in disks; later 8 in and $5\frac{1}{4}$ in became common, helped by the expanding market in desktop computers.

12.16 Floppy disks

Floppy disks are the result of a search for a fast yet cheap nonvolatile memory for the programmable control store of a processor under development at IBM in the late 1960s. Both magnetic tape and hard disk were ruled out on grounds of cost since only intermittent duty was required. The device designed to fulfil these requirements — the floppy disk drive — incorporated both magnetic-tape and disk technologies.

The floppy concept was so cost-effective that it transcended its original application to become a standard in industry as an online data-storage device. The original floppy disk, or diskette as it is sometimes called, was 8 in in diameter, but a $5\frac{1}{4}$ in diameter disk was launched to suit more compact applications. More recently Sony introduced the $3\frac{1}{2}$ in floppy disk which has a rigid shell with sliding covers over the head access holes to reduce the likelihood of contamination.

Strictly speaking the floppy is a disk, since it rotates and repeatedly presents the data on any track to the heads, and it has a positioner to give fast two-dimensional access, but it also resembles a tape drive in that the magnetic

One-quarter revolution

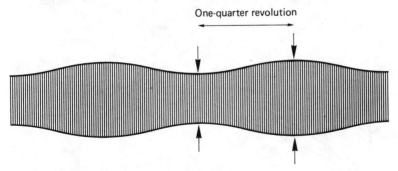

Figure 12.30 Sinusoidal amplitude modulation of floppy disk output due to anisotropy of medium.

medium is carried on a flexible substrate which deforms when the read/write head is pressed against it.

Floppy disks are stamped from wide, thick tape, and are anisotropic, because the oxide becomes oriented during manufacture. On many disks this can be seen by the eye as parallel striations on the disk surface. A more serious symptom is the presence of sinusoidal amplitude modulation of the replay signal at twice the rotational frequency of the disk, as illustrated in Fig.12.30.

Floppy disks have radial apertures in their protective envelopes to allow access by the head. A further aperture allows a photoelectric index sensor to detect a small hole in the disk once per revolution.

Fig.12.31 shows that the disk is inserted into the drive edge-first, and slides between an upper and a lower hub assembly. One of these has a fixed bearing which transmits the drive; the other is spring-loaded and mates with the drive hub when the door is closed, causing the disk to be centred and gripped firmly. The moving hub is usually tapered to assist centring. To avoid frictional heating and prolong life, the spindle speed is restricted when compared with that of hard disks. Recent drives almost universally use direct-drive brushless DC motors; older machines used an induction motor and belt drive. Since the rotational latency is so great, there is little point in providing a fast positioner, and the use of leadscrews driven by a stepping motor is universal. The permanent magnets in the stepping motor provide the necessary detenting, and to seek it is only necessary to provide a suitable number of drive pulses to the motor. As the drive is incremental, some form of reference is needed to determine the position of cylinder zero. At the rearward limit of carriage travel, a light beam is interrupted which resets the cylinder count. Upon power-up, the drive has to reverse-seek until this limit is found in order to calibrate the positioner.

One of the less endearing features of plastics materials is a lack of dimensional stability. Temperature and humidity changes affect plastics much more than metals. The effect on the anisotropic disk substrate is to distort the circular tracks into a shape resembling a dog bone. For this reason, the track width and pitch have to be generous. There are only 77 tracks on standard 8 in disks.

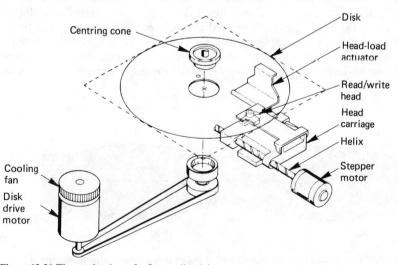

Figure 12.31 The mechanism of a floppy disc drive.

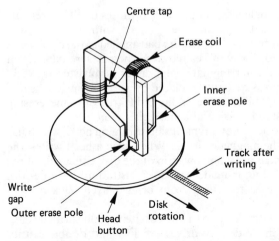

Figure 12.32 The poor dimensional stability of the plastic diskette means that tunnel erase or side trim has to be used. The extra erase poles can be seen here.

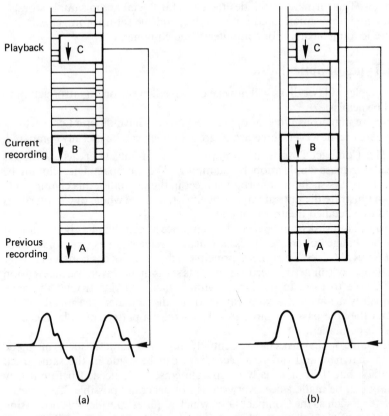

Figure 12.33 The effect of side trim is to prevent the traces of a previous recording from interfering with the latest recording: (a) without side trim; (b) with side trim.

The read/write head of a single-sided floppy disk operates on the lower sur-face only, and is rigidly fixed to the carriage. Contact with the medium is achieved with the help of a spring-loaded pressure pad applied to the top surface of the disk opposite the head. Early drives retracted the pressure pad with a solenoid when not actually transferring data; later drives simply stop the disk. In double-sided drives, the pressure pad is replaced by a second sprung head.

Because of the indifferent stability of the medium, side trim or tunnel erasing is used, because it can withstand considerable misregistration.

Fig.12.32 shows the construction of a typical side-trimming head, which has erase poles at each side of the magnetic circuit. When such a head writes, the erase poles are energized, and erase a narrow strip of the disk either side of the new data track. If the recording is made with misregistration, the side-trim prevents traces of the previous recording from being played back as well (Fig.12.33).

As the floppy-disk drive is intended to be a low-cost item, sophisticated chan-nel codes are never used. Single-density drives use FM and double-density drives use MFM. As the recording density becomes higher at the inner tracks, the write current is sometimes programmed to reduce with inward positioner travel.

The capacity of floppy disks is in the range of hundreds of kilobytes to a few megabytes. This virtually precludes their use for digital audio sample storage, but they find application in edit-list storage, console set-up storage, and as a software-loading medium for computer-based equipment.

12.17 Types of optical disk

The principles of laser disks will now be described, based on an introduction to optical principles.

There are numerous types of optical disk, which have different characteris-tics.[1] There are, however, three broad groups which can be usefully compared.

(1) The Compact Disc is an example of a read-only laser disk, which is designed for mass duplication by stamping. The Compact Disc cannot be recorded. As it is such an important subject in digital audio, this chapter only serves to illustrate the optical physics behind it, and the whole of Chapter 13 is devoted to a detailed treatment of CD.

(2) Some laser disks can be recorded, but once a recording has been made, it cannot be changed or erased. These are usually referred to as write-once-read-many (WORM) disks. The general principle is that the disk contains a thin layer of metal; on recording, a powerful laser melts spots on the layer. Surface tension causes a hole to form in the metal, with a thickened rim around the hole. Subsequently a low-power laser can read the disk because the metal reflects light, but the hole passes it through. Clearly once a pattern of holes has been made, it is permanent.

(3) Erasable optical disks have essentially the same characteristic as magnetic disks, in that new and different recordings can be made in the same track indefinitely, but there is usually a separate erase cycle needed before a new recording can be made since overwrite is not generally possible. To contrast with systems such as the Compact Disc, which requires considerable processing after the write stage before reading is possible, such systems are called direct-read-after-write (DRAW) disks.

12.18 Optical theory

All of these technologies are restricted by the wave and quantum nature of light, and depend heavily on certain optical devices such as lasers, polarizers and diffraction gratings. These subjects will be outlined here.

Wave theory of light suggests that a plane wave advances because an infinite number of point sources can be considered to emit spherical waves which will only add when they are all in the same phase. This can only occur in the plane of the wavefront. Fig.12.34 shows that at all other angles, interference between spherical waves is destructive.

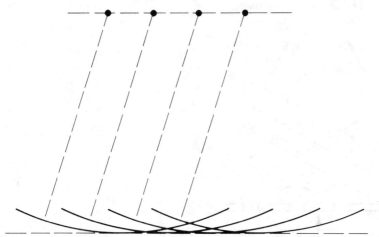

12.34 Plane-wave propagation considered as infinite numbers of spherical waves.

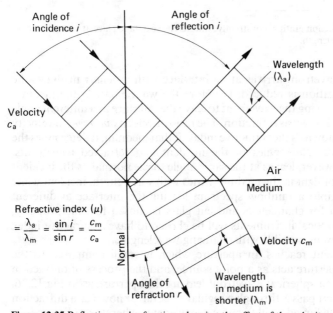

Angle of incidence i

Angle of reflection i

Wavelength (λ_a)

Velocity c_a

Air

Medium

Refractive index (μ)

$$= \frac{\lambda_a}{\lambda_m} = \frac{\sin i}{\sin r} = \frac{c_m}{c_a}$$

Normal

Velocity c_m

Angle of refraction r

Wavelength in medium is shorter (λ_m)

Figure 12.35 Reflection and refraction, showing the effect of the velocity of light in a medium.

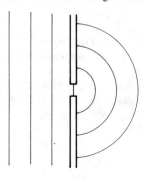

Figure 12.36 Diffraction as a plane wave reaches a small aperture.

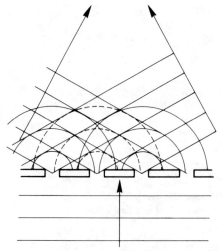

Figure 12.37 In a diffraction grating, constructive interference can take place at more than one angle for a single wavelength.

When such a wavefront arrives at an interface with a denser medium, the velocity of propagation is reduced; therefore the wavelength in the medium becomes shorter, causing the wavefront to leave the interface at a different angle (Fig.12.35). This is known as refraction. The ratio of velocity *in vacuo* to velocity in the medium is known as the refractive index of that medium; it determines the relationship between the angles of the incident and refracted wavefronts. Reflected light, however, leaves at the same angle to the normal as the incident light. If the speed of light in the medium varies with wavelength, incident white light will be split into a rainbow spectrum leaving the interface at different angles. Glass used for chandeliers and cut glass is chosen for this property, whereas glass for optical instruments will be chosen to have a refractive index which is as constant as possible with changing wavelength.

When a wavefront reaches an aperture which is small compared to the wavelength, the aperture acts as a point source, and the process of diffraction can be observed as a spherical wavefront leaving the aperture as in Fig.12.36. Where the wavefront passes through a regular structure, known as a diffraction grating, light on the far side will form new wavefronts wherever radiation is in

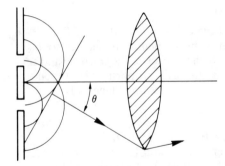

Figure 12.38 Fine detail in an object can only be resolved if the diffracted wavefront due to the highest spatial frequency is collected by the lens. Numerical aperture (NA) = sin θ, and as θ is the diffraction angle it follows that, for a given wavelength, NA determines resolution.

phase, and Fig.12.37 shows that these will be at an angle to the normal depending on the spacing of the structure and the wavelength of the light. A diffraction grating illuminated by white light will produce a rainbow spectrum at each side of the normal. To obtain a fixed angle of diffraction, monochromatic light is necessary.

For a given wavelength, the greater the spatial frequency of the grating (bars per unit of distance) the greater will be the angle of diffraction. A corollary of this effect is that the more finely detailed an object is, the greater the angle over which light must be collected to see the detail. The light-collecting angle of a lens shown in Fig.12.38 is measured by the numerical aperture (NA), which is the sine of the angle between the optical axis and the wavefront carrying the finest detail in the image. All lenses thus act as spatial filters which cut off at a spatial frequency limited by NA. The response is known as the modulation transfer function (MTF). Light travelling on the axis of a lens is conveying the average brightness of the image, not the detail, as this is conveyed in the more oblique light collected at the rim of the lens. Lenses can fall short of their theoretical MTF because of shortcomings in manufacture. If a lens is made accurately enough, a wavefront which has passed through it will have the same phase over its entire area. Where wavefront aberrations have a variance of less than the square of the wavelength divided by 180, the lens is said to meet the Maréchal criterion, which essentially means that the performance of the lens is as good as it is going to get because it is now diffraction-limited rather than tolerance-limited.

When a diffraction-limited lens is used to focus a point source on a plane, the image will not be a point owing to exclusion of the higher spatial frequencies by the finite numerical aperture. The resulting image is in fact the spatial equivalent of the impulse response of a low-pass filter, and results in a diffraction pattern known as an Airy pattern, after Sir George Airy, who first quantified the intensity function. It is the dimensions of the Airy pattern which limit the density of all optical media, since it controls the minimum size of features that the laser can produce or resolve. The only way a laser disk could hold more data would be if the working wavelength could be reduced, since this would reduce the size of the spot.

By the same argument, it is not much use trying to measure the pit dimensions of a laser disk with an optical microscope. It is necessary to use an electron microscope to make measurements where conventional optics are diffraction-limiting.

12.19 The laser

The semiconductor laser is a relative of the light-emitting diode (LED). Both operate by raising the energy of electrons to move them from one valence band to another conduction band. Electrons which fall back to the valence band emit a quantum of energy as a photon whose frequency is proportional to the energy difference between the bands. The process is described by Planck's Law:

Energy difference $E = H \times f$

where H = Planck's Constant = 6.6262×10^{-34} joules/hertz.

For gallium arsenide, the energy difference is about 1.6 eV, where 1 eV is 1.6×10^{-19} joules. Using Planck's Law, the frequency of emission will be:

$$f = \frac{1.6 \times 1.6 \times 10^{-19}}{6.6262 \times 10^{-34}} \text{ Hz}$$

The wavelength will be c/f, where c = the velocity of light = 3×10^8 m/s.

$$\text{Wavelength} = \frac{3 \times 10^8 \times 6.6262 \times 10^{-34}}{2.56 \times 10^{-19}} \text{ m}$$

$$= 780 \text{ nanometres}$$

In the LED, electrons fall back to the valence band randomly, and the light produced is incoherent. In the laser, the ends of the semiconductor are optically flat mirrors, which produce an optically resonant cavity. One photon can bounce to and fro, exciting others in synchronism, to produce coherent light. This can result in a runaway condition, where all available energy is used up in one flash. In injection lasers, an equilibrium is reached between energy input and light output, allowing continuous operation. The equilibrium is delicate, and such devices are usually fed from a current source. To avoid runaway when temperature change disturbs the equilibrium, a photosensor is often fed back to the current source. Such lasers have a finite life, and become steadily less efficient. The feedback will maintain output, and it is possible to anticipate the failure of the laser by monitoring the drive voltage needed to give the correct output.

12.20 Polarization

In natural light, the electric-field component will be in many planes. Light is said to be polarized when the electric field direction is constrained. The wave can be considered as made up from two orthogonal components. When these are in phase, the polarization is said to be linear. When there is a phase shift between the components, the polarization is said to be elliptical, with a special case at 90 degrees called circular polarization. These types of polarization are contrasted in Fig.12.39.

To create polarized light, anisotropic materials are convenient. Polaroid material, invented by Edwin Land, is vinyl which is made anisotropic by stretching it while hot. This causes the long polymer molecules to line up along the axis of stretching. If the material is soaked in iodine, the molecules are rendered

Polarization

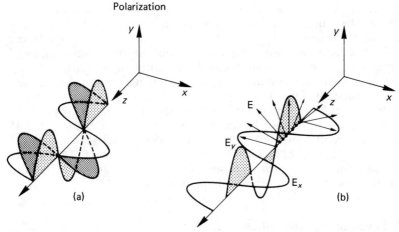

(a)   (b)

Figure 12.39 (a) Linear polarization: orthogonal components are in phase. (b) Circular polarization: orthogonal components are in phase quadrature.

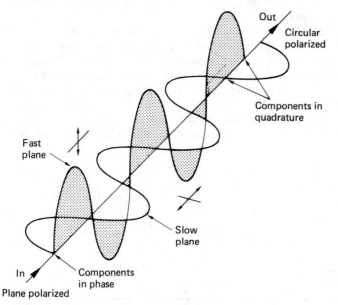

Figure 12.40 Different speed of light in different planes rotates the plane of polarization in a quarter-wave plate to give a circular-polarized output.

conductive, and short out any electric-field component along themselves. Electric fields at right angles are unaffected; thus the transmission plane is at right angles to the stretching axis.

Stretching plastics can also result in anisotropy of refractive index; this effect is known as birefringence. If a linearly polarized wavefront enters such a medium, the two orthogonal components propagate at different velocities, causing a relative phase difference proportional to the distance travelled. The plane of polarization of the light is rotated. Where the thickness of the material is such that a 90-degree phase change is caused, the device is known as a quarter-wave plate. The action of such a device is shown in Fig.12.40. If the plane of polarization of the incident light is at 45 degrees to the planes of greatest and least refractive index, the two orthogonal components of the light will be of equal magnitude, and this results in circular polarization. Similarly, circular-polarized light can be returned to the linear-polarized state by a further quarter-wave plate. Rotation of the plane of polarization is a useful method of separating incident and reflected light in a laser pickup. Using a quarter-wave plate, the plane of polarization of light leaving the pickup will have been turned 45 degrees, and on return it will be rotated a further 45 degrees, so that it is now at right angles to the plane of polarization of light from the source. The two can easily be separated by a polarizing prism, which acts as a transparent block to light in one plane, but as a prism to light in the other plane.

12.21 Thermomagneto-optics

A relatively recent and fascinating field is the use of magneto-optics,[2] also known more fully as thermomagneto-optics, for data storage where the medium can be rerecorded.

Writing in a DRAW device makes use of a thermomagnetic property possessed by all magnetic materials, which is that above a certain temperature, known as the Curie temperature, their coercive force becomes zero. This means that they become magnetically very soft, and take on the flux direction of any externally applied field. On cooling, this field orientation will be frozen in the material, and the coercivity will oppose attempts to change it. Although many materials possess this property, there are relatively few which have a suitably low Curie temperature. Compounds of terbium and gadolinium have been

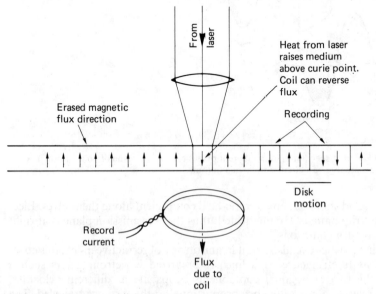

Figure 12.41 The thermomagneto-optical disk uses the heat from a laser to allow a magnetic field to record on the disk.

used, and one of the major problems to be overcome is that almost all suitable materials from a magnetic viewpoint corrode very quickly in air.

Fig.12.41 shows how a DRAW disk is written. If the disk is considered to be initially magnetized along its axis of rotation with the north pole upwards, it is rotated in a field of the opposite sense, produced by coils, which is weaker than the room-temperature coercivity of the medium. The coils will therefore have no effect. A laser beam is focused on the medium as it turns, and a pulse from the laser will momentarily heat a very small area of the medium past its Curie temperature, whereby it will take on a reversed flux due to the presence of the field coils. This reversed-flux direction will be retained indefinitely as the medium cools. The storage medium is thus clearly magnetic, but the writing mechanism is the heat produced by light from a laser; hence the term thermo-magneto-optics. The advantage of this writing mechanism is that there is no physical contact between the writing head and the medium. The distance can be several millimetres, some of which is taken up with a protective layer to prevent corrosion. In prototypes, this layer is glass, but it is expected that commercially available DRAW disks will be plastic.

The laser beam will supply a relatively high power for writing, since it is supplying heat energy. For reading, the laser power is reduced, such that it cannot heat the medium past the Curie temperature, and it is left on continuously. Readout depends on the so-called Kerr effect, also known as the Faraday effect, which is a rotation of the plane of polarization of light due to a magnetic field. The magnetic areas written on the disc will rotate the plane of polarization of incident polarized light to two different planes, and it is possible to detect the change in rotation by passing the reflected light through a further polarizing screen. The light whose plane of polarization is more nearly parallel with the transmission plane of the screen will pass more easily than the light whose plane of polarization is rotated away from the transmission plane, and a photosensor will detect an intensity change which re-creates the write waveform. The read-out signal is very small, since the Kerr effect is subtle. The plane of polarization is rotated only a fraction of a degree in typical devices, which makes the replay signal prone to noise. In order to change a recording, it must first be erased. The laser is set to the power level required for writing, but the coils adjacent to the disk are fed with a reversed current to that used in the write process. As the laser scans the old recording, the heat raises the track above its Curie temperature, and causes it to take on the direction of the applied field, which is that of the erased state. The coil current is then set back to the write direction, and the disk track can be rewritten with laser pulses as before. The erase process is necessary because the write process can only set the magnetic state. It cannot reset it.

Experimental recordable Compact Discs have been made based on this principle.[3,4]

12.22 Structure of laser drive

A typical laser disk drive resembles a magnetic drive in that it has a spindle drive mechanism to revolve the disk, and a positioner to give radial access across the disk surface. The positioner has to carry a collection of lasers, lenses, prisms, gratings and so on, and cannot be accelerated as fast as a magnetic-drive positioner. A penalty of the very small track pitch possible in laser disks, which gives the enormous storage capacity, is that very accurate track following is needed, and it takes some time to lock on to a track. For this reason tracks on laser disks are usually made as a continuous spiral, rather than the concentric rings of magnetic disks. In this way, a continuous data transfer involves no more than track following once the beginning of the file is located. The track-following and focus mechanisms of laser disks are treated in Chapter 13.

12.23 Defect handling

The protection of data recorded on disks differs considerably from the approach used on other media in digital audio. This has much to do with the intolerance of data processors to errors when compared with audio. In particular, it is not possible to interpolate to conceal errors in a computer program or a data file.

In the same way that magnetic tape is subject to dropouts, magnetic disks suffer from surface defects whose effect is to corrupt data. The shorter wavelengths employed as disk densities increase are affected more by a given size of defect. Attempting to make a perfect disk is subject to a law of diminishing returns, and eventually a state is reached where it becomes more cost-effective to invest in a defect-handling system.

There are four main methods of handling media defects in magnetic media, and further techniques needed in WORM laser disks, whose common goal is to make their presence transparent to the data. These methods vary in complexity and cost of implementation, and can often be combined in a particular system.

12.24 Bad-block files

In the construction of bad-block files, a brand new disk is tested by the operating system. Known patterns are written everywhere on the disk, and these are read back and verified. Following this the system gives the disk a volume name, and creates on it a directory structure which keeps records of the position and size of every file subsequently written. The physical disk address of every block which fails to verify is allocated to a file which has an entry in the disk directory. In this way, when genuine data files come to be written, the bad blocks appear to the system to be in use storing a fictitious file, and no attempt will be made to write there. Some disks have dedicated tracks where defect information can be

	1	1	1	1	1	1	1	1	1	1	1	0	0	0	0	0	A
A	0	0	0	0	0	0	1	1	1	1	1	1	1	1	1	1
	1	1	1	1	1	1	1	1	1	1	1	1	1	1	1	1
	1	1	1	1	1	1	1	0	0	0	0	1	0	0	0	0	B
	0	0	1	1	1	1	1	1	1	1	1	1	1	0	0	0
	0	0	0	0	0	0	0	0	e	tc.						

Figure 12.42 A disk-block-usage bit map in sixteen-bit memory for a cluster size of eleven blocks. Before writing on the disk, the system searches the bit map for contiguous free space equal to or larger than the cluster size. The first available space is the second cluster shown at A above, but the next space is unusable because the presence of a bad block B destroys the contiguity of the cluster. Thus one bad block causes the loss of a cluster.

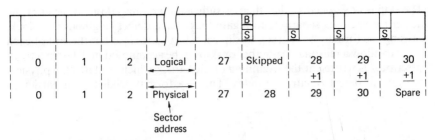

Figure 12.43 Skip sectoring. The bad block in this example has a physical sector address of 28. By setting the skip-sector flags in the header, this and subsequent logical blocks have one added to their sector addresses, and the spare block is brought into use.

written during manufacture or by subsequent verification programs, and these permit a speedy construction of the system bad-block file.

In association with the bad-block file, many drives allocate bits in each header to indicate that the associated block is bad. If a data transfer is attempted at such a block, the presence of these bits causes the function to be aborted. The bad-block file system gives very reliable protection against defects, but can result in a lot of disk space being wasted. Systems often use several disk blocks to store convenient units of data called clusters, which will all be written or read together. Fig.12.42 shows how a bit map is searched to find free space, and illustrates how the presence of one bad block can write off a whole cluster.

12.25 Sector skipping

In sector skipping, space is made at the end of every track for a spare data block, which is not normally accessible to the system. Where a track is found to contain a defect, the affected block becomes a skip sector. In this block, the regular defect flags will be set, but in addition, a bit known as the skip-sector flag is set in this and every subsequent block in the track. When the skip-sector flag is encountered, the effect is to add one to the desired sector address for the rest of the track, as in Fig.12.43. In this way the bad block is unused, and the track format following the bad block is effectively slid along by one block to bring into use the spare block at the end of the track. Using this approach, the presence of single bad blocks does not cause the loss of clusters, but requires slightly greater control complexity. If two bad blocks exist in a track, the second will be added to the bad-block file as usual.

12.26 Defect skipping

The two techniques described so far have treated the block as the smallest element. In practice, the effect of a typical defect is to corrupt only a few bytes. The principle of defect skipping is that media defects can be skipped over within the block so that a block containing a defect is made usable. The header of each block contains the location of the first defect in bytes away from the end of the header, and the number of bytes from the first defect to the second defect, and so on up to the maximum of four shown in the example of Fig.12.44. Each defect is overwritten with a fixed number of bytes of preamble code and a sync pattern.

The skip is positioned so that there is sufficient undamaged preamble after the defect for the data separator to regain lock. Each defect lengthens the block, causing the format of the track to slip round. A space is left at the end of each track to allow a reasonable number of skips to be accommodated. Often a track descriptor is written at the beginning of each track which contains the physical position of defects relative to index. The disk format needed for a particular

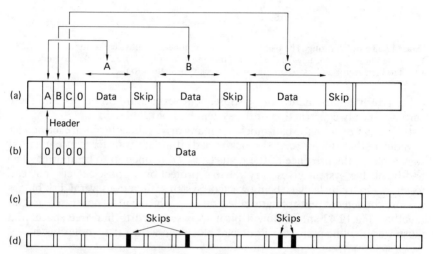

Figure 12.44 Defect skipping. (a) A block containing three defects. The header contains up to four parameters which specify how much data is to be written before each skip. In this example only three entries are needed. (b) An error-free block for comparison with (a); the presence of the skips lengthens the block. To allow for this lengthening, the track contains spare space at the end, as shown in (c), which is an error-free track. (d) A track containing the maximum of four skips, which have caused the spare space to be used up.

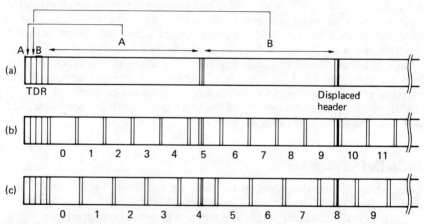

Figure 12.45 The purpose of the track descriptor record (TDR) is to keep a record of defects independent of disk format. The positions of the defects stored in the TDR (a) are used by the formatter to establish the positions relative to the format used. With the format (b), the first defect appears in sector 5, but the same defect would be in sector 4 for format (c). The second defect falls where a header would be written in (b) so the header is displaced for sector 10. The same defect falls in the data area of sector 8 in (c).

system can then be rapidly arrived at by reading the descriptor, and translating the physical defect locations into locations relative to the chosen sector format. Fig.12.45 shows how a soft-sectoring drive can have two different formats around the same defects using this principle.

In the case where there are too many defects in a track for the skipping to handle, the system bad-block file will be used. This is rarely necessary in practice, and the disk appears to be contiguous error-free logical and physical space. Defect skipping requires fast processing to deal with events in real time as the disk rotates. Bit-slice microsequencers are one approach, as a typical microprocessor would be too slow.

12.27 Revectoring

A refinement of sector skipping which permits the handling of more than one bad block per track without the loss of a cluster is revectoring. A bad block caused by a surface defect may only have a few defective bytes, so it is possible to record highly redundant information in the bad block. On a revectored disk, a bad block will contain in the data area repeated records pointing to the address where data displaced by the defect can be found. The spare block at the end of the track will be the first such place, and can be read within the same disk revolution, but out of sequence, which puts extra demands on the controller. In the less frequent case of more than one defect in a track, the second and subsequent bad blocks revector to spare blocks available in an area dedicated to that purpose. The principle is illustrated in Fig.12.46. In this case a seek will be necessary to locate the replacement block. The low probability of this means that access time is not significantly affected.

12.28 Error correction

The steps outlined above are the first line of defence against errors in disk drives, and serve to ensure that, by and large, the errors due to obvious surface defects are eliminated. There are other error mechanisms in action, such as noise and jitter, which can result in random errors, and it is necessary to protect disk data against these also. The error-correction mechanisms described in Chapter 7 will

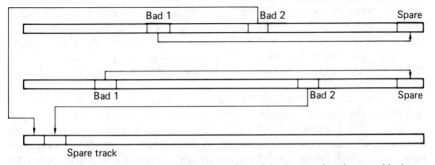

Figure 12.46 Revectoring. The first bad block in each track is revectored to the spare block at the end of the track. Unlike skip sectoring, subsequent good blocks are unaffected, and the replacement block is read out of sequence. The second bad block on any one track is revectored to one of a number of spare tracks kept on the disk for this purpose.

be employed. In general each data block is made into a codeword by the addition of redundancy at the end. The error-correcting code used in disks was, for a long time, Fire code, because it allowed correction with the minimum circuit complexity. It could however only correct one error burst per block, and it had a probability of miscorrection which was marginal for some applications. The advances in complex logic chips meant that the adoption of a Reed–Solomon Code was a logical step, since these have the ability to correct multiple error bursts. As the larger burst errors in disk drives are taken care of by verifying the medium, interleaving is not generally needed.

In some systems, the occurrence of errors is monitored to see if they are truly random, or if an error persistently occurs in the same physical block. If this is the case, and the error is small, and well within the correction power of the code, the block will continue in use. If, however, the error is larger than some threshold, the data will be read, corrected and rewritten elsewhere, and the block will then be added to the bad-block file so that it will not be used again.

12.29 Defect handling in WORM disks

In erasable optical disks, formatting is possible to map out defects in the same way as for magnetic disks, but in WORM disks, it is not possible to verify the medium because it can only be written once. The presence of a defect cannot be detected until an attempt has been made to write on the disk. The data written can then be read back and checked for error. If there is an error in the verification, the block concerned will be rewritten, usually in the next block along the track. This verification process slows down the recording operation, but some drives have a complex optical system which allows a low-powered laser to read the track in between pulses of the writing laser, and can verify the recording as it is being made.

12.30 Digital audio disk system

In order to use disk drives for the storage of audio samples, a system like the one shown in Fig.12.47 is needed. The control computer determines where and when samples will be stored and retrieved, and sends instructions to the disk controller which causes the drives to read or write, and transfers samples between them and the memory. The disk drive cannot supply samples at a constant rate, because of gaps between blocks, defective blocks and the need to move the heads from one track to another. In order to accept a steady audio sample stream for storage, and to return it in the same way on replay, a silo or FIFO memory is necessary.[4,6] The operation of these devices was described in Chapter 3.

The essentials of a disk controller are determined by the characteristics of drives and the functions needed, and so they do not vary greatly. For digital audio use, it is desirable for economic reasons to use a commercially available disk controller intended for computers. A disk controller consists of two main parts, that which issues control signals to and obtains status from the drives, and that which handles the data to be stored and retrieved. Both parts are synchronized by the control sequencer.

The execution of a function by a disk subsystem requires a complex series of steps, and decisions must be made between the steps to decide what the next will be. There is a parallel with computation, where the function is the equivalent of an instruction, and the sequencer steps needed are the equivalent of the micro-instructions needed to execute the instruction. The major failing in this analogy is that the sequence in a disk drive must be accurately synchronized to the rotation of the disk.

Most disk controllers use direct memory access, which means that they have

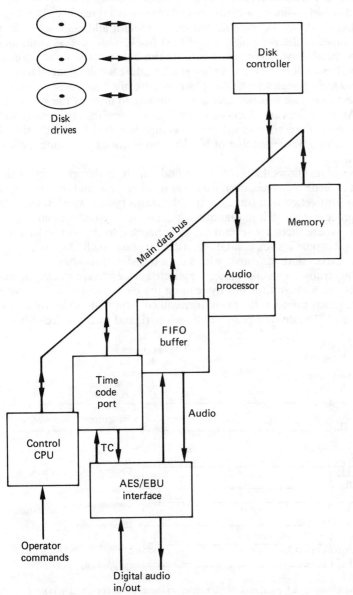

Figure 12.47 The main parts of a digital audio disk system. Memory and FIFO allow continuous audio despite the movement of disk heads between blocks.

the ability to transfer disk data in and out of the associated memory without the assistance of the processor. In order to cause an audio-file transfer, the disk controller must be told the physical disk address (cylinder, sector, track), the physical memory address where the audio file begins, the size of the file and the direction of transfer (read or write). The controller will then position the disk heads, address the memory, and transfer the samples. One disk transfer may consist of many contiguous disk blocks, and the controller will automatically increment the disk-address registers as each block is completed. As the disk turns, the sector address increases until the end of the track is reached. The track or head address will then be incremented and the sector address reset so that transfer continues at the beginning of the next track. This process continues until all of the heads have been used in turn. In this case both the head address and sector address will be reset, and the cylinder address will be incremented, which causes a seek. A seek which takes place because of a data transfer is called an implied seek, because it is not necessary formally to instruct the system to perform it. As disk drives are block-structured devices, and the error correction is codeword-based, the controller will always complete a block even if the size of the file is less than a whole number of blocks. This is done by packing the last block with zeros.

The status system allows the controller to find out about the operation of the drive, both as a feedback mechanism for the control process, and to handle any errors. Upon completion of a function, it is the status system which interrupts the control processor to tell it that another function can be undertaken.

In a system where there are several drives connected to the controller via a common bus, it is possible for nondata-transfer functions such as seeks to take place in some drives simultaneously with a data transfer in another.

Before a data transfer can take place, the selected drive must physically access the desired block, and confirm this by reading the block header. Following a seek to the required cylinder, the positioner will confirm that the heads are on track and settled. The desired head will be selected, and then a search for the

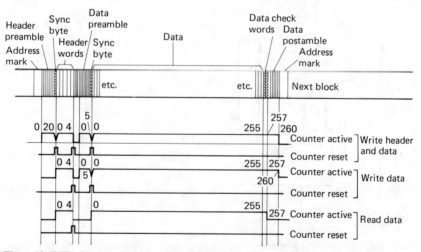

Figure 12.48 The format of a typical disk block related to the count process which is used to establish where in the block the head is at any time. During a read the count is derived from the actual data read, but during a write, the count is derived from the write clock.

correct sector begins. This is done by comparing the desired sector with the current sector register, which is typically incremented by dividing down servo-surface pulses. When the two counts are equal, the head is about to enter the desired block. Fig.12.48 shows the structure of a typical disk track. In between blocks are placed address marks, which are areas without transitions which the read circuits can detect. Following detection of the address mark, the sequencer is roughly synchronized to begin handling the block. As the block is entered, the data separator locks to the preamble, and in due course the sync pattern will be found. This sets to zero a counter which divides the data-bit rate by eight, allowing the serial recording to be correctly assembled into bytes, and also allowing the sequencer to count the position of the head through the block in order to perform all the necessary steps at the right time.

The first header word is usually the cylinder address, and this is compared with the contents of the desired cylinder register. The second header word will contain the sector and track address of the block, and these will also be compared with the desired addresses. There may also be bad-block flags and/or defect-skipping information. At the end of the header is a CRCC which will be used to ensure that the header was read correctly. Fig.12.49 shows a flowchart

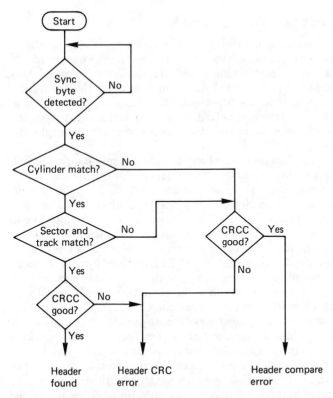

Figure 12.49 The vital process of position confirmation is carried out in accordance with the above flowchart. The appropriate words from the header are compared in turn with the contents of the disk-address registers in the subsystem. Only if the correct header has been found and read properly will the data transfer take place.

of the position verification, after which a data transfer can proceed. The header reading is completely automatic. The only time it is necessary formally to command a header to be read is when checking that a disk has been formatted correctly.

During the read of a data block, the sequencer is employed again. The sync pattern at the beginning of the data is detected as before, following which the actual data arrive. These bits are converted to byte or sample parallel, and sent to the memory by DMA. When the sequencer has counted the last data-byte off the track, the redundancy for the error-correction system will be following.

During a write function, the header-check function will also take place as it is perhaps even more important not to write in the wrong place on a disk. Once the header has been checked and found to be correct, the write process for the associated data block can begin. The preambles, sync pattern, data block, redundancy and postamble have all to be written contiguously. This is taken care of by the sequencer, which is obtaining timing information from the servo surface to lock the block structure to the angular position of the disk. This should be contrasted with the read function, where the timing comes directly from the data.

12.31 Sampling rate and playing time

Now that the basic hardware of a disk system has been described, the way in which it can be used for digital audio recording and editing can be treated.

The bit rate of a digital audio system is such that high-density recording is mandatory for long playing time. A disk drive can never reach the density of a rotary-head tape machine because it is optimized for fast random access, and so it would be unwise to expect too much of a disk-based system in terms of playing time. In practice, the editing power of a disk-based system far outweighs this restriction.

One high-quality digital audio channel requires about a megabit per second, which means that a megabyte of storage (the usual unit for disk measurement) offers about eight seconds of monophonic audio. A typical mid-sized Winchester disk drive offers a capacity of 300 megabytes, which translates into about 40 min of monophonic audio. There is, however, no compulsion to devote the whole disk to one audio channel, and so two channels could be recorded for 20 min, or four channels for 10 min and so on. For broadcast applications, where an audio bandwidth of 15 kHz is imposed by the FM stereo transmission standard, the alternative sampling rate of 32 kHz can be used, which allows about an hour of monophonic digital audio from 300 megabytes. Where only speech is required, an even lower rate can be employed.[7] Clearly several disk drives are necessary in most musical post-production applications if stereo or multitrack working is contemplated. In practice, multitrack working with disks is better than these calculations would indicate, because on a typical multitrack master tape, all tracks are not recorded continuously. Some tracks will contain only short recordings in a much longer overall session. A tape machine has no option but to leave these tracks unrecorded either side of the wanted recording, whereas a disk system will only store the actual wanted samples. The playing time in a real application will thus be greater than expected.

12.32 Editing in a disk system

When audio samples are fed into a disk-based system, from an AES/EBU interface or from a converter, they will be placed in a memory, from which the disk controller will read them by DMA. The continuous-input sample stream will be split up into disk blocks for disk storage. The AES/EBU interface carries a timecode in the additional bits in each sample period, and this timecode can be used to assemble a table which contains a conversion from real time to the physical disk address of the corresponding audio files. As an alternative, an interface may be supplied which allows conventional SMPTE or EBU timecode to be input. Wherever possible, the disk controller will allocate incoming audio samples to contiguous disk addresses, since this eases the conversion from timecode to physical address.[8] This is not, however, always possible in the presence of defective blocks, or if the disk has become chequerboarded from repeated recording and erasing.

The table of disk addresses will also be made into a disk file and stored in a different area of the disk from the audio files. Several recordings may be fed into the system in this way, or one long recording which contains perhaps much superfluous sound such as the inevitable 'ums and ers' and hesitations.

If it is desired to play back one or more of the recordings, then it is only necessary to specify the starting timecode and the filename, and the system will look up the physical address of the first and subsequent sample blocks in the desired recording, and begin to read them from disk and write them into the memory. The disk transfers must by definition be intermittent, because there are headers between contiguous sectors. Once all the sectors on a particular cylinder have been read, it will be necessary to seek to the next cylinder, which will cause a further interruption to the reading sequence. If a bad block is encountered, the sequence will be interrupted until it has passed. The instantaneous data rate of a typical drive is roughly ten times higher than the sampling rate, so that there is time for the positioner to move whilst the audio output is supplied from the FIFO memory. In replay, the drive controller attempts to keep the FIFO as full as possible by issuing a read command as soon as one block space appears in the FIFO. This allows the maximum time for a seek to take place before reading must resume. Fig.12.50 shows the action of the FIFO during reading. Whilst recording, the drive controller attempts to keep the FIFO as empty as possible

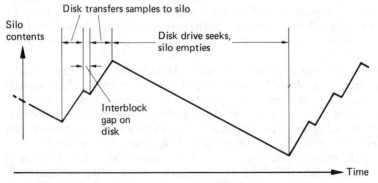

Figure 12.50 During an audio replay sequence, silo is constantly emptied to provide samples, and is refilled in blocks by the drive.

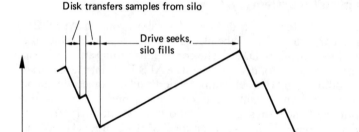

Figure 12.51 During audio recording, the input samples constantly fill the silo, and the drive attempts to keep it empty by reading from it.

by issuing write commands as soon as a block of data is present, as in Fig.12.51. In this way the amount of time available to seek is maximized in the presence of a continuous audio sample input. In order to edit the raw audio files fed into the system, it is necessary to listen to them in order to locate the edit points. This can be done by playback of the whole file at normal speed if time is no object, but this neglects the random access capability of a disk-based system. If an event list has been made at the time of the recordings, it can be used to access any part of them within a few tens of milliseconds, which is the time taken for the heads to traverse the entire disk surface. This is far superior to the slow spooling speed of tape recorders.

If an event list is not available, it will be necesary to run through the recording at a raised speed in order rapidly to locate the area of the desired edit. Clearly if the disk can access fast enough, this can be achieved simply by raising the sampling-rate clock, so that the timecode advances more rapidly, and new data blocks are requested from the disk more rapidly. If a constant sampling-rate output is needed, then rate reduction via a digital filter will be necessary.[9,10] Some systems have sophisticated signal processors which allow pitch changing, so that files can be played at nonstandard speed but with normal pitch or vice versa.[11] An alternative approach to processing on playback only is to record spooling files[12] at the same time as an audio file is made. A spooling file block contains a sampling-rate-reduced version of several contiguous audio blocks. When played at standard sampling rate, it will sound as if it is playing faster by the factor of rate reduction employed. The spooling files can be accessed less often for a given playback speed, or higher speed is possible within a given access-rate constraint.

Once the rough area of the edit has been located by spooling, the audio files from that area can be played to locate the edit point more accurately. It is often not sufficiently accurate to mark edit points on the fly by listening to the sound at normal speed. In order to simulate the rock-and-roll action of edit-point location in an analog tape recorder, audio blocks in the area of the edit point can be transferred to memory and accessed at variable speed and in either direction by deriving the memory addresses from a hand-turned rotor. A description of this process was included in Chapter 8 where rotary-head editing was discussed.

Using one or other of these methods, an edit list can be made which contains an in point, an out point and an audio filename for each of the segments of audio

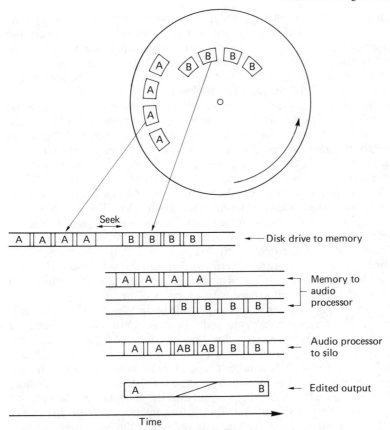

Figure 12.52 In order to edit together two audio files, they are brought to memory sequentially. The audio processor accesses file pages from both together, and performs a crossfade between them. The silo produces the final output at constant steady-sampling rate.

which need to be assembled to make the final work, along with a crossfade period and a gain parameter. This edit list will also be stored on the disk. When a preview of the edited work is required, the edit list is used to determine what files will be necessary and when, and this information drives the disk controller.

Fig.12.52 shows the events during an edit between two files. The edit list causes the relevant audio blocks from the first file to be transferred from disk to memory, and these will be read by the signal processor to produce the preview output. As the edit point approaches, the disk controller will also place blocks from the incoming file into the memory. It can do this because the rapid data-transfer rate of the drive allows blocks to be transferred to memory much faster than real time, leaving time for the positioner to seek from one file to another. In the memory there will be simultaneously the end of the outgoing recording and the beginning of the incoming recording. The signal processor will use the fine edit-point parameters to work out the relationship between the actual edit points and the audio-block boundaries. This will allow it to address the memory to obtain samples with the correct timing. Before the edit point, only samples from the outgoing recording are accessed, but as the crossfade begins, samples from the incoming recording are also accessed, multiplied by the gain parameter and then mixed with samples from the outgoing recording according to the crossfade period required. The output of the signal processor becomes the edited preview material, which can be checked for the required subjective effect. If necessary the in or out points can be trimmed, or the crossfade period changed, simply by modifying the edit-list file. The preview can be repeated as often as needed, until the desired effect is obtained.

Once the editing is finished, it will be necessary to transfer the edited material to some external storage, since the Winchester drives in the editor have fixed media. It is only necessary to connect the AES/EBU output of the signal processor to a digital tape recorder, and then the edit list is executed once more. The edit sequence will be performed again, exactly as it was during the last preview, and the results will be recorded on tape. It is important to realize that at no time during the edit process were the original audio files modified in any way. The editing was done solely by reading the audio files. The power of this approach is that if an edit list is created wrongly, the original recording is not damaged, and the problem can be put right simply by correcting the edit list. The advantage of a disk-based system for such work is that location of edit points, previews and reviews are all performed almost instantaneously, because of the random access of the disk. This can reduce the time taken to edit a program to a quarter of that needed with a tape machine.[13]

During an edit, the disk drive has to provide audio files from two different places on the disk simultaneously, and so it has to work much harder than for a simple playback. If there are many close-spaced edits, the drive may be hard-pressed to keep ahead of real time, especially if there are long crossfades, because during a crossfade the source data rate is twice as great as during replay. A large buffer memory helps this situation because the drive can fill the memory with files before the edit actually begins, and thus the instantaneous sample rate can be met by the memory's emptying during disk-intensive periods. In practice crossfades measured in seconds can be achieved in a disk-based system, a figure which is not matched by tape systems.

Disk formats which handle defects dynamically, such as defect skipping, will also be superior to bad-block files when throughput is important. Some drives rotate the sector addressing from one cylinder to the next so that the drive does not lose a revolution when it moves to the next cylinder. Disk-editor performance is usually specified in terms of peak editing activity which can be achieved, but with a recovery period between edits. If an unusually severe editing task is necessary where the drive just cannot access files fast enough, it will be necessary to rearrange the files on the disk surface so that files which will be needed at the same time are on nearby cylinders.[8] An alternative is to spread the material between two drives so that overlapped seeks are possible.

12.33 Broadcast applications

Editing is not the only application of disk-based systems. In a radio broadcast environment it is possible to contain all of the commercials and jingles in daily use on a disk system.[14] They can be played instantly by specifying the file name of the wanted piece. Adding extra output modules means that several audio files can be played back simultaneously if a station broadcasts on more than one channel. A disk-based machine of this kind can compete with the traditional analog-cartridge spot player. If a commercial break contains several different spots, these can be chosen at short notice just by producing a new edit list.

A multitrack recording can be stored on a single disk and, for replay, the drive will access the files for each track faster than real time so that they all become present in the memory simultaneously. It is not, however, compulsory to play back the tracks in their original time relationship. For the purpose of synchronization,[15] or other effects, the tracks can be played with any time relationship desired, a feature not possible with multitrack tape drives.

References

1. BOUWHUIS, G. et al. Principles of Optical Disc Systems. Bristol: Adam Hilger (1985)

2. OHR, S., Magneto-optics combines erasability and high-density storage. Electronic Design, 11 Jul. 1985, 93-100

3. SCHOUHAMER IMMINK, K.A. and BRAAT, J.J.M., Experiments towards an erasable Compact Disc digital audio system. Presented at 73rd Audio Engineering Society Convention (Eindhoven, 1983), preprint 1970(E2)

4. KURAHASHI, A., et al., Development of an erasable magneto-optical digital audio recorder. Presented at 79th Audio Engineering Society Convention (New York, 1985), preprint 2296(A-1)

5. WEISSER, A. and KOMLY, A., Description of an audio editing system using computer magnetic hard disk. Presented at 80th Audio Engineering Society Convention (Montreux, 1986), preprint 2317(A5)

6. INGBRETSEN, R.B. and STOCKHAM, T.G., Random access editing of digital audio. J. Audio Eng. Soc.,32, 114-122 (1982)

7. MACINTYRE, C., The Sirius-100 digital audio memory. Int. Broadcast Eng., 18, 51-52 (1987 Mar.)

8. MCNALLY, G.W., GASKELL, P.S. and STIRLING, A.J., Digital audio editing. BBC Research Dept Report, RD 1985/10

9. MCNALLY, G.W., Varispeed replay of digital audio with constant output sampling rate. Presented at 76th Audio Engineering Society Convention (New York, 1984), preprint 2137(A-9)

10. GASKELL, P.S., A hybrid approach to the variable speed replay of audio. Presented at 77th Audio Engineering Society Convention (Hamburg, 1985), preprint 2202(B-1)

11. GRAY, E., The Synclavier digital audio system: recent developments in audio post production. Int. Broadcast Eng., 18, 55 (1987 Mar.)

12. MCNALLY, G.W., Fast edit-point location and cueing in disk-based digital audio editing. Presented at 78th Audio Engineering Society Convention (Anaheim, 1985), preprint 2232(D-10)

13. TODOROKI, S., et al., New PCM editing system and configuration of total professional digital audio system in near future. Presented at 80th Audio Engineering Society Convention (Montreux, 1986), preprint 2319(A8)

14. ITOH, T., OHTA, T. and SOHMA, Y., Real time transmission system of commercial messages in radio broadcasting. Presented at 67th Audio Engineering Society Convention (New York, 1980), preprint 1682(H-1)

15. MCNALLY, G.W., BLOOM, P.J. and ROSE, N.J., A digital signal processing system for automatic dialogue post-synchronisation. Presented at 82nd Audio Engineering Society Convention (London, 1987), preprint 2476(K-6)

Chapter 13

The Compact Disc

The Compact Disc is of particular importance to the subject of digital audio, since it is simultaneously an everyday consumer product available in large numbers, and a technically advanced device. CD results from the marriage of many disciplines, including laser optics, servomechanisms, error correction and both analog and digital circuitry in VLSI form. Since this is a book about technology, no attempt will be made to chart the history of CD, which resulted from a cooperation between Philips and Sony, and this chapter simply describes the final product.

The equipment necessary to produce the master recordings used to make Compact Discs has been discussed in Chapter 8, to which the reader is referred. The principles of optics which are assumed in this chapter are outlined in Chapter 12.

13.1 Advantages of CD

Fig.13.1 shows that the information layer of CD is an optically flat mirror upon which microscopic bumps are raised. A thin coating of aluminium renders the layer reflective. When a small spot of light is focused on the information layer, the presence of the bumps affects the way in which the light is reflected back, and variations in the reflected light are detected to read the disc. Fig.13.1 also illustrates the very small dimensions involved. For comparison, some sixty CD tracks can be accommodated in the groove pitch of a vinyl LP. These dimensions demand the utmost cleanliness in manufacture.

The optical readout of CD is a non-contact process, so there is no wear mechanism. The optical system will focus on the information layer which is far below the disc surface, so that debris and surface scratches will be well out of focus, and their effect will be minimized. Combined with a powerful error-correction strategy, this results in a medium which is highly resistant to handling. The use of a disc containing data in the form of mechanical dimension changes allows rapid mass-production using pressing and, as with vinyl disks, access to the desired band is rapid. CD access is enhanced by the use of subcodes buried in the data stream which permit the beginning of each band to be located precisely. The small size of the disc allows production of car dashboard and portable players.

The CD process, from cutting, through pressing and reading, produces no

constant. This constant linear velocity (CLV) results in rather longer playing time than would be obtained with a constant speed of rotation. Owing to the minute dimensions of the track structure, the cutter has to be constructed to extremely high accuracy. Air bearings are used in the spindle and the laser head, and the whole machine is resiliently supported to prevent vibrations from the building from affecting the track pattern.

The blank is then developed, which hardens the resist in unexposed areas. Etching removes the exposed areas to create pits in the surface of the resist. The process is halted when a monitoring laser detects the correct pit depth. The surface is given a coating of silver by evaporation to render it electrically conductive. In a similar fashion to the production of vinyl records, a father is made by electroplating with nickel, which is itself electroplated to produce a mother. From the mother, a number of sons are produced which will become the actual dies used to stamp discs. Once the stampers are checked, the valuable blank can be stripped of resist and used again. Stamping transfers the pit structure to the transparent disc material. Since every step in the process creates a mirror image, the fact that there are an even number of processes – father, mother, son, disc – means that the disc will resemble the blank, and will have pits on its surface. A thin layer of aluminium is applied to the reflecting layer, followed by a protective coat of lacquer. The disc is centred by optically optimizing track runout,

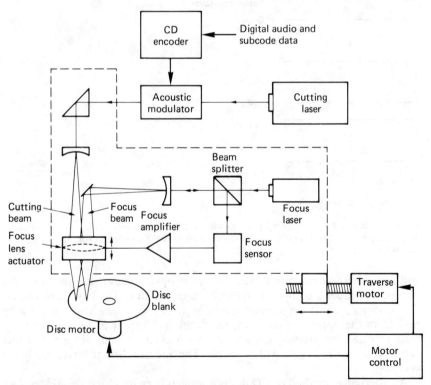

Figure 13.3 CD cutter. The focus subsystem controls the spot size of the main cutting laser on the photosensitive blank. Disk and traverse motors are coordinated to give constant track pitch and velocity. Note that the power of the focus laser is insufficient to expose the photoresist.

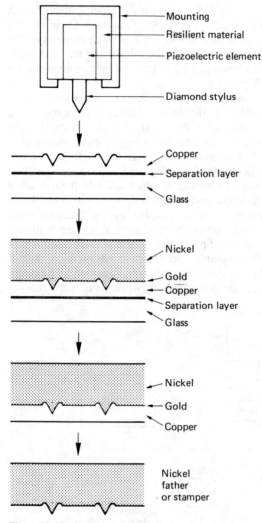

Figure 13.4 In direct metal mastering, a piezoelectric element enbosses a copper layer, which is plated over with nickel and subsequently etched away to make a father, or for direct use as a stamper for short runs.

and the centre hole can be punched and the periphery trimmed, although some stampers produce a completely trimmed, punched disc. The label is placed on the lacquer side, and can be printed on directly, or stuck on. As the disc will be read from the opposite side to the label, the pits appear as bumps from the readout side. The pressing quality can be checked optically since any defect which would corrupt data will be visible. The disc can then be boxed ready for shipping.

An alternative method of CD duplication has been developed by Teldec.[3] As Fig.13.4 shows, the recording process is performed by a diamond stylus which embosses the pit structure into a thin layer of copper. The stylus is driven by a piezoelectric element using motional feedback. The element is supported in an

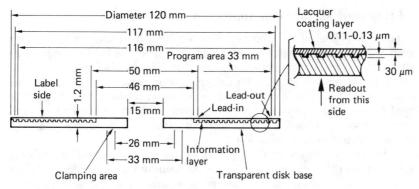

Figure 13.5 Mechanical specification of CD. Between diameters of 46 and 117 mm is a spiral track 5.7 km long.

elastic medium so that its own centre of gravity tends to remain stationary. Application of drive voltage makes the element contract, lifting the stylus completely off the copper between pits. Since the channel code of CD is DC-free, the stylus spends exactly half its time in contact with the copper, and therefore the embossing force is exactly twice the static force applied. The pits produced are vee-shaped, rather than the flat-bottomed type produced by the photoresist method, but this is not of much consequence, since the diffraction- limited optics of the player cannot determine any more about the pit than its presence or absence. It is claimed that this form of pit is easier to mould.

A glass master disc is prepared as before, and following a thin separation layer, a coating of copper about 300 nm thick is sputtered on. The recording is made on this copper layer, which is then gold-coated, and nickel-plated to about 0.25 mm thick. The resultant metal sandwich can then be peeled off the glass master, which can be re-used. The recording is completely buried in the sandwich, and can be stored or transported in this form.

In order to make a stamper, the copper is etched away with ferric chloride to reveal the gold-coated nickel. This can then be used as an electroplating father, as before. For short production runs, the nickel layer can be used as a stamper directly, but it is recommended that the gold layer be replaced by rhodium for this application.

Fig.13.5 shows the mechanical specification of CD. Within an overall diameter of 120 mm the program area occupies a 33 mm-wide band between the diameters of 50 and 116 mm. Lead-in and lead-out areas increase the width of this band to 35.5 mm. As the track pitch is a constant 1.6 μm, there will be

$$\frac{35.6 \times 1000}{1.6} = 22\,188$$

tracks crossing a radius of the disc. As the track is a continuous spiral, the track length will be given by the above figure multiplied by the average circumference.

$$\text{Length} = 2 \times \pi \times \frac{58.5 + 23}{2} \times 22\,188 = 5.7\,\text{km}$$

These figures give a good impression of the precision involved in CD manufacture.

13.3 Rejecting surface contamination

A fundamental goal of the Compact Disc was that it should not require any special working environment or handling skill. The bandwidth required by digital audio is such that high-density recording is mandatory if reasonable playing time is to be obtained, and this implies short wavelengths. Using a laser focused on the disc from a distance allows short wavelength recordings to be played back without physical contact, whereas magnetic recording requires intimate contact and implies a wear mechanism, the need for periodic cleaning, and susceptibility to contamination.

The information layer of CD is read through the thickness of the disc. Fig.13.6 shows that this approach causes the readout beam to enter and leave the disc surface through the largest possible area. The actual dimensions involved are shown in the figure. Despite the minute spot size of about 1.2 μm diameter, light enters and leaves through a 0.7 mm-diameter circle. As a result, surface debris has to be three orders of magnitude larger than the readout spot before the beam is obscured. The size of the entry circle is a function of the refractive index of the disc material, the numerical aperture of the objective lens and the thickness of the disc. The method of readout through the disc thickness tolerates surface scratches very well, and in extreme cases of damage, a scratch can often be successfully removed with metal polish. By way of contrast, the label side is actually more vulnerable than the readout side, since the lacquer coating is only 30 μm thick. For this reason, writing on the label side is not

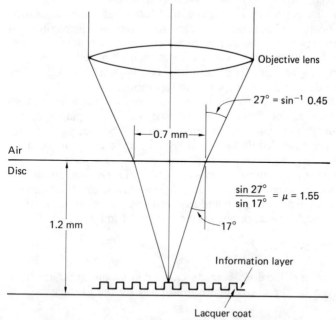

Figure 13.6 The objective lens of a CD pickup has a numerical aperture (NA) of 0.45; thus the outermost rays will be inclined at approximately 27° to the normal. Refraction at the air/disk interface changes this to approximately 17° within the disk. Thus light focused to a spot on the information layer has entered the disk through a 0.7 mm diameter circle, giving good resistance to surface contamination.

recommended. Pressure from a ballpoint pen could distort the information layer, and solvents from marker pens have been known to penetrate the lacquer and cause corruption. The common party-piece of writing on the readout surface with a felt pen to show off the error-correction system is quite harmless, since the disc base material is impervious to most solvents.

The base material is in fact a polycarbonate plastic produced by Bayer under the trade name of Makrolon. It has excellent mechanical and optical stability over a wide temperature range, and lends itself to precision moulding and metallization. It is often used for automotive indicator clusters for the same reasons. An alternative material is polymethyl methacrylate (PMMA), one of the first optical plastics, known by such trade names as Perspex and Plexiglas, and widely used for illuminated signs and aircraft canopies. Polycarbonate is preferred by some manufacturers since it is less hygroscopic than PMMA. The differential change in dimensions of the lacquer coat and the base material can cause warping in a hygroscopic material.

13.4 Spot size and track dimensions

Fig.13.1 showed the basic principle of the readout process. The height of the bumps in the mirror surface has to be one-quarter of the wavelength of the light used, so that light reflected from a bump has travelled half a wavelength less than light reflected from the mirror surface, and will be out of phase with it. This results in destructive interference in light returning to the source, and the light will escape, in any direction where constructive interference allows, as a diffraction pattern primarily along a disc radius. Effectively a bump scatters light, reducing the amount of reflected light. Clearly the light source must be monochromatic. The wavelength in the medium is determined by the refractive index.

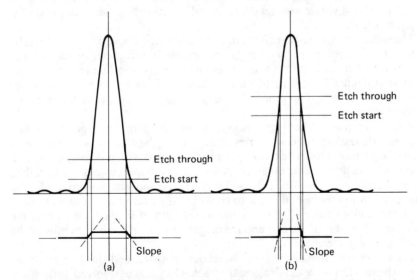

Figure 13.7 The two levels of exposure sensitivity of the resist determine the size and edge slope of the bumps in the CD. (a) Large exposure results in large bump with gentle slope; (b) less exposure results in smaller bump with steeper sloped sides.

The specified light source has a wavelength of 780 nm in air, and inside the medium of the disc the refractive index of 1.55 causes this to become 500 nm. The bump height is one-quarter of this figure at 0.11–0.13 μm. The dimensions of the track structure are closely comparable with those of the Laservision videodisc developed by Philips, on whose optical technology CD is based.[4] Both are working at a recording density which is diffraction-limited, which is to say that the dimensions on the disc are as small as is permitted by the wave nature of light.

It is not possible to focus light to a point even with a lens which is free from aberrations. When this is attempted the result is an Airy disc, whose size is a function of the wavelength used and the NA of the lens.

When the master is cut, the effective spot size is about 0.4 μm. The effective spot size is determined by balancing the power of the laser against the sensitivity of the resist. In Fig.13.7 the resist will be seen to have two sensitivity thresholds of note, one where etching will just begin, and one where etching will go right through to the glass blank. Increasing the exposure produces pits with gradually sloping edges, which are optically inferior, but which allow the disc to release from the mould easily. Exposure is controlled to achieve the desired compromise.

In order to achieve the small spot size needed in the cutter, the resist sensitivity is set to about the half-power level of the Airy intensity function, and a helium cadmium or argon ion laser with the shorter wavelength of 400–500 nm is used, with a working numerical aperture of 0.9. The optimum size for the playback spot is rather larger than that of the cutting spot since, for destructive interference to cause complete cancellation in the direction of the pickup, the energy falling on the top of the bump should be the same as that falling on the mirror surface beside it. This simplistic condition is never obtained in practice, and the presence of a long bump typically reduces the reflected power by about 75 %. A larger player spot also eases the task of track following, and permits the use of a low cost visible wavelength laser and a smaller NA, which improves the depth of focus.

The specified wavelength of 780 nm and the numerical aperture of 0.45 results in an Airy function where the half-power level is at a diameter of about 1 μm. The first dark ring will be at about 1.9 μm diameter. As the illumination follows an intensity function, it is really meaningless to talk about spot size unless the relative power level is specified. The analagy is quoting frequency response without dB limits.

Allowable crosstalk between tracks then determines the track pitch. The first ring outside the central disc carries some 7 % of the total power, and limits crosstalk performance. The track spacing is such that with a slightly defocused beam and a slight tracking error, crosstalk due to adjacent tracks is acceptable. Since aberrations in the objective will increase the spot size and crosstalk, the CD specification requires the lens to be within the Maréchal criterion. Clearly the numerical aperture of the lens, the wavelength of the laser, the refractive index and thickness of the disc and the height and size of the bumps must all be simultaneously specified.

The cutter spot size determines the reader spot size, and this in turn determines the shortest wavelength along the track which can be resolved. If the track velocity is specified, the wavelength limit becomes a frequency limit. The optical

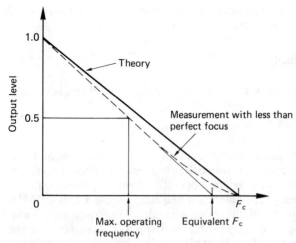

Figure 13.8 Frequency response of laser pickup. Maximum operating frequency is about half of cut-off frequency F_c.

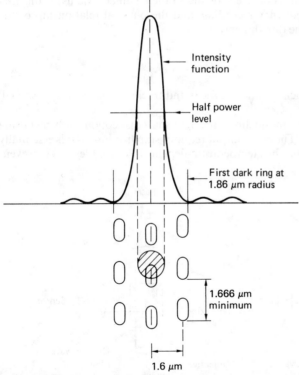

Figure 13.9 The structure of a maximum-frequency recording is shown here, related to the intensity function of an objective of 0.45 NA with 780 micrometre light. Note that track spacing puts adjacent tracks in the dark rings, reducing crosstalk. Note also that as the spot has an intensity function it is meaningless to specify the spot diameter without some reference such as an intensity level.

cutoff frequency is that frequency where the amplitude of modulation replayed from the disc has fallen to zero, and it is given by

$$F_c = \frac{2NA}{\text{wavelength}} \times \text{velocity}$$

The minimum linear velocity of CD is 1.2 m/s, giving a cutoff frequency of

$$F_c = \frac{2 \times 0.45 \times 1.2}{780 \times 10^{-9}} = 1.38 \text{ MHz}$$

Fig.13.8 shows that the frequency response falls linearly to the cutoff, and that actual measurements are only a little worse than the theory predicts. Clearly, to obtain any noise immunity, the maximum operating frequency must be rather less than the cutoff frequency. The maximum frequency used in CD is 720 kHz, which represents an absolute minimum wavelength of 1.666 μm, or a bump length of 0.833 μm, for the lowest permissible track speed of 1.2 m/s used on the full-length 75 min-playing discs. One-hour-playing discs have a minimum bump length of 0.972 μm at a track velocity of 1.4 m/s. The maximum frequency is the same in both cases. This maximum frequency should not be confused with the bit rate of CD since this is different owing to the channel code used. Fig.13.9 shows a maximum-frequency recording, and the physical relationship of the intensity function to the disc dimensions.

13.5 Focus systems

The structure of CD pickups and the focus and tracking systems necessary will now be dealt with.

The requirement for a monochromatic light source is economically met using a semiconductor laser. The laser output requires stabilization, as it is essentially a regenerative device and has temperature-dependent output level. To prevent

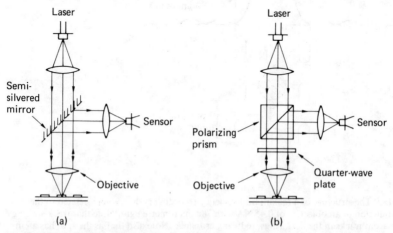

Figure 13.10 (a) Reflected light from the disc is directed to the sensor by a semisilvered mirror. (b) A combination of polarizing prism and quarter-wave plate separate incident and reflected light.

thermal runaway, a feedback photodiode adjacent to the laser controls a current source in the laser power supply.

In order to extract a signal, the pickup must be capable of separating the reflected light from the incident light. Fig.13.10 shows two systems. In (a) a semisilvered mirror reflects some of the returning light into the photosensor. This is not very efficient, as some of the light is lost by transmission straight on. In the example at (b) separation is by the plane of polarization. A polarizing prism passes light from the laser which is polarized in a plane at right angles to the plane of the page. This light is passed through a quarter-wave plate, which rotates the plane of polarization through 45 degrees. Following reflection from the disc, the light passes again through the quarter-wave plate and is rotated a further 45 degrees, such that it is now polarized in the plane of the page. The polarizing prism reflects this light into the sensor.

Since the residual stresses set up in moulding plastic tend to align the long-chain polymer molecules, plastics can have different refractive indices in different directions, a phenomenon known as birefringence. It is possible accidentally to rotate the plane of polarization of light in birefringent plastics, and there were initial reservations as to the feasibility of this approach for playing moulded CDs. The necessary quality of disc moulding was achieved by using relatively high temperatures where the material flows more easily. This has meant that birefringence is negligible, and the polarizing beam-splitter is widely used.

Since the channel frequency response (nothing to do with the audio response) and the amount of crosstalk are both a function of the spot size, care must be taken to keep the beam focused on the information layer. Disc warp and thickness irregularities will cause focal-plane movement beyond the depth of focus of the optical system, and a focus servo system will be needed. The depth of field is related to the numerical aperture, which is defined, and the accuracy of the servo must be sufficient to keep the focal plane within that depth, which is typically $\pm 1 \, \mu m$.

The focus servo moves a lens along the optical axis in order to keep the spot in focus. Since dynamic focus-changes are largely due to warps, the focus system must have a frequency response in excess of the rotational speed. A moving-coil actuator is often used owing to the small moving mass which this permits.

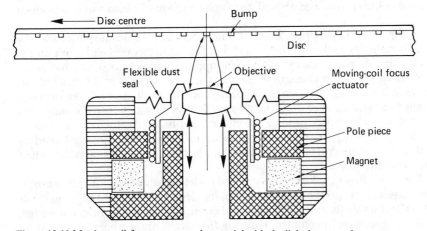

Figure 13.11 Moving-coil-focus servo can be coaxial with the light beam as shown.

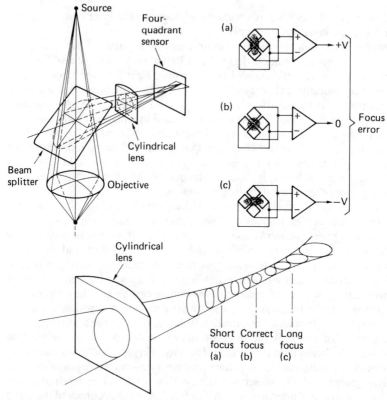

Figure 13.12 The cylindrical-lens focus method produces an elliptical spot on the sensor whose aspect ratio is detected by a four-quadrant sensor to produce a focus error.

Fig.13.11 shows that a cylindrical magnet assembly almost identical to that of a loudspeaker can be used, coaxial with the light beam.

A focus-error system is necessary to drive the lens. There are a number of ways in which this can be derived, the most common of which will be described here.

In Fig.13.12 a cylindrical lens is installed between the beam splitter and the photosensor. The effect of this lens is that the beam has no focal point on the sensor. In one plane, the cylindrical lens appears parallel-sided, and has negligible effect on the focal length of the main system, whereas in the other plane, the lens shortens the focal length. The image will be an ellipse whose aspect ratio changes as a function of the state of focus. Between the two foci, the image will be circular. The aspect ratio of the ellipse, and hence the focus error, can be found by dividing the sensor into quadrants. When these are connected as shown, the focus-error signal is generated. The data readout signal is the sum of the quadrant outputs.

Fig.13.13 shows the knife edge-method of determining focus. A split sensor is also required. At (a) the focal point is coincident with the knife edge, so it has little effect on the beam. At (b) the focal point is to the right of the knife edge, and rising rays are interrupted, reducing the output of the upper sensor. At (c)

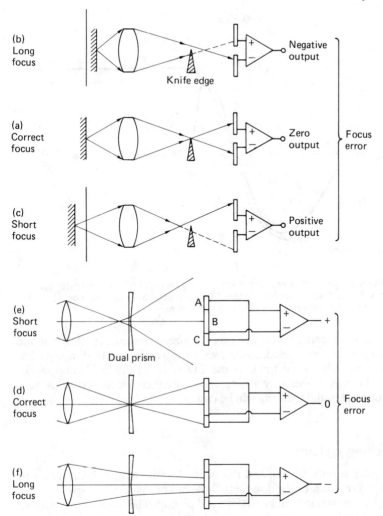

Figure 13.13 (a)–(c) Knife-edge focus method requires only two sensors, but is critically dependent on knife-edge position. (d)–(f) Twin-prism method requires three sensors (A, B, C), where focus error is $(A + C) - B$. Prism alignment reduces sensitivity without causing focus offset.

the focal point is to the left of the knife edge, and descending rays are interrupted, reducing the output of the lower sensor. The focus error is derived by comparing the outputs of the two halves of the sensor. A drawback of the knife-edge system is that the lateral position of the knife edge is critical, and adjustment is necessary. To overcome this problem, the knife edge can be replaced by a pair of prisms, as shown in Fig.13.13(d)–(f). Mechanical tolerances then only affect the sensitivity, without causing a focus offset.

The cylindrical lens method is compared with the knife-edge/prism method in Fig.13.14, which shows that the cylindrical lens method has a much smaller capture range. A focus-search mechanism will be required, which moves the

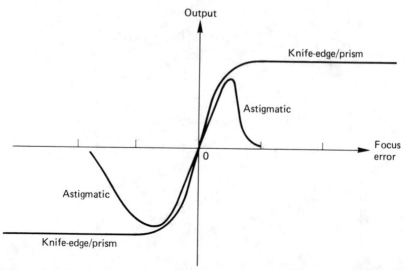

Figure 13.14 Comparison of captive range of knife-edge/prism method and astigmatic (cylindrical lens) system. Knife edge may have range of 1 mm, whereas astigmatic may only have a range of 40 micrometres, requiring a focus-search mechanism.

focus servo over its entire travel, looking for a zero crossing. At this time the feedback loop will be completed, and the sensor will remain on the linear part of its characteristic. The spiral track of the CD starts at the inside and works outwards. This was deliberately arranged because there is less vertical runout near the hub, and initial focusing will be easier.

13.6 Tracking systems

The track pitch is only 1.6 μm, and this is much smaller than the accuracy to which the player chuck or the disc centre hole can be made; on a typical player, runout will swing several tracks past a fixed pickup. The non-contact readout means that there is no inherent mechanical guidance of the pickup: there is no groove and no stylus. In addition, a warped disc will not present its surface at 90 degrees to the beam, but will constantly change the angle of incidence during two whole cycles per revolution. Owing to the change of refractive index at the disc surface, the tilt will change the apparent position of the track to the pickup, and Fig.13.15 shows that this makes it appear wavy. Warp also results in coma of the readout spot. The disc format specifies a maximum warp amplitude to keep these effects under control. Finally, vibrations induced in the player from outside, particularly in portable and automotive players, will tend to disturb tracking. A track-following servo is necessary to keep the spot centralized on the track in the presence of these difficulties. There are several ways in which a tracking error can be derived.

In the three-spot method, two additional light beams are focused on the disc track, one offset to each side of the track centre-line. Fig.13.16 shows that, as one side spot moves away from the track into the mirror area, there is less destructive interference and more reflection. This causes the average amplitude

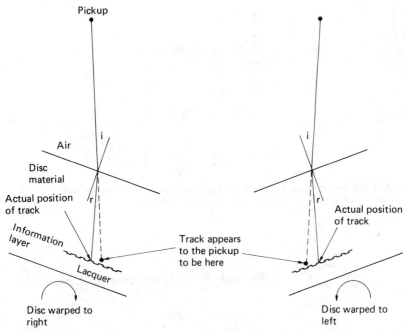

Figure 13.15 Owing to refraction, the angle of incidence (*i*) is greater than the angle of refraction (*r*). Disc warp causes the apparent position of the track (dotted line) to move, requiring the tracking servo to correct.

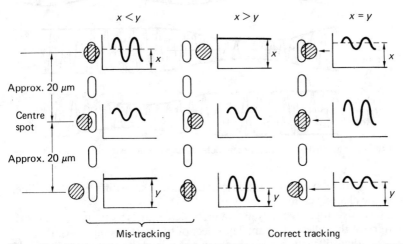

Figure 13.16 Three-spot method of producing tracking error compares average level of side-spot signals. Side spots are produced by a diffraction grating and require their own sensors.

of the side spots to change differentially with tracking error. The laser head contains a diffraction grating which produces the side spots, and two extra photosensors onto which the reflections of the side spots will fall. The side spots feed a differential amplifier, which has a low-pass filter to reject the channel-code information and retain the average brightness difference. Some players use a delay line in one of the side-spot signals whose period is equal to the time taken

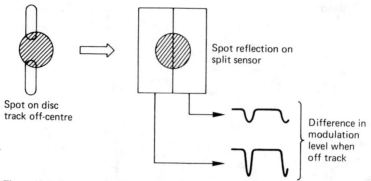

Figure 13.17 Split-sensor method of producing tracking error focuses image of spot onto sensor. One side of spot will have more modulation when off track.

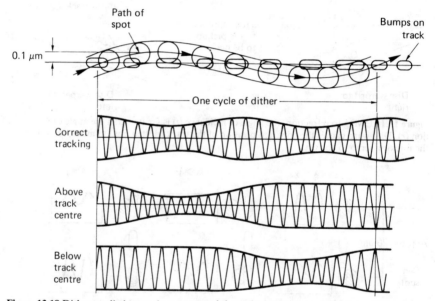

Figure 13.18 Dither applied to readout spot modulates the readout envelope. A tracking error can be derived.

for the disc to travel between the side spots. This helps the differential amplifier to cancel the channel code.

The alternative approach to tracking-error detection is to analyse the diffraction pattern of the reflected beam. The effect of the spot's being off-centre is to rotate the radial diffraction pattern about an axis along the track. Fig.13.17 shows that, if a split sensor is used, one half will see greater modulation than the other when off track. Such a system may be prone to develop an offset due either to drift or to contamination of the optics, although the capture range is large. A further tracking mechanism is often added to obviate the need for periodic adjustment. Fig.13.18 shows this dither-based system, which resembles in many respects the track-following method used in C-format professional videotape recorders. A sinusoidal drive is fed to the tracking servo, causing a radial oscillation of spot position of about $\pm$ 0.1 μm. This results in modulation of the envelope of the readout signal, which can be synchronously detected to obtain the sense of the error. The dither can be produced by vibrating a mirror in the light path, which enables a high frequency to be used, or by oscillating the whole pickup at a lower frequency.

13.7 Typical pickups

It is interesting to compare different designs of laser pickup. Fig.13.19 shows a Philips laser head.[5] The dual-prism focus method is used, which combines the output of two split sensors to produce a focus error. The focus amplifier drives

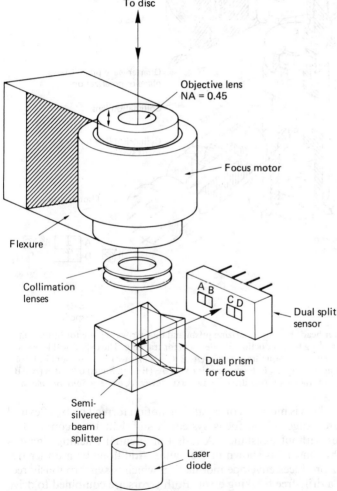

Figure 13.19 Philips laser head showing semisilvered prism for beam splitting. Focus error is derived from dual-prism method using split sensors. Focus error $(A+D)-(B+C)$ is used to drive focus motor which moves objective lens on parallel action flexure. Radial differential tracking error is derived from split sensor $(A+B)-(C+D)$. Tracking error drives entire pickup on radial arm driven by moving coil. Signal output is $(A+B+C+D)$. System includes 600 Hz dither for tracking. (Courtesy *Philips Technical Review*)

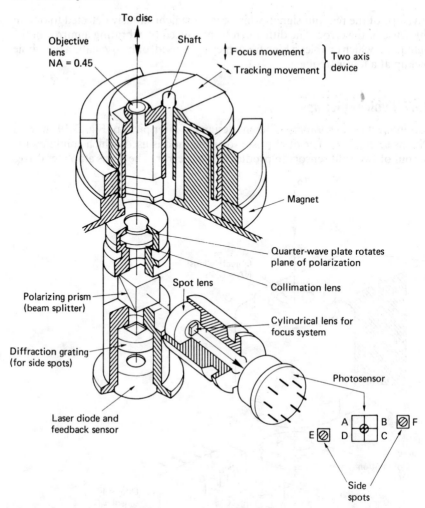

Figure 13.20 Sony laser head showing polarizing prism and quarter-wave plate for beam splitting, and diffraction grating for production of side spots for tracking. The cylindrical lens system is used for focus, with a four-quadrant sensor (A, B, C, D) and two extra sensors E, F for the side spots. Tracking error is E − F; focus error is (A + C) − (B + D). Signal output is (A + B + C + D). The focus and tracking errors drive the two-axis device. (Courtesy *Sony Broadcast*)

the objective lens which is mounted on a parallel motion formed by two flexural arms. The capture range of the focus system is sufficient to accommodate normal tolerances without assistance. A radial differential tracking signal is extracted from the sensors as shown in the figure. Additionally, a dither frequency of 600 Hz produces envelope modulation which is synchronously rectified to produce a drift-free tracking error. Both errors are combined to drive the tracking system. As only a single spot is used, the pickup is relatively insensitive to angular errors, and a rotary positioner can be used, driven by a moving coil. The assembly is statically balanced to give good resistance to lateral shock.

Fig.13.20 shows a Sony laser head used in consumer players. The cylindrical-lens focus method is used, requiring a four-quadrant sensor. Since this method

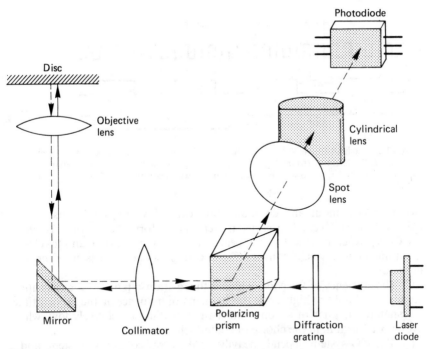

Figure 13.21 For automotive and portable players, the pickup can be made more compact by incorporating a mirror, which allows most of the elements to be parallel to the disc instead of at right angles.

has a small capture range, a focus-search mechanism is necessary. When a disc is loaded, the objective lens is ramped up and down looking for a zero crossing in the focus error. The three-spot method is used for tracking. The necessary diffraction grating can be seen adjacent to the laser diode. Tracking error is derived from side-spot sensors (E, F). Since the side-spot system is sensitive to angular error, a parallel-tracking laser head traversing a disc radius is essential. A cost-effective linear motion is obtained by using a rack-and-pinion drive for slow, coarse movements, and a laterally moving lens in the light path for fine rapid movements. The same lens will be moved up and down for focus by the so-called two-axis device, which is a dual-moving coil mechanism. In some players this device is not statically balanced, making the unit sensitive to shock, but this was overcome on later heads designed for portable players. Fig.13.21 shows a later Sony design having a prism which reduces the height of the pickup above the disc.

13.8 Channel code

The channel code used for the digital recording on the Compact Disc will now be described. The reader is also referred to Chapter 6 for a general treatment of channel-coding theory.

The CD channel code has to operate under a number of constraints.[6] These are:

(1) The DC content of the code should be as small as possible for several

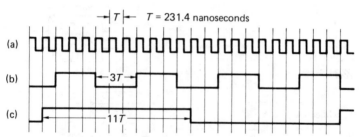

Figure 13.22 The limit frequencies of CD channel code: (a) the master clock frequency of 4.3218 MHz, $T = 231.4$ ns; (b) the highest recorded frequency with transitions $3T$ apart, frequency 720 kHz; (c) the lowest recorded frequency with transitions 11 T apart, frequency 196 kHz.

reasons. Disc runout and contamination cause low-frequency noise in the replay signal, which can be rejected if there is no information at these frequencies. Code DC content will also appear as noise in the tracking, and to a lesser extent the focus servos. Finally a DC-free code simplifies the design of the data separator.

(2) The efficiency of the code, which is the relationship of bit rate to channel bandwidth, should be high, since this has a major influence on the playing time. Fortunately the jitter of a non-contact rigid medium is relatively low, which gives more freedom in the choice of coding scheme.

(3) The CD system depends heavily on the error-correction system, and a group code using symbols of the same size as the error-correction mechanism will be at an advantage as error propagation can be minimized.

(4) The bit rate of CD is low compared to that of computer disks and digital video recorders; thus no simplification of the code is required to achieve the necessary operating speed. A complex encoding system is a relatively small penalty, because few encoders are needed. The complexity of the decoder is of greater significance since this more directly affects the cost of the player.

It has been shown that there is a cut-off frequency due to the numerical aperture of the optics and the track velocity. All recorded frequencies must be below this by a sensible margin to allow a noise margin in the presence of coma due to disc warps and focus errors. This determines the minimum time period between transitions. It is fundamental to the CD channel code that the time between successive transitions (bump edges) is an integer multiple of one-third the minimum period. The basic time period T is one cycle of 4.3218 MHz or 231.4 ns. Fig.13.22 shows that the minimum wavelength allowable is $6T$ and that this corresponds to 720 kHz. The minimum period between transitions is $3T$, but the period can also be $4T$, $5T$ etc. In order to retain a reasonable clock content for immunity to jitter, the maximum period between transitions (the run length limit) is $11T$, corresponding to a frequency of 196 kHz. There are thus only nine different time periods used in all CD recording. The basic clock period is one-third the minimum transition length, and so the resolution of the medium has apparently been increased by a factor of three. This gain cannot be fully realized because some data patterns cannot be recorded if the $3T$ spacing rule is to be obeyed. Data to be recorded must be converted to a form which accepts this restriction.

Symbols of $14T$ period are assembled. If all combinations of a fourteen-bit symbol are examined, it will be found that there are some 267 where the run

Data

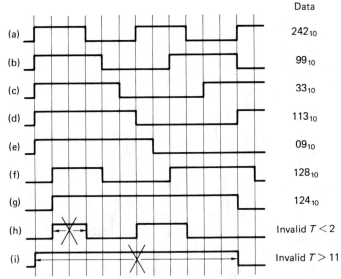

(a) 242_{10}

(b) 99_{10}

(c) 33_{10}

(d) 113_{10}

(e) 09_{10}

(f) 128_{10}

(g) 124_{10}

(h)   Invalid $T < 2$

(i)   Invalid $T > 11$

Figure 13.23 (a–g) part of the codebook for EFM code showing examples of various run lengths from $3T$ to $11T$. (h, i) Invalid patterns which violate the run-length limits.

length is neither less than $3T$ nor more than $11T$. From these, 256 patterns are selected to describe uniquely any combination of eight data bits. Some of the remaining valid patterns are used for synchronizing. Fig.13.23 shows some valid and invalid symbols for comparison. This conversion process gave rise to the name of eight-to-fourteen modulation (EFM) for the CD channel code. To prevent violation of the rules by certain symbols following others, and to control the DC content of the code, three packing bits are placed between each symbol. Each eight bit data symbol thus requires $17T$ to be recorded. This coding is 8/17 efficient, and when multiplied by the resolution improvement of three, yields the actual density ratio of EFM:

$$\frac{3 \times 8}{17} \times 100\% = 141\%$$

Although the highest frequency in the channel code is 720 kHz, or 1.44 million transitions per second, the bit rate is given by:

$$4.3218 \times \frac{8}{17} \text{ Mbits/s} = 2 \text{ Mbits/s}$$

The choice of packing bits for DC control[7] is determined as follows. The digital sum value (DSV) of the channel patterns is derived as in Fig.13.24. If a channel bit is true during a T period, one is added to the DSV. If it is false, one is subtracted. Clearly if the channel code is to be DC-free, the DSV must average to zero. In Fig.13.24(b) two successive $14T$ symbols are shown, each of which has positive DSV. By adding a transition in the packing bits, the second symbol is inverted, and the overall DSV is reduced. This inversion has no effect on the data, as the only parameter of interest is the period between transitions.

The interference-readout process causes reflected light to increase and decrease about some average, which superimposes a DC level on the readout signal, in addition to a component at the rotation frequency of the disc and its

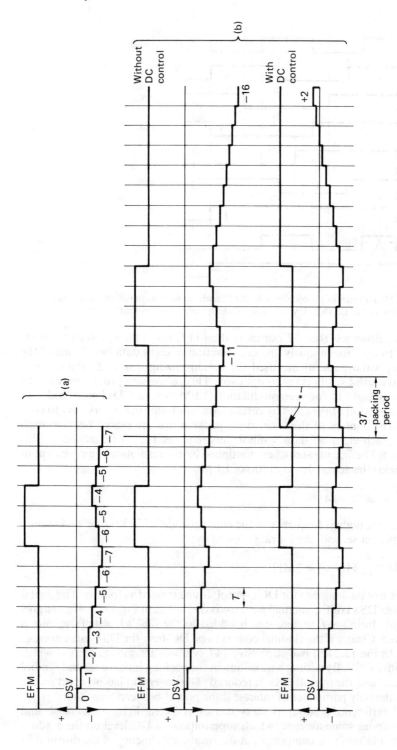

Figure 13.24 (a) Digital sum value example calculated from EFM waveform. (b) Two successive 14T symbols without DC control (upper) give DSV of −16. Additional transition (*) results in DSC of +2, anticipating negative content of next symbol.

harmonics. Since the code is DC-free a simple coupling capacitor can be used to remove these effects.

If a typical readout signal is observed on an oscilloscope which triggers on a positive zero crossing, the next zero crossing could be $3T,4T$ etc. later as shown in Fig.13.25. The oscilloscope superimposes all of these waveforms to give the characteristic eye pattern of CD. The $3T$ minimum and the $1T$ increments can be seen. Note that the amplitude of the shorter-period signals is smaller because of the linear fall in response to the cutoff frequency.

The quality of the optics and the focus servo can be assessed by comparing the $3T$ amplitude with maximum amplitude.

The first step in data separation is to locate the crossings in the signal and produce a binary waveform. This is done by comparing the input waveform with a reference voltage, a process referred to as slicing. Since the code is DC-free, the reference voltage, or slicing level, can be obtained by integrating the binary output (Fig.13.26). This re-creates the binary channel code. Every readout transition is used to synchronize a phase-locked loop running with period T. This clock is used to count the number of T periods between transitions, and thus recreate the $14T$ symbols. These are converted back to data bytes using a ROM or gate array. The truth table of the EFM conversion is computer optimised to minimize the complexity of the decoder.

As with most channel codes, EFM requires a preamble to synchronize the read circuitry to the $14T$ symbol boundaries. This unique preamble consists of three transitions separated by $11T$.

Each data block or frame shown in Fig.13.27 consists of 33 symbols $17T$ each following the preamble, making a total of $588T$ or $136\,\mu s$. Each symbol represents eight data bits. The first symbol in the block is used for subcode, and the remaining 32 bytes represent 24 audio sample bytes and 8 bytes of redundancy for the error-correction system. The subcode byte forms part of a subcode block which is built up over 98 successive data frames, and this will be described in detail later in this chapter.

Fig.13.28 reveals the timing relationships of the CD format. The sampling rate of 44.1 kHz with sixteen-bit words in left and right channels results in an audio data rate of 176.4 kb/s (k = 1000 here, not 1024). Since there are 24 audio bytes in a data frame, the frame rate will be:

$$\frac{176.4}{24}\,\text{kHz} = 7.35\,\text{kHz}$$

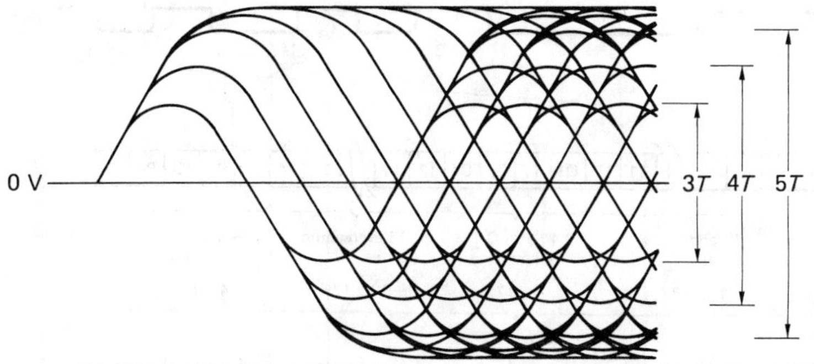

Figure 13.25 The characteristic eye pattern of EFM observed by oscilloscope. Note the reduction in amplitude of the higher-frequency components. The only information of interest is the time when the signal crosses zero.

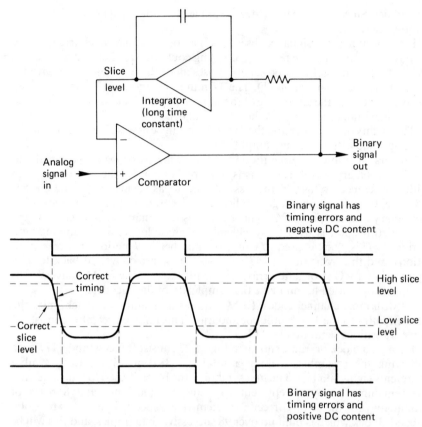

Figure 13.26 Self-slicing a DC-free channel code. Since the channel code signal from the disc is band-limited, it has finite rise times, and slicing at the wrong level (as shown here) results in timing errors, which cause the data separator to be less reliable. As the channel code is DC-free, the binary signal when correctly sliced should integrate to zero. An incorrect slice level gives the binary output a DC content and, as shown here, this can be fed back to modify the slice level automatically.

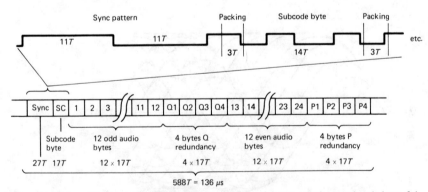

Figure 13.27 One CD data block begins with a unique sync pattern, and one subcode byte, followed by 24 audio bytes and eight redundancy bytes. Note that each byte requires $14T$ in EFM, with $3T$ packing between symbols, making $17T$.

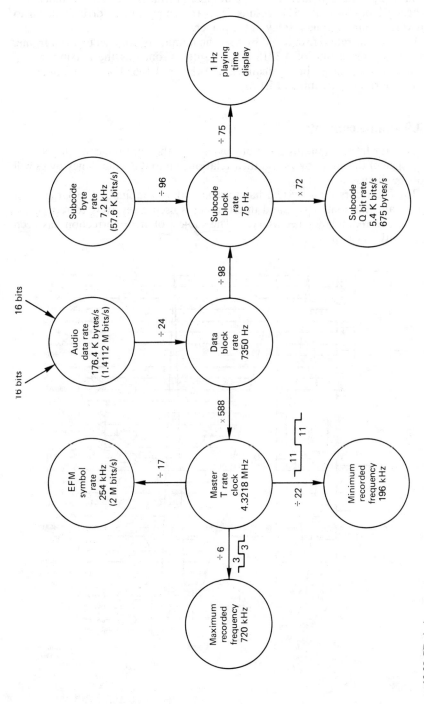

Figure 13.28 CD timing structure.

If this frame rate is divided by 98, the number of frames in a subcode block, the subcode block rate of 75 Hz results. This frequency can be divided down to provide a running-time display in the player.

If the frame rate is multiplied by 588, the number of channel bits in a frame, the master clock-rate of 4.3218 MHz results. From this the maximum and minimum frequencies in the channel, 720 kHz and 196 kHz, can be obtained using the run length limits of EFM.

13.9 Frame contents

Each data frame contains 24 audio bytes, but they are noncontiguous. The sequence of the audio bytes and their relationship to the redundancy bytes will now be discussed.

The error-correction system has to deal with a combination of large burst errors and random errors, and interleaving is used extensively to reduce the amount of redundancy necessary.[7,8] The subject of error correction has been dealt with in Chapter 7.

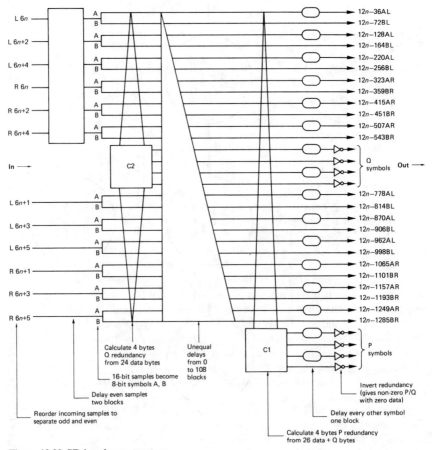

Figure 13.29 CD interleave structure.

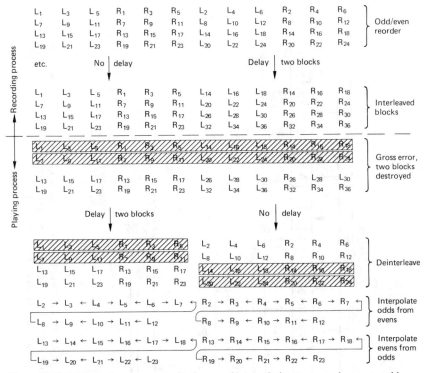

Figure 13.30 Odd/even interleave permits the use of interpolation to conceal uncorrectable errors.

There are a number of interleaves used in CD, each of which has a specific purpose. The full interleave structure is shown in Fig.13.29. The first stage of interleave is to introduce a delay between odd and even samples. The effect is that uncorrectable errors cause odd samples and even samples to be destroyed at different times, so that interpolation can be used to conceal the errors, with a reduction in audio bandwidth and a risk of aliasing. The odd/even interleave is performed first in the encoder, since concealment is the last function in the decoder. Fig.13.30 shows that an odd/even delay of two blocks permits interpolation in the case where two uncorrectable blocks leave the error-correction system.

Left and right samples from the same instant form a sample set. As the samples are sixteen bits, each sample set consists of four bytes, AL, BL, AR, BR. Six sample sets form a 24-byte parallel word, and the C2 encoder produces four bytes of redundancy Q. By placing the Q symbols in the centre of the block, the odd/even distance is increased, permitting interpolation over the largest possible error burst. The 28 bytes are now subjected to differing delays, which are integer multiples of four blocks. This produces a convolutional interleave, where one C2 codeword is stored in 28 different blocks, spread over a distance of 109 blocks.

At one instant, the C2 encoder will be presented with 28 bytes which have come from 28 different codewords. The C1 encoder produces a further four bytes of redundancy P. Thus the C1 and C2 codewords are produced by crossing an array in two directions. This is known as crossinterleaving.

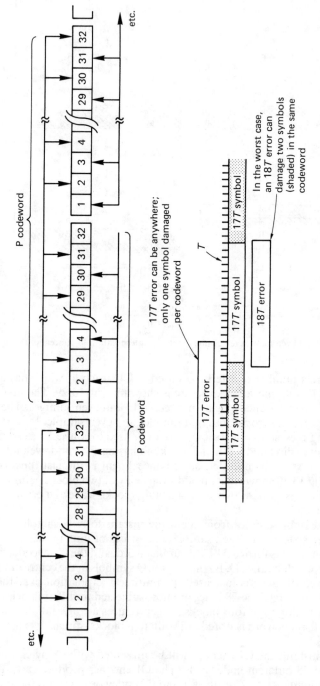

Figure 13.31 The final interleave of the CD format spreads P codewords over two blocks. Thus any small random error can only destroy one symbol in one codeword, even if two adjacent symbols in one block are destroyed. Since the P code is optimized for single-symbol error correction, random errors will always be corrected by the C1 process, maximizing the burst-correcting power of the C2 process after deinterleave.

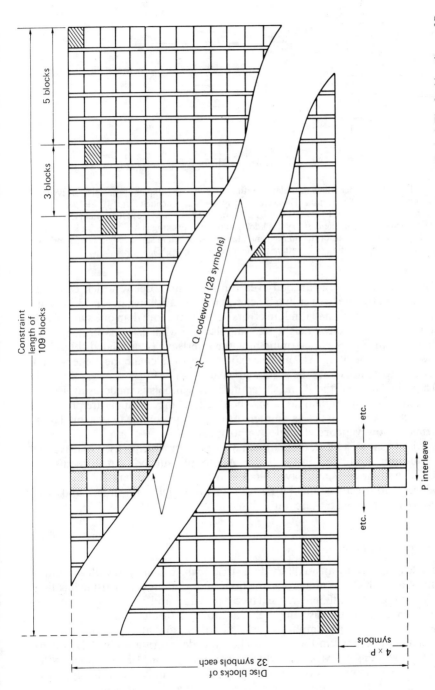

Figure 13.32 Owing to crossinterleave, the 28 symbols from the Quencode process (C2) are spread over 109 blocks, shown hatched. The final interleave of P code words (as in Figure 13.31) is shown stippled. Result of the latter is that Q code word has 5, 3, 5, 3 spacing rather than 4, 4.

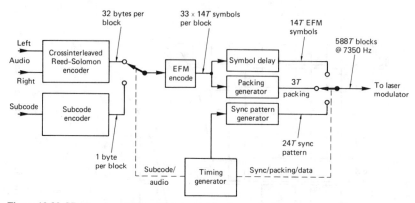

Figure 13.33 CD encoder which modulates cutting laser. Audio samples are crossinterleaved and combined with subcode data. These eight-bit symbols are encoded into 14*T* EFM symbols. The packing generator prevents run-length violations and provides DC content control via 3*T* packing symbols. The EFM symbol delay allows the packing generator to look ahead. Two of the many functions of the timing generator are to switch in subcode bytes (left) and to assemble blocks by selecting sync patterns, data and packing (right).

The final interleave is an odd/even output symbol delay, which causes P codewords to be spread over two blocks on the disc as shown in Fig.13.31. This mechanism prevents small random errors destroying more than one symbol in a P codeword. The choice of eight-bit symbols in EFM assists this strategy. The expressions in Fig.13.29 determine how the interleave is calculated. Fig.13.32 shows an example of the use of these expressions to calculate the contents of a block and to demonstrate the crossinterleave.

The calculation of the P and Q redundancy symbols is made using Reed–Solomon cyclic polynomial division. The P redundancy symbols are primarily for detecting errors, to act as pointers or error flags for the Q system. The P system can however correct single-symbol errors.

Fig.13.33 shows a block diagram of a CD encoder which is used to drive the acousto-optic modulator in the cutter. Audio and subcode data streams are supplied, and the crossinterleaved block structure is created. The EFM encoder produces a fourteen-channel-bit pattern for every eight-bit symbol, and sync patterns and merging bits are multiplexed in.

13.10 CD subcode

Subcode is essentially an auxiliary data stream which is merged with the audio samples, and which has numerous functions. One of these is to assist in locating the beginning of the different musical pieces on a disc, and providing a catalogue of their location on the disc and their durations. A further vital function is to convey the status of pre-emphasis in the recording, so that de-emphasis can be automatically selected in the player. The subcode information in CD is conveyed by including an extra byte, which corresponds to one EFM symbol, in the main frame structure. As the format of the disc is standardized, the player is designed to route the subcode byte in the frame to a different destination from that of the audio sample bytes. The separation is based upon the physical position of the subcode byte in the frame. The player uses the sync pattern at the

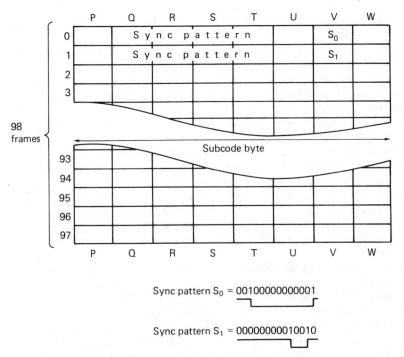

Sync pattern S_0 = 00100000000001

Sync pattern S_1 = 00000000010010

Figure 13.34 Each CD frame contains one subcode byte. After 98 frames, the structure above will repeat. Each subcode byte contains one bit from eight 96-bit words following the two synchronizing patterns. These patterns cannot be expressed as a byte, because they are 14-bit EFM patterns additional to those which describe the 256 combinations of eight data bits.

beginning of the frame to reset a byte count so that it always knows how far through the frame it is. As a result, subcode bytes will be separated from the data stream at frame frequency.

It has been shown that there are 98 bytes in a subcode block, since this results in a subcode block rate of exactly 75 Hz. This frequency can be used to run the playing-time display.

It is necessary for the player to know when a new subcode block is beginning. This is the function of the subcode sync patterns which are placed in the subcode byte position of two successive frames. There are more than 256 legal fourteen-bit patterns in EFM, and two of these additional legal channel-bit patterns are used for subcode-block synchronizing. The EFM decoder will be able to distinguish them from the patterns used to represent subcode-data bytes. For this reason it is impossible to describe the subcode sync patterns by a byte, and they have to be specified as fourteen channel bits.

Fig.13.34 shows the subcode sync patterns, and illustrates the contents of the subcode block.

After the subcode sync patterns, there are 96 bytes in the block. The block is arranged as eight 96-bit words, labelled P Q R S T U V and W. The choice of labelling is unfortunate because the letters P and Q have already been used to describe the redundancy in the error-correction system. The subcode P and Q data have absolutely nothing to do with that. The eight words are quite independent, and each subcode byte in a disc frame contains one bit from each word.

This is a form of interleaving which reduces the damage done to a particular word by an error.

The P data word is used to denote the start of specific bands (having the same meaning as the bands on a vinyl disk) in the sound recorded. The entire word is recorded as data ones during the start-flag period. It can be used even where there is no audible pause in the music, since the start point is defined as where the P data become zeros again. The CD standard calls for a minimum of two seconds of start flag to be recorded. This seems wasteful, but it allows a very simple player to recognize the beginning of a piece easily by skipping tracks. The fact that every bit is a one means that it is not necessary to wait for subcode block sync to be found before finding pause status on the disc track. The two second-flag period means that the status will be seen a few tracks in advance of the actual start-point, helping to prevent the pickup from overshooting. If a genuine pause exists in the music, the start flag may be extended to the length of the pause if it exceeds two seconds. Again, for the benefit of simple players, the start flag alternates on and off at 2 Hz in the lead-out area at the end of the recording.

At the time of writing the only other defined subcode data word is the Q word. This word has numerous modes and uses which can be taken advantage of by CD players with greater processing and display capability.

Fig.13.35 shows the structure of the Q subcode word. In the 96 bits following the sync patterns, there are two four bit words for control, a 72-bit data block, and a sixteen-bit CRC character which makes all 96 bits a codeword.

The first four-bit control word contains flags specifying the number of audio channels encoded, to permit automatic decoding of future four channel-discs, the copy-prohibit status and the pre-emphasis status. Since de-emphasis is often controlled by a relay in the analog stages of the player, the pre-emphasis status is only allowed to change during a P code start flag.

The second four-bit word determines the meaning of the subsequent 72-bit block. There can be three meanings: mode 1, which tells the player the number and start times of the bands on the disc; mode 2, which carries the disc catalogue

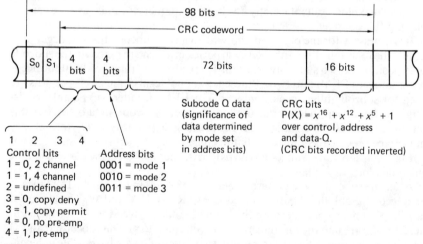

Figure 13.35 The structure of the Q-data block. The 72-bit data can be interpreted in three ways determined by the address bits.

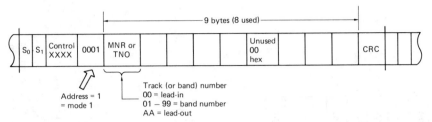

Figure 13.36 General format of Q subcode frame in mode 1. There are eight unused bits, leaving eight active bytes. First byte is music or track number, which determines meaning of remaining bytes.

number; and mode 3, which carries the ISRC (International Standard Recording Code) of each band. Of all the subcode blocks on a disc, the mode 1 blocks are by far the most common.

Mode 1 has two major functions. During the lead-in track it contains a table of contents (TOC), listing each piece of music and the absolute playing time when it starts. During the music content of the disc, it contains running time.

Fig.13.36 shows that the 72-bit block is subdivided into nine bytes, one of which is unused and permanently zero. Each byte represents two hexadecimal digits where not all codes are valid. The first byte in the block is the music number (MNR), which specifies the number of the track on the disc; where in this context 'track' corresponds to the bands on a vinyl disk. The tracks are numbered from one upwards, and the track number of 00 indicates that the pickup is in the lead-in area and that the rest of the block contains an entry in the table of contents.

The table of contents is built up by listing points in time where each track starts. One point can be described in one subcode block. Fig.13.37 shows that the second byte of the block is the point number. The absolute time at which that point will be reached after the start of the first track is contained in the last three bytes as point minutes, point seconds and point frames. These bytes are two BCD digits, where the maximum value of point frame is 74. As there is only error detection in the Q data, the point is repeated in three successive subcode blocks. The number of points allowed is 99, but the track numbering can continue through a set of discs. For example, in a two-disc set, there could be five tracks, 1 to 5, on the first disc, and six tracks, 6 to 11, on the second disc. Clearly the first point on the second disc is going to be point 6, and to prevent the player fruitlessly looking for points that are absent, the point range is specified.

If the point byte has the value A0 hex, the point-minute byte contains the number of the first track on the disc, which in the example given would be 6. If the point byte has the value A1 hex, the point-minute byte contains the number of the last track on the disc, which would here be 11. A further point is specified, which is the absolute running time of the start of the lead-out track, which uses the point code of A2 hex. These three points come after the actual music start points. During the lead-in track, the running time is counted by the minute, second and frame bytes in the block.

If the first byte of the block is between 00 and 99, the block is in a music track, and the meaning shown in Fig.13.38 applies. The running time is given in three ways. Minute, second and frame are the running time from the start of that track, and A(bsolute)min, Asec and Aframe are the running time from the start

First disc: five bands 1-5

Frame no.	Point	Point (min,sec,frame)		
$n, n+1, n+2$	01	00	02	00
$n+3, n+4, n+5$	02	12	09	10
$n+6, n+7, n+8$	03	24	11	20
$n+9, n+10, n+11$	04	36	59	74
$n+12, n+13, n+14$	05	48	50	22
$n+15, n+16, n+17$	A0	01	00	00
$n+18, n+19, n+20$	A1	05	00	00
$n+21, n+22, n+23$	A2	59	27	31

Second disc: six bands 6-11

Frame no.	Point	Point (min,sec,frame)		
$n, n+1, n+2$	06	00	02	10
$n+3, n+4, n+5$	07	10	03	20
$n+6, n+7, n+8$	08	20	05	11
$n+9, n+10, n+11$	09	30	04	03
$n+12, n+13, n+14$	10	40	02	19
$n+15, n+16, n+17$	11	50	59	70
$n+18, n+19, n+20$	A0	06	00	00
$n+21, n+22, n+23$	A1	11	00	00
$n+24, n+25, n+26$	A2	59	20	74

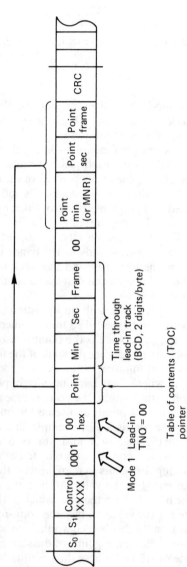

| S_0 | S_1 | Control XXXX | 0001 | 00 hex | Point | Min | Sec | Frame | 00 | Point min (or MNR) | Point sec | Point frame | CRC |

Mode 1   Lead-in TNO = 00

Time through lead-in track (BCD, 2 digits/byte)

Table of contents (TOC) pointer

Figure 13.37 During lead-in TNo. is zero, and Q subcode builds up a table of contents using numbered points with starting times. For multidisc sets, the band numbering can continue from one disc to the next, and there are point-limit codes A0 and A1 which specify the range of bands on a given disc. The example of a two-disc set is given, with five bands on the first disc and six bands on the second. Point = 00–99, point = music number, and point (min, sec, frame) denotes absolute starting time of that music number. This forms an entry in TOC. Point = A0 hex, point min byte = music number of *first* band on this disc, denotes beginning MNR of TOC. Point = A1 hex, point min byte = music number of *last* band on this disc, denotes end MNR of TOC. Point = A2 hex, point (min, sec, frame) denotes absolute starting time of lead-out track.

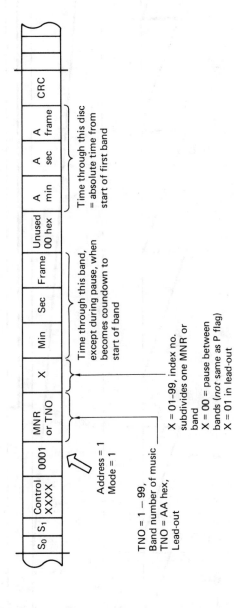

Figure 13.38 During music bands TNo. is 01–99, and subcode shows time through band and time through disc. The former counts down during pause. Each band can be subdivided by index count X.

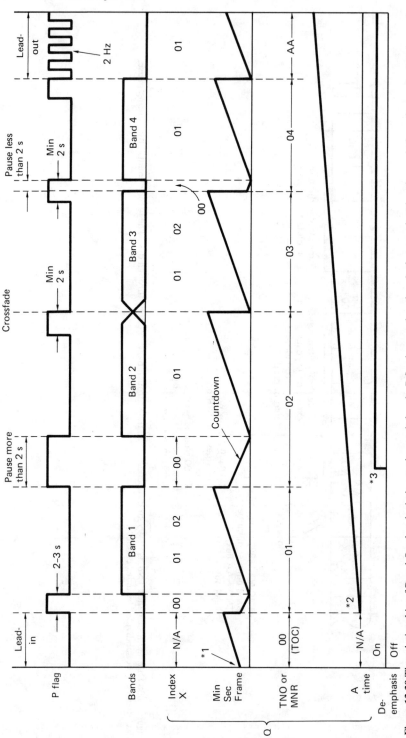

Figure 13.39 The relationship of P and Q subcode timing to the music bands. P flag is never less than 2 s between bands, whereas index reflects actual pause, and vanishes at a crossfade. Time counts down during index–00.
*1: lead-in time does not have to start from zero.
*2: A time must start from zero;
*3: de-emphasis can only change during pause of 2 s or more.

of the first track on the disc. The third running-time mode employs the index or X byte. When this is zero, it denotes a pause, which corresponds to the P subcode's being 1. During this pause, which precedes the start of a track, the running time counts down to zero, so that a player can display the time to go before a track starts to play. The absolute time is unaffected by this mode. Non-zero values of X denote a subdivision of the track into shorter sections. This would be useful to locate individual phrases on a language-course disc, or the individual effects on a sound-effects disc. Fig.13.39 shows an example of the use of P and Q subcode and the relationship between them and the music bands.

Mode 2 of the Q subcode allows the recording of the barcode number of the disc, and is denoted by the address code of 2 in the block as shown in Fig.13.40. The 52-bit barcode, along with twelve zeros and a continuation of the absolute frame count, are protected by the CRC character. If this mode is used, it should show up at least once in every 100 subcode blocks and the contents of each block should be identical. The use of the mode is not compulsory.

Mode 3 of Q subcode is similar to mode 2, except that a code number can be allocated to each track on the disc. Fig.13.41 shows that the ISR code requires five alphanumeric characters of six bits each and seven BCD characters of four bits each. Again the mode is optional but, if used, the mode 3 subcode block must occur at least once in every 100 blocks.

The R to W subcode is currently not standardized, but proposed uses for this data include a text display which would enable the words of a song to appear on

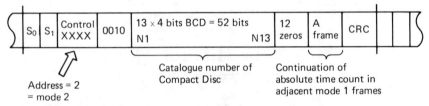

Figure 13.40 In mode 2, the catalogue number can be recorded. This must always be the same throughout the disc, and must appear in at least one out of a hundred successive blocks.

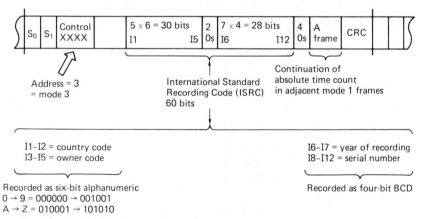

Figure 13.41 ISRC format in mode 3 allows each band to have a different code. All mode 3 frames must be the same within same TNO. Must appear in at least one out of every hundred successive blocks. Not present in lead-in or lead-out tracks.

a monitor in synchronism with the sound played from the disc. A difficulty in this area is the requirement to support not only the kind of alphanumerics in which this book is written but also the complex Kanji characters which would be needed for the Japanese market.

The second proposed mode is to support colour graphics display, and the third mode would be to store colour television stills. A frame store would be necessary in the player to refresh the CRT. The large number of pixels needed for a TV still would require some 2.5 s of playing time to read each one from the disc.

13.11 Player structure

The physics of the manufacturing process and the readout mechanism have been described, along with the format on the disc. Here, the details of actual CD players will be explained.

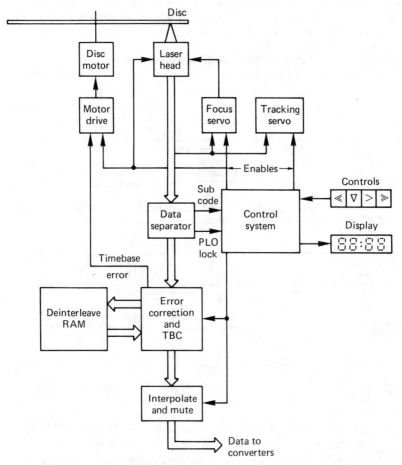

Figure 13.42 Block diagram of CD player showing the data path (broad arrow) and control/servo systems.

One of the design constraints of the Compact Disc and its format was that it should allow the construction of players to be straightforward, since they were to be mass-produced.

Fig.13.42 shows the block diagram of a typical player, and illustrates the essential components. The most natural division within the block diagram is into the control/servo system and the data path. The control system provides the interface between the user and the servo mechanisms, and performs the logical interlocking required for safety and the correct sequence of operation.

The servo systems include any power-operated loading drawer and chucking mechanism, the spindle-drive servo, and the focus and tracking servos already described.

Power loading is usually implemented on players where the disc is placed in a drawer. Once the drawer has been pulled into the machine, the disc is lowered onto the drive spindle, and clamped at the centre, a process known as chucking. In the simpler top-loading machines, the disc is placed on the spindle by hand, and the clamp is attached to the lid so that it operates as the lid is closed.

The lid or drawer mechanisms have a safety switch which prevents the laser operating if the machine is open. This is to ensure that there can be no conceivable hazard to the user. In actuality there is very little hazard in a CD pickup. This is because the beam is focused a few millimetres away from the objective lens, and beyond the focal point the beam diverges and the intensity falls rapidly. It is almost impossible to position the eye at the focal point when the pickup is mounted in the player, but it would be foolhardy to attempt to disprove this.

The data path consists of the data separator, timebase correction and the deinterleaving and error-correction process followed by the error-concealment mechanism. This results in a sample stream which is fed to the converters.

The data separator which converts the readout waveform into data was detailed in the description of the CD channel code. LSI chips have been developed to perform the data-separation function: for example, the Philips SAA 7010 or the Sony CX 7933. The separated output from both of these consists of subcode bytes, audio samples, redundancy and a clock. The data stream and the clock will contain speed variations due to disc runout and chucking tolerances, and these have to be removed by a timebase corrector.

The timebase corrector is a memory addressed by counters which are arranged to overflow, giving the memory a ring structure as in Fig.13.43. Writing into the memory is done using clocks from the data separator whose frequency rises and falls with runout, whereas reading is done using a crystal-controlled clock, which removes speed variations from the samples, and makes wow and flutter unmeasurable. The timebase-corrector will only function properly if the two addresses are kept apart. This implies that the long-term data rate from the disc must equal the crystal-clock rate. The disc speed must be controlled to ensure that this is always true, and there are two contrasting ways in which it can be done.

The data-separator clock counts samples off the disc. By phase-comparing this clock with the crystal reference, the phase error can be used to drive the spindle motor. This system is used in the Sony CDP-101, where the principle is implemented with a CX-193 chip, which was originally designed for DC turntable motors. The data-separator signal replaces the feedback signal which would originally have come from a toothed wheel on the turntable.

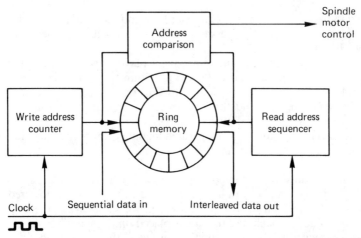

Figure 13.43 Deinterleaving is achieved by the use of a ring memory which is addressed linearly on one side and by a sequencer at the other side. Time base correction may also be performed by the same unit, and the relationship of read and write addresses can be used to control the disc spindle.

The alternative approach is to analyse the address relationship of the timebase corrector. If the disc is turning too fast, the write address will move towards the read address; if the disc is turning too slowly, the write address moves away from the read address. Subtraction of the two addresses produces an error signal which can be fed to the motor. The TBC RAM in Philips players, which also serves as the deinterleave memory, is a 2 kbyte SSB 2016, and this is controlled by the SAA 7020, which produces the motor-control signal. In these systems, and in all CD players, the speed of the motor is unimportant. The important factor is that the sample rate is correct, and the system will drive the spindle at whatever speed is necessary to achieve the correct rate. As the disc cutter produces constant bit density along the track by reducing the rate of rotation as the track radius increases, the player will automatically duplicate that speed reduction. The actual linear velocity of the track will be the same as the velocity of the cutter, and although this will be constant for a given disc, it can vary between 1.2 and 1.4 m/s on different discs.

These speed-control systems can only operate when the data separator has phase-locked, and this cannot happen until the disc speed is almost correct. A separate mechanism is necessary to bring the disc up to roughly the right speed. One way of doing this is to make use of the run-length limits of the channel code. Since transitions closer than $3T$ and further apart than $11T$ are not present, it is possible to estimate the disc speed by analysing the run lengths. The period between transitions should be from 694 ns to 2.55 μs. During disc runup the periods between transitions can be measured, and if the longest period found exceeds 2.55 μs, the disc must be turning too slowly, whereas if the shortest period is less than 694 ns, the disc must be turning too fast. Once the data separator locks up, the coarse speed control becomes redundant. The method relies upon the regular occurrence of maximum and minimum run lengths in the channel. Synchronizing patterns have the maximum run length, and occur regularly. The description of the disc format showed that the C1 and C2 redundancy was inverted. This injects some ones into the channel even when the audio is muted. This is the situation during the lead-in track—the very place that lock must be achieved. The presence of the table of contents in subcode during the lead-in also helps to produce a range of run lengths.

Owing to the use of constant linear velocity, the disc speed will be wrong if the pickup is suddenly made to jump to a different radius using manual search controls. This may force the data separator out of lock, and the player will mute briefly until the correct track speed has been restored, allowing the PLO to lock again. This can be demonstrated with most players, since it follows from the format.

Following data separation and timebase correction, the error-correction and deinterleave processes take place.

Because of the crossinterleave system, there are two opportunities for correction, firstly using the C1 redundancy prior to deinterleaving, and secondly using the C2 redundancy after de-interleaving.

In Chapter 7 it was shown that interleaving is designed to spread the effects of burst errors among many different codewords, so that the errors in each are reduced. However, the process can be impaired if a small random error, due perhaps to an imperfection in manufacture, occurs close to a burst error caused by surface contamination.

The function of the C1 redundancy is to correct single-symbol errors,[10] so that the power of interleaving to handle bursts is undiminished, and to generate error flags for the C2 system when a gross error is encountered.

The EFM coding is a group code which means that a small defect which changes one channel pattern into another will have corrupted up to eight data bits. In the worst case, if the small defect is on the boundary between two channel patterns, two successive bytes could be corrupted. However, the final odd/even interleave on encoding ensures that the two bytes damaged will be in different C1 codewords; thus a random error can never corrupt two bytes in one C1 codeword, and random errors are therefore always correctable by C1. From this it follows that the maximum size of a defect considered random is $17T$ or $3.9\,\mu$s. This corresponds to about a $5\,\mu$m length of the track. Errors of greater size are, by definition, burst errors.

The deinterleave process is achieved by writing sequentially into a memory and reading out using a sequencer. The RAM can perform the function of the timebase-corrector as well. The size of memory necessary follows from the format; the amount of interleave used is a compromise between the resistance to burst errors and the cost of the deinterleave memory. The maximum delay is 108 blocks of 28 bytes, and the minimum delay is negligible. It follows that a memory capacity of $54 \times 28 = 1512$ bytes is necessary.

Allowing a little extra for timebase error, odd/even interleave and error flags transmitted from C1 to C2, the convenient capacity of 2048 bytes is reached.

The C2 decoder is designed to locate and correct a single-symbol error, or to correct two symbols whose locations are known. The former case occurs very infrequently, as it implies that the C1 decoder has miscorrected. However, the C1 decoder works before deinterleave, and there is no control over the burst-error size that it sees. There is a small but finite probability that random data in a large burst could produce the same syndrome as a single error in good data. This would cause C1 to miscorrect, and no error flag would accompany the miscorrected symbols. Following deinterleave, the C2 decode could detect and correct the miscorrected symbols as they would now be single-symbol errors in many codewords. The overall miscorrection probability of the system is thus quite minute. Where C1 detects burst errors, error flags will be attached to all symbols in the failing C1 codeword. After deinterleave in the memory, these flags will be used by the C2 decoder to correct up to two corrupt symbols in one C2 codeword. Should more than two flags appear in one C2 codeword, the errors are uncorrectable, and C2 flags the entire codeword bad, and the interpolator will have to be used. The final odd/even sample deinterleave makes interpolation possible because it displaces the odd corrupt samples relative to the even corrupt samples.

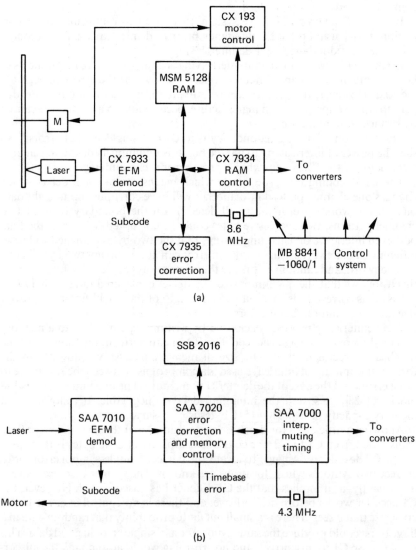

Figure 13.44 (a) The LSI chip arrangement of the CDP-101, a first-generation Sony consumer CD player. Focus and PLO systems were SSI/discrete. (b) LSI chip arrangement of Philips CD player.

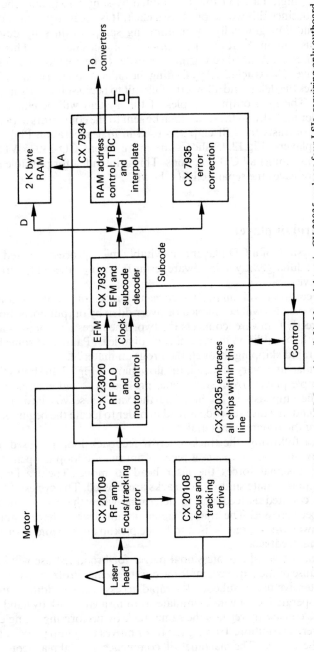

Figure 13.45 Second-generation Sony LSIs put RF, focus and PLO on chips (left). New eighty-pin CX 23035 replaces four LSIs, requiring only outboard deinterleave RAM. This chip is intended for car and Walkman-type players.

If the rate of bad C2 codewords is excessive, the correction system is being overwhelmed, and the output must be muted to prevent unpleasant noise. Unfortunately digital audio cannot be muted by simply switching the sample stream to zero, since this would produce a click. It is necessary to fade down to the mute condition gradually by multiplying sample values by descending coefficients, usually in the form of a half-cycle of a cosine wave. This gradual fadeout requires some advance warning, in order to be able to fade out before the errors arrive. This is achieved by feeding the fader through a delay. The mute status bypasses the delay, and allows the fadeout to begin sufficiently in advance of the error. The final output samples of this system will be either correct, interpolated or muted, and these can then be sent to the convertors in the player.

Fig.13.44 contrasts the LSI chip sets used in first-generation Philips[11] and Sony[12] CD players. Fig.13.45 shows the more recent CD-23035 VLSI chip which contains almost all CD functions. This is intended for portable and car players, and replaces the separate LSIs shown.

13.12 Control of player

The control system of a CD player is inevitably microprocessor-based, and as such does not differ greatly in hardware terms from any other microprocessor-controlled device.

Operator controls will simply interface to processor input ports and the various servo systems will be enabled or overridden by output ports. Software, or more correctly firmware, connects the two. The necessary controls are Play and Eject, with the addition in most players of at least Pause and some buttons which allow rapid skipping through the program material.

Although machines vary in detail, the flowchart of Fig.13.46 shows the logic flow of a simple player, from start being pressed to sound emerging. At the beginning, the emphasis is on bringing the various servos into operation. Towards the end, the disc subcode is read in order to locate the beginning of the first section of the program material.

When track-following, the tracking-error feedback loop is closed, but for track crossing, in order to locate a piece of music, the loop is opened, and a microprocessor signal forces the laser head to move. The tracking error becomes an approximate sinusoid as tracks are crossed. The cycles of tracking error can be counted as feedback to determine when the correct number of tracks have been crossed. The 'mirror' signal obtained when the readout spot is half a track away from target is used to brake pickup motion and re-enable the track following feedback.

The control system of a professional player for broadcast use will be more complex because of the requirement for accurate cueing. Professional machines will make extensive use of subcode for rapid access, and in addition are fitted with a hand-operated rotor which simulates turning a vinyl disk by hand. In this mode the disc constantly repeats the same track by performing a single track-jump once every revolution. Turning the rotor moves the jump point to allow a cue point to be located. The machine will commence normal play from the cue point when the start button is depressed or from a switch on the audio fader. An interlock is usually fitted to prevent the rather staccato cueing sound from being broadcast.

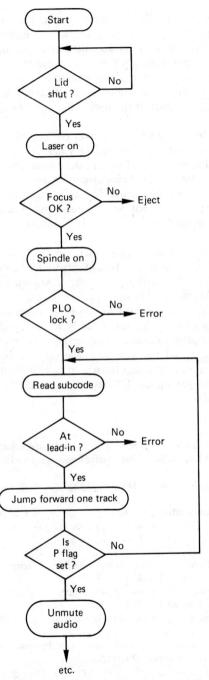

Figure 13.46 Simple flowchart for control system, focuses, starts disc, and reads subcode to locate first item of program material.

Another variation of the CD player is the so called Karaoke system, which is essentially a CD jukebox. The literal translation of Karaoke is 'empty orchestra'; well-known songs are recorded minus vocals, and one can sing along to the disc oneself. This is a popular pastime in Japan, where Karaoke machines are installed in clubs and bars. Consumer machines are beginning to follow this trend, with machines becoming available which can accept several discs at once and play them all without any action on the part of the user. The sequence of playing can be programmed beforehand.

Another development of the CD system is CD-V. The player is a combined unit which would also be a Laservision videodisc player. A CD-V disc contains about five minutes of video with digital stereo, and a further fifteen minutes or so of digital audio only. A common spindle and laser pickup can be used, with different processing circuitry for the two kinds of signals. This is intended as a boost for the Laservision system; since it could not record, most consumers chose videocassettes instead, and sales were disappointing. With a built in CD player it would look more attractive.

Finally, a non-audio use of the Compact Disc must be mentioned. As CD offers a tremendous storage capacity in digital terms, and the ability to duplicate rapidly, it has come into use as a digital distribution medium known as CD-ROM (Compact Disc Read Only Memory).[13] In one application, encyclopaedias can be stored on disc and read from a player linked to a computer terminal. Another use is to distribute computer programs. Clearly, in computer instructions, error concealment is not appropriate, and a further layer of error correction is necessary to provide the increased data integrity necessary for this kind of information. Since early digital audio machines borrowed heavily from computer technology, it is interesting to see that in CD-ROM the wheel has turned full circle.

References

1. VERKAIK, W., Compact Disc (CD) mastering —an industrial process. In *Digital Audio*, edited by B.A. Blesser, B. Locanthi and T.G. Stockham Jr, New York: Audio Engineering Society 189–195 (1983)
2. MIYAOKA, S., Manufacturing technology of the Compact Disc. In *Digital Audio, op. cit.* 196–201
3. REDLICH, H. and JOSCHKO, G., CD direct metal mastering technology: a step toward a more efficient manufacturing process for Compact Discs. *J. Audio Eng. Soc.*, **35**, 130–137 (1987)
4. Various authors, Video long-play systems. *Appl. Opt.*, **17**, 1993–2036 (1978)
5. Various authors, *Philips Tech. Rev.*, **40**, 149–180 (1982).
6. OGAWA, H., and ScHOUHAMER IMMINK, K.A., EFM —the modulation system for the Compact Disc digital audio system. In *Digital Audio, op. cit.* 117–124
7. SCHOUHAMER IMMINK, K.A. and GROSS, U., Optimization of low-frequency properties of eight-to-fourteen modulation. *Radio Electron. Eng.*, **53**, 63–66 (1983)
8. PEEK, J.B.H., Communications aspects of the Compact Disc digital audio system. *IEEE Commun. Mag.*, **23**, 7–15 (1985)
9. VRIES, L.B. *et al.*, The digital Compact Disc —modulation and error correction. Presented at 67th Audio Engineering Society Convention (New York, 1980) preprint 1674.
10. VRIES, L.B. and ODAKA, K., CIRC —the error correcting code for the Compact Disc digital audio system. In *Digital Audio, op. cit.* 178– 186
11. MATULL, J., ICs for Compact Disc decoders. *Electron. Components Appl.*, **4**, 131-141 (1982)
12. ODAKA, K., FURUYA, T. and TAKI, A., LSIs for digital signal processing to be used in Compact Disc digital audio players. *J. Audio Eng. Soc.*, **30**, 362 (1982)
13. WATKINSON, J.R., CD: the 600 megabyte ROM. *Electronics and Wireless World*, **93**, 1046–1049 (1987)

Index

Given here are section number(s) of main reference(s) to a subject.